Arnulfo L. Oliveira Memorial Library

George

THE POOR LITTLE RICH BOY WHO BUILT THE YANKEE EMPIRE

Peter Golenbock

WILEY
John Wiley & Sons, Inc.

For Charlie, my son. I couldn't be prouder.
And for Debra.

Contents

Illustrations start on page 151

Preface

I was supposed to be a lawyer, but two months before the bar exam, I got punched in the face by a mugger in the deserted Rahway, New Jersey, train station, and a few days later, in the elevator of the New York University law library, I had a seizure that knocked me out and put me in the hospital. I was told to avoid stress, but how to you do that when you have to take the bar exam? I sat in a large hall, ready to take the exam, and on the cover of my blue book, the first question was, "What is your name?" Searching my scrambled brain to answer the question, I drew a blank. I closed the book and walked out.

I got a job working for a prestigious law firm located on Fifty-ninth Street just off Fifth Avenue anyway. But I left after eight weeks. I had been assigned to a negligent lawyer and quit rather than act as his apologist. Shortly afterward, I espied an ad in the *New York Times* for a writer with a legal background. I had been the sports editor of the *Dartmouth*, and I had been the Dartmouth correspondent to both the *New York Times* and the *Boston Globe*. I was the perfect man for the job, and when I called and talked to the director of personnel, I was told to drive to the offices of Prentice Hall on the banks of the Hudson River in New Jersey just north of the George Washington Bridge.

In the summer of 1972, I was hired as an assistant editor for the munificent salary of $7,500 a year to write a weekly report on President Richard M. Nixon's wage and price controls. After a month chafing at the corporate culture and angry they could pay me a low salary because I had failed to pass the bar, I joined with several others in the legal department to meet with the Teamsters about starting a union for the lawyers on the staff at Prentice Hall. We had several meetings with Jimmy Hoffa's boys, and we were well on our way to doing something about the low pay of the company when one lunchtime I ran across a catalog of Prentice Hall's trade books. Among the tomes in the catalog was *Bread and Butter Basketball* by my old Dartmouth basketball coach, Doggie Julian. I wanted to write a book about the New York Yankees, my childhood team. Perhaps Prentice Hall would publish it.

I drove to Yankee Stadium, and I asked for the public relations department. I was ushered in to see a young guy by the name of Marty Appel. He was the assistant PR guy for the Yankees, and he looked to be about sixteen years old. "If I can get a contract to write a book about the Yankees," I asked, "will you allow me to spend time looking through your newspaper morgue?"

"If you can get a contract," Marty said with a smile and obvious skepticism, "you're welcome to research our archive."

I had just turned twenty-six. I had no notion of how the world worked. *Why wouldn't Prentice Hall want to publish my book?* I thought. I left my desk around noon and went looking for the head trade book editor, wandering the maze of jail-yellow halls and asking for directions until I found my man. Without as much as an appointment, I knocked on the door of Nick D'Incecco.

Nick yelled, "Come in," and I walked into his office. We shook hands, and I talked up this book I wanted to write about the Casey Stengel–era Yankees of my blessed childhood. I gave him my credentials—how could he turn down a writer who had been the sports editor of the *Dartmouth*? I told him I worked upstairs in the legal department, and I told him that in the sixteen seasons I wanted to write about, the Yankees had drawn almost twenty million fans.

"If I could sell a book to one percent of those people," I said, "we'd have a big seller."

Luckily for me, Nick loved the Yankees as much as I did.

"Write me up a proposal," he said.

In my four pages of bullshit (as it turned out, I really had no clue how I was going to do this), I listed all the great players I was going to write about from the years 1949 through 1964, a period in which the Yankees won fourteen pennants and nine world championships. I also wrote that the Yankees had agreed to give me access to their private newspaper morgue.

A week later I got a call from D'Incecco.

"Come down and sign your contract," he said.

It seemed too easy, and over the years the enormity of it all grew. I was literally doing the impossible. I often wondered whether Prentice Hall gave me the contract to stop my union organizing. Later,

I discovered, management defeated the union efforts. I have always felt guilty about that.

I had started a business renting rooms in the Penn Garden Hotel to college students, and every day I would drive my little Mercedes 230 SL from my Manhattan garage on First Street to Yankee Stadium, where I would sit among the literally hundreds of thousands of newspaper articles and take notes. It was a gargantuan task, but I was undaunted, in part because Marty Appel kept his word and let me have access to the Yankee archive, and because the people working for the Yankees were so supportive. Led by Yankee president Michael Burke, these were some of the finest people I have ever known.

After several weeks, Freddie Bachman, a large, jovial born salesman in charge of special projects and also in charge of employee lunch, began inviting me to go with them. Freddie had this special restaurant he and his friends patronized. It was a small steak joint where Joe DiMaggio and Mickey Mantle used to eat. It was also owned by the mob. Large men wearing pinkie rings sat in the corner eating huge slabs of steak. We ordered a New York strip streak. For us Yankee employees, the tab was two dollars each.

Before long I was answering the phones, "New York Yankees," when the PR people were out of the office. I was leading a most amazing life, working at Yankee Stadium by day, playing camp counselor for my hundred-plus college students at night.

I had started my research in August, when the Yankees were still playing. The team was improving slowly and would finish second that year to the Baltimore Orioles. The star of the team was the catcher Thurman Munson, and Bobby Murcer was proving a talented player, though he never did become the second coming of Mickey Mantle like they said he was going to. The team had several talented pitchers, including Mel Stottlemyre, Fritz Peterson, and Mike Kekich. It also had Ron Blomberg, the first American League designated hitter and a delight to be around. Several times Ronnie and Hal Lanier would ask if I would shag for them. One pitched while the other hit, and at first I stood where I usually did when I played the outfield on my softball teams, sure I could catch anything they hit.

The first time I tried it, I watched every ball Blomberg hit go over my head. The only way I could catch a ball was to stand with my back to the low outfield fence and run in for the ones I could reach. I had often wondered how much better I would need to be in order to make the major leagues. On this day it became crystal clear: a *hell* of a lot better.

In January 1973, out of the blue, the Yankees called a press conference to announce that CBS had sold the team to a group of investors led by Michael Burke and a Cleveland shipbuilder by the name of George Steinbrenner III. Most of the Yankee employees were surprised by the news. I certainly hadn't heard anything about it. The sale was for ten million dollars, and after it was announced everyone was assured that their jobs were safe and nothing was going to change. We were told that Burke would continue to be in charge and that Steinbrenner, the money man in the deal, was going to remain in Cleveland where he would continue to run his ship-building business.

About a week later Freddie Bachman came to see me. "I want you to hear this," he said. We walked over to the elevators on the bottom floor of the stadium. He motioned for me to put my ear to the elevator door. I could hear two men screaming at each other at the top of their lungs. I wasn't able to make out what they were saying, but an occasional "Fuck you" could be clearly heard amid the din. The two men were Michael Burke and George Steinbrenner III.

A month later Michael Burke was gone, having been hired by Madison Square Garden. Mike took exec Howard Berk with him. Two other Yankee employees, Marty Appel and Joe Garagiola, joined forces to start a sports agency enterprise, and Freddie Bachman left to help bring a hockey team to Hartford, Connecticut. I went off to spend the next year interviewing old Yankees.

My book on the Yankees would take another two years to finish. After going through thousands of clippings, I sat down ready to write, but I discovered that you can't write a book on old clips. I needed to go see the players. D'Incecco, fortunately, kept sending me $2,500 advances until I finished the year of interviewing most of the Yankees who played during the era I was focusing on. I saw Joe Page outside of Pittsburgh, Clete Boyer in his bar in Atlanta, Mickey Mantle in the Yankee clubhouse, and Yogi Berra in his stately mansion in Montclair, New Jersey. Whitey Ford even came to my hotel apartment to talk to me. I had one of the last interviews with Roger Maris before he died. I went to see Jim Bouton, who lived in nearby Englewood, and he and I became close like brothers.

I went on to write *Dynasty*, my history of those Casey Stengel Yankees, and from that experience I was asked by former Yankee player Billy Martin to help him write his autobiography. Martin's agent, Doug Newton, also represented the pitcher Sparky Lyle, and Doug encouraged me to find a way to make Sparky some money writing a book. Our collaboration, which was called *The Bronx Zoo*, for a long time was the best-selling sports book ever. My book with Martin, called *Number 1*, was a big hit, as was *Balls*, the book I wrote with third baseman Graig Nettles. I also managed to squeeze in a charming little book called *Guidry*, with pitcher Ron Guidry.

I am convinced that a large part of the success of *The Bronx Zoo*, *Number 1*, and *Balls* in particular was the deep and abiding interest of the public in how Sparky, Billy, and Graig portrayed team owner George Steinbrenner.

I moved to Florida in 1989 to write a book on the Senior Professional Baseball League called the *Forever Boys*. My son, Charlie, was born in 1987, and during the winter of 1997 I brought him to Yankee Stadium, where my buddy Arthur Richman gave him a bat and led him out to home plate so he could stand in the same spot where Mickey Mantle, Babe Ruth, and Lou Gehrig once stood.

Then during the summer of 2001 I was teaching a course on the art and history of sports journalism at Rutgers University. I saw that Old-Timers' Day was coming up, and I decided I would take Charlie, now thirteen, to meet some of my coauthors, Sparky Lyle, Graig Nettles, and Ron Guidry, as well as some old friends like Jim Bouton and Goose Gossage.

I called Rick Cerrone, the Yankees public relations director. I had known Rick for a long time. He had started a magazine called *Baseball*, and I had helped him out by allowing him to excerpt for free a section of my book *Dynasty* for his magazine. We had been good friends then, and I felt warmly toward him. When I called him and asked for two press passes to the clubhouse before the game, he was cordial and helpful.

He asked me who the other pass was for.

"My son, Charlie," I said. "He's thirteen, and I'm bringing him with me to the game."

"You can come down," Cerrone said, "but you can't bring your son. No children are allowed in the clubhouse. It's the rules."

After I parked, Charlie and I walked to the press entrance. I instructed him to sit on a bench in the lobby while I went downstairs to the clubhouse for a few minutes to see the gang. As I stood in front of the elevator I was greeted by Barry Halper, a close friend who not only had the largest baseball memorabilia collection in the world, but owned a share of the Yankees.

"Where's Charlie?" he asked.

"Over there," I said. "Rick Cerrone said he can't come into the clubhouse."

"Oh, bullshit," Barry said. "Bring him along."

"Are you sure?" I asked. Barry motioned for Charlie to join us.

We took the elevator down, and the three of us entered the hallowed sanctuary that is the Yankee clubhouse. I could feel the ghosts of Mickey, Roger, Lou, and the Babe. The old-timers were in various stages of getting dressed for the two-inning preliminary game, and about a dozen kids were wildly scurrying about the place. *I thought kids weren't allowed in the clubhouse*, I said to myself.

I went over to Sparky, and we hugged, and I chatted with Graig, shook hands with Goose and Moose Skowron, gave Ron Guidry a hug, and spoke to Yogi for a minute. Charlie, it turned out, had no interest in "those old guys." He wanted to meet Derek Jeter, Bernie Williams, and Paul O'Neill, and he was thrilled when O'Neill walked past.

Charlie and I were crossing the clubhouse when Rick Cerrone happened by. He looked at Charlie, and then he looked at me.

"Is that your son?" he demanded.

Before I could say that Barry Halper had told me to bring him, he bellowed, "You defied me. You defied me." Like a referee throwing a player out of the game, he pointed toward the door and screamed, "Get out. You are banned from Yankee Stadium for life."

I went over to Barry. "What do I do now?" I asked.

"The hell with him," Barry said. "Let's get out of here." I grabbed Charlie, and we walked out the clubhouse door. I'm sure the players must have been wondering what that was all about. I'm sure Charlie did too.

I had tickets elsewhere, but Barry said to me, "Come on up with me. We'll watch the game in the owner's box."

We arrived on the mezzanine level, and we walked through a door marked private. We entered a large office with a big couch shaped like a five-fingered fielder's glove. Barry had one in his office at his home in Jersey. Barry said George Steinbrenner liked it so much, he bought one too.

George wasn't there that day, but his son-in-law Steve Swindal, daughter Jennifer, and grandson were. The grandson was about Charlie's age, and the two quickly began playing catch across George's big mahogany desk. There were photos on the walls, and I waited for the tinkle of broken glass, but since Jennifer didn't object, I kept quiet.

And so while Barry, his lovely wife, Sharon, and I watched the Yankee game, Charlie and George Steinbrenner's grandson played catch across his office.

When the game was over, Jennifer, who clearly was bored and glad her son had someone to play with, came over to me. "Your son," she said, "is wonderful. How would you like to bring him back again for tomorrow's game?" She gave me a phone number to call. I thanked her, but after having gritted my teeth through the excruciating traffic-congested car ride from Princeton, New Jersey, across the George Washington Bridge to the Bronx, I decided that I didn't have the stomach to do it two days in a row.

But I couldn't help thinking how crazy it was to be involved with the Yankees, if only for a day. I had been thrown out of the Yankees' clubhouse and banned from Yankee Stadium for life by a crazed PR guy one minute, and the next minute I was invited to return to the stadium to sit in the owner's box by the owner's daughter.

Since I lived in Florida, being banned from Yankee Stadium for life didn't mean all that much, practically speaking, though after a time I began to see it as a badge of honor. Even Jim Bouton had been invited back, some thirty years after having written *Ball Four*. I thought, *Rick Cerrone, what has working for George Steinbrenner done to you?* Like all other PR directors under George, Cerrone was fired. I wonder, *Does that mean my lifetime ban has been lifted?*

In 1981, I had signed a contract to write a book about Steinbrenner for Crown, the company that published *The Bronx Zoo*. I didn't know it at the time, but there were two other Steinbrenner books in the works, one by Ed Linn and another by Dick Schapp. My contract gave me exactly one year to write my book, and when it turned out there was no way I could make the deadline and beat out the other two books, my editor, Daphne Abeel, informed me that Crown had no interest in publishing a third Steinbrenner book, and it was canceling my contract.

Tempus fugit. Fast-forward to the year 2008, and a few days after selling the idea of a Steinbrenner biography to John Wiley & Sons, I was informed that Bill Madden, the talented *New York Daily News* sportswriter, is also writing a Steinbrenner book, making Hana Lane, my new editor, very nervous. As Yogi Berra would say, it's déjà vu all over again.

Acknowledgments

This book is an example of that old saying "Good things happen to those who wait." When I began the research for *George*, I lived in Englewood, New Jersey, with my wonderful wife, Rhonda, and my two loving dogs, Sparky and Mickey. When I finished the research, I was living in St. Petersburg, Florida, without my wife, but with my son, Charles, and my two loving dogs, Fred and Doris. Twenty years separated the two. As that other old saying goes, "I wonder where the time goes."

At any rate, in addition to those men and women who asked not to be identified, I wish to thank those who weren't so reticent. I couldn't have written this book without you:

Jack Adams, Jerry Adams, Bruno Aldrino, Maury Allen, Marty Appel, Fred Bachman, Ket Barber, Jim Beardsley, Alex Belk, Joe Bennett, Howard Berk, Steve Blasky, Jim Bouton, Bruce Breckenridge, Jack Brody, Michael Burke, Tony Butterfield, Bill Callahan, Peter Callahan, Bill Crippen, Sam Curtain, Pearl Davis, Len Dawson, Ruben DeAlba, Tony DeSabio, Tom Evans, Louis Figone, Joe Flaherty, Ben Fleiger, Ben Froelich, Bill Gabriel, Ike Ganyard, Charlie Glass, Otto Graham, Dick Greco, David Halberstam, Pete Hensil, Leo Hindery, Dr. Jim Hull, Paul Hornung, Catfish Hunter, Ken Irvine, Pat Irvine, Dan Joy, Tom Keys, Dick Kraft, John LeCourt, Mitch Lukevics, Sparky Lyle, Billy Martin, Don Martin, Dan Mason, Tom McBride, John McClendon, Jack Melcher, Roy Meyers, William Mixson, Jeanette Montgomery, John Moore, Mr. Morris, Charles Mosher, John Nagy, Graig Nettles, Warren Ornstein, Gabe Paul, Jim Polk, Lee Robinson, Marc Rosenman, Lou Saban, Robert Sauvey, John Schanz, Bill Sharman, Bud Shockley, Robert Simpson, A. Coke Smith, Pete Smythe, Bob Stecher, Patsy Stecher, George Steinbrenner, George Steiner, Bob Sudyk, Burt Sugar, Dan Swartz, Pam Thomas, Frank Treadway, Fay Vincent, Len Watters, and Harold Zeig. I also want to thank Hana Lane, my editor, for all her support; Paul Fedorko, my agent; and Neil and Dawn Reshen, longtime friends and advisers. It's been twenty years since I started researching this book. Ed Linn and Dick Schapp are no longer with us. They were two talented friends, and I miss them.

Personality Disorders

Traits of Obsessive-Compulsive Personality Disorder

Perfection is a goal one can never reach. As Yogi Berra once said, "If the world were perfect, how would we know?" We may be able to strive to improve things, but we can never make things perfect. A person suffering from obsessive-compulsive personality disorder often exhibits these behaviors:

He has an obsessive need to avoid failure, and he works hard to prevent it. Everything he does is to ensure that he does not fail.

He tries to be perfect because his greatest fear is to be viewed as flawed.

He has an excessive devotion to work.

He is almost never involved in leisure activities.

He postpones leisurely activities such as vacations.

He doesn't take time off because leisure is a waste of time.

He doesn't delegate tasks. He feels he must do everything himself.

If he does become involved in tasks with others, the task must be done his way. He leaves detailed instructions as to how the task must be done.

The emphasis is on perfect performance. He has an all-or-nothing approach to life. Either he is perfect or he is useless. Either he wins the race or he is a loser.

He is a moralist who is hypercritical of others.

He seeks the illusion of virtue to hide his own vices.

He sets unattainable, unrealistic goals and attempts them anyway.

Traits of Narcissistic Personality Disorder

While the person who has obsessive-compulsive personality disorder thinks he's never done enough, that he's never perfect, the narcissist thinks he is perfect and everyone else is wrong. The following are characteristics of a person with narcissistic personality disorder:

He has a grandiose sense of himself, exaggerating his talents and inflating his accomplishments.

He believes he is special and unique.

He has a sense of entitlement, which lets him feel he is above the law. If he should get caught, he is certain he will be treated less harshly than others.

He doesn't tolerate others because they aren't as good as he.

He needs constant admiration from others or else he doesn't feel important.

He sees all publicity as good.

He is boastful.

His self-esteem is vulnerable to criticism because criticism makes him feel humiliated and degraded. Any criticism is seen as an attack, and his reaction often is rage. The narcissist will scream at the waiter if the food doesn't meet his standards. Instead of learning from criticism, the narcissist lashes out or fires the one who criticizes him.

He takes advantage of others to achieve his own needs.

He lacks empathy for others. He identifies only with his own feelings.

He is arrogant.

Even if he has wealth, he becomes envious and jealous of others.

He feels he should only associate with and be understood by people of very high status.

He has fantasies of success and power.

People are complex. They may have a combination of disorders, which psychiatrists call a "mixed personality."

Since I'm not a psychiatrist, I cannot tell you that George Steinbrenner is a man who exhibits obsessive-compulsive and narcissistic traits. Since my good friend, Dr. Irving Kolin, a renowned clinician, researcher, and educator, hasn't examined Mr. Steinbrenner, he can't either. But if you want to understand George Steinbrenner, the traits found in these disorders might well be a step in the right direction.

Prologue: The Final Game

I came to say good-bye. Like Ebbets Field and the Polo Grounds, Yankee Stadium, which opened in April 1923, was headed for the wreckers' ball, only this time, unlike the Dodgers and Giants, the team isn't headed anywhere. Thanks to the largesse of former mayor Rudy Giuliani, the city of New York gave George Steinbrenner a huge handout as part of the deal for the Yankees to move into a brand-new, billion-dollar retro–Yankee Stadium next door. Passed without a referendum of any kind, it will enable the Yankees to stay in the Bronx forever, living like pashas in a Yankee Valhalla where top tickets will be $2,500 a seat a game. One can only imagine how much moolah Giuliani would have given away to his rich friends had he been elected president.

The day—September 21, 2008—was glorious, as was befitting the last day of summer. To get to the stadium, I rode the 4 train on the Lexington Avenue line straight up the East Side of Manhattan into the Bronx. My car was filled with fans wearing a mélange of uniforms, mostly white with blue pinstripes, but some dark blue. All had various numbers on their backs—51, 20, 2, 13, and 46. In front of me, a young girl wearing 42 was kissing her beau, who was wearing 51. Ah, young love.

The game was scheduled to start at eight-thirty, but I arrived just before three, anxious to walk out onto Monument Park and offer my last good-byes. A lot of old friends have been memorialized there, some dead, some living. Billy and Mickey, Roger and Ellie, players of my generation, are no longer with us; Whitey and Yogi are still kicking; and, of course, there was Babe and Lou and Miller Huggins, Yankees from my father's day. For years, many people thought Babe and Lou were actually buried there, side by side for eternity.

Colonel Ruppert is remembered there. He was, after all, the man who paid for and built Yankee Stadium and created the first Yankee dynasty. I was saddened that the man who built the current Yankee dynasty, George Steinbrenner, was not present, either in bronze or in body. Steinbrenner, who has owned the Yankees since 1973, and who has generated large headlines and hundreds of pages of newspaper copy, has been laid low by his health, and his medical condition has deteriorated to the point where he can no longer travel. During the summer, he attended the All-Star Game at the stadium. Looking like a wax figure from Madame Tussaud's museum, he rode around in a cart, feebly waving to the cheering fans. He held two baseballs, which were taken from him and given to two waiting former stars, Reggie Jackson and Yogi Berra, men he had treated shabbily in the past, but who showed they had obviously forgiven him when they both kissed him affectionately on the cheek. It seemed as though Jackson and Berra were saying good-bye for all of us. My guess is we will never see Steinbrenner—or the likes of him—again.

Yogi provided one of the moving moments of the evening. In an address that was broadcast on the JumboTron, Berra, eschewing his patois of sayings featured in his AFLAC commercials, eloquently told the crowd, "Baseball is inside me. This is my life. And this is where I lived it."

The evening of the final game at the old Yankee Stadium drew fifty-seven thousand fans, many of whom were wearing Yankee attire. It used to be that only men wearing suits and ties and bowler hats came to major league baseball games. On this day there were almost as many women as men, and a lot of those women were decked out in Derek Jeter garb.

The evening ceremony started bizarrely, with members of the grounds crew dressed in old-time Yankee uniforms impersonating the Yankee greats who have passed away, including Ruth, Gehrig, DiMaggio, Lefty Gomez, Allie Reynolds, and Joe Page. Then relatives of more recent Yankee greats Mantle, Maris, and Martin were introduced, and they received a nice reception, but nothing as raucous as that for the Yankees responsible for the latest string of Yankee world championships, players like Derek Jeter, who soldiers on superbly, and his retired mates Tino Martinez, Paul O'Neill, Scott Brosius, and the most popular Yankee of them all, Bernie Williams, a perennial All-Star who had been given his pink slip by the Yankees two years earlier without even a fare-thee-well. As flashbulbs popped all over the stadium, Bernie stood in the outfield waving as the crowd chanted his name, "Ber-nie Will-yams, Ber-nie Will-yams," over and over. If Bernie questioned where he stood in the hearts and minds of Yankees fans, he needn't wonder any longer.

I was curious as to who would or would not attend. Despite the fact that Steinbrenner had tried to ruin his career, Dave Winfield, wearing his famed number 31, appeared and received a nice hand, as did Reggie Jackson, who once was so angry with Steinbrenner he came *this* close to punching him. My traded erstwhile coauthors, Sparky Lyle and Graig Nettles, attended, as did another former collaborator, Ron Guidry, who had been fired as pitching coach by Steinbrenner. My other Yankees coauthor, Billy Martin, who had been hired and fired five times by Steinbrenner, was represented by his son Billy Joe. On Old-Timers' Day, Billy's last wife, Jill, stood in his place, infuriating Billy Joe and Billy's friends. This time Billy Joe, who loved his father dearly, got his due.

Bobby Richardson came, but Tony Kubek, the Yankees shortstop and later a sportscaster who for years has borne a deep loathing for the way Steinbrenner has treated people, did not attend. Don Mattingly, a Yankee star during the years when Steinbrenner's meddling kept the team from winning and who was dismissed as batting coach when Joe Torre was fired as manager after the 2007 season, attended and received a nice ovation. Torre, who got no mention, was in Los Angeles managing the Dodgers to the division championship while the 2008 Yankees were mired in third place, out of playoff contention for the first time in thirteen years. Torre received awfully short shift considering he had led the Yankees to six American League pennants and four world championships.

Despite the presence of so many former Yankees, to me the most important Yankee personage was still George Steinbrenner, whose booming voice and stentorian demeanor hovered over everything. It was he who rejuvenated the Yankees after buying the team from CBS. It was he who spent big bucks to buy the first of the important free agents, including Catfish Hunter and Reggie Jackson. It was he who saw baseball not as a game but as an entertainment, and the fact that the Yankees were drawing four million fans a year for the fourth year in a row was evidence of that. It was he who wanted All-Stars at every position, and in 2008 the team featured a lineup of Damon, Jeter, ARod, Giambi, Abreu, Nady, Cano, and Pettitte. Jose Molina, who hit the last home run in the old stadium, caught in place of Jorge Posada, who would have been the ninth All-Star had he been healthy. Even the pageantry of the evening was a page from the George Steinbrenner playbook. It wasn't as dramatic as the two times Billy Martin was announced as manager on Old-Timers' Days, but it came close. The House that Ruth Built was closing. Beginning in 2009, the Yankees would move into the House that George Steinbrenner built. What is sad is that it will open without him.

Henry and George

The Steinbrenner family got into the shipbuilding business because of a disaster on the Great Lakes. The steamer involved, called the *Western Reserve*, had been built in 1888 by Peter Minch, the oldest son of shipping baron Philip Minch, who started building boats on the Great Lakes back in the 1850s.

When Philip died in 1887, Peter took over the ten-ship company, which was in the business of transporting ore, grain, and other commodities. An experienced seaman, Peter had been a ship captain since the age of twenty-one. He was fifty-one years old in August 1892 when he left Cleveland harbor on the *Western Reserve* for a run across the lakes along with his wife and two of his children, Charles and Florence. His wife's sister and her son also went along.

The *Western Reserve* was three hundred feet long, the largest in its class on the lakes. There were twenty crewmen and eleven passengers on board. On August 30, the ship cleared the Soo locks, and Captain Albert Myers pointed the ship into the teeth of a fierce storm about sixty miles beyond Whitefish Point at the entrance to Lake Superior. The vessel had weathered many similar storms without any trouble.

As the ship's bell struck nine, suddenly the vessel shuttered strangely. The captain sounded the alarm, and all hands rushed to the lifeboats. The ship's steel mast had snapped halfway up and fallen to the deck around amidships. After the two lifeboats were lowered into the water, one of them collapsed immediately, while the other stayed afloat only to run aground and capsize less than a mile from land. There was only one survivor.

The bodies of Captain Minch and his wife's sister were recovered a day later. A funeral was held at the family home on Kinsman Street in Cleveland. The flags of all his ships were flown at half mast.

Several months later the *Western Reserve*'s starboard lantern floated to shore along a bleak section of the Canadian coast. It was returned to Peter Minch's son Philip, who kept it burning constantly in memory of his lost family.

The wreck of the *Western Reserve* was what brought the Steinbrenner family into the shipping business. The Minch Transit Co. limped along until 1901, when it was taken over by the husband of Sophie Minch—Philip's daughter and Peter's sister. Sophie's husband, Henry Steinbrenner, had a thriving career as a lawyer and businessman, and at first he was reluctant to get involved in the shipping business, but the vitality of the company was at stake, and in 1901 he agreed to try and save it. That year he formed the Kinsman Marine Transit Company.

Henry was assisted by his son George II, who then took over and was assisted by his son Henry, a track star at MIT and first in his class of 1927. When Henry took over the company in the 1930s, he was a wealthy, respected baron of the industry.

Henry Steinbrenner, George Steinbrenner III's father, was a control freak, a Prussian from the old school who let everyone around him know that it was his way or the highway. As Henry saw it, this was a man's world, and women were to be treated as servants. They had no business in business; their place was in the home, cooking, doing the dishes, or raising babies.

There was another thing Henry believed in: himself. No one else could do the job as well as he, so delegating authority was a no-no. As a result, if Henry wanted something done, he would either do it himself or would assign an underling with the job and stay on top of him until he got it done or screwed up, in which case the underling would suffer a terrible tongue-lashing. If he messed up badly enough, his fate was certain: he would be fired. Since employees were interchangeable, Henry taught George, you never got close to employees, never invited them to social functions. No employee of Henry's was ever allowed to make a decision, even about a simple task. Only one person in the Kinsman Marine Transit Company made decisions, and that was the boss, Henry Steinbrenner.

Steinbrenner's family was dominated by his rules and his iron fist that enforced those rules. For his children, he would choose punishment over affection every time, sure that fear begot respect. Love would play no part. Love was for weaklings. He didn't have many friends, but Henry Steinbrenner didn't need friends. He had his shipping business, and he worked long hours almost every day, taking no holidays or vacations. He taught his children that to succeed, one needed to keep one's nose to the grindstone and a close watch on one's employees to make sure they weren't slacking off and wasting your hard-earned money. For Henry Steinbrenner, his employees were to be treated not as servants but as slaves.

The Steinbrenners—Henry, wife Rita, son George, and daughters Judy and Susan—lived in Lakewood, Ohio, a town ten miles west of Cleveland, in a large home, one of the largest in town. They spent summers in nearby Bay Village, because Henry liked the ambiance of the sleepy town with the open fields so much that in 1912 he bought twelve acres of property across the road from the Lake Erie shore. After he took over Kinsman Marine from his father in 1939, he remodeled the quaint farmhouse on the land into a modern, substantial two-story home. George was eight years old when the family moved into their Bay Village home.

Henry built a sturdy white fence to surround the property, and at the front of his estate he placed the anchor of a lake freighter and a capstan. He named his home the Anchorage.

George's friends were deathly afraid of his father. George feared him, for sure, but he never could get himself to admit it. He recalled a bucolic childhood that was seemingly carefree, except that he was constantly under the thumb of a rigid, domineering father.

"Bay Village was a small place, and it was a great life," George told me. "It was a rural community and very friendly. You walked or rode ponies or bicycles. I had my own pony. Later my sisters had horses. I rode in pony races at the Cuyahoga State Fair when I was a kid.

"My family was not flamboyant and did not live extravagantly. My dad had a lot of money. I know my grandfather was very well-to-do.

He left a lot to the grandchildren. In fact, the grandchildren got a good portion of his money.

"Most of the people who came from the West Side of Cleveland were very conservative. I'm not that way. I can't tell you where that comes from. Not from my father. Not from my mother, who was five foot one and quiet. She was the strength of the family. She held it all together. My mother, Rita, is a lovely, lovely woman.

"My father was the disciplinarian, but my mother provided the love that was necessary in a strong disciplinarian system. You have to have somebody like my mother in there—there has to be a human strain through it too.

"I had rules—written and unwritten—that I had to live under at home. Rules about when you could listen to the radio and when you had to do your studies and when you had to have your work and chores done. We were never allowed to feel that anything my dad was fortunate enough to have could be used by us. We had to work. He was a pusher. He led, and we followed. You could run three races in one day and get two firsts and a second, and the only thing he wanted to talk about was, How did you get beat? What did you do wrong? One lesson he taught me that stayed with me more than anything is that you can learn more from your mistakes than you can from your successes."

The other lesson he learned from that was that winning was all that mattered. "I was mad at him all the time. I was mad a lot. But I found myself working that much harder to prove to him I could do it, or prove to him something, whatever it was, and sometimes that's a good psychology, and sometimes it isn't. You have to know how to handle it, to get your athlete or the person working for you to say, 'I'll show that son of a bitch.' You have to go by a fine line, or it can be difficult and destructive.

"My sisters and I had to live with that pressure every day, but I don't regret it now. It means more to me as I look back on it than it did while I was going through it. In a sense, I thank God he did what he did for me, because he taught me an awful lot. And you had to respect the man.

"He never crushed my spirit. Some people think I'm a case for an institution maybe. But it never crushed my spirit at all.

"My dad was very well respected and liked. He was elected councilman. He got the highest votes of anyone who ran. In those days politics was not the fishbowl it is today. Your private life was your own. My father in a lot of ways was a very, very private guy.

"My dad liked teaching his kids and educating us. From the time I was a kid, I worked. We all knew how to keep books and a ledger from the time we were nine years old. I had chickens to raise. We never got an allowance. We were given chickens, and we sold eggs, and that's the way we made our money. We had a little cart and ponies to pull the cart, and I used to sell eggs all through Bay Village. Then when I went away to school in the ninth grade, Dad had me sell my egg company to my two sisters. The George Company became the S&J Company. I sold the company to them for fifty dollars, and it took them two years to pay me, but I got my money. I made sure of it.

"I'd have to get up every morning before I went to school, clean the chicken roost, collect the eggs, get the chickens fed, and I can remember a couple of times forgetting to take the eggs out of my pockets in school, and egg stuff would be dripping. I went to Bay Village Elementary School, and I was the only one who had to wear a coat and tie.

"My father always was interested in having his kids in sports. My dad is six foot three, and he knows his sports. In 1928, he had everyone beaten in the high hurdles for the Olympics. He was one of the three best hurdlers in the world at that time. And he would have made the U.S. Olympic team, but he didn't try, because he and my mother decided to get married instead."

I asked George if he had seen the movie *Chariots of Fire*, about an English runner who leaves his girl behind so he can try out for the Olympics.

"A great movie," George said. "Isn't that a great movie? My dad did just the opposite. And they are still together," he said proudly. "He's a very competitive man, and he had all three of his children doing sports at a very young age, my sisters as well, both of them."

Ike Ganyard, who was a year older than George, was a close childhood friend of George's. He recalled what it was like growing up in rural Bay Village in the years before and after the war.

"George's white, big old farmhouse was on the south side of Lake Road," he said. "I thought it was the biggest house in Bay Village. It was huge, three stories with a gabled roof. It was a modern, beautiful home; because the rest of us lived in little, tiny houses and we were very impressionable. We all knew Mr. Steinbrenner owned a shipping company. We were aware.

"George and I were friends since we were kids. We lived about a quarter of a mile to a half a mile away. We would ride bikes and meet. We would leave home at eight in the morning in the summertime, and our parents never saw us until dark. We went swimming. God, people went swimming morning, noon, and night in the summertime.

"We used to play baseball and football in the backyard of what we called the Little Red Schoolhouse. Playing sports was all a kid had to do back then.

"George was big for his age. I can remember in the fifth and sixth grade we played hardball, and George pitched because he was tall and he could throw the ball faster than the rest of us.

"We also played football. It wasn't organized like they do today. We didn't have uniforms or teams. When we had six guys, we played three-on-three, but we played tackle with no equipment. As in everything, we had good players and bad players. Anybody who showed up could play.

"I was aware that George sold eggs to the neighbors and people he knew, because I remember the chicken coop. He didn't have that many eggs, but he could keep people supplied, a dozen for the next-door neighbor, that type of thing. We didn't know whether it was George's hobby because he was interested in it or because of his father wanting him to do it. I remember George wearing a shirt and tie to school in grammar school. Most of us wore open shirts and knickers."

Joe Bennett, who knew George when they were children, remembered Henry Steinbrenner most vividly. To Bennett, George's father was someone to fear.

"The old man was a tough son of a bitch, difficult to all the people who knew George," said Bennett. "He was a tough cookie, a good old boy, and you were either on his side, or there was no side.

"Henry was an autocrat. He was overbearing to his wife. I would say he ruled the roost with an iron hand. His wife was timid. She swallowed it. She had to. She was scared of him. I'm sure George was scared of him. As we all were. We all laughed about his old man. We called him 'the son of a bitch.'

"George's father never asked George to do anything. He told him. I don't care what George says, I think George was scared of his dad. I was petrified of him. Scared to death. I was so scared of him, when he came into the house, I ran out.

"I never saw his father hug or kiss George. Definitely not, nor joke with him. Henry was a very straitlaced person. Henry had no sense of humor, for Christ's sake. He was tough on George."

Frank Treadway, another of George's childhood friends, recalled that though he rarely was around George's father, Henry loomed as the dominant factor in his son's life.

"Henry didn't have anything to do with any of George's young friends. My father was the same way. My mother used to say, 'Rusty loves his own children, but he doesn't really care for anybody else's kids.' To me, my father was polite to my friends when I brought them home, but as far as taking them on picnics, he didn't care for that. And Henry was the same way."

Treadway couldn't help notice that despite his wealth, Henry Steinbrenner lived modestly, sometimes even cheaply. "Henry Steinbrenner had a little dinky white Ford with standard shift and no air-conditioning," he said. "My father was driving one of these big four-door Lincolns, and we'd tool down Lake Avenue on the way to work in the morning, and we'd come by this beat-up old car with the roof crushed in. Something had fallen on Henry's car, and it took him a year to fix it. And here was old Henry driving along. He wasn't going to ride the bus, but he sure didn't need anything fancy."

What Treadway recalled more than anything were the stories George told about his father. The most famous was his "Egg Story." As George saw it, the story is about Henry's temper. But Treadway viewed it as more about George's never taking responsibility for his actions and using his father to fight his battles.

"George used to tell some wonderful stories about himself," said Treadway. "George is a wonderful storyteller. He'd get wound up at a party—it was never liquor-induced. When I knew him he wasn't much of a drinker. There was nothing he loved more than to tell stories about himself.

"He would tell the story about his getting a C on his report card, showing it to his father at night, and saying, 'My teacher doesn't like me.' And the next day George goes to school with eggs in his pocket, and his father comes to talk to the principal about George getting a C in a course, and he starts to shake George, and he breaks all the eggs in his pocket. Now, George is not being shaken as a disciplinary measure. His father was going to school to stick up for George against this teacher who is picking on him.

"I just think his father is steaming under his collar, and he's shaking George because he can't shake the principal or shake himself. George is this eighth-grade kid. He's the only kid in the school who has to wear a coat and tie to school and where else is he going to carry the eggs but his coat pocket? Again, we got this story from George. George could very well have embellished it. Henry came to talk to the principal, and his father is all pissed off. 'How can you give him a grade like that?' And he ends up shaking George and breaking the eggs. George would tell that story, and we'd laugh so hard the tears would come down our eyes.

"George also used to tell another story of how Mrs. Steinbrenner lived in fear of her husband at times. Henry didn't like the sound of water at night past eight o'clock. George came home from a date one night, went downstairs, and there was the sound of splashing water coming from the basement. George said, 'Mother, is that you?' Poor Rita was giving herself a sponge bath in the laundry tub because Henry didn't want to hear the water running. It was only eight-thirty.

"Then there was the story Rita told my mother—how she and Henry had been married about a week, and they came home after the honeymoon, and Rita made a casserole, thinking that was a legitimate form of food, and Henry didn't, and he threw it at her. A tough old German, Henry didn't like food that was cooked twice.

"The world is full of things like this behind closed doors. You meet him in public, and he is a gentleman, but this is behind closed doors.

"George didn't really have any adversity in his life like so many people. He went to summer camp, and he lived in a nice home, and there was always good food on the table, so he had no adversity. If you're rich when you grow up, and you're still rich when you're fifty, it's 'Let's make it out that I had to climb a few mountains when I was a kid, make all the stories sound so much better.'"

Patsy Stecher, who lived in Bay Village and was close to the Steinbrenners, also saw the tyrannical nature of Henry Steinbrenner. "He fixed the rules, and you did it his way," she said. "When you have a father like George had, either you end up being nothing, or, like George, you become competitive. My theory was that what drove George was trying all the time to please his father."

2

It was unquestionably true that George used his
father to get what he wanted.
—Lee Robinson

Culver Military Academy

Culver Military Academy was founded in 1894 in Indiana by
Henry Harrison Culver, who got rich selling four-hundred-
pound potbellied stoves door-to-door in the Midwest. As the company
gained prosperity, he fought with his brothers, and in 1883 a worn-down
Henry Culver left the company in ill health. A wealthy man, he sought
tranquillity, and he bought land on the shores of Lake Maxinkuckee.
In 1888, he built a tabernacle, a hotel, and some cottages on his property and arranged for a series of revival meetings. When his religious
penchant waned, he built a fairground on the site with a racetrack, and
when nothing came of that, in 1896, he founded a school, deciding it
best to mix liberalism with a Christian education. The result was Culver
Military Academy.

Among Culver's illustrious alumni were Walter O'Malley, the
owner of the Brooklyn Dodgers and the man who took them to Los
Angeles; Gene Siskel, the movie critic; Jonathan Winters, the come-
dian; Hal Holbrook, the movie and stage star; bandleader Horace
Heidt; Jack Eckerd, the founder of Eckerd Pharmacy and Eckerd
College in St. Petersburg, Florida; Alberto Bailleres, the third richest
man in Mexico; and George Steinbrenner, the owner of the New York
Yankees and perhaps the school's most visible and talked-about alum.

In 1941, when George began attending Culver summer camp as a nine-year-old, the school looked like something out of a King Arthur tale, a Gothic castle with battlements and parapets on the roof. From the administration building you could see beautiful Lake Mixinkuckee, surrounded by trees and with green, rolling hills stretching into the distance.

The Culver summer program was devoted to the usual camp activities like baseball, tennis, boating, canoeing, swimming, and arts and crafts. It was a leisurely way to pass a summer. George Steinbrenner would attend Culver for four summers before enrolling in the school as a thirteen-year-old freshman. He recalled his introduction to the Culver summer program. From a young age George had displayed a "the whole world is against me" attitude, and the way he tells it, he was such an exceptional camper that by the time he arrived as a plebe, the other kids already had it in for him.

"I went to the summer school for four years, and I had risen to a high rank," he remembered. "In Woodcraft, you attain a bronze C, a silver C, and a gold C, and I got my bronze C the first year, then the next two Cs my second year, when it's supposed to take you three years. Then they sent me back almost a postgrad year—and I was aide to the commandant, and then I went right into the winter school.

"In winter school they were laying for me because I came in with this big rank from the Woodcraft camp. You know the way the cadets are. When I started there, I didn't adapt to it as well as I should have."

Lee Robinson, who met George when they were both ten, questioned George's telling of events. "That isn't true," said Robinson, who hails from Manhasset, New York. "George didn't win any more Woodcraft camp badges than anyone else. We were in the same group of campers, and he wasn't a particularly outstanding camper. He wasn't below average. He was just an average guy. As a boy, I liked George well enough.

"I remember he would say, 'The kids are down on me.' But George was picked on more than most because he came from a wealthy family, and he had a tendency to gloat and talk a lot about how rich his family was, and that irritated the kids. I would say that was much more of a reason they picked on him than any awards he won.

"If George wasn't liked, it was a question of attitude. He acted superior, because he was from a very wealthy family. He had few friends because his arrogance set him apart."

When George enrolled for his freshman year in 1945, Culver was perhaps the finest military academy in the country from an academic standpoint. Students went there for several reasons. George attended because his father was a man who valued discipline and structure über alles, and he feared that his son wouldn't fare as well academically in an unstructured public school environment. Without saying so, George indicated that going to Culver certainly wasn't his idea.

"I don't know why my father wanted me to go to Culver," George said. "He appreciated the school. It represented more discipline than an ordinary school, and that's what he wanted for me."

At Culver, every minute was structured. Don Martin, a star student who started with George in the ninth grade, recalled the routine. "At six twenty-five the bells rang," he said. "The cannon went off and the bugle blew, and a man at the head of each corridor said, 'Good morning. Six twenty-five. Time to get up.' You had three minutes until another bell rang, at which point if your feet were not on the floor, you got demerits.

"We had tough, white-glove inspections all the time, and kids were always thinking of ways to pull pranks on other kids, like short-sheeting the bed or putting worms in the bed, but you couldn't get away with too much.

"We were under a strict plebe–Old Man system like West Point. I can remember when I was a plebe, I was told, 'You watch that lightbulb straight ahead of you, and when it turns red, white, and blue, stand up and sing the "Star Spangled Banner."' We were fifteen years old, and we were intimidated. You didn't deviate. People fell in line."

During his plebe year, George roomed with Lee Robinson, who went to Culver because the war was on and his father thought military training would be good for him. Robinson recalled George as a mediocre student who hated the plebe–upper class system but who had an abiding interest in sports.

"His plebe year I remember he very much resented the authority of the upperclassmen," said Robinson. "He would often do things out of line."

George saw the constant disciplining by the upperclassmen as abusive, and he felt he was unfairly singled out and picked on. He admitted that his freshman year was traumatic at times.

"In those days there was a great deal of hazing at Culver," George said. "The plebe system was very strong, and hazing was strong. They'd look for you to make a little mistake, but for some other guy they'd overlook a big mistake. It was that way, it seemed, during my freshman year at Culver.

"There were always times you wanted to quit something like that. Yes, but I never called my dad and said, 'Get me out of here.' No, I was scared to do that. But there were times I wanted to quit, and there was more than one night I went to bed a little misty-eyed, because it was really tough."

The discipline of Culver didn't turn George into a better student as his father had wished. "George was *not* a good student," said Robinson. "I never thought of George as being very bright academically. He's smart in a business sense. He just barely had a C average at Culver, and as far as I knew, he studied the same as everyone else. George was very interested in athletics, specifically track, and to a lesser extent football. I had a feeling he was competing with his father's record in the athletic world. I remember George stressing track, and at one point he talked of becoming an actor. He had been in a Gilbert and Sullivan play in junior high school.

"I also remember his talking about money a lot. He gave the impression he was already rich. He said his father was very, very wealthy. He let it be known that if someone gave [him] a hard time, he'd see to it his father would fix it."

When the time came for the students to go home for Thanksgiving, it was too far and too expensive for Robinson to go back to Long Island, so George's mother invited him to their Bay Village home for the holiday. Said Robinson, "Whenever I was with Mr. Steinbrenner, I always thought he was a very gracious, pleasant man. He was a wealthy, self-made man who had worked hard and enjoyed the fruits of his labor. George had always described him as tough, but I never saw that. In fact, George worshipped his dad. You got the feeling that whatever George was going to do in life, he was going to do his utmost to measure up to his father."

George had taken piano lessons since he was five years old, and for four years took drum lessons from a Clevelander by the name of Charlie Wilcoxon, whom he described as "the premier drum teacher in the United States."

"He taught all the great ones," said George. "My dad was interested in my knowing music, and so he wanted me in the band at Culver.

"I took voice lessons and was in the choir, and I played in the drum and bugle corps in the summer school, and I went into the band in the winter. I was not a great drummer, but I enjoyed it. I loved the band, and I will never regret a minute of the time I spent in the band or in the glee club. To me that was as important as athletics."

The band played at all military functions, and none was as important or as grand as the parade held every Sunday morning when all eight hundred cadets would mass in an elaborate ceremony. The infantry formed up in platoons, with the captains out front. Eight hundred men would snap to attention, the captains would all raise their sabers, and the men would come forward and salute.

Then the trucks would pass by pulling the cannons, and the cavalry would march by the reviewing stand. As they passed the stand, the cadets on horseback would drop their lances and look to the right, the infantrymen would snap to attention, and they would all present arms. Throughout, the band would play march tunes. It was a stirring, impressive ceremony.

"The band was kind of a renegade unit," said Ket Barber, a Michigander who went to camp and to high school with George. "Nobody quite knew what to do with us. We were part of the infantry, but our activities were so varied—our task was to perform at military functions—we were a bit different from the rest. We were kind of a unit unto ourselves. The band as a military unit was generally not all that highly regarded.

"We had a concert band. We had our own special concerts, and of course we had the marching band. We were thoroughly versatile. And as an offshoot we had a jazz band. George was the drummer. He had talent. I didn't."

Barber met George their freshman year. He remembered him as "not altogether orthodox. He had a sense of humor. He enjoyed a practical joke."

At the end of their freshman year, Ket Barber asked Lee Robinson, George's roommate, if he would room with him the following year. Robinson agreed. Said Robinson, "Later on I told George I wasn't going to room with him, and our relationship was a little strained by then. George was difficult to get along with. I couldn't take his arrogance, the feeling he gave that he was above it all, that he didn't have to work the way the rest of the kids did because he had his father up there in Cleveland to get things straightened out for him. We didn't have proof. But you put two and two together."

The feeling by some of his classmates, especially those in the band who were closest to him, that George was getting preferential treatment because of his father's influence would dog him for the rest of his Culver career.

Culver was run on a strict demerit system. If a cadet was given demerits, at noontime he would report to the officer in charge of his barracks, usually an older retired military man who acted as a counselor, and the officer would read the charge. "You were late getting up in the morning. What do you have to say?" The cadet would have to give his explanation and, based on that, he would get demerits or not. If a cadet didn't seem to be sorry, demerits were automatic. If you were awarded a large number of demerits in a short span of time, the punishment was marching around the square in front of the administration building carrying a rifle. It was rare for a cadet to amass that many, but George was one who managed to do so.

Ket Barber recalled George's penchant for hijinks in the face of authority. "We used to eat in the mess hall, which had a very high ceiling. We'd march in and take our assigned seats, and on the table they would serve us butter patties. One of the sports we partook in was flicking the butter patties up onto the ceiling so they would stick by launching them with a knife. When they melted, they would drop back down onto the table or onto somebody's head or clothes.

"George managed to get two or three of them up there, when a counselor came over. Had he caught George in the act, he was going to be in deep yogurt.

"Of course George denied doing it. As the counselor spoke, one of the patties came back down onto the table. It was an awkward situation. George kept his cool, looked at it, looked around, and said, 'You guys gotta quit sticking the butter patties up on the ceiling.'

"George had a sense of humor. Some of the guys had a little trouble handling it, of course. He took a little understanding, but we were great friends."

Barber, however, was not amused when George played one of his pranks on him. One morning George came down to Barber's room and said to him, "Come over to the Inn with me. It's Nancy Sutherland's birthday, and I want to get her a present, and I want you to help me."

The Inn had a fancy gift shop, and George bought some toilet water. He said to the saleswoman, "Wrap it," and he signed a little card for it. When Barber started to leave, George said, "I want to give it to her, but I don't have enough time to visit with her, so just come over with me, and we'll give it to her and leave." Barber agreed.

Nancy Sutherland, one of the few females on the all-male campus, was the daughter of a faculty member. George and Ket Barber knocked on the door, and as the handle began to turn and Nancy opened the door, George jammed the little box into Barber's chest and ran. Barber grabbed for it, and when Nancy opened the door, George shouted to her, "Ket told me it was your birthday, and I forgot all about it. He got you a present, and I just wanted to come over and wish you a happy birthday." Then he said, "I gotta leave right away. You two have a good time. I'll see you later."

Barber, who George knew had no designs on the girl, was left having to go through with the charade. "There was no way I could explain it," said Barber, "because George had put my name on the card. Well, what do you say? My reaction was a little bit unkind. I knew it was a prank, but sometimes when it becomes your turn, you don't think it's quite so funny."

The dorms at Culver in the 1940s were named after World War I battles. The band members lived on the first floor of a brick building named Argonne and in half of another building called Château-Thierry. George lived in Argonne all four years. One of his classmates was Pete Hensil, a band member who played flute and piccolo. Hensil remembers playing electronic football with George almost every Friday night. "The game had a lightbulb," Hensil recalled, "and you pulled out a slide, and you had plays."

Hensil also remembered fondly that George spent several weeks trying to teach him how to dance. "He was a good dancer, and he tried to teach me. We used to call George 'Hot Lips.' He had a girlfriend, Mary Bishop, the daughter of our history instructor. It was a feather in his cap."

Going into their sophomore year, George asked Hensil if he would room with him. Hensil said no. Commented Hensil years later, "As

I look back, I really blew it. I ended up rooming with a guy who became a programmer for a beer outfit."

Hensil remembered George for his devotion to athletics. They both played on the band intramural basketball team, a recreational activity that was coached and organized. The team practiced every day in the winter. George was a forward. Hensil recalled that George had an uncanny, off-balance shot from the corner. "And he could make it," Hensil said. "In the spring," he added, "George also ran track on the varsity, and he did very well. He was outstanding at Culver. We had intramural track at Culver, and George talked me into running on a relay for the band team. I didn't have any track shoes, and he lent me his shoes."

In the three years he ran varsity track at Culver, George's track team was undefeated, the class of the private school league. George Steiner, who was also on the track team, felt he got to know Steinbrenner "pretty well, having spent time with him on trips as well as at practice. I knew at the time his family was wealthy, that they were involved with ships," he said. "I never knew how much they had, whether they were millionaires, but a lot of people at Culver were well-off. That wasn't that unusual. I always felt George was very personable, a nice guy. I really liked him."

Jim Beardsley, another team member, recalled that though George was the best hurdler on the Culver team, his times were only average. Beardsley argued that one reason their times weren't better was that the rigors of military school wore everybody out.

"George liked track a lot," he said. "He didn't have that much speed. He was like a lot of us, going to military school, drilling, going to all these parades, and by the time we got to doing sports, we were kind of worn out. Sometimes we had a tough time getting through the day. And the academic standards were pretty high too—that was part of it."

The coach of the track team from 1943 through his retirement in 1974 was a faculty member by the name of A. Coke Smith. When Smith talked about George, I could hear deep affection—and disappointment. That George hadn't worked as hard in track as he did in football. That he had loved his football coach, Russ Oliver, more than he had Smith. In 1981 Smith also wondered what had happened to George that as owner of the New York Yankees he had turned into a tyrant Smith barely recognized.

"George was a marvelous young man," said Smith. "He got along fine with everyone. He was a gentleman of the first order. He was very gentle and very kind, and much of a family man."

I asked Smith whether Henry Steinbrenner had been tough on George. "Oh heavens to Betsy no," he said. "Hank was a wonderful father. And his mother was wonderful. See, I grew fond of the whole family. I could say that George was somewhat of a disappointment to me, but I was never frustrated by George because he was always such a gentleman, always such a good man to be around. He didn't argue. He didn't fight. He just did what you told him to—up to a point. I just liked him so much.

"He was a fine competitor but not very enthusiastic about working. George was kind of lazy. He was pretty good, but he could have gotten better. He could get by with what he was doing not working too hard. George was a member of one of the best track teams Culver ever had. He had lots of natural ability, was one of the top runners. By the time he was a senior, he could run the 120 hurdles in 15.2 [seconds], which may not be very good according to Texas standards, but good according to Indiana standards. He could have been better at track, but I don't think George had his heart in it. At Culver he had more on his mind than academics. I think he was interested in football and track more than academics. That's not unusual for a boy that age. I still do [think that], though I wish I could change his attitude. He does not seem like the George Steinbrenner I used to know. But when he gets into the competition of making money, he's like the man behind the wheel of an automobile. He turns into an ogre."

George made the Culver football team his junior year, and as a senior he started at end over junior George Steiner, who said that George got to play "because he was a year older and just a little bit better." Ket Barber played fullback, guard, or tackle, depending on where he was needed, and he recalled George's enthusiasm for football and the fact he had a hard time accepting defeat.

"He was hard on himself," said Barber. "Yeah, he didn't like to lose. He would talk about it. He'd say, 'I should have done this.' He was known to slam a locker or two, as opposed to the guy who would sit down and look at his shoes and go into a corner and hide."

Lee Robinson admitted that George was a better athlete than he was, but he said he and his friends didn't think he deserved to start at end. In his opinion, the specter of George's doting dad influenced the coaching staff to promote George. "I don't know for sure if there was a connection," he said, "but I just had the general feeling there were better-qualified people who didn't get to play because George was on the team." George probably did deserve his starting role, but the fact that his classmates felt the way they did about him says a lot about him during his years at Culver.

During his senior year, George and his class were handed the reins of power, and so the newbie plebes were at his mercy. Ket Barber recalled when the company officers, including George, inspected the plebes for their uniforms and shoe shines. Said Barber, "George was known to bend down and inspect a plebe's shoes and check for how well they were shined, and a time or two he'd tie their shoelaces together. Of course, at the first command, [the plebe] fell over."

By the time George became a senior, he was outspoken and brash, and if he felt strongly enough about something, he took a position. He was on the yearbook committee and had his own ideas how it ought to be structured. That there was a photo of him in the yearbook catching a touchdown pass could not have been a coincidence. In his own way, George was learning leadership at Culver, and though he didn't have rank to indicate his status, by his senior year he was usurping leadership in areas he thought he should control. Though he was drawing resentment for it, he remained unfazed.

"George tended to polarize people," said Barber. "You tended to be for or against him. George was very much an extrovert. He was no shrinking violet. Some kids from the upper strata resented him because they were used to having people look after them, and here was a peer who had no respect for that in itself. He wasn't deferential just because of their economic status. Nor did he expect anything from anyone else. He just did his thing.

"George had his share of detractors, and that in itself set him back a little bit. But if he wanted something, he was pretty much able to organize things and get it."

When classmates discussed what they remembered most about George, inevitably they would start to talk about his father, who by George's senior year had become a familiar figure on the Culver campus. Some students, like Pete Hensil, expressed admiration for George's father's interest in his son.

"He would visit him quite often," said Hensil. "His father always managed, and I appreciated that."

But Ket Barber saw something else. He saw a father who was constantly rushing to campus to stick up for George when he got in trouble. From his perspective, George was a victim of his father's overprotectiveness.

"The problem," said Barber, "was that George's father took a personal interest with everything that happened with George, and as a matter of fact, George somewhat resented it. If his father felt the faculty or anyone else was treating George unfairly, he would drive over and address his complaints to the faculty, and he'd embarrass George somewhat. If George came back with his fair share of demerits, and he told his father there was prejudice going on, his father would react to that.

"It wasn't unusual for kids to feel that way [that prejudice was going on]," said Barber. "The unusual part was to have a father who would get involved. Hank Steinbrenner was a rather large man with a stentorian voice, and he wasn't the kind of guy who would speak in whispers. He'd go to the superintendent's office or the counselor's office, and everybody knew he was there. Hank didn't hold back when he got his dander up. He let everybody know about it, and sometimes the faculty members would talk about it. But they didn't hear him telling George he had to shape up and do his part. Nevertheless, those actions on his dad's part would have held him back more than it got him ahead. We had people there who came from very wealthy families, so we're talking about money and status abounding, and it wasn't a matter of paying attention to someone who was rich."

Lee Robinson saw the George-Henry relationship differently. According to Robinson, George used the influence of his wealthy, powerful father like a billy club to get what he wanted. "George would talk about what a tough guy his father was," said Robinson, "but I never could understand that. I never saw his father scream at him or make him cry. Nothing like that. He treated George the same way he treated me, easygoing and a nice guy. George seemed to be able to get just about anything he wanted to from his father.

"It was unquestionably true that George used his father to get what he wanted," he continued. "He used his father's influence any chance he could to further his career at Culver. That's how the students looked on it, and they used to tease him about it.

"He'd get in trouble—not serious trouble, but something like not shining his shoes—and he'd get some demerits, and the kids would say, 'George, you don't have to worry about that. Your pop will get those wiped off for you.' Sometimes when he got demerits he'd joke, 'I don't have to worry about those things.'

"He gave everyone the attitude that he was throwing his weight around not based on his own merit or achievement but on the wealth of his family. He flaunted that, and that created resentment in a number of his fellow students, some of whom used to ride him about it. Not that he cared how we felt. George seemed very self-assured in those days. It was water off a duck's back. He learned at an early age that if he had a goal to reach, he wouldn't hesitate to use his or anyone else's money to achieve that goal."

George's promotion to lieutenant in November of his senior year was one such event. Promotions usually were made at graduation, and at the graduation ceremony after his junior year, George looked at the promotion list, only to find that his name wasn't on it. He was disappointed and hurt, but his promotion had been held up by several faculty members who felt that he had a lot more ability than he showed in their classes, that he didn't prepare, didn't study, and didn't care that he was getting mediocre grades. They also saw that he had trouble with military discipline and tended to be argumentative in class. The truth was, George was bored within the severity of the military system and couldn't wait to leave.

Said Pete Hensil, "George really didn't show that much leadership. He was more on the goof-off side."

According to Ket Barber, when George, still a lowly sergeant, returned to school in the fall of his senior year, he had a different attitude toward his studies. "When he came back," said Barber, "it had an ameliorating effect on him, and he got a bit more serious, and he started doing things more conventionally. So when he was promoted to second lieutenant in November, it was almost automatic."

Lee Robinson, when asked how it was that George had been promoted, immediately laughed. "That's a question I heard my classmates ask for years," he said. "It was June of 1947, right after a visit from his father. His father must have done something, because none of us could ever figure out what George did to deserve it. The kids had a pretty good idea of the standards you had to meet in order to become an officer, and they also had a pretty good idea that George did not meet those standards. And so they drew their own conclusions. A lot of us were mad about it."

In the spring of his senior year George learned that he had been turned down by MIT, where his father had graduated number one in his class, but he did get into Williams College, a small, prestigious liberal arts college in western Massachusetts. On graduation day, George was presented by his father with a brand-new 1947 Buick convertible. It was maroon, and classmates noticed.

"Most of us didn't get anything more than a wristwatch," said Lee Robinson.

"I ended up with a fairly good record," said George. "The last year I won the Callahan award for overall excellence, which my dad couldn't believe."

His classmates couldn't believe it either, but with graduation at hand, they were looking forward, not back.

"George's senior year he won the Callahan award for excellence in the band, and that was Colonel Payson's doing," said Lee Robinson. "George's father was the one who had the relationship with Colonel Payson. His father would come down to Culver all the time and spend hours with Colonel Payson. They got to know each other well, and so George got to know him too.

"I know some eyebrows were raised, but that was the end of our senior year, and the kids didn't have much time to discuss it. They were more anxious to get out of that school and get on to bigger and better things. They weren't concerned about George."

3

George is the last puritan.
—Charlie Glass

Williams College

Located in the Berkshire Mountains north of Pittsfield in western Massachusetts, Williams College has been said by some to have the prettiest campus and to be the best liberal arts school in the United States. Founded in 1793 as a men's college, it was funded from the estate of Ephraim Williams, a wealthy landowner and officer of the Massachusetts militia who was killed at the battle of Lake George on September 8, 1755.

When George Steinbrenner entered Williams in the fall of 1948 as a member of the class of 1952, he was accompanied by a group of friends and acquaintances from the greater Cleveland area, including Peter Callahan, William Callahan, Robert Simpson, Dave Andrews, Jim Krill, and Chuck Harris, whose father was mayor of Shaker Heights, a wealthy suburb on the East Side of Cleveland. As high schoolers, all had attended the same parties and knew one another socially. Pete Smythe, a friend of George's from Bay Village, had been accepted to Williams the year before. According to Simpson, it was Smythe who interested the others.

Confirmed George, "I went to college at Williams because all my pals were going to Williams: Bill Callahan, Chuck Harris, that group."

Since George had been a mediocre student at Culver, mostly because academics hadn't interested him very much, the question remains, how did he get into such a prestigious school?

One answer: his father's connections. Henry Steinbrenner, whose ships on the Great Lakes were involved in the war effort, had a network of influential friends in high places that was spread across the country. According to one Deke fraternity mate of George's, Charlie Glass, one of Hank Steinbrenner's friends was James Phinney Baxter III, the president of Williams. It would not be the last time that Henry would use his clout to make sure George succeeded in getting where he wanted to go.

During his freshman year, George shared a room in the dorm with fellow Culver grad Don Martin. During the Culver graduation, George's father had been duly impressed when Martin kept trotting up to the podium to accept awards for academic achievement. When Henry Steinbrenner heard that Martin was going to Williams he told George, "It would be beneficial for you to room with someone who is smart and knows how to study and do his homework. He'd be a good person to room with."

"George picked me," said Martin. "I didn't pick him. The third person, Dick Kraft, came to us as the luck of the draw."

Dick "Pusher" Kraft came to Williams from a small town in New Jersey. Like George, he was a football player, and he would go on to become the captain of the freshman team. (Martin played soccer.) Kraft, who came from a public high school, at first was envious that George and Martin knew each other, but quickly friendships materialized.

Martin recalled most vividly that his Cleveland roommate was fanatical about sports, especially the Cleveland Browns and the Cleveland Indians, and well he should have been, because in 1948 the Browns, playing in the All-America Football Conference, at 15–0 went through the season undefeated, the first pro football team ever to do so. Led by quarterback Otto Graham and captain Lou Saban, the Browns dominated the AAFC, losing only four games in four years before joining the NFL in 1950.

The 1948 Indians also were champions, world champions, victors over the Boston Braves. The Indians were owned by Bill Veeck, a brilliant promoter and a pioneer in that he signed Larry Doby, the first black to play in the American League. Led by player-manager Lou

Boudreau, Bob Feller, Bob Lemon, and another black star, Satchel Paige, the Indians won their first pennant since 1920. For Cleveland fans, 1948 was a year to remember.

As a symbol of George's love of the Indians, he placed a small, doll-like statue of a Cleveland Indian baseball player on the mantel in his dorm room.

"Bill Veeck owned the Indians at the time," said Don Martin, "and he really admired Veeck as being a super-owner because of his promotional instincts. One day George picked up that little Indian and he said to me, 'What I would like to do one day is own the Cleveland Indians.' I thought he was kidding. But that's what he really wanted, right from when he was a freshman at Williams. Very few people at an early age can identify what they want to do, and even fewer are able to do it. It's very unusual for an individual to be able to perform and achieve what he really desires."

One of George's other loves was football. He came to Williams with a strong desire to play, but, he said, what stopped him from making the freshman football team was a separated shoulder, an injury he said had occurred during his senior year at Culver.

Len Watters, the Williams head football coach from 1948 to 1962, recalled that George had a real loose shoulder. "When that arm got over his head, it would go out of joint, and it was a painful thing each time you had to put it back," he said. "He quit on my advice and that of his doctors. But George wasn't a bad halfback. He could run like nobody's business."

George would not go out for football again until his junior year. Instead, he concentrated all his energies on running track. An important part of three consecutive undefeated Culver track teams, he was intent not just on making the Williams team but on running in the 1952 Olympics, an unreachable, unrealistic goal considering the level of his talent.

Living next door to George was another track enthusiast by the name of Jack Brody, who remembers the horseplay of the freshmen who lived in Williams Hall. "Dick Kraft was usually the noisy one, but George would go along," said Brody. "I have a clear picture of my two roommates, Dick Edwards and Kenny Moffitt, sliding down the banister on one leg, and everyone thinking it the funniest thing."

Brody was a track nut who came out of Brooklyn with a reputation as a sprinter. George and Jack Brody would go on to become the top runners on the Williams varsity. They would avidly read the statistics-laden *Track and Field* magazine, perusing the long lists of times to see who was doing what in meets around the country.

George's times were only average compared to those of the star runners—George's track coach at Culver said he had been clocked in the 220 hurdles at 15.2 seconds, and George would cite that as his best time, but in comparison to the best in the world, Harrison Dillard, who ran it in 13.7, he didn't come close to measuring up to Olympic stature. Nevertheless, Brody noticed, no one on the track team—not even he—worked harder at improving himself than George.

"We were both track nuts," said Brody. "We went through the same training, day in and day out. He would do a morning session as well as an afternoon session. I only did that about half the time.

"George was really determined to get the most out of himself. He dieted. He never smoked, never drank. So he was really serious. George really used all his talent. He had a great Christian work ethic."

George and Jack Brody became the closest of friends during their first two years at Williams. They walked from the dorm to the gym together, and they'd walk back together. In the winter they practiced outdoors on the dirt track. The wind would blow, and they'd take a deep breath, and their throats would burn. George's nose would get very red. In the biting cold, said Brody, it looked like it was on fire.

During their grueling workouts, George and Brody would run side by side and tease each other. Though neither carried much extra poundage, they called each other "fat," and they'd brag how each was better than the other, and would laugh a lot to break the monotony of training. George didn't realize it, but in Jack Brody he had a loyal, supportive friend, a rarity for the socially awkward, blustery freshman.

One of the first things Brody noticed about George was that his life was deeply colored by his relationship with his father. It was George's favorite subject, it seemed. One minute George would talk glowingly about him, regaling anyone within earshot, including those on the track team, with stories about how his father had qualified for the Olympics in 1928 but how he chose to get married instead, and how he was the captain of a fleet of ships that crisscrossed the Great

Lakes. The next minute George would tell stories about the martinet Henry, about his father's rules that forced everyone to be silent in the house after 8 p.m., about his egg business, how his father broke the eggs in his pocket one day at school, and about how second place was never good enough for his father. George made it clear he was both in awe of his father and terrified of him. "His father seemed to be a force even when we were five hundred miles away," said Brody. "George was always talking about his father. In general, Henry didn't approve. There was always a lot of fear in that. Respect, awe, and yeah, fear. George imparted this to everyone else, so we referred to his father as 'the Baron,' a scary, powerful man, and we were very uneasy."

Later, when Brody actually met Henry Steinbrenner, he came away confused. Like some others before him, he could see the fear George had of his father, but whenever Brody was in the great man's presence, Henry Steinbrenner seemed polite and almost kind.

"When George and his father were together, George was very polite, but he was scared polite. When his father talked to me, I was shocked to find he was very affable. He seemed very nice. I could only conclude it was in George's head."

Brody began to see that it was George's father's influence that prompted George to train at track as hard as he did. "George had a great need to be loved by this person who he was afraid of, and that had something to do with his knocking himself out at track. If George wasn't going to be great, at least he'd do his best."

Friends wondered why George entered prestigious events like the Knights of Columbus meet in Cleveland, where he raced against the legendary Harrison Dillard, only to get smoked by the competition. Said Frank Treadway, "I felt sorry for him because there was no race at all. Here's this rich white kid trying to beat the black hurdlers, and there was no race. But he had paid the entrance fee. Why? Whether he was trying to please his dad, I don't know. At least he had the pull and the gumption to go down there and do it."

Jack Brody noticed that George showed contempt for those on the track team who were slipshod about practicing. One of the members of the team, whose last name was Jones, was the best quarter-miler on the team. George thought it a disgrace that Jones trained only rarely and told him so. They were like oil and water.

For his part, Jones, who read poetry and enjoyed opera, would call George "the fat ass from Cleveland," or he'd say, "Hey, George, how is the baron?"

George, who had no sense of humor about anyone for whom things came so easily, would retort, "Why don't you go and listen to your goddamn opera."

Brody noticed something else about George: he desperately wanted the approval of the older athletes on the track team, especially the war veterans, who comprised about 60 percent of the students. "I assumed his need to be associated with older athletes was all about his father," said Brody. "He was very respectful to the veterans and to the coaches particularly. His association with coaches had an awful lot to do with the association with his father—strong, dominating figures."

Once track practice began, Brody noticed George's desperate need to be accepted by the team's armed services veterans, especially Kevin Delaney, the track team captain, men who showed little patience for a freshman with a modicum of talent who too often strolled over and tried to horn in on their conversations. He particularly sought out Delaney, a former marine, who at times could be cruel to him.

"Kevin was captain of the track team, and George was always kissing his ass," said Steve Blasky, George's student adviser. "Kevin always made fun of him. Kevin would call him an asshole."

"The veteran track members would say to him, 'Beat it,'" recalled Jack Brody, "but George was remarkably thick-skinned about it, at least on the outside. They couldn't get rid of him. They'd tell him to stop hanging around them, to stop it, and he wouldn't. Nothing would stop him. He'd get very red and come right back. I would hear people talking about him out of his presence. They'd say, 'I don't know why he keeps hanging around Kevin Delaney.' Kevin used to tell him to get lost all the time.

"George idolized this other runner, a war veteran, a quarter-miler, and George kept after him to teach him to run the quarter. George just wouldn't go away, and finally when George asked him again, the guy said, 'You just have to run faster.' That's a put-down. But no one else would have asked that question. It's a funny question. The way you run faster? You train.

"This is hard to talk about because I felt such fondness for George. I would think, Jesus, don't they recognize the guy is really trying? I was sensitive about that."

Fraternity life was extremely important at Williams back in 1949. Freshmen rushed the fraternities almost as soon as they got off the train. George had a love of sports, but he also had his artistic side. He was a musician who could play the drums and the piano, and he had a pleasant singing voice. He enjoyed literature, and he ended up majoring in English. His senior thesis was on the works of Jane Austen. But more than anything else, George saw himself as a jock. With his love of sports, he was attracted to Delta Kappa Epsilon, where the jocks hung out. Though he didn't go out for the football team, he saw himself as a football player, and the people he wanted to hang out with most were the football players. Delta Kappa Epsilon, which was called the Deke House, was filled with them.

Charlie Glass, who joined Deke a year after George, recalled that sports was the main topic of discussion at every meal. "George would pretend he was the general manager of the Indians, and he'd try to figure out what to do to make the team better. And everybody knew all the statistics. It was four years of that. Sports was the key topic."

His junior year George was the fraternity's rush chairman. Charlie Glass was one of the freshmen rushing that year. He recalled that during Hell Week, the week in which the upperclassmen terrorized the pledges much as the upperclassmen had terrorized the plebes at Culver, George was more vocal than most.

"He made the pledges take their clothes off and stand in the chimney fireplace," said Glass. "He'd holler, 'Stand up and sing.' 'Recite obscene stuff.' George was the biggest yeller, but no one paid a whole lot of attention."

As far as Peter Callahan was concerned, Deke made a mistake by taking too many jocks their year. The combination of testosterone and booze turned the Deke House into Animal House. "The Deke House got a little too Dekey," said Callahan. "We were responsible for bringing the Deke House and the fraternity system down. The Deke House is gone now, and so is the whole fraternity system." While everyone was on vacation in August 1959, the college administration announced its end. Genteel eating clubs took their place.

The Deke House had living quarters only for about eighteen of its fraternity brothers, so it was mostly seniors and a couple juniors who lived in the house. Their sophomore year George and Don Martin shared a double in Sage Hall. In the room next door was one of the more memorable personages on campus, Chuck Salmon, a star of the football team. Like Kevin Delaney, Salmon was someone George sought out, and unlike Delaney, Salmon allowed him into his inner circle. They were an odd couple, George and Salmon. They were both Dekes, but they couldn't have been more different. George came from culture and class, and though Salmon's father had owned the Port Jervis, New York, newspaper, he had run into financial problems, and Salmon turned to friends from the other side of the tracks. A rough-and-tumble guy who had life experience far beyond his years, he relished getting drunk and into bar fights. He enjoyed the company of prostitutes, and he wasn't shy about talking about his sexual encounters. Chuck had been around; George, who had lived a sheltered life, hadn't been anywhere.

Don Martin remembered Salmon, and not fondly. "Chuck was a tough guy, and he could be mean," he said. "He wasn't one of my favorites."

Pete Callahan, who earned eleven letters in football, baseball, and skiing and played alongside Salmon on the football field, tremendously admired his leadership ability. He too was aware that Salmon was a loose cannon that could go off at any moment. "Chuck was one of my best friends, a fantastic guy," said Callahan. "He was the captain of the football team my senior year, and he was a good boxer. In football he was a guard, a tackle, or a linebacker, depending on who was injured. He was a good basketball player. He could do anything.

"Our junior year we were playing Amherst, and I was playing defensive right end, and I was right next to Chuck, who was at right tackle that day. The whole first quarter—Christ—Amherst was running through him because he was standing there pounding the shit out of the guy across from him.

"I went over to Coach Watters and I said, 'Hey, you better get Chuck out of here and cool him off. They're running around him while he's boxing.' Coach Watters took him out and cooled him off, and when he came back, it was all over." Callahan wasn't surprised when Salmon befriended George. He recalled that Chuck was in the habit of befriending people who "were not exactly in." As he did with George.

Bruce Breckenridge, who would room with George their senior year, recalled the friendship between the roughneck Salmon and the gentlemanly George, who became junior-year roommates. "Chuck and George were such opposites," said Breckenridge. "That was the fun thing about them. Chuck was an interesting character, as interesting as George. To Chuck, George was an interesting new factor in his life.

"Chuck and George enjoyed each other. They had a lot of laughs together." One ritual the two performed constantly was arguing the merits of the starting players on the Cleveland Indians versus the starters on the New York Yankees. Said Breckenridge, "George would take the Indians' side, and Salmon would argue for the Yankees. They'd argue over whether Joe DiMaggio was better than Larry Doby, or whether Lou Boudreau was a better manager than Casey Stengel. They'd argue lineups, Al Rosen and Doby versus Mickey Mantle and Billy Martin. They'd also do it in football, the Cleveland Browns versus the New York Giants, but not as much. They'd do this for hours."

George and Chuck Salmon were both named freshman advisers their junior year, a post of distinction. Freshman advisers had to live in the dorm of the freshmen they advised. When they agreed to room together, Don Martin, who was no fan of Salmon, was left to find himself another roommate.

"Chuck didn't like me, but George would defend me to Chuck in conversations he didn't know I heard," said Martin. "I always admired George for his loyalty to me. That showed me he could stand up to Salmon. I wouldn't put too much weight on George's hero worship of Salmon, because, quite frankly, Salmon wasn't hero material."

The legend of Chuck Salmon grew after his heroics during the Korean War. He had joined the air force as a fighter pilot, just as he said he would, and against orders; after the armistice he crossed the Yalu River and shot down the last MIG of the war. When the war ended, Salmon joined the Thunderbirds, the elite flying team that entertained thousands of enthralled spectators each year at air shows. On March 12, 1959, flying out of Nellis Air Force Base, Salmon was practicing with the Thunderbirds when his and another plane collided. He ejected out of the plane, but the ejection mechanism malfunctioned and his seat ripped through his parachute. He died over the Mojave Desert outside of Las Vegas, Nevada.

Steve Blasky had run into Salmon in a Las Vegas casino only two weeks before he died. "He was still a wild man," said Blasky. "We were in a nightclub, and he said, 'Don't say anything. This is not my wife.' It was a Las Vegas lady. Chuck was just the same. When he saw me, he picked me up and damn near threw me across the room.

"I was on a bus in New York City and opened up the *Daily News* and saw the headline, THUNDERBIRD CAPTAIN KILLED, and I saw Chuck's picture, and I burst into tears. He was a beautiful human being, though the meanest, dirtiest football player I had ever seen."

Jack Brody, for one, observed how important it was for George to hang around with and make friends with the top athletes like Salmon. He blamed that on George's father. Brody also saw something else: George made friends based on his needs, not on how well he was treated by others. Brody had been George's closest companion their first two years together, but then when George roomed with Salmon his junior year, he spent less and less time with Brody, until by their senior year Brody rarely saw him except at the track. Brody was almost wistful when he talked about George's choice of friends.

"He was motivated by social ambition and tremendous energy," said Brody, "and the need not to be alone. It's why he sought out coaches and football players and track veterans. If only the janitor was left, he would have gone on talking to him.

"I always had the feeling that his father in some way roughed him up, but I couldn't be sure, because when his father was around, it didn't come across. But in some way his father said, 'George has to be the best,' and George couldn't be the best, so he started to hang around with the people he felt were the best. What George didn't understand was that they weren't the best. They were tin best.

"George liked to be around 'important' people, and he spent a lot of time at it. At first I didn't see it, but then after people started talking to me about it, I noticed. And George would be teased about it. They'd make a wisecrack, but it didn't deter him.

"To be clear, George was not an ass-kisser or sycophant. He just wanted to be one of the boys. He wouldn't let himself be a sap. But some of the athletes didn't treat him very well. They didn't think he was that good, and they felt he was pushy. When I tell people George isn't Jewish, they don't believe me. But he wasn't pushy like the stereotypical Jew. He was pushy as the Protestant water boy.

"He was a person who didn't make commitments. He was so busy testing everyone out to see if they liked him, it was very obvious no one was going to like him—because they knew they were being tested rather than being approached as a friend. He made people edgy.

"I hate to play psychologist, but George was in a trap. If a father makes a son feel lousy, the son can only try to emulate him or try to be better. But George couldn't be better. And that's his self-image. He's not as good as he's supposed to be, so he has to go outside to get his praise.

"He somehow confused in his mind the excellence of athletics with an association of those people. Since he wasn't good, and his father was good, he wanted an association with those guys who were good. But none of them had the affection for him that I had. I really think their criticism was totally inappropriate. He wasn't bad company. He should have been given a better reception. I saw him as a sweet guy trying very hard.

"George developed a real tolerance for pain. He was thick-skinned, and he was a terrible, terrible judge of character. He didn't know who his friends were, didn't know who really liked him.

"George was so surprised when I was loyal. In front of him at Williams I would tell people what a great guy he was, and he would become embarrassed, and he couldn't handle the normal reciprocal emotion. He had no knowledge of what friendship among men might be."

Some questioned how he handled matters having to do with the birds and the bees. During one vacation break, George and Charlie Glass were driving back to Cleveland with Tony Butterfield and a girl from Bennington. After drinking a few beers, Butterfield and the girl began making out.

"George pulled the car over to the side of the road, leapt out of the car, opened the rear door, and pulled Butterfield out of the car. He said, 'You touch that girl again, I'll kill ya.' He didn't want anything to happen to her while she was in his car. Of course, she didn't care. We got going again, and they started making out again.

"George was a Christian Scientist, but you didn't have to be a Christian Scientist to be puritanical in those days," said Glass. "This was the fifties. The real guilt trip was about sex, and George was smack in the middle of it, like the rest of us.

"George didn't have much luck with girls. I don't think they thought he was sincere. I don't know why. I really don't. I have to say that George didn't enjoy himself very much. George was very puritanical, more than most. Even though he was a member of Animal House. But he wasn't part of it. He never seemed to be enjoying himself when I saw him. Getting him to relax was a tough thing. He can't relax. George is the last Puritan."

Despite his bum shoulder and being an important member of the track team, George never quit on the idea of making the football team. He tried out junior year but didn't make it. During the two days of tryouts, he played halfback but had a terrible time holding on to the ball and was cut.

Said Peter Callahan, one of the stars of the team, "I don't think George had the heart for football physically. He wasn't that physical a guy. You have to be physical to play in that game, and George never had that. He wasn't gutsy, wasn't a killer. He was much more into the mental aspect of the game."

Steve Blasky, George's student adviser, witnessed the tryout. According to him, George wasn't very good. "I will say this," he said. "George has always had a big pair of balls. He ended up coaching football in college, and anyone who had the nerve to create the athletic background for himself that got him those jobs, you got to have a lot of chutzpah. That's one thing George always had."

If you look in the Williams yearbook for George's senior year, you will find a series of remarks that say a lot about how he was viewed by his classmates. It says: Best athlete, Jon Kosar. Then it says: Thinks he is, George Steinbrenner. For best build it says: Billy Callahan and Peter Callahan. Then it says: Thinks he is, George Steinbrenner. And then: Class president, Dick Curtis. Thinks he should be, George Steinbrenner.

"It was written as a joke," said Peter Callahan, "I don't think there was anyone who didn't like him."

If you look at the picture of the Williams varsity football team in the yearbook his senior year, George is in the picture. But according to teammates, he was given a uniform because of his close friendship with head coach Len Watters, which developed while he was co–sports editor of the *Williams Record*. Callahan related the story.

"Coach Watters wanted a spokesman, and George was his spokesman," he said. "Consequently, they were both using each other. George wanted to be on the team because Salmon and Billy Callahan and Dick Kraft were his best friends, the guys he really respected. His senior year, Coach Watters, who was a wonderful guy, put him on the squad, but he didn't play. Anyone else would have gotten cut, but these are the subtleties. George was a very complex guy. He did get his picture in the yearbook."

Though George never got on the field as a player, he nevertheless managed to package himself in a way that got him coaching jobs at both Northwestern and Purdue universities. Some classmates admired him for being able to do that.

"No one takes a guy who can't even make a stupid little college team and makes him a coach at Northwestern, but George was able to do it," said Callahan. "You don't have to play if you love the game the way George did.

"Football is strategy, like a battle, and George is a strategist," he said. "The rules are firmly drawn, but within those rules you can do a lot of things. You can move people around, like a game of chess. He was always intrigued with people, and he knew how to titillate things in people. The point is, he loved football, and he loved the strategy of it and the people end of it, and he became a coach not only at Northwestern but at Purdue."

What bothered the football players, though, was that after George left Williams there was an article in the *Cleveland Plain Dealer* that said George had been the captain of the Williams team. This was after Chuck Salmon, the real captain, had been killed.

Said Don Martin, "When George got out of school, the articles about his athletic prowess made him better and better, and that upset some people who knew what the truth was."

"It was the only time I quarreled with George," said Pete Callahan. "I screamed about that."

Until the day Len Watters died on December 10, 1986, in Venice, Florida, George held him in high esteem and went out of his way to repay him for his kindness. After George bought the Yankees in 1973, he brought in more than a dozen of Watters's captains and colleagues from Williams for Old-Timers' Day, put them up at a fancy hotel in Manhattan, and shuttled them around in limousines. For Watters's eightieth birthday, George got him a cake so big he had to hire a van and two kids to drive it all the way to Vermont along with a magnum of champagne. "That's the kind of guy he is," said his Williams school-mate Pete Smythe.

George may not have made the football team, but he had a solid list of other accomplishments. In the fall of his junior year the edi-torial board of the *Williams Record*, the school newspaper, named him sports editor, a position that allowed him access to the varsity ath-letes and enabled him to ingratiate himself further with the coaches. From that post he also learned the power of the press. At Williams he discovered how to get headline-making quotes by setting one player against another.

"He'd go to one guy and say, 'You should have been named football captain and not so-and-so,'" said Peter Callahan. "And then he'd go to the captain and say, 'So-and-so thinks he should have been captain and not you.' That was the newspaperman in him. He later did that with Reggie Jackson and Billy Martin. That was his style."

For the rest of his life, no matter what he was doing, George would manipulate the press, attempting to turn local newspapermen covering him into his private public relations team.

When George was named sports editor, Robert Simpson, an ac-quaintance from Cleveland who also was a member of the Deke House, was designated his assistant. Simpson, who felt he deserved better, was sure he had been given the lesser slot after he was openly critical of the student editor in chief from the year before. He complained to Dick Duffield, the incoming editor in chief, and to George. According to Simpson, both were sympathetic to Simpson's slight and rectified it immediately. The solution was relatively simple: since the paper came out twice a week, George would be sports editor one day and Simpson would have the job the next. Simpson, who has not seen George since 1953, was forever grateful that George came to his defense.

In addition to his duties as sports editor, George also sang in the glee club, and his senior year he was captain of the track team. The account of the winter track season in the yearbook was sketchy, but showed enough to indicate George was one of the best hurdlers in New England.

In spring track, George led the team with six victories, three seconds, and a third, as well as forty points earned in the hurdles. The critics in his class could scoff that he couldn't hold Harrison Dillard's jock, but then again, neither could anyone else.

Jack Brody, the co-captain with George of the indoor track team and the other point-getter, recalled how even if they didn't qualify for the big meets in New York or Boston, George would drive Brody to see them, and when the two went alone, George would stay in Brody's home in Brooklyn. Brody recalled one weekend when they drove to Madison Square Garden to compete in a big meet, and in Brody's only try in the broad jump, he soared 22.5 feet and scored points for Williams. However, on the jump he tore a hamstring muscle and was in terrible pain. During the drive back, he sat in the backseat moaning while George drove him straight to the infirmary.

"I remember with great fondness how he would worry about me," said Brody. "I never once recall a time when George was unkind." The highest honor bestowed by one's peers at Williams College was to be chosen for Gargoyle, the secret society made up of the top students on campus. Of the eight hundred students in the junior class, only sixteen were chosen, and George Steinbrenner was one of them.

Jack Brody, another who made Gargoyle, felt that George richly deserved the honor. "George made Gargoyle because he was captain of the track team, ran the glee club, wrote sports for the paper, and was an editor. That's how he made it."

What bothered some who knew him, though, was how and why he was able to make Gargoyle. They wondered whether he had joined certain activities solely for the purpose of being recognized. The term they used was "merchandising himself" as they questioned whether George was "genuine."

"In our day it wasn't considered good form to merchandise yourself," said Callahan. "For instance, you never would be seen wearing your letter sweater. You didn't do it. In fact, you went the other way. But George was a little different. He did it. That's why he stood out. Most guys wouldn't dare, but he wasn't afraid.

"We were good friends, but I saw him for what he was. I knew he wasn't completely sincere, that it was practiced, too practiced for me, and I always resented it. He was a striver. He worked at it damn hard.

"Being a political animal, George was self-serving, getting up front on everything. I took George with a grain of salt. He didn't bother me. A lot of people took him a lot more seriously, and they got upset.

They saw this guy getting all these accolades, pushing himself—not the college or the team—felt he was out for number one, which is not uncommon, and they might have disliked that."

Charlie Glass concurred. "I was once asked, 'How do you account for George's great success?' I said, 'He had this great drive.' You can do a lot of amazing things if you just try. That's why so many people don't do a hell of a lot. They just give up. George just doesn't give up. He was just a bundle of perpetual motion. Why not buy the Yankees? It's amazing how far that desire can carry you despite your shortcomings."

Bruce Breckenridge, George's senior-year roommate, is one who denies that George joined organizations for the recognition. "He never ran for office," he said. "He wasn't even an officer in the Deke House. He didn't mind being recognized, but to say he was seeking it, no. He did it because he enjoyed the activities. George liked to have a certain amount of peer approval in a certain funny way, not in a traditional way. He wasn't trying to be one of the boys, but he still wanted recognition, and he did it through these groups.

"George didn't work hard at books," said Breckenridge. "Not at the books, but other things. His father used to get on him a lot for his grades. But George was more a social animal than a student. He liked the action. He never sat and gassed with the boys. He would run over to the track at Saratoga for the trotting races. And he liked girls, though he never mixed the two. We went on road trips, so having George along was a pretty good deal, because he didn't drink. We had him as the driver. And he had good cars, better cars than I ever had, and he was very generous with his car. But he did his thing. He did what he wanted to do. He wasn't the pensive type. Never has been. It revolved around a lot of activity.

"No one ever accused George of being lazy. Ever. That would be the last adjective to use with him. When George ran track, his father was always saying, 'Why aren't you doing better?'

"I liked George," said Breckenridge. "We had good fun together. George was lively and interesting. He wasn't a fool. It was fun to be with him."

Williams College wasn't for everybody. All male, it was a jock school. The Stephen Sondheims and John Frankenthalers were the exception.

"I didn't fit in at all," said Charlie Glass. "Williams wasn't for me, even though I was accepted. I didn't feel terribly at home with these guys. This was a time when you didn't make a big deal out of going to the library. There were no long philosophical discussions, and so I wanted to get the hell out of there. I wanted to go to Yale. And I did."

Jack Brody, one of the few Jews at Williams, felt much the same way, only his self-awareness came much later. When Brody looked back on his years at Williams, one of the things that struck him was how badly George was treated by those whose friendship he desired most. Brody was astounded that George was able to ignore or bury the slights and put-downs and found it in his heart over the years to reward Williams College with substantial donations.

"I don't think George had any idea how unhappy he was at Williams," said Brody. "It was just dawning on me when I got there. I had a wonderful time in prep school, and to be stuck away in a place like Williams was cruel and unusual punishment, and George never had the courage to say that."

Quite the contrary, in addition to donating money, George has gone out of his way to honor Williams in unusual ways. In a story he related to Peter Callahan and other classmates meeting at Yankee Stadium in 1973, he said he was asked one year to give financial support for the North-South All-Star college game. The way George told the story, he said he would donate a substantial sum of money if the best football player at Williams College would be added to the North squad. The first response was no. George repeated his demand: no Williams player, no money.

Finally, they gave in; they chose a player from Williams and played him at defensive back. Said George, "He made two interceptions and a key tackle, and he got the game ball."

Callahan said George told him that when he took over the Yankees, he ordered his scouting staff to sign a Williams College pitcher and place him on a minor league team. As Callahan told it, the Williams pitcher was assigned to a fall league team in Arizona, and every week George would come in and look at the scouting reports. One week he saw that the kid's chart had been placed on the top of the stack of evaluations. His earned run average was 11.

"He knew what they were doing," said Callahan, "giving him the old razz. Finally he called them all in and said, 'I don't give a shit what you do with him, make him a DH [designated hitter], but goddamn, you're going to use him.'" And according to George, said Callahan, "they made a DH out of him, and he hit the cover off the ball."

4 What George wants, he wants, and if he can't get
it one way, he's going to get it another. And if you
don't believe it, you don't know George Steinbrenner.

—Jeanette Montgomery

Lockbourne Air Force Base

While George Steinbrenner was a freshman home from
college, he and his friend were at a party when he
informed everyone that he knew the governor. Bob Stecher, one of his
pals who was there, remembered thinking, *What a joke! What college
freshman knows the governor?* But George, to stem the skepticism, got
the governor on the phone.

"We didn't think he could do that, but he did," said Stecher. "He
just knew a lot of people. You have to remember George's father ran
boats on the Great Lakes. His father was a very important man. And
George knew the governor as a young kid. The point is, he knew him,
and most kids don't know the governor, and if they did, they wouldn't
have the guts to call him, but George did."

Knowing powerful people is what separates the rich and powerful
from the rest of us.

George Steinbrenner, the self-proclaimed patriot who was born
on the Fourth of July, graduated from Williams College in the spring
of 1952, smack-dab in the middle of the deadly Korean conflict. Like
Chuck Salmon, he joined the air force, but unlike Salmon, who shot
down MIGs in Korea, George never was subjected to enemy fire. In

fact, thanks to his father's influence, he would never have to set foot in Korea. He was assigned a base three hours away from his Bay Village, Ohio, home.

He had taken air force ROTC at college, protecting him from getting drafted while he was in school and binding him to two years of active military service after graduation, and so when he joined the military in the summer of 1952, he began his air force career as an officer. After doing six weeks of basic training at the Lackland base in Houston, he was assigned to Lockbourne Air Force Base, twelve miles southeast of Columbus, Ohio.

Lockbourne, which today is called Rickenbacker Air Force Base, had been activated in June 1942. A wing of the Strategic Air Command, the base's primary role was to spy on the Soviet Union and to protect America from a Soviet nuclear attack.

"Nobody at Lockbourne was involved in Korea," said William Mixson, an officer on the base at the time George arrived. "We were going to England. We were strictly reconnaissance against the Big Bear over there." George's assignment, it turned out, was a safe haven close to home.

Jeanette Montgomery, who worked closely with George's superior officers as a secretary, was told by Colonel Esmay, who was in charge of personnel, "George was sent to Lockbourne, and a congressman had done it, because Georgie's mother wanted Georgie close to home."

According to Colonel Jerry Adams, who knew George well, Henry Steinbrenner had used his influence to get his son safely placed at Lockbourne. "George's father was a big deal in Ohio, so that's where it sprang from," said Adams. "I was told George's father pulled some strings to get George [assigned to Lockbourne]."

John Moore, a major who would be George's commanding officer during his two years at Lockbourne, recalled the day that Charlie Wilson, who headed the War Production Board under President Harry Truman and would soon be secretary of defense, arrived on the base along with Henry Steinbrenner. "Wilson was the contact," said Moore. "He was the big cheese. He was the Caspar Weinberger of his day. That would put him all over the military."

Major Moore recalled the day when his superior, Colonel Charles "Bo" Dougher, the base commander, called him down to the office to tell him there was a "special problem" coming up. Dougher told

Moore that "a very special young man" was coming onto the base, and he was to "look after him." The "special problem" was twenty-two-year-old George Steinbrenner.

"It's very rare to have a commanding officer worry about some second lieutenant," said Moore, who immediately understood that Dougher—and only Dougher—would be giving George orders. When George reported for duty, he was named an aide to Dougher, in charge of running the base athletic program.

According to Moore, George confided to him that in exchange for Dougher, who was near retirement and had already been a colonel for ten years, to look after him, his father would see to it that Dougher would be promoted to one-star general. (Dougher got his star on August 25, 1953.) "Dougher was close to retirement," said Moore, "and it was now or never, and so the Steinbrenners were just what he needed. Dougher was the one who told me not to be too hard on George, and it happened more than once."

You would think if you were under the protection of the base commander, you would want to keep such an arrangement quiet, if only to prevent jealousy and gossip. Not George. Very quickly he let everyone know that he was playing by his own rules, and if the other officers didn't like it, well, there wasn't a damn thing they could do about it.

Most officers didn't have much money, so they lived in the substandard quarters on the base or else two or three of them shared an apartment off the base. George lived by himself in a fancy apartment off base, and he came and went pretty much as he pleased. This alone created an intense dislike of him among other junior officers. But George stuck needles in their eyes by thumbing his nose at protocol.

All of the other officers were required to be at formation each day at eight in the morning. George not only skipped formation with regularity, but there were times when he'd be off base and incommunicado for days at a time. Periodically when the base held a parade and everyone had to show up, George would be late or he wouldn't come at all. And he never seemed to get in trouble for it.

Said Moore, "He would be inaccessible for duty for three and four days at a time. Any other officer would have gotten court-martialed. But Jerry Adams, a colonel under Dougher, would say, 'He's young, and he has to be handled carefully. You know, he's a special case.'"

Too many times after trying unsuccessfully to reach him by phone, Moore would send someone to his home, only to find out he was in Cleveland.

George did not pal around with the other lower-grade officers. Away from home and lonesome, they would go to a bar and sit around drinking beer. George didn't drink, and he was not sociable that way.

"George didn't go out of his way to be nice to junior officers," said Moore. "He went out of his way to be nice to colonels. Among his peers he had a reputation of sucking up; that is, polishing the apple with the brass."

According to Moore, George let it be known he had money and that he was willing to pay for something if he wanted it badly enough. Some people on the base resented his wealth and status.

"He was a rich kid," said Jeanette Montgomery. "He told me his father owned a steamship line, and his mother had a lot of influence with Congress. I distinctly remember saying to George, 'If you're so rich, why don't you get a new coat?' Because he had a blue trench coat, and the belt was kind of raggedy. He just ignored me. That's typical of rich people. They don't replace things until they find something they want to replace it with."

Money may create resentment in some, but in others it breeds attraction. When it became known around Columbus that George came from money, his standing with the local gals soared. "He was a popular young bachelor," said Moore. "He looked nice in a uniform, and he had more money than most to spend. He was very popular with the society matrons, who were always asking me, 'Do you know George?' If he hadn't met their daughter, they were figuring out ways he could. He would have been a good catch."

When George arrived at Lockbourne, he was assigned the job of base special service officer. His assignment was to be the athletic director of the base, putting him in charge of intramurals and the baseball and basketball teams. He also ran the base dances at the Airmen's and NCO clubs. Despite his frequent absences from the base, the general impression was that he did his job excellently. The intramural program ran without a hitch; the base basketball and baseball teams, which he coached very well, were winners; and his USO dances were a hit.

As at Williams College, when George took over an organization, he made sure not to miss a trick. His superior offices had reservations about other aspects of his personality, but of one thing they were certain: George was a leader who knew how to get things done.

"His sports program was very well organized," said Colonel Adams. "As far as George was concerned, that took priority over everything else that was going on."

To run any successful organization, George needed underlings who were loyal. For his right-hand man, he chose a sergeant by the name of Lefty (those who remember Lefty say his last name sounded Polish). Lefty had been an athlete, and he had been around at Lockbourne for years. He took George under his wing, took care of him, covering George's tracks whenever he needed to. When Lefty had problems at home, George gave him money. If Major Moore needed to find George, he would call Lefty over at the gym, and Lefty's inevitable reply would be, "He's not here. I'll have him call you as soon as he gets in." Other sergeants were just as loyal.

"It was run very efficiently," said Moore. "He had them very loyal. I do know they were very fond of him, though once or twice if they had a difference of opinion, he would stop his generosity, and they would turn. They learned he was generous with those who were loyal.

"Don't get me wrong. George in his way did many good things. But his theory was, in order to win it doesn't make any difference who you step on. We never had any knock-down, drag-outs, but there was nothing I could do. You put up with it. We stood and glared at each other a few times."

Added Jeanette Montgomery, "What George wants, he wants, and if he can't get it one way, he's going to get it another. And if you don't believe me, you don't know George Steinbrenner."

Usually when George got his way, there were no repercussions, but every once in a while he would do something so outside the laws of the land—the rules of the road, the spirit of society—that he would end up in hot water.

"He was always into some kind of mess, getting called on the carpet," said Major Moore. "He pulled so many things. I frequently tried to stop George from doing what he wanted, but I was never successful. George would say to me, 'I will do better.' But it didn't last very long, because, as I say, winning was his way, and he wasn't used to having people stand in his way."

One time George spent his own money for a band to play at the enlisted club dance. The problem: the regular band wasn't getting paid, and the musicians' union was up in arms. Ruffled feathers had to be smoothed out by higher-ups.

On another occasion, George as athletic director for the base took one look at the lights on the baseball field and decided they weren't up to his standards. He went to the Welfare Board, which controlled the money for sports and recreational activities, and tried to bludgeon them into budgeting $20,000 for state-of-the-art lights. Major Moore was the secretary of the board, which turned him down not once, but twice.

"George asked us to pay for the lights, but there was no money in the budget, and we couldn't afford it," said Moore. "He went and arranged with a local contractor to put them up, and he just assumed the military would pay for them. He said, 'If they don't, I'll pay for them myself.'" George had the lights installed the week Moore was on vacation. When he returned, the major couldn't help but notice a couple hundred floodlights illuminating the field.

Most of the board felt that George should pay for the lights as he had promised. They felt that if he made a commitment like that, he ought to pay or his father ought to pay for him. "Throwing that kind of money around with that frequency made him popular with some people," said Moore, "but it didn't make him popular with the career officers. And the base engineer was mighty perturbed."

In the end, Moore suspects that Colonel Dougher twisted the arm of the Welfare Board to pay for the lights. Once again, much to Moore's consternation, George got away scot-free.

The one time George almost was court-martialed occurred after a baseball tournament in Japan. George was the coach of the Lockbourne team, and he arranged to replace some of the airmen on the team with professional ballplayers. The Lockbourne team won the tournament, but a sportswriter recognized a couple of the pros wearing air force uniforms and cried foul.

Said Moore, "He was always pulling some deal like that, doing whatever he wanted because he had the bucks. He violated something on that base, so if there was going to be a court-martial, it was going to be in Japan.

"The military is a very closed outfit, and news travels very, very fast, and by the time we heard about it, our response was, 'It couldn't have happened to a more deserving character.' We thought, *He finally got into a situation where he's going to get his just rewards.*"

But in the end nothing came of it, as usual, and George returned to Lockbourne unbowed.

George's tour of duty ended in June 1954. A few months later a warrant officer, whose job it was to take an inventory of the sports equipment, began opening the boxes of footballs and basketballs that sat from floor to ceiling along the long wall of the athletic director's office. All were empty.

During the two years he had served as base athletic director, George had been the speaker at a lot of high school banquets, and he would give away basketballs and footballs signed by the members of the high school team. The balls had come from the base supplies. The warrant officer, who had no idea what had happened to the equipment, would have taken the rap had Colonel Adams, who instinctively knew what had become of the balls, not stepped in and gotten him off the hook.

Said Jeanette Montgomery, "The warrant officer had taken over George's account, so when he went to open the boxes, the balls were missing. George had . . . Well, it was typical of his whole life. He just has to get his way: *This is what I want, and this is what I'm going to do, and the rules don't apply to me. I'm going to do it my way.* He was not considerate of other people. It was about what he wanted to do.

"George was very difficult for the base to control, and it was frustrating because you couldn't do anything to him. Back in those days the military was rigid, and he had Bo Dougher."

Major Moore would later find out just how completely George and Henry Steinbrenner had Dougher in his pocket. "It's very difficult to keep secrets in the air force," said Moore. "Years later I ran into a friend of mine from personnel, and he told me that George's father was able to get Dougher a second star after Dougher was able to clean up George's record at the Pentagon. I have no idea how this was done, but if you looked at George's service record, you'd think he had a halo."

Coach George

With carte blanche to come and go as he pleased, Lieutenant George Steinbrenner honed his skills of self-promotion, using his two years as athletic director and coach at Lockbourne Air Force Base as a way to make himself known in the greater Columbus athletic community. He also used his position as a way to get outstanding Ohio State athletes like Heisman Trophy candidate Howard "Hopalong" Cassady to speak at his banquets and to meet the other Buckeye jocks.

In Columbus, George could be found at a fancy sports club, the Wigwam, where the Columbus power brokers went. Among others, he met the king makers—the big money families and businessmen.

George also hung out at two of Columbus's top hot spots for Ohio Staters, the Agonis Club and a swanky dance place in Columbus called Valley Dale. It was through Lou Pepy, brother of the great swimming coach at Ohio State and the owner of Valley Dale, that George met a lot of OSU people, including Dr. Jimmy Hull. The former All-American basketball player at Ohio State had read of George in the newspapers. As athletic director of the Lockbourne base, George was accorded access to nearby colleges so he could get to meet the Buckeye athletes and invite them out to speak to his teams.

While at Lockbourne, George met Ohio State athletic director Dick Watkins and head football coach Woody Hayes, and he got to know a number of the players, including halfback "Hopalong Cassady, who in his thirty-six games playing for Ohio State between 1952 and 1955 scored thirty-seven touchdowns and won the Heisman Trophy twice, in 1954 and 1955. Said George's future father-in-law, Harold Zeig, "George all his life was active helping football players get through school. He helped Hop all the way through school, and he helped others."

Though his immediate supervisor, Major John Moore found it infuriating that George had the protection of the base commander and did not have to follow everyone else's rules, he nevertheless marveled at his promotional skills. "George's newspaper abilities got his name and his Lockbourne Skyhawks' name in the Columbus paper more than the name of Colonel Dougher," said Moore. "George was very conscious of getting in the newspapers. He would write stories about his teams and bring them in to the papers.

"He wasn't the base PR officer, but he worked closely with him. I can picture him arranging theater tickets for the PR officer, saying, 'You don't mind if I handle the sports aspect by myself?' I'm sure he wined and dined anyone who could give him good coverage. Because, as I said, you read more about him in the local papers than you did the commanding general."

Tom Keys, the sports editor of the *Columbus Citizen-Journal*, recalled George as a kind of PR man for the Lockbourne Air Force Base. "He made us very much aware of the athletic program down there," said Keys.

"He would camp in my office and say, 'Here it is.' George was so thorough and complete. We got information daily."

George cultivated the sportswriters, inviting them out to his sports banquets at the base and at the various high schools where he spoke or donated trophies or footballs. When it came to promotion—and self-promotion—Columbus had never seen anyone quite like him.

At night he also chased women. George ran the USO dances, and all sorts of girls were invited—college girls, town girls, nurses—and George had his pick, because they were enlisted men's dances, and he'd be the only officer there. Others might be embarrassed by their special protected status. George used it to his advantage.

Said Major Moore, "Among the gals you heard, 'He's the lieutenant who has the base commander in his pocket.' That was the scuttlebutt in town, and I had nothing to do with it. But it was free access to all the young lovelies in town. He was nice-looking, and he had better manners and better presence than the average young guy. I don't know how many beds he got into, but if the rumor holds, he did more than okay. I'm sure some of the girls thought, I'm going to snag this guy, and they would put out, and nothing happened. I remember a couple of nurses who really thought they would be Mrs. Steinbrenner, the Millionaire.' He didn't marry them."

George was introduced to the girl whom he would eventually marry by Dr. Jimmy Hull, one of the Ohio State jocks he had met and who had become an orthodontist. "I was treating Joan [pronounced 'Jo-ann'] Zeig. She was eighteen or nineteen, an orthodontic patient, wearing braces. She was a beauty who wore clothes beautifully. I'm sure George had seen pretty girls, but he never saw one as pretty as that Joan. At the time she was studying dental hygiene at Ohio State.

"During the next two or three weeks Joan came into the office for an appointment. When I gave her the next appointment, I made a duplicate card for George. I gave him her card, and I said, 'If you want to meet a lovely girl, you get down here to my office.'

"George showed up, and I introduced him, and he took it from there. He went for her in a big way. He knew he had a jewel when he met Joan. They started to go out, and I was with them the night he gave her the engagement ring on Christmas Eve of 1955. They were married in June of 1956, and I was his best man, and I always sign my letters, 'Your best man and still the best man.'"

Harold Zeig, Joan's father, didn't see anything special when George showed up for their first date. Some years later, he would soften. But for a number of years he wondered why of all the eligible men in the world she had married George.

Jimmy Hull recalled how nervous George was on his wedding day. "Right before the wedding we had George back in the First Community Church, and they started playing 'Here Comes the Bride,' and George says, 'Get me out of here.'

"I said, 'I'll get you out of here. Get out there and marry Joan.'

"George was kidding. I said, 'George, you've talked too much, as usual.'

"It was a beautiful wedding, a lovely, sophisticated wedding, one of the prettiest weddings of that season or any other season. The Zeigs knew how to do things in top fashion. Everyone, even George's father, wore tails." According to Harold Zeig, about a hundred people attended, and football players Hopalong Cassady, Otto Graham, and Curly Morrison were among the ushers.

The reception was held at the Sciotto Country Club. "It was the nicest, most fashionable country club in Columbus," said Don Martin. "George just loved the sports scene, and it was a great break for him to get this assignment at Lockbourne. I know he pulled some strings. He doesn't let fate decide."

In addition to befriending Ohio State jocks and becoming the squire of Columbus, George's arrangement with Colonel Dougher enabled him to pursue his greatest love: coaching. One might wonder where George Steinbrenner found the time to do so many things. As his college classmates attested, his energy and stamina seemed superhuman.

George first made his name coaching the Lockbourne Skyhawks baseball and basketball teams. Led by six-foot-nine-inch center Bill McCauley, the Skyhawks became All-Service champs in basketball. George's superior, Major Moore, was impressed when George told him he had played in college and then a year of pro football. Moore was skeptical, but he didn't question it.

In the spring of 1952, George scheduled a baseball game for his Skyhawks against the Ohio State varsity. But when the bus arrived at the base, George learned that the Ohio State players were members of the junior varsity, not the varsity. Bob Sudyk, who later would write about sports for the *Cleveland Press*, was a sophomore first baseman on the JV team. He recalled seeing a man screaming in a high-pitched soprano, "Stay on the bus. We're not playing you, and that's final. The game's off. We're scheduled to play the varsity, not the JV scrubs."

"I was as puzzled as the rest of my teammates," said Sudyk. "Our manager got out and tried to calm the caterwauling. Finally, it was agreed the game would go on. What followed wasn't a ball game, it was a nine-inning circus. With the baseball rule book in his hand,

Lockbourne's screaming manager kept shuffling his lineup and berating the umpires."

" 'Who is this guy?' I asked as we boarded the bus after the game.

" 'That was Lieutenant George Steinbrenner.' "

But despite his rages and his notoriety, his Lockbourne teams won, and in sports that is usually the bottom line.

"George was skilled at coaching," said John Moore. "Many of his players were older than he was, but he was a very good coach. But winning was more important than how he won. Winning was more important than winning by the rules. The rules never meant much to George."

As much as George enjoyed coaching basketball and baseball, his true love was football. Because there was no Lockbourne football and because Woody Hayes had a rather strong hold on the job at Ohio State, George became involved in coaching high school teams.

While still in the service, George asked John Montgomery, the head football coach at Lyndon McKinley High School in Columbus, if he could be an unpaid assistant. The coach had met George through his wife, Jeanette Montgomery, who worked as a secretary at Lockbourne. George volunteered to scout Lyndon McKinley's opponents, and before the game against powerful Central High, he talked John Montgomery into letting him devise a defense he felt could stop their rival.

John LeCourt, a star halfback on the team, recalled, "We were scheduled to play Central Catholic, a powerhouse because of Paul Skooley, a tremendous running back. We were three- or four-touchdown underdogs. We should not have been on the same field with them. Central ran a buck-lateral series, a direct snap back to the quarterback standing behind the guard. The running back then takes the ball and hands it back to the quarterback, who pitches it out to the one or two back. It was complicated, but George scouted them, and he came in with a whole new concept for a defense, a New York Giants–style eagle defense, a man-to-man defense. My job was to guard Gene Dennis, who was second or third in the state in the hundred-yard dash—I had him one-on-one, and our defense stopped them time after time, and we beat them seven to six. You had to say George's eagle defense won the game for us. Central's Coach Parks had never seen it before."

After George left the air force in June 1954, he remained in Columbus to pursue an advanced degree in physical education at Ohio State. In the fall of that year he became the head football coach of a small Catholic high school called Aquinas. Jimmy Hull, who had found him a wife, also found him his first head coaching job in football. "At this time George was coming out of the service," said Hull. "They hired George with the understanding he would continue with his education and get his master's degree in physical education. I called Dr. Oberturfer, the head of the physical education department at Ohio State, and set George up to start."

One of George's players at Aquinas was Tony DeSabito, who that year was chosen by *Columbus Monthly* magazine as the best high school football player in the state. What impressed DeSabito and the other players was that here was a man from money—everyone had noticed his snazzy convertible—who was willing to take the time, without pay, to help them.

"He didn't have to come," said DeSabito. "We never had anything. We didn't have a locker room, and he made us one. He had a carpenter come in and make one out of chicken wire. We never had a jock strap, and he made sure we had a clean one every day. When you're a kid from a poor family, busted . . . He didn't have to do that. He didn't even get paid. He did it because he liked doing it.

"We all thought he was a man coming down from heaven."

More than anything, George brought discipline to the team, both on and off the field. "He made you be in shape," said DeSabito. "Drills, man, drills. He also wanted to make sure the players were well behaved, that we didn't do anything wrong at night, made sure we didn't stay out late, that nobody drank or smoked cigarettes. You didn't get to play if he found out you were smoking or running around at night. And he wouldn't give in. The priest, Father Taylor, would. George wouldn't. He was a disciplinarian, very strong.

"George would do anything to help us have a winning season. One time he brought in two Cleveland Browns to scout an opponent. He was trying to make us good."

Over the years, George has singled out hundreds of disadvantaged high school kids and provided them with scholarships to college. Because he does it privately, it's hard to know exactly how many youngsters he has helped. One of the first was John LeCourt. LeCourt was a high school track star, but after watching him at a meet one evening, George felt he could be even better. He was certain that if LeCourt trained harder, he could be a champion. It would be the same sort of demonic training George had put himself through while running track at Williams College.

To train under this stranger, LeCourt had to submit completely to George, who required nothing less than slavish devotion and total commitment. LeCourt, poor kid with little going for him but his athletic talent, was wise enough to go along. As a result, after some strong-arming by George, he set state track records and went on to Ohio University, albeit kicking and screaming. Though he told the story many years after it happened, the awe and wonder of being the recipient of George's attention and largesse never left him.

"I'm from a little town in the southern part of Ohio called Glouster, population a few hundred. It's a coal-mining town," said LeCourt. "We didn't have organized athletics in Glouster, Ohio, a hillbilly town. We had alley ball, pickup football, pickup basketball. When I struck out thirteen times in high school baseball, our baseball coach said, 'John, I notice you're pretty fast running the bases.' By the time I was a junior in high school, for two consecutive years I had been the Columbus high school track champion. In four events, I would win three, and sometimes I'd win all four, because I was also good in the long jump.

"I was at Dennison University at an indoor track meet. I won the 55-meter dash, and I won the 200 meters, and I ran a leg in the 880-meter relay, which we won.

"After the meet an individual came up to me, and he said, 'You have to be one of the worst track runners I have ever seen in my life. You have a very poor start, and . . .' on and on and on.

"In my mind I thought, Who are you to say? But instead I said, 'I appreciate that.'

"He said, 'I can really help you. My name is George Steinbrenner.'

"I explained to George that I didn't want to insult Mr. White [LeCourt's coach]. Plus the fact I was taught not to take up with strangers, right? When you first meet George Steinbrenner it's not a sensational feeling. This was on a Sunday afternoon, and the following Monday Steinbrenner came over to Lyndon McKinley High School from Lockbourne wearing his uniform. He was a first lieutenant, and he drove a '53 Pontiac convertible, plush red with a white top. I thought, My God. Who is this guy?

"He walked up to me and told me Mr. White had agreed that he could help me out after my regular practice, and then handed me a book about track and field, a list of foods I could eat, and a schedule.

"He said, 'Are you ready to go to work?'

"I said, 'I'm going to take a shower. I'm done.'

"He said, 'No, you haven't even started yet.'

"I looked at him, and he looked at me, and then I thought, This man is taking his own time to come out here and volunteer.

"'What do you want me to do, George?' I asked.

"'We're going to start at the starting block,' he said. He changed everything about the way I ran. Normally the right foot is up, and the left foot is back. He switched it.

"He said, 'I want you to come out of the starting block like a shotgun, and it's going to be very awkward at first.'

"'George,' I said, 'this is very uncomfortable. How can you criticize me on my start when no one has ever beaten me? I'm the city champion.'

"He said, 'John, I'll tell you, you have the worst start in the world. You have to improve your timing and your start if you're going to be halfway decent in track.'

"'What's halfway decent?' I asked.

"From that point we went to the 120-yard dashes, the 220s; I ran 330s, 440s, and 660s. And then for some strange reason he felt I had talent in the 180-yard low hurdles.

"I said, 'George, I never ran the 180-yard low hurdles in my life.'

"At first I would knock down three hurdles, and my right kneecap was nothing but blood and cinders. Did he say, 'Let's quit right now'? No, it was, 'Get back up, and let's do it again. Get the two and a half steps between each hurdle. Let's go. Cut your timing down. Cut your movement down. Cut your legs down going over the hurdles.'

"I said, 'George, I cannot run the 180-yard low hurdles.'

"He said, 'LeCourt, I don't want to argue about it. This is the way it's got to be done.'

"I had had a football coach, a basketball coach, and a track coach, but I had never had a coach talk to me this way. I thought, Why am I taking this from him?

"I said, 'I'll run everything else, but forget the 180-yard low hurdles.'

"He said, 'John, you're running the 180-yard low hurdles.'

"Needless to say, seven days later in a dual track meet I ran the 180-yard low hurdles against Clemens Central High School's Paul Skooley, the city champion, and I beat him by two and a half hurdles. It was just totally amazing, and I credit that to George Steinbrenner.

"I became a product, as though I was a racehorse. I had a timetable. I had to get up at a certain time. My parents were gone, and I lived with my brother and sister-in-law, but I didn't eat there. I had to go to a restaurant by the name of Jim Clark's, where my menus were set up by George. If I needed spending money or needed to borrow his convertible, Mr. Steinbrenner was there. I was like a colt. Most track athletes train during the week and take the weekends off. Not George Steinbrenner. We trained seven days a week.

"There was a track magazine out of Cleveland that listed the best runners, and he made a study of it. George knew who my opponents were and what their strong and weak points were.

"I entered the Worthington Relay in Columbus. Twelve teams entered. It was raining so hard that day that it could have been called off. George couldn't be there that day. He told me I needed to run the 220 in 22.4 if I was going to win, and I did win, setting a record. I set a record in the 100-yard dash, and keep in mind I had to run through puddles. He had me enter the 440-yard dash, which isn't my race because I have very short legs. And to run a good 400 on a cinder track you are talking to a horse, because mentally I was a horse. That's the type of program he had me under. In the 440, I set a record. I took one jump in the long jump and won, and in the *Columbus Journal* the next day in bold print there was a headline: 'LeCourt breaks three records, wins four first places.'

The next day he was called into the principal's office and told he had a phone call. "I picked it up," LeCourt continued, "and it was George.

"'LeCourt,' he said, 'what the hell happened to you last night?'

"I said, 'What?'

"He said, 'Jesus, I saw those times. I could have run those times backwards.'

"I said, 'Didn't you read the newspaper? I broke three records last night.'

"He said, 'That's not good enough. I'll see you at the gym tonight.'

"You can give a hundred and twenty percent, and that's not good enough for George Steinbrenner. You are going to be the best, no matter what it takes.

"My wife and I went together three years all through high school, and George tried to break us up. He would say, 'Look, LeCourt, let me tell you something. Practice track. Practice football. Girls are secondary. You're spending too much time with her.'

"You can't tell that to a high school athlete. He couldn't impress on me enough that he wanted me to go to college and get a business degree. He wanted me to continue in sports in college. He wanted me to find out what life was all about.

"He gave me those golden opportunities. If it hadn't been for George Steinbrenner coming to my house in June of 1954, taking me down to Ohio University . . . I didn't want to go to college. I said, 'I'm not going.'

"He said, 'Yes, you are.' And off we went. He drove me there. The next thing I knew, I was living in the best hall at Ohio University. All because of George Steinbrenner.

"Through the years he has shown me what life is about. And he's asked nothing of me. Nothing. How do you repay a guy like that? He doesn't want anything. He doesn't want a thing. Believe it or not.

"I'm a little guy, a nobody, but I'll tell you one thing about Steinbrenner. It's not how big you are in this world. This guy has a heart of gold, and I'm blessed, very lucky. I can't say enough about him."

George Steinbrenner's early career goal was to become a head college football coach. So in the spring of 1955, after coaching at Aquinas for one year, he walked into the Evanston, Illinois, office of Northwestern head football coach Lou Saban and asked for an assistant coaching job. He had built himself a reputation around Columbus, saying that not only had he been a star at Williams, but that he also had played a year of pro ball with the New York Giants. This was publicly known because George told people it was so, and no one bothered to check. George had a leg up on the job because Henry Steinbrenner had been a big Browns football fan, went to the games, and became friends with Saban, the captain and star linebacker of the team.

George had also known Saban since 1948, when George worked with Saban on starting the Junior Olympics. Saban, the coordinator, needed to find organizers for the districts. George, who loved track, volunteered to coordinate Cleveland's West Side.

Paul Hornung, a sportswriter for the *Columbus Citizen*, recalled Saban calling him to get his impressions of George. "I told Saban," said Hornung, "I thought George had made a conscious effort to learn as much as possible about football, that he was very wrapped up in sports and was making an effort to find out what it was all about."

Saban, an assistant coach at Northwestern who had been promoted to the top spot, hired George to be his end coach. Ben Froelich, one of George's freshman ends, was particularly fond of Saban and George as coaches and noted the difference in tone when martinet Ara Parseghian came in the next year with a whole new staff. "We had a bunch of rag-tag ends," said Froelich, "but George was so proud of us all; we'd stand around and talk to George. He was always one of the boys. When George showed up, I wondered what he knew about playing end. George was a complete character. He was fun to work with, a very, very nice guy who wasn't much older than we were. He was a friend to everyone and not a real disciplinarian by any means. He didn't know a whole lot about coaching ends, and it showed because we tied one game and lost every other, and at the end of the season all the coaches were gone. Ara Parseghian and new people like Alex Agassi came in with a new athletic director, and I never saw or heard from George again until he showed up as the owner of the New York Yankees."

"We had a bitter experience," said Steinbrenner. "Lou got fired with the staff. It's a funny story that nobody else will have. I'll tell it to you. Stu Holcombe came in as the athletic director. They took him from Purdue. This was 1955. It was in November, right after the season was over. Stu came in and invited all of us to breakfast at the Georgian Hotel in Evanston. And then he fired the entire staff.

"Ten years later Stu Holcombe was a flunky with the Chicago White Sox when I first owned the Yankees. I walked into a meeting, and he kept looking over at me, and he walks over and says, 'I know you from somewhere. Where do I know you from?'

"I said, 'Think hard, Mr. Holcombe. Think back to 1955. The Georgian Hotel. A dark and stormy morning.' I gave him the whole bit. 'At nine-thirty you walked in and said, "Lou Saban and his entire staff is fired."' His mouth began to drop. I said, 'I was the end coach.' And I turned and walked away."

After he was canned, George went home to work with his father at Kinsman. But it was not long before Purdue athletic director Red Mackie called and asked George if he would come to Purdue to coach his freshmen.

Henry Steinbrenner, whose shipping company was struggling, didn't want George going off again. He told George, "Goddammit, either in or out of this business."

George told his father, "I have to get it out of my system. I have to have one year to know what I can do and whether I want to do it."

George's job at Purdue was to take the freshmen and have them mimic the opposing teams' offenses and defenses. His head coach was Jack Mollenkopf, whose 84–39–9 record made him the winningest coach in the school's history. Mollenkopf, elected into the College Football Hall of Fame in 1988, was a master who stressed fundamentals, preparation, and execution. He appreciated George's dedication and hard work and at midseason rewarded him with added duties.

One of the ends on the 1957 Purdue team was Big Dan Mason from West High in Cleveland. Mason enjoyed his association with George. "I thought he was a real good coach, and a real good guy. He was dynamic then and he hasn't changed a bit. I just think George is a super-great guy."

Mason recalled the annual freshman scrimmage, known as the Gold and Black game. George was assigned half the team, with Coach Parker taking the other.

"We were supposed to use plays we had been using during the year," said Mason. "The other team used a dipsy-doodle, and they scored. We were ahead seven to zero, and when they put up the score, George called time out and said, 'Take it off the board.'

"They said, 'For what?'

"He said, 'That play wasn't in the playbook. You can't use it. We went with the plays we used during the year, and that's what you were supposed to do.'"

"They disagreed. George said, 'If you don't take it off, I'm going to take my squad off the field.' They said, 'Nah,' and we started walking off, and they took the seven points off the board. He was right. That's the kind of guy he is.

"George is still a Purdue backer, and he did a tremendous job pushing for Purdue athletes." One player on whom he had a major impact was Purdue's All-American quarterback Len Dawson. "George was instrumental in something he probably didn't even know about," said Dawson. "He did a great sales job on me. My senior year I injured my shoulder, had a bone bruise. It was painful, and I wasn't playing as often as I could.

"George and I had coffee, and he convinced me. And I did [play more despite the pain], and I didn't have any problems. And it taught me a lesson and really helped me in professional football because so many times I had aches and pains I had to get over and play. I'm sure he used psychology on me, to get at my pride, and whatever it was, he did it."

George would only coach at Purdue for one year, but his loyalty to the Boilermakers remained. He had had no intention of leaving, but at the end of the season he was waylaid by his father, who needed him, and a wife who was unhappy with the low-paying, itinerant life of an assistant college coach.

"My wife was pregnant at the time," said George. "I was gone until late at night. I would start in the morning, work all day, and I'd spend extra time working with guys like Lenny Dawson. Lenny will tell you that he was ready to throw it in, and I got him back up." (Dawson was wrong about George's not remembering. George knew full well how he was affecting him.)

"I wanted to stay on at Purdue. If I had my way today, that's what I would want to be, an educator.

"If I had gone back to Purdue, I'm not sure what my dad would have done. It was either, 'Come back and get going or we're going to get out of the business like some of the other independents.'

"If I had stayed in coaching, I think I could have been a head coach at a big school. I think I was good enough at the game to do that. I didn't lack any confidence in my ability to do it."

6

Goddammit, George, you can't get your hair
cut on company time.

—Henry Steinbrenner

Come to Papa

Collage football lost a dedicated young coach when George
Steinbrenner left Jack Mollenkopf's Purdue staff to return
to the Cleveland area to help his father run Kinsman Marine. It could
not have been an easy decision for him to make. He knew that working for his father would be no picnic. And yet he was also aware that
his wife, Joan, desired a more stable life, where she could count on his
coming home after work. That it didn't turn out that way was a
function of George's personality and his father's work ethic. Henry
Steinbrenner believed his employees were obligated to work long
hours and never take vacations or holidays.

George was on call twenty-four hours a day to troubleshoot if there
were problems with the business, and in addition to his suburban West
Side social life, he also would develop a circle of friends in Cleveland
among the sports figures, politicians, and movers and shakers of the
city. As it had been back at Williams, his friends were amazed at his
stamina and his range of interests. How did the young man find the
time to do all the things he did?

Upon George's return to Kinsman, his father immediately gave
him a position of tremendous responsibility. He was named the dis-

patcher, the man who kept track of the boats. It was a twenty-four-hour-a-day, seven-day-a-week job. If Henry wanted to talk to George at three o'clock in the morning, George better take the call if he knew what was good for him. George also was given the job of selling contracts to Republic Steel and the other companies. He was much more personable than Henry, and he was an adept salesman.

"Many times George would leave a party on a Saturday night and fly to Duluth, Minnesota, to spring a drunken sailor out of jail," said Frank Treadway, a friend from George's social circle.

Because Henry Steinbrenner was such a perfectionist, no matter how well George performed, it seemed it was never good enough. Bill Crippen, who worked in the Rockefeller Building in downtown Cleveland on the same floor as the Steinbrenners, recalled that yelling by the father at the son was the natural order of things. "As a matter of fact, Henry's father, George, was there then [at Kinsman Marine in 1947]. It was old George yelling at young Henry, and after old George died, it was old Henry yelling at young George. Hell, it was the days before air-conditioning. In the summertime everyone left their doors and windows open. You could hear them bellowing back and forth. The nature of the beast. Outside the office there were no finer gentlemen you'd ever meet. But once the door closed, they became tigers."

Ben Fleiger, who worked for George as general manager of the Cleveland Pipers, recalled visiting the Kinsman offices and finding the atmosphere funereal: "Those people looked like something out of Charles Dickens. They didn't have chains to their desks, but those people, you could see it in their eyes, the long faces, not a smile, not a look of pleasure. People were glum, almost cowering. You could almost visualize the leg irons. These people were bitter, frustrated, unhappy, but they needed their jobs."

Joe Bennett, a close friend of George's, would go visit George at the Kinsman offices to discuss which football games they wanted to bet on. Henry wouldn't stand for it. "One day George and I were betting football games, and the old man threw me out," said Bennett. "He wanted George to go back to work.

"George was a heavy better. I don't think the old man liked that at all. He bet a lot of money on football, baseball, and a lot of basketball, as much as a thousand dollars a game, and sometimes more than that."

Frank Treadway would also visit George at the Kinsman offices. He saw firsthand the tug-of-war between father and son. "There was a barbershop in the basement, and George would sneak down there and get his hair cut, and the telephone would ring in the shop, and the call would be for George," said Treadway. "It was Henry, who was angry George was getting his hair cut instead of working. Henry would bang on the pipes that he knew ran down to the barbershop, and this was George's message, and if George didn't come up, the old man would come downstairs, and they'd have a big fight.

"Henry'd say, 'Goddammit, George, you can't get your hair cut on company time.' George would say, 'Goddammit, it grows on company time.' The two guys would be yelling at each other, eyeball to eyeball."

Despite George's obvious competency, the hard-to-please Henry often would find fault, and every once in a while he would "fire" George.

Bob and Patsy Stecher were among George and Joan Steinbrenner's closest friends. In 1957, not long after George returned to Kinsman, the four of them and another couple took a trip on the *Finlay*, one of Kinsman's lake freighters. When they returned, the Stechers witnessed Henry Steinbrenner's displeasure over something George had done.

"We were coming in from Buffalo, and we were heading the dock at Sandusky, Ohio," recalled Patsy Stecher. "George looks off in the distance, and he sees a figure standing on the dock. The figure was no more than two inches tall. And he says, 'My father is mad.'

"We came up to the dock, and the boat smashed into it, and Henry got on board. George was working for Kinsman at the time, and George had done something against his father's wishes. He had taken disciplinary action into his own hands.

"The father came on board, took him into a room, gave him holy hell, and fired George.

"The next morning George was going to get up real early and clean out his office so he could have one-upmanship on his father.

"George and Joan were living in Rocky River at the time, and there was a knock at the door. George went to the door, and it was his father, who was carrying all the contents of his office desk. He dumped it all on their living room floor and left. His father beat him to it."

George remembered the incident vividly. "When my dad came into the business, he found it very tough working for his father, as I found it working for him," he said. "I know they used to have arguments, and he'd come home, and I'd hear him talk about it, saying that my grandfather didn't want to do this or that, and he felt we should be doing it. And he quit. And I had the same thing. My God, after I was first married, I remember one time my dad bringing all my stuff out of my desk and sitting it outside our apartment door. And that was the end. I was finished."

The "firings" were gut-wrenching for George, but his friends knew how badly Henry needed him, and friends like Joe Bennett thought it "kind of silly." Said Bennett, "Henry was probably firing him and giving him stock at the same time."

Said Frank Treadway, "He and his father fought like cats and dogs. Henry was always firing George, but it never meant anything. The passion was there." But George told Treadway, "I wish I could get along with my father the way you do with yours. In other words, I wish I had a relationship." One would think George wouldn't have had time for a social life, but after he moved into a home in Bay Village about half a mile from the family farmhouse, he joined a crowd of upwardly mobile young executives who called themselves the Conservatives. In addition to the Steinbrenners, the group included Bill Gabriel and his wife, Frank Treadway and his wife, the Westovers, the Stouffers, and Joe and Patsy Stecher, all West Siders. On the weekends, one of the couples would throw a party, and everyone would attend, with the women sitting in one room and the men in another talking sports. Or they would all go out for dinner and a movie. One time they went to a burlesque house. A couple of the wives were scandalized at having seen bare breasts.

The Treadways lived four doors down from George and Joan. Frank recalled how close they were. "I was raising four children," said Frank Treadway. "Joan had a lovely home, and she would not allow my kids, or anyone else's kids, in the house unless they took their shoes off. When it was time for dinner, and I couldn't find the kids, I'd go over there, and if there were ten pairs of little shoes sitting on the Steinbrenners' front porch, I'd go in, and my kids would be there, and George would be sitting there playing the organ. These little kids would be completely enraptured by him. He'd hire a bus, a Cleveland Transit System bus, and he would take fifty or sixty people to the circus."

Their friends also recall how stormy George and Joan's marriage was.

"People like to fight," said Joe Bennett. "Yeah."

"Joan said something amusing to me," said Patsy Stecher. "She said, 'I don't know why I married George. I should have known, because when I went out with him on our first date, he talked for three hours about himself.'

"She made no bones about the fact that George is very difficult. They don't live together that much, so life isn't that difficult. His life-style is very difficult for her. It isn't that she isn't interested in what he's doing, but George has an insatiable ego, so everything is based on his ego. She's a very beautiful woman, and if she's around George, my guess is the cameras will home in on her, not him. That's my own observation."

Part of the conflict had to do with George's very Victorian notion—handed down by Henry—that the man is the king of his castle, and the woman has to go along. Combine that with George's dictatorial nature and his volcanic temper, and it's easy to see why Joan often became upset.

Frank Treadway recalled how dogmatic George could be when it came to Joan. "We had a picnic supper down at Clifton Beach, a cold day in late May or June. George had come up from town, and Joan came with my wife, and she had the audacity to wear slacks, and she looked great, because she was a young, trim, beautiful woman. When he saw what she was wearing, he ordered her to go home and change. He said, 'If you don't take those pants off, don't bother coming back to the party.' He publicly humiliated her. He felt she shouldn't be show-ing off her cute little rear end."

Treadway also saw a wife who was convinced that while George was traveling on business, he was entertaining other women. "Joan used to come over and sit on our back porch and cry her eyes out. Joan thought George was womanizing. He'd go away with a pair of pajamas and come home, and the bottoms would be missing, and Joan would read into it. I never thought George was the type to chase skirts. But he was an attractive guy who spent money easily. But Joan was from a family where people loved each other, and she finally got a bellyful of George hollering and screaming at her and telling her what to do."

At one point George ended up living at the YMCA, and finally she went back to Columbus and there was a trial separation. Eventually there was a reconciliation. Over the years the effect on Joan became obvious. She developed a thick skin and she became quicker to anger.

Frank Treadway witnessed the transformation. "From living with George, Joan had to become tough, tough, tough," he said.

On one occasion he saw her become livid in public when she didn't get recognition for her contribution to a charity event. "I thought, *Joan, what has happened to you? How you've changed living with George.* The point is she had to get just as tough as George in order to live with the guy. This was not the girl who George married. She just became hard as nails, still pretty but no longer soft."

During the football season, George's passion was the Cleveland Browns. He had only to drive down the street to hang out with one of the greatest Browns of all time, quarterback Otto Graham, who moved to Bay Village not long after coming to the team. Graham, who starred at Northwestern University, had been quarterback of the Browns during the first ten years of their existence, from 1946 to 1955, and during that span led them to a championship game every single year. Only Jim Brown would rate above him in the entire history of Cleveland Browns football.

Graham recalled his friendship with the Steinbrenners. "George, who lived down the street, was a tycoon in those days, very personable," he said. "I can remember a very funny story. George, Jake Davis, and myself and our wives went to an Indians baseball game. As we walked to the stadium, I pretended like I was going to goose George's wife. I just pretended, and she swung her purse and whacked me in the head, and we all laughed about it. Whenever I see George, I kid him about the purse.

"George and I are very good friends. I love the guy, frankly." But he added, "After I was fired by the Washington Redskins as coach in 1967, George was talking about getting involved in Florida. He was going to buy this farm in Ocala. He asked me if I wanted to go down and run his Florida businesses. I was thinking about it seriously, and I realized I could make a hell of a lot of money working for George, but it also was obvious there would be a lot more headaches. In business you're going to get more headaches than if you are athletic director of the Coast Guard Academy. And I was aware when you worked for George, you have headaches."

One of the ways Steinbrenner gained status in the Cleveland sports society was his work with the Junior Olympics, a program he had helped start when he was a student at Williams College. John Nagy, the head of the Cleveland parks department when the Junior Olympics was started in 1951, recalled how George would come home for the summer and work on the playgrounds coaching kids in track.

"We started the Junior Olympics on the playgrounds of Cleveland. George was involved from the beginning. He worked on the playground, and he was nuts about track. I liked the guy very much. He was a hell of a guy. George had a lot to do with its success. We had this idea, and we talked to him, and he helped structure the whole thing. And later, after he became a successful businessman, he funded the Junior Olympics with a group called Group 66. He was the head of that."

George also funded a program to provide training for Bay Village's youngsters. As a result of these and other charitable undertakings, George Steinbrenner in 1960 was named the Junior Chamber of Commerce Man of the Year.

There were also wonderful acts of kindness by George that no one ever knew about. "George did some things that really made me love the guy," said longtime Bay Village parks commissioner John Nagy. "A family got burned out of their home on the south side of Cleveland, and they were poor, and George rebuilt their house for them. George did it on his own. Nobody knew about it, but I knew the family. He didn't know them. He just read about it in the paper. That's the kind of heart the guy has. A fantastic man."

7

The thing that I would tell anyone who has experienced George is that you can't let him destroy you. He has that need—I now call it Steinbrenner Syndrome—to take credit for everything. You have to be amused by it, then move on to better days.

—John McClendon

The Cleveland Pipers

Ed Sweeney, a Cleveland plumbing and heating contractor, loved sports, especially boxing, but he also had a keen interest in amateur basketball, and so in 1958 he fulfilled a fantasy when he entered a team of amateur hoopsters in the Cleveland City League. After his team, which he called the Sweeney Pipers, won the title, he decided to raise the financial stakes considerably by joining the prestigious National Industrial Basketball League (NIBL).

This was no Mickey Mouse operation. The Industrial League teams had excellent players. There were only eight National Basketball Association (NBA) teams, and turnover was so low in the NBA that if you were a second-round draft choice, chances were you didn't make the team. Many of those who were cut ended up in the NIBL. They were deemed amateurs because the companies paid them to work for them, not play basketball for them.

Sweeney had a daunting task. He was starting from scratch against high-quality competition. Goodyear, for example, had ten thousand employees making tires. It was nothing for the company to pick out whatever college basketball players it coveted, give them jobs, and sign them up to play. Sweeney not only had to find a winning coach, but he had to find talented free agent players who could compete.

To assist him, Sweeney chose as his general manager a bright young man by the name of Mike Cleary. They came across the sterling record of John McClendon, who had led Tennessee State to two NAIA championships and was in the process of leading it to a third. Sweeney and Cleary figured correctly if they could hire McClendon, they could get his talented players as well.

There was one fact the statistics didn't tell Ed Sweeney: John McClendon was black, and in 1959 no white team anywhere, pro or college, had ever hired a black coach. This was 1959 in segregated America, before the Birmingham bus boycott, a year before the Freedom Rides. Sweeney, looking for the best candidate he could find, didn't care.

"He told me at the time, 'I didn't realize you were black,'" said McClendon. "He said to me, 'Does it make a difference to you?'

"I said, 'Of course not, if it doesn't make a difference to you,' and that was the end of that."

After Tennessee State won a third straight National Association of Intercollegiate Athletes (NAIA) national championship, John McClendon quit what surely was a lifetime job to coach the Pipers. He wanted to bring with him five members of his Tennessee State team, but Sweeney was afraid of the backlash—all of McClendon's players were black, and five black starters in white America was way too many. From his three-time NAIA champions, McClendon brought with him John Barnhill and Ronald Hamilton. Another Tennessee State starter, Dick Barnett, had signed with the Syracuse Nats. A fourth big talent, Ben Warley, was a junior at Tennessee State and would join the Pipers the following year after graduation.

In their first season the Pipers finished with a 16–16 record, fourth in the league, the highest finish ever for a first-year team in the NIBL and the highest finish ever for a first-year coach.

The Pipers were an even better team in 1960, but they were losing money, and Ed Sweeney's mother and siblings were becoming alarmed because he was siphoning serious money from the plumbing and heating business to run his team. Before the season was over, Sweeney's kin sued to throw him into bankruptcy in order to prevent him from contributing any more money to his team.

On the day the Pipers defeated the Denver-Chicago Truckers in Denver in a one-game playoff for the 1959–1960 NIBL title, Coach McClendon was informed that Sweeney was out of funds and that no more money would be forthcoming to pay bills. Since the Pipers were seeded first in the Amateur Athletic Union (AAU) national tournament, held in Denver that year, Coach McClendon and the team decided to stick it out and play even though they were virtually penniless. They severely cut their expenses during the weeklong tournament, moving into the YMCA, stopping eating in restaurants, and, to cut transportation costs, relying on the kindness of strangers or hitchhiking to the games. Coach McClendon was told that a new group of investors had bought the Pipers, but he was unable to reach the new owners to get them to send him some money so he could finish out the tournament.

When the Pipers reached the semifinals, Coach McClendon was desperate. Bravado was admirable, but he was at the point where he had no choice but to seriously consider withdrawing the Pipers from the tournament. Then an AAU official by the name of Willard Grimes, learning of the team's plight, stepped in with the needed money. The Pipers went on to win the tournament.

When Ed Sweeney was forced by his family to give up the Pipers, Ed Uhas, the business manager for the team, took steps to find someone to keep the franchise going. His first choice was thirty-year-old George Steinbrenner. Uhas knew a bit about his background—his coaching, his work with the Junior Olympics program, that he was Ohio Man of the Year—and he also knew Steinbrenner came from money.

When Uhas called him, Steinbrenner, who all his life had yearned to own a big-time sports franchise, jumped at the opportunity. He raised about fifty thousand dollars, borrowing money from the National City bank and selling some of his Kinsman Marine stock—infuriating his father, who wanted George running the shipping company, not wasting time on a foolish lark. He also decided to raise more capital the way Bill Veeck did it, by bringing in some friends. He called nine of his closest buddies and asked them to put up a thousand dollars each along with another three thousand dollars in notes just in case. He was sure, he told them, that the team would be such a hit that he wouldn't need the other three grand. He paid off Ed Sweeney's debts, totaling about twenty-five thousand dollars, and took over the team.

When the players returned to Cleveland from playing eight exhibition games in Russia, they learned something about the dark side of George Steinbrenner. He had wanted the State Department to promote him and the Pipers, asking that the team go over to Russia as the Cleveland Pipers, not the U.S. team. When the State Department refused, George decided to take it out on his players by not paying their monthly salaries earned while they were overseas.

Said Jack Adams, the team's captain, "Ben Fleiger, a sportswriter for the *Cleveland Plain Dealer*, got hold of the story. McClendon told Fleiger because the blacks were the ones Steinbrenner really didn't treat right. The white guys he really couldn't do enough for. He was trying to get everyone, particularly the blacks, for nothing, and was paying a lot to guys like [Larry] Siegfried and [Jerry] Lucas, who didn't even play. I got to know Lucas pretty good. He was getting money. It was their only livelihood, and he [George] wasn't going to pay them, and they had to have their money."

After the team returned from Russia, the players found out something else about their new head guy: George Steinbrenner was ambitious. Wanting a bigger stage, the new owner had quit the NIBL and joined a new league, the American Basketball League.

Abe Saperstein, the owner of the world-renowned Harlem Globetrotters, was the ABL's founder. He was convinced there was room on the American sports landscape for a second professional basketball league to rival the NBA.

When George Steinbrenner entered his franchise in Saperstein's new league, he had one overriding goal: winning the league. That he was able to do so was a tribute to his ingenuity and leadership. At the same time, the 1960–1961 Pipers would allow George Steinbrenner to display all his many characteristics—the good and the bad. By the time the year was over, Steinbrenner would be one of the most talked-about figures in Cleveland's sporting community.

George's first objective as the new owner of the franchise was to add the best players he could find. John McClendon wanted the existing Pipers players to form the nucleus of the team. George, as head honcho, felt it was entirely up to him and that McClendon had no say in the matter. He negotiated with the players one-on-one, leaving McClendon out of the decision-making process. Steinbrenner left some of the players and McClendon wondering whether they would even have a job.

The start-up of the ABL meant the demise of the NIBL, and so George had to outrecruit the other teams for the top talent available from the NIBL teams that had folded. He got the lion's share the old-fashioned way: he offered them more money than anyone else. George recruited Jack Adams, the highest-scoring player on the Peoria Caterpillars when that team folded, and Dan Swartz, the leading scorer of Wichita. Roger Brown, a high-scoring forward with San Francisco, was another important addition to the team. George also signed up Gene Tormohlen, a fierce rebounder from Tennessee; Woody Akins, a teammate of Jerry West's at West Virginia; Larry Siegfried, a teammate of Jerry Lucas's at Ohio State; and Johnny Cox of Kentucky, whom George almost lost because of his crassness.

"Cox knew a lot of our players," said John McClendon. "He was on the original All-Star team. I wanted him. Some people didn't. George wanted him. Johnny and I were sitting at a table waiting for George. George walked in, and he threw the contract across the table and said, 'Here, sign this.' He didn't even say, 'Glad to see you.' He just walked in and threw the contract clear across the table. 'Sign it, and let's get out of here.'

"Cox said, 'I'm not going to accept this kind of treatment.' He got up and left, went back to his room, and left the hotel. I went after him and called him back.

"I told Johnny, 'Don't pay any attention to him. After all, he's not the team.'"

George, who, like Sweeney, cared more about talent than about skin color, signed three of John McClendon's Tennessee State players, Dan Warley, John Barnhill, and Ron Hamilton. He decided to take on the NBA directly when he went after a fourth, offering Dick Barnett $14,000 to quit the Syracuse Nats and come play for the Pipers.

George had put together a team of talented players, but not long after he took over the Pipers, he stirred up controversy when he let it be known that although the Pipers had won everything under the sun the year before, he wanted a more famous, feistier coach than the tremendously popular John McClendon. McClendon was one of the great gentlemen of the coaching ranks. He never raised his voice, never argued with the referees. But George wanted box office. He wanted a dramatic coach like Red Auerbach. He couldn't stand that McClendon sat quietly while the referees kept making obviously bad calls.

Uncharacteristically, George didn't get his way: he was forced to keep McClendon on because everyone else—the players and the other board members—had great respect for his abilities and wanted him back.

"George never did want me as a coach," said McClendon, "and to be fair with him, I think he didn't want me because he didn't know me. I believe he didn't think I was well-known enough. He wanted someone everyone knew. He was looking for a name coach."

The team was fortunate that George didn't get his way. In an age of segregation, this integrated team from Cleveland would go on to boast a 47–11 record, and it would be the first team ever to defeat a U.S. Olympic team, which included a lineup of Hall of Fame greats Oscar Robertson, Jerry West, and Jerry Lucas. Stuck with John McClendon as coach, George decided that if a bad call was made, he would be the one to object. He also was quick to criticize McClendon publicly if he felt he was doing something he didn't like. McClendon was so popular that everyone ended up taking the coach's side against George.

The Pipers may have been a second-tier attraction, but George constantly kept them in the headlines by his actions. Part of the fun of going to games was to sit in the stands and boo George. The publicity about Steinbrenner's boorish behavior should have silenced him, but it didn't. George, it seemed, was impervious to criticism. What's more, the publicity seemed to fuel him.

After the Pipers defeated the U.S. Olympic team, the *Cleveland Press* the next day played the story on the first sports page, not on the front page of the paper. George became furious, called up sportswriter Bob August, and gave him hell.

In the paper the next day, August called George "congenitally unsuited" to run a pro sports team. When George read that, he proved August's point by ordering all team personnel to cancel their subscriptions to the *Press* and to call fifteen of their friends and have them cancel their subscriptions as well.

"One night George went out onto the floor and chewed out the referee in the middle of the game," said Bob Sudyk, a reporter for the *Cleveland Plain Dealer*. "He came out of the stands and stood nose to nose with him. The referee threw him out, and the people in the stands were screaming, going wild. Everyone knew it was George doing it, too."

On another night he became so irate, he rushed from his seat, knocking down chairs and spectators in a stampede to the bench to chastise Coach McClendon. He could often be heard suggesting strategy and loudly criticizing players when he felt they were giving a subpar effort. Part of the fun of going to the games was to sit in the stands and boo George.

In late August 1960, George Steinbrenner made more headlines for himself and the Pipers when he brought Dick Barnett over from the NBA's Syracuse Nationals. Barnett suited up to play a game, but just before tip-off a process server walked out onto the court with an injunction, and Barnett had to sit out. Barnett had a non-compete clause in his contract, and Syracuse was making sure that if he didn't play for the Nats, he wasn't going to be playing anywhere else either.

In court Barnett argued that playing for Syracuse was damaging his career. The reason, he said, was that Syracuse had been using him as a guard, not a forward, and as a result he was out of sync and not very productive. Even though the court held against Barnett and the Pipers, the Syracuse Nats gave the unhappy forward his release. Once in Cleveland playing for his old college coach, Barnett would display the uncanny shooting ability that later made him famous with the New York Knicks.

Getting Barnett was a huge coup for the Pipers, and that afternoon the Pipers PR department sent out a press release that was supposed to be embargoed until the next day, when the *Cleveland Press* was going to run a front-page article.

Gib Shanley, a new announcer at an AM station in Cleveland, got the Barnett story from the wire services, ignored the embargo, and went on the air with it at 6:15 that night. Chuck Heaton, a sportswriter for the morning paper, the *Cleveland Plain Dealer*, heard Shanley on the radio, and he broke the story himself the next morning. As a result, the *Cleveland Press*, no longer having a scoop, moved the story inside the paper.

George's first big splash was ruined, and he was apoplectic. Heads would roll.

"I was the general manager, and it was my job to control everything," said Mike Cleary. "When I came in the next morning, George was all over me. I explained what happened. I said, 'George, you cannot help a situation like that. It just happens.'

"He said, 'Nothing just happens,' and he said, 'You're fired.'"

"I said, 'No, before you do that, I quit.' And I was gone that day. So I had the privilege of being the first general manager ever fired by George Steinbrenner."

Now Steinbrenner had to find another general manager. The man he chose was the *Cleveland Plain Dealer's* Ben Fleiger. Fleiger had been a beat reporter covering the Cleveland Indians in 1959 and 1960, and he was tired of the grind of being on the road, so when Steinbrenner asked him if he would take over as general manager of the Pipers, he agreed. George indicated he'd have a contract drawn up, and Fleiger foolishly took the job before he signed it. Steinbrenner withheld that contract during Fleiger's entire tour of duty with the Pipers.

"I don't know why he picked me for the job," said Fleiger. "I'm sorry he did, although it was a hell of an experience, and I survived. Had I known how little money they had, I never would have left my job at the newspaper.

"George had also promised the job to Pipers business manager Eddie Uhas, who when he found out George had also offered me the job resigned to join the Cleveland Indians publicity staff. Again, that was George double-talking and playing one off against the other. He couldn't help himself."

To his credit, George had built one of the great pro basketball teams of his generation in the 1960–1961 Pipers. All he had to do was sit back and let Hall of Fame basketball coach John McClendon lead his men to victory. But George Steinbrenner was never a dynasty builder, because he was incapable of leaving well enough alone. He was a compulsive meddler who had to be in complete control over every aspect of the organization, and his most detrimental flaw was that he always thought that because he had once been a coach, he knew more about the sport than his coaches. The other part had to do with his narcissism, the personality disorder in which the one suffering from it is convinced that he is better than everyone else, is smarter than everyone else, and knows better than everyone else.

His second-guessing was constant and annoying, and his meddling often counterproductive and sometimes downright hurtful to his team. There was a constant struggle between George and Coach McClendon. George rarely gave his coach a moment's peace.

Said Frank Treadway, "He'd stand there and wave his arms and tell McClendon, 'Take that son of a gun out of there and put him on the bench.' We had a terrible time sitting on him.

"One time after a game when George came to the dressing room to complain, McClendon told him, 'I don't allow anyone in my dressing room, and I don't let anybody talk to me in that manner in front of my players. You're going to have to leave.'"

Said McClendon, "George wanted to be part of the thing, but his behavior was derisive, and the players weren't used to that. We were used to people who would stay with you up or down."

George, looking to improve the team even more, was intending to trade for Connie Hawkins, the star of the league, until Coach McClendon told George he wouldn't play him.

Said center Dick Brott, "McClendon felt he had seen real evidence that proved that Hawkins had been involved in a fix. He said, 'He's a bad boy, and I don't want him.'" Years later Hawkins sued the NBA for banning him and won.

Always looking for an edge, George hired the coach of the championship high school team in Ohio to sit up in the stands with a walkie-talkie. His job was to relay formations down to Coach McClendon. For his part McClendon refused to talk to him. The task was left to one of the bench players.

McClendon was certain that George had no idea of his basketball philosophy, and that if he did, he didn't subscribe to it. As a result, McClendon felt that George's man-in-the-stands stunt was more to second-guess him than anything else. The bottom line, though, was that McClendon just didn't think it served a purpose.

John McClendon's philosophy was to maximize the skills of his players. He didn't expect them to be all-around players. What he wanted was for the talented rebounders to rebound, the talented passers to pass, and the talented shooters to shoot.

Steinbrenner wanted big men in the center from his experience coaching the dominating Bill McCauley at Lockbourne. McCauley, at six nine, was almost always the most talented player on the court, and he scored a lot of points. Steinbrenner liked having a high-scoring center, and he was scornful of the play of the Pipers' center, Dick Brott, whose function on the team under McClendon's system was to dish the ball to his teammates and to rebound. McClendon, who asked

Brott not to shoot, constantly praised him for his play. At the same time, during the games Steinbrenner would be in his ear constantly screaming at him from his seat close to the bench to shoot more.

Said McClendon, "Brott and I had an understanding. He wanted to stay in the role we had for him, but at the same time he was under pressure to do what George wanted. I thought the world of Brott. I loved him. He was a fighter. But before it was over Brott became a real nervous wreck."

Brott resented George for the way he treated McClendon, whom he called "one of the finest people you will ever meet," and he absolutely hated the way the Pipers owner treated him. "I was never in a place I disliked more than Cleveland," said Brott. "I just didn't like Steinbrenner. Nobody liked him as far as I knew. He would do things like call you into the office and tell you you were a loser. I said nothing. He paid my salary." Steinbrenner traded Brott to Hawaii just before the end of the first half of the season. The Pipers had a slim lead over the Pittsburgh Rens, led by Connie "the Hawk" Hawkins, and Steinbrenner saw that the Rens had to play three games against Hawaii right at the end. He also knew that Brott was the most effective defender against Hawkins in the league. The Hawk was averaging forty-two points a game, except when he played against Brott, who held the star to seventeen points a game. George acquired center Connie Dierking, and he traded Brott to Hawaii so he could help them beat Pittsburgh and give the Pipers the first-half championship. Remarkably, it turned out just that way.

John McClendon was unruffled by the owner's constant interference. "I wasn't shaken by all these things," he said. "I tried to level it off by having my players take the same attitude I did. I'd tell them, 'Go out on the court and do your best. As long as you're winning, what can anybody say?'"

The first American Basketball League (ABL) season began in October 1960. Everything went fairly smoothly until December, when the Los Angeles team folded, leaving San Francisco by itself on the West Coast. Saperstein, who was very successful running the Globetrotters, was a disaster as ABL commissioner. When George enlisted his investors, he had made it seem that a roaring success was inevitable. A born salesman, he stressed Saperstein's experience and connections and how there was plenty of room for a second professional basketball league.

Frank Treadway was one of the original investors in the Pipers, and he recalled George's leadership and his unflagging optimism. "There was a fledgling company trying to get started at the time, Western Reserve Life Assurance Company, and several of the directors were in the group," said Treadway. "There was Skain Bowler, my cousin Tim Treadway, and the Smythe brothers, Pete and his brother Cragin. The Smythes were old West Side Cleveland people, friends with my mother and father, who in turn were friends with the Stouffers and the Steinbrenners, and all this started out with a bunch of guys out having a lark. If we lost a few bucks, okay. That type of thing. It wasn't until down the road when George became obsessed with this business that alarms went off."

Treadway was swayed to invest, he said, because of George's super salesmanship. It was clear from the start that George would be the decision maker, which was fine with everyone. George sold him on the team's move to the ABL in part by relying on Abe Saperstein's business acumen.

"We all knew who Saperstein was," said Treadway, "and we knew the Globetrotters were successful, because every time they came to Cleveland—twice a year—they sold out the Cleveland Arena." Treadway admitted that the investors didn't ask the right questions. "What does a traveling team of comedians have to do with a professional basketball league?" he asked.

Saperstein failed because the teams and the league were undercapitalized. When Los Angeles folded, chaos ensued. And it wasn't bad enough that the league was falling apart. Serious problems arose in Cleveland with the Cleveland Arena, and attendance dropped off. George had no choice but to move the games to the old, decrepit Public Hall—called the world's largest morgue—a move that ultimately killed any chance the Pipers had to stay solvent. By January 1962, the Pipers were hemorrhaging money. For the first time, some of the investors were questioning George's ways.

"It wasn't a month when George was hitting up the directors for more money," said Treadway. "Within six to eight months the original investment was gone. George would pull out his big checkbook, and he'd say, 'We need fifteen thousand dollars.' And he'd start the ball rolling with a check, and then he'd turn to Jim Stouffer and the others, and Jimmy would write out a check for five thousand dollars.

Jimmy wrote fairly large ones. It was like being in church, and George expected us to put in our tithing.

"It's like being in love with a prostitute. You know it's wrong, but you can't help yourself. 'Gimme my money. I want to give it to George.' It was an obsession with some of these people." Years later Treadway sought out the accountant and discovered that, all along, while other investors were writing checks, George never deposited the checks he wrote.

One of the reasons some of the stockholders turned on George when things started to go bad was that George operated in a vacuum. He did not communicate to anyone—not even to general manager Ben Fleiger—anything about the financial situation of the team other than "Things are fine," and even when the team started losing a lot of money, the stockholders were kept in the dark. In March 1962, the losses were far outrunning the income. There was no money coming in, and the Pipers were in the red about $240,000. Without notice, the locks on the team's offices were changed. The uniforms went unwashed. Employees went home at the end of the week without payment.

According to those who knew George and Joan, George's financial troubles were causing a rift in his marriage. He should have trod softly if he wanted to keep it intact. To show just how desperate he was to keep himself and the Pipers afloat, he went so far as to sell some of his wife's stock without her knowledge so he could raise money. In 1962, Joan filed for divorce.

"George was a stockholder in Western Reserve Life," said Frank Treadway. "He owned stock and he needed some money, and two weeks before Christmas he called me up to sell a thousand shares. I knew the stockholders had restricted stock, called letter stock, meaning it had to be held for six months before it could be sold." George told Treadway it was his account and not letter stock.

"Five days later, George came in to get his money, and he had to deliver the securities. They were registered under his wife's name, and it was in fact letter stock. The divorce was pending at the time, and he was selling her stock.

"The stock was in Joan's name, and it was restricted, and somehow she left it where George knew where it was, and he came in, and to top it off, he told me he wanted to buy her a Christmas present, a new car.

"He's so quick on his feet, almost coming up with excuses that sound legitimate.

"When she found out about it, she was furious. I kept waiting for someone to blow the whistle on him."

Joan never went through with the divorce. George made her an offer she couldn't refuse, and she withdrew her petition.

"Why didn't Joan leave him?" asked Frank Treadway rhetorically. "You've known attention, the bright lights, pretty dresses, fancy things. The promise of all that was on the horizon. And maybe her parents said to her, 'Come on, Joan, stick it out.'"

The question is: why did George want so badly to stay married?

"He wanted to maintain the image of marriage," said Treadway. "A divorce for a lot of people is painful. And it is an admission of defeat, where it's your fault or hers."

They are still married.

If you look at George's actions from the perspective of an investor, it seemed incredible that he was able to keep the team going as long as he did. At no point did he quit seeking financial relief. He had so many ideas, plots, and schemes going, it was hard to keep track of them all. Frank Treadway was always amazed that George was involved in so many projects at once. He said, "He was like a juggler in his mind. He always had a dozen balls bouncing, and somebody would make a proposition to him, and he'd say, 'Yeah, sure.'

"I was in the securities business, and sometimes George would call me, and sometimes I'd call him. I'd say, 'I'd like you to buy something.'" When George agreed, he would sometimes hedge it. "But I would get myself in trouble because I'd call George on Monday, and he'd say, 'Okay, buy me twenty-five thousand dollars worth and have them deliver them to the bank.'

"The bank was Central National, and five or ten days later—whenever they'd come in from New York—they'd take them to the bank for payments.

"I'd say, 'George, don't get me in trouble. Tell your banker to have the money there and sign the papers.' And it would be weeks, or even months, before George would sign the papers and deposit the sufficient funds to complete the transaction. It's not completely illegal, but it certainly is unethical.

"You'd be on the phone, and he'd put you on hold. The other line was ringing, and it was somebody talking about the Ground Round, his restaurant in Buffalo, that needed attention, and George would forget about me and go on to the next fellow. Always too many deals, not enough money, and not enough time to think about them. Maybe I'm too conservative, but if I am, George was too impetuous."

Treadway also noticed another trait of George's: he was willing to take chances that a lot of other people wouldn't. "One time during the Piper days," he said, "George wanted to bring down a shipment or two of grain from the Minnesota area, just before the lakes were shut down for the winter. If we each put in five thousand dollars, he said, he would guarantee that we'd all make twenty-five. But the insurance company had the good sense to say no."

At the end of the first half of the split season, the Pipers uncharacteristically lost seven of nine games. When the second half began, George decided to shake the team up with a big trade. It was also the excuse he needed to fire John McClendon. Though Jack Adams was one of the players traded to the New York Tuck Tapers, George nevertheless asked him whether he would take over as coach.

"I told him, 'No, I don't feel right replacing Coach McClendon. You already made your decision. I'm going with New York,'" said Adams.

"George was so vindictive," Adams continued. "He will do anything for someone as long as he does what he wants. If you don't do what he wants, he will go to extremes to get even with you." Trading three of his players was only the beginning. Because Adams would not take over as coach, McClendon still had the job.

After the Pipers lost two games to one in the first-half-season playoff series against Kansas City, George told the players that because the team had lost, he wasn't going to pay them. McClendon was incredulous. "It was a complete surprise," said McClendon. "Guys had played their hearts out, and when we lost, they didn't get paid. We had heard that some of his friends had gambled on the team, and they were upset, so he, in answer to their being upset, didn't pay the guys.

But the point was: the bad sport's attitude was the thing. The guy can't take it, and here we had another half coming up right away."

McClendon was not about to let George get away with this. He phoned *Cleveland Plain Dealer* reporter Bob Sudyk to tell him that Steinbrenner was refusing to pay his players their salary. He told Sudyk they were going to boycott the evening's game against the Pittsburgh Rens unless they got paid. In the article, Sudyk reported that the players had a "seething resentment" of Steinbrenner. McClendon had called early enough for the story to make the afternoon paper.

When the article came out, Steinbrenner called Sudyk on the phone, ranting. He said, "Who told you my players aren't being paid? That's a pack of lies. I'll have your job for this. You're through in the newspaper business. You won't be able to get a job anyplace in the country after I'm done. Don't ever speak to me again. Get a lawyer."

Sudyk was shaking in his boots. Steinbrenner obviously meant business, and he had the money to back up his threats.

George, enraged that he had been outmaneuvered, turned Machiavellian. He composed a letter under the signature of Jack Adams, whom he had just traded, refuting Sudyk's story of dissention and of their not getting paid. (When I asked Adams about the letter years later, he said he knew nothing about it.) He then ordered the players to sign the letter, telling Roger Brown that if they refused, he would fold the team and no one would be paid for the rest of the year. He then sent the letter signed by the players to the *Cleveland Press*.

When John McClendon learned what Steinbrenner was doing, the principled coach called the newspapers to announce he was resigning. McClendon in a statement said he felt he could not be true to his players or to his own conscience unless he resigned.

After McClendon quit, Steinbrenner tried to repair the damage by retaining McClendon in the job of vice president in charge of player personnel. The truth was, this was what George wanted from the start. Keeping John McClendon on and giving him a fancy title did not obscure from the public the fact that Steinbrenner had tried to intimidate his players into lying and had placed a principled, able, beloved coach in an untenable, compromising position.

"When John quit, there was a great hullabaloo in the papers," said Ben Fleiger. "A seaman on one of Kinsman Transit's ships wrote to the *Cleveland Press* and said, 'I'm not surprised by what George Steinbrenner did to John McClendon. I worked for Kinsman Transit on a ship, and George's father made Captain Kidd look like Little Lord Fauntleroy.'"

After George accepted John McClendon's resignation, he had the gall to ask him to help hire his replacement, Boston Celtics great Bill Sharman. McClendon, always the gentleman, gladly did so. McClendon and Sharman were good friends. McClendon knew him through Sam Jones, the Celtic great who had played for McClendon in college.

Sharman had coached the Los Angeles team in the ABL before it folded. A huge name, he was just what Steinbrenner had wanted all along, and with his arrival, the owner stopped the second-guessing of his coach.

"Things calmed down after Bill came," said John McClendon. "They had to, after the dissatisfaction caused by the players not getting paid. Bill was the right person at the right time."

Sharman, who led the Pipers to the second-half championship, had nothing but praise for his boss, who, because of Sharman's fame, treated him with a lot more respect than he gave McClendon. "George actually was a great guy to work for," said Sharman, "because when I was there, we were lucky enough to win. If we would win, George would be very happy. If we would lose, he'd be very upset. He wanted to win so badly, I could see how he could make things very tough. But he treated me very, very well.

"Everything started going good for us, and we ended up winning the championship."

"The championship series was Cleveland against Kansas City," said Ben Fleiger. "The Pipers won, and we took the trophy, and I ended up with it, and even though John wasn't the coach, I gave it to him. I told him that after all he went through, he had earned it more than I did."

By late March 1962, George was looking for a white knight to come along and rescue the Pipers from insolvency, but because he had made so many enemies in the press with his bizarre series of actions against his players and John McClendon, he had lost a great deal of credibility in the Cleveland financial community. George's actions—spitefully not paying his players, forcing the players to lie about not getting paid—had been those of a psychopath. Who would be crazy enough to throw in with him? Yet it didn't stop him from continuing to seek financial help.

Art Modell, the purchaser of the Cleveland Browns, was new in town, and he had heard about the Pipers' plight. Not knowing how bad it was, he asked Ben Fleiger and Lou Mitchell to come see him about the possibility of his investing in the team. When Modell asked Fleiger when he had been paid, Fleiger explained it had been a month since his last paycheck arrived. Hearing that, Modell offered him a job on a part-time basis. Fleiger gladly went to work for Modell.

With the season coming to an end and the Pipers in deep financial trouble, any normal owner would have considered throwing in the towel and letting the franchise go under. But George Steinbrenner was no ordinary man. One trait of a narcissistic personality is that the person needs to be involved with only the best—the best doctor, the best lawyer, the best institutions. For Steinbrenner, the best institution in the sport of basketball meant the National Basketball Association. Somewhere along the line—some say it was his plan from the beginning—he boldly took steps to take his championship Cleveland Pipers team into the NBA.

He would have a legitimate shot, he determined, if he could sign the number one college player in the country, Ohio State center Jerry Lucas. In a league that was becoming blacker and blacker, Lucas was the Great White Hope of the NBA. He had been drafted by the Cincinnati Royals and offered $30,000. Steinbrenner, determined to make Lucas a Cleveland Piper, offered him $45,000 in cash and stocks, contingent on the Pipers getting into the NBA. George and investor John Schanz shepherded Lucas around Cleveland, selling him on the city, and George talked him into playing.

Ben Fleiger watched from afar as George, who was broke, staged a big press event at the Hotel Cleveland to announce Lucas's signing. George was able to get him because Lucas wanted to play a shorter ABL schedule and be closer to home. All it took was money. Said Frank Treadway, "Lucas wanted forty-five thousand, and we had already spent our money.

"We were out of money, and George didn't have any more strings to pull, so he was making a lot of promises and worrying about paying later on. George was sweet-talking Jerry into coming into the NBA.

I used to fret. I'd say, 'George, we have a history of financial losses, and here you are making these promises.'

"George would say, 'Frank, don't worry about it. You're always worrying about things.'

"We had been told if we could sign this guy, we could have an NBA franchise for two hundred and fifty thousand. The network TV people were concerned about the black players causing the white people not to watch basketball on TV. Lucas was the Great White Hope to rescue the Pipers and the NBA. George wanted him, and he was willing to sign him for a forty-five thousand dollars worth of Chinese money."

With the great Jerry Lucas under contract, all George had to do was raise $250,000, and he would have had an NBA franchise. But George had no money—his wealthy father, who thought George foolish to get involved with the Pipers in the first place—had refused to invest a penny, and because of the ugly publicity surrounding his stewardship of the Pipers, most serious investors who might have been interested in owning a pro basketball franchise decided that they weren't about to get in bed with crazy George Steinbrenner.

George was able to raise a little more than half of the $250,000 entry fee. At the NBA league meeting at which he was to get his franchise, he showed the NBA executives a pile of telegrams representing the rest of the down payment. According to John McClendon, when the NBA officials checked, the telegrams turned out to be bogus, and George got asked out of the meeting. Said McClendon, "It threw basketball in Cleveland back six or seven years because no one would touch Cleveland after that, and it wasn't until George left Cleveland that Cleveland was able to get a franchise."

After his fake telegrams were found out, a determined George Steinbrenner continued his quest to come up with the money. Here's how close he came: he called Pipers director Lou Mitchell at his investment firm. Mitchell recalled the conversation.

"George called me from the meeting at Ball, Burch, and Krause. He said, 'Unless we can get a hundred thousand dollars down here, they are not going to let us into the league, and they won't give us a second chance.'

"I counted up all the money I had at the time. I went through my stocks, and they were worth eighty-seven thousand dollars. I thought for a minute whether I wanted to blow it, and I decided not to. That was the end of the Pipers."

When the Pipers ended up in the red to the tune of about $240,000, George, to his credit, decided he would do what he could to pay back his creditors. Bob Stecher, a close friend, recalled what George did to settle his debts incurred by the Pipers, working a deal by selling an old freighter to get money he used to pay off the investors.

Bill Sharman, for one, was surprised to get paid several years after the Pipers' demise. "We went to the playoffs, and none of us got play-off money," he said. "About three years later, George sent me the money he owed me. About three thousand dollars. It was money I never expected. So I think George is as good as his word. If he says he's going to do something, he does it."

Said investor John Schanz, "George likes to gamble. He likes the horses. He likes sports. He likes to bet. And he isn't afraid of losing. He once said, 'I'll die broke or a millionaire.' But he would feel terrible if he died owing anyone."

Though George had ruffled feathers and made himself the object of derision by his antics, a significant number of investors had nothing but praise for their charismatic owner. The Pipers had been, they knew, a risky investment, and he had given his all in an attempt to turn the team into a winner and a financial score.

"We all enjoyed the experience," said Bud Shockley. "It was a fun thing to do and great to be part of. I remember the whole experience fondly."

Bob Ferry was another investor who held no ill will toward George. "I'm a great admirer of George Steinbrenner. What he has done is incredible. I think George Steinbrenner is the stuff America is made of. You have to understand you are dealing with a hell of a competent guy. He believed if he could put the money together, it could go.

"George was very concerned about some of his friends losing money, and he made his best efforts to pay people back. He tried. We were all involved. It was pride. Who wants to walk down the street and have the laundry man look at you and know you owe him money?

"George's philosophy was 'What's the point of playing unless you want to win?' And I think that's commendable. That's why they won the championship. He pushed them. He wanted to win even though we weren't making any money, because he figured if we had a championship team, why, we'd draw fans. He didn't have the money he needed, and he still went out and got the players. The only thing was, we didn't draw fans. In a way he was way ahead of his time. He was on the right track, wanted to raise money, but not with that crew.

"He was determined never to enter a deal without having enough money behind it. He learned that. He was determined not to make that mistake again. And he never did."

8

Gartland went out of business because George was
the one who ran them out.

—Robert Sauvey

George Builds an Empire

T wo years after the demise of the Cleveland Pipers, in 1963, George Steinbrenner bought Kinsman Marine Transit from his father. Six years earlier, after the 1957 season coaching at Purdue, his father had said to him, "Come back and get going or we're going to get out of the business like some of the other independents." George returned, and for six years he and his father locked horns.

Their biggest battle of wills was over finances. Henry Steinbrenner was very conservative. He had a half dozen old freighters that carried coal and grain across the Great Lakes. The way the business worked, the fleet owner depreciated the boats like any other piece of machinery, and twenty years down the line he would sell the boat to another shipping company family, like the Hutchinsons, the Woods, or the Sullivans, and then the Sullivans would depreciate the boat, and they would then sell their old boat to Henry, and Henry would depreciate the boat all over again. This is how the shipping lines made much of their money. Moreover, Henry was perfectly satisfied to earn a low-six-figure but not spectacular living at a time when most people were making six or seven thousand dollars a year. As far as Henry was concerned, he was living a good life, and he had no desire to seek anything more.

The other way Henry made money was to keep costs down, setting rigid rules. He kept on top of everything that was happening. Robert Sauvey, who worked on Kinsman ships, starting as a deckhand and working his way up to first mate, remembered Henry as "really tight-fisted" and a "bitchy old bastard."

George was different from his dad—he wanted more. He wanted bigger things.

"One day George was fussing," said childhood friend Frank Treadway. "He said, 'Jesus Christ, Kinsman has a million dollars in a checking account, not even getting interest from anyone. It can buy things. If Kinsman has a million in the bank, I might be able to borrow ten million more.'"

Over time, Henry Steinbrenner grew weary of the business and of fighting with George, and slowly he began to relinquish control. George borrowed money from his banker friends to better the company, and according to Treadway, "more of his moves worked out than didn't work out."

In 1963, Henry Steinbrenner decided to retire. "George bought Kinsman out from his father," said Harold Zeig, George's father-in-law. "He had a chance to get it at a good price, and he thought the possibilities were great on the Great Lakes, and this is very important for your book, by the way: no one else favored the Great Lakes because shipping on the lakes had been going down. George alone felt the shipping business had a great future on the Great Lakes, especially grain and coal. And I'll give him credit, because no one helped him. He did it on his own. His father was around, but his father didn't have the same vision he did. He gradually replaced the ships that were not too valuable with big ones he got from U.S. Steel, and from there on he had a real fleet. He was making a million dollars a year in a very short time."

Another Cleveland friend, Pete Smythe, recalled the time when George was trying to borrow the money to buy Kinsman from his father. "George came to me hat in hand," said Smythe. "He needed ten thousand dollars to get back in business. He had the opportunity to buy all of Kinsman Transit's ships. The rest of the family was involved as well. George got his sisters, Sue and Judy, to stay in.

"I didn't like the deal, so I said, 'Let me think about it over the weekend.' When we talked next, he said, 'Never mind. I have someone else.' That guy, who turned out to be Tom Roulston, made ninety thousand dollars on his investment."

Part of George's vision for making Kinsman Marine viable was to expand his fleet.

"When George took over Kinsman, the company had four freighters," said Cleveland newspaperman Bob Sudyk. "He expanded it to twenty-two ships." Years later he was able to triple the value of the company.

The other part of George's plan was to put as many competing independent shipping companies out of business as he could. One such company was Gartland Steamship, which Robert Sauvey had worked for. Said Sauvey, "Gartland went out of business because George was the one who ran them out.

"George said to me, 'You might as well come to work for us, because I'm going to run Gartland out of business anyway.' And he did that about 1967.

"George took over Kinsman from his dad. He shoved his dad out, really. We bought out the Republic Steel fleet. We had two of the newest self-loaders on the Great Lakes and twenty-some ships. We named one ship the *Paul Thayer* and the other the *William R. Rush*. I was first mate on the *Rush*. Those ships were built strictly for Jones and Laughlin Steel. We had a contract for J and L."

Said Jack Melcher, who worked for a long time as an attorney for George, "The contracts for grain, coal, and ore came from a fellow by the name of Paul Peacham, who used to be with Jones and Laughlin. Paul was an old buddy of George's father, and Paul would feed him some contracts, and other people who were friends of his father would feed him contracts, and so George survived off the crumbs on the table."

But he did survive, when most of his competitors did not. Then in 1967, George was involved in a deal that saw him take over one of the largest shipbuilding companies in the United States, the American Ship Building Company.

By 1970, however, the steel industry was in steep decline, and everyone in the business was running scared. The American Ship Building Company was still one of the biggest builders of Great Lakes ships, and so in 1971 it came as a shock to the industry when George Steinbrenner, the owner of a relatively small shipping company called Kinsman Marine Transit, announced that he had taken over the much larger American Ship.

Much as George had done when he took the Cleveland Pipers from the Industrial League to within inches of getting into the National Basketball Association, Steinbrenner had managed to turn his relatively small company into a bigger, more powerful one. The man who chose him to lead the reorganization of the company was an AmShip executive by the name of Tom Roulston, the same man who had lent George the money to buy Kinsman Marine Transit from his father.

"Tom Roulston was approached by a group of people in New York who had rather significant holdings in American Ship Building to see what could be done about changing management," said Jack Melcher. "Roulston thought, Steinbrenner is the kind of guy who would be a good CEO for American Ship. One of the stumbling blocks to the takeover was George's insistence that American Ship acquire Kinsman. That was resisted, but after George became CEO of American Ship, eventually AmShip acquired Kinsman. And that's where I first got involved with Steinbrenner.

"George got a lot of money when American Ship bought Kinsman," said Melcher. "It wasn't spendable cash. It was restricted stock. I suspect he borrowed money against it. One of the things that happened when the public offering occurred in 1971, he sold some of his own.

"As chairman of American Ship, George was in a position to do people favors, and he expected reciprocation and got it. His fortune started out that way. It wasn't the shares of stock, though on paper it made him a millionaire. There was a great deal of clout, and George was a master of using it in a rather forceful way."

Melcher had a front-row seat as Steinbrenner sold Kinsman Marine to two brilliant business associates, Shelley Guren and Ed Ginsburg. He put his father, Henry, in charge of running the company. George also began to vertically integrate his new company, buying the firm that was supplying dockworkers for his ships. Guren and Ginsburg helped him buy it.

"George and the twins—Shelley Guren and Ed Ginsburg—bought the Stevedore Company," said Melcher. "There was a lot of political business going on. I felt there was something not quite kosher about it. This is owned by the Cleveland Port Authority, and it was interesting because one of the guys who was originally on the board, a fellow by the name of Tom Coakley, owned their competitor, the Cleveland Stevedore Company, which had most of the stevedoring business in the Cleveland port. Coakley was on the board, and then he and George didn't get along, and after a year or two, Coakley walked away from it.

"This is typical of what George would do. He gets mad at Coakley, so what does he do? He buys the other stevedoring company just to stick it to Coakley."

Guren and Ginsburg also helped George buy a towing company, even though by doing so George was circumventing the antitrust laws.

"Shortly before I left American Ship, George came to me and said, 'What I want you to do is figure out some way we can get Kinsman back into the Steinbrenner family,'" said Melcher. "After I left, this was done."

George became involved in a campaign for governor by liberal Democrat Jack Gilligan. He needed to be politically active because of a very important bill he desperately needed to have passed in Congress. It was called the Merchant Marine Act of 1970, and it provided for the Great Lakes to be recognized as a seacoast. In 1936, a bill was passed benefiting shipbuilders on the East and West coasts. The subsidy law guaranteed Title XI mortgages and put them in a capital construction fund. Tax was deferred, and the money saved was used to build new ships. The builders could also depreciate the vessels.

Were the Great Lakes shipbuilders able to gain an equal recognition, the business interests, including the union, could obtain tax advantages in terms of appreciation, write-offs, and acceleration of tax advantages that were being enjoyed by shipbuilders on the East and West coasts. The purpose of the bill was to encourage shipbuilding on the Great Lakes.

George led a movement to include the Great Lakes shipbuilders on both coasts. He lobbied Ted Kennedy and Richard Nixon. In a speech in Seattle, Nixon promised to help the Great Lakes shippers. After he was elected president in 1968, he signed the Merchant Marine Act of 1970. One of George's allies was Charles Mosher, a congressman from

Cleveland and one of a group of politicians who would receive illegal campaign contributions from Steinbrenner. Mosher, who had no idea the donations were illegal, would be terribly embarrassed by the whole episode. Even so, he felt it important to get the bill passed and expressed pride in doing so.

"We had meetings with George," said Mosher. "His office was in Lorain. He's a character. I've never known a person with such ambitions and competitive energy and at that point, cocksureness. He sought power. He's a great believer in power and manipulation. At that time he believed he could buy power with money anywhere, including Washington. He had been chairman on the Democratic committee for raising funds for Senate candidates. And he had this strange, paradoxical situation of being chairman to raise funds for Democratic senators and yet contributing to the Republicans such as I, and even at one point contributing to the Nixon campaign. He was pretty cynical, but in a fascinating way. In a way he's a great big, rambunctious sort of teenage kid who's just overflowed with self-confidence."

I asked Mosher about George's role in the passage of the bill.

"You know George," he said. "He doesn't take less than a lead role in anything like that. It all evolved later into a very embarrassing situation for me. He was so pleased with the success of this effort that three years later, in the election campaign of 1972, he contributed funds to a dozen or more members of Congress, among them I—and when I say he contributed, he did it in an illegal fashion, as you well know. He gave bonuses to certain trusted employees, who then out of the blue sent contributions to my campaign, and a good many others. We accepted them on face value. They were personal checks. And we deposited them only to find out later that it had been an illegal arrangement.

"Even though my campaign committee and I handled this in what we considered to be a completely aboveboard, legal, routine fashion, just being associated with all the headlines in the newspapers, 'Illegal Contributions,' was a tremendous embarrassment.

"We had accepted the money in good faith. Two years had passed, and we spent it. There was nothing illegal in the way we handled it.

"The funny thing, the bill was significant after the fact. As a result of this legislation literally hundreds of people had jobs in my district that they wouldn't have had otherwise. It did stimulate a very significant amount of ship business, including nine-hundred- to one-thousand-foot freighters."

The contributions to Mosher were not the only "funny money" donated during the 1972 elections. George, who was being hounded by the Justice Department for antitrust violations, decided he would give a significant donation to the Nixon reelection campaign in the hope that he might influence the men in power. As a result, he gave $100,000 to the Committee to Re-elect the President, known disparagingly to Nixon's detractors as CREEP. Later it came out that a portion of the money was given underhandedly and illegally. When George then lied to the feds about it, he got himself in serious legal trouble. It wouldn't be the first or the last time he didn't play by the rules, but it was the first time he would have to suffer the consequences.

9

There are people who step on people on the way to
the top, and George is one of those people.
—Frank Treadway

Vernon Stouffer's Revenge

After the Cleveland Indians won a pennant in 1954, the fortunes of the team sank like a stone. Some of the reason was
bad luck when phenom left-hander Herb Score was hit in the face by a
line drive and nearly killed. Some of it was bad management and abject
stupidity: future stars like Roger Maris, Rocky Colavito, and Norm
Cash were traded away.

By 1957, the Indians were losing money. They drew only 722,000
fans all season. Owner William Daley wanted his general manager,
Frank "Trader" Lane, to keep the Indians in the newspapers and in
the public eye. Lane had the sobriquet of "Trader" because he was
addicted to moving players around. He would become known as the
"Man Who Destroyed the Indians."

Lane did keep the team on the front burner with his trades, most
of them unpopular: he dealt Early Wynn, one of the most popular
Indians in the history of the franchise, and Norm Cash, who would go
on to star for the Detroit Tigers. That first season Lane made thirty-
one trades involving seventy-six players. Twice it was reported that
he was trying to trade Colavito, the most popular player. Colavito hit
long home runs, and no one had a better outfield arm. Lane felt he

struck out too often and talked about trading him for a hitter with a higher batting average.

On June 15, 1958, Lane made another awful trade, sending to Kansas City a young outfielder by the name of Roger Maris, and on August 23, he sold Hoyt Wilhelm to Baltimore. Both were future Hall of Famers. Both moves were monumental blunders.

In addition, Lane sacked managers as though they had no value. George Steinbrenner, who ran the American Ship Building Company and would be known for firing managers, certainly was watching closely when in 1959 Lane fired manager Joe Gordon, whom he had been second-guessing all season, with two weeks to go in the season, even though the Indians were fighting for a pennant. Three days later the Indians were eliminated from the race. With a promising season, in shambles, Lane decided to replace Gordon with—Gordon. He brought his manager back, something Steinbrenner would do with manager Billy Martin five times. In 1960, Lane would trade Gordon to the Detroit Tigers for their manager, Jimmy Dykes.

The spring of 1960 was filled with the bitter salary dispute between Rocky Colavito and Lane. Colavito argued that he had had a better year than Mickey Mantle, who was making $66,000. Rocky was making $28,000 and he wanted a raise to boost him to $45,000. Colavito would sign for $35,000.

After announcing that he would not trade Colavito, the day before the 1960 season began Lane shipped the slugger off to Detroit for American League batting champion Harvey Kuenn. It might have been the dumbest trade anyone had ever made. Lane had done what the owner wanted: put the Indians on the front page and in the minds of the Indians fans—except that those Indian fans wanted to take a hatchet to Lane and scalp him.

In 1960, the Indians finished fourth with a 76–78 record and Lane was through in Cleveland. But right before he resigned, he traded Harvey Kuenn to the San Francisco Giants for Johnny Antonelli, who had a sore arm, and Willie Kirkland, a power hitter who struck out more often than Colavito did. Lane resigned on January 4, 1961, only to go to Kansas City, where he was reunited with manager Joe Gordon.

On April 27, 1961, Gabe Paul was named Indians general manager. He would preside over a lot of bad baseball for twenty of the next twenty-three years in Cleveland, but he was still better than Trader Lane. Paul would become known for his bad trades. One of his worst was that in 1964 of Jim "Mudcat" Grant to the Minnesota Twins for Lee Stange and George Banks. The next year Grant finished 21–7 for the Twins. Grant became a World Series hero, winning two games and homering.

No one questioned what qualified Lane or Gabe Paul to be a general manager. Back in the days before computers, the most important qualification was the ability to get along with the owner. Gabe Paul was a master at that. He made enough money to buy an 11 percent share of the ball club. Once he became part owner, he was virtually fireproof.

When Paul took over as GM of the Indians in 1961, he quickly learned that the team owners had very little money. When owners Bill Daley and Nate Dolan talked to Paul about moving the Indians to another city, Gabe talked them out of it. In 1962, Daley decided to sell the team, and Paul put together a group that bought it. He and his group owned it from 1963 to 1966, when Paul decided he needed to find an owner with means. Paul sold the team in 1967 to Vernon Stouffer, the cofounder of Stouffer's foods and Stouffer hotels.

Just one generation back, the Stouffers had lived in a rented house. Vernon's parents opened a six-seat coffee stand in Cleveland in an old office building. Every morning they served coffee and hot soup, and one day Mrs. Stouffer brought in a pie or a cake she had baked; pretty soon the little restaurant became very popular. From that beginning, their two sons, Vernon and Gordon, together built a national empire selling frozen foods. Then Gordon died at a relatively young age, leaving Vernon all by himself to run the business.

Though it was said that Vernon Stouffer "didn't know a baseball from a tennis racquet," Gabe Paul convinced him to buy the Indians to save the franchise from being moved out of the city by other interests. Paul, who remained as general manager, figured that with a wealthy owner, he could lead the Indians into contention. Two years into ownership of the team, Vernon Stouffer suffered severe reversals, both financial and personal, and he no longer could afford to own the team. A quiet man, he began drinking more often and more heavily, until the disease of alcoholism overtook him.

The year 1969 had been a difficult one for Gabe Paul. He had hired Alvin Dark, the former New York Giants star, as an adviser, and Dark, a religious man known for his duplicitous ways, convinced Stouffer that he, not Gabe Paul, should be in charge of player development. Gabe told Vernon he was crazy to do that, but Stouffer, charmed by Dark, did it anyway. Paul, the team president, stayed on because he knew Stouffer eventually would see the error of his ways. In 1970, the Indians finished dead last under Dark, and the following year Stouffer fired Dark and reinstated Paul.

The team was in a terrible state, and Gabe Paul thought he had a solution. To buy the Indians he put together the threesome of George Steinbrenner, Al Rosen, and Gabe's closest friend, entrepreneur Steve O'Neill. Gabe would have a piece of the team and remain as general manager. He had known Steinbrenner, a rabid Indians fan, for a long time. They had met at social functions, and Paul was sure that Steinbrenner could return the team to glory.

George put together a group of investors. Gabe would run it. George told Gabe he would not be too active. He had a shipbuilding company to run. Vernon's son Jim had grown up with George, and they worked out a deal. The price was between $8.6 million and $9 million in cash.

"We were all in George's office," said Gabe. "He called Vernon in Scottsdale, where he had a home. There had been a leak in the press, which I think upset Vernon. When George called, Vernon was very noncommittal. He said, 'Ah, I'm not going to take a deal like that.' Vernon just didn't want it.

"It was a shock, because of the way it had been structured. Jim had set the price. After George hung up, there was no discussion. The deal was off. Vernon was so definite.

"George was surprised. You must remember there was a family relationship there, different from most deals. It would have been a great deal for Vernon, a decent amount of cash. I don't know. I think he was irked by the leak in the press. I just think they talked to Vernon at the wrong time of day."

Jack Melcher, who was George's attorney at American Ship, heard that when George first went into the meeting with Stouffer, whom Melcher categorized as "a very sweet guy," the characterization was that "George and Gabe went in like protection guys going into a drugstore. They were very heavy-handed. 'Look Vernon, you either sell to us, or you're going to lose your shirt.' And I guess Vernon threw them out, and George was offended by that."

The likelihood is that in the end Vernon Stouffer didn't sell the team to George Steinbrenner because of several underhanded things George had done when he was running the Cleveland Pipers years earlier.

Said Ben Fleiger, "I heard that Jim Stouffer was very, very unhappy—in fact, bitter—about George after the Pipers, because George didn't square with the guys, and he spent the federal withholding money, which left all the directors liable for the federal pen. The Stouffers made peace with George a year or two later."

At least Jim did. Those close to Vernon say he *never* forgave George for something else he did while running roughshod over the Pipers.

Said Frank Treadway, "When George went to buy the Indians, I was told Vernon Stouffer refused to sell it to him because of what George had done to him.

"There were difficult times between the Stouffers and the Steinbrenners, because George took advantage. A Stouffer check was signed by Steinbrenner using Stouffer's name. A five-digit figure. And there was another story that went around. A party was given at the Westwood Country Club on the West Side of Cleveland, and Jimmy was to pay for the band and George was to pay for the liquor, and George never paid. Again, George would do something like promising Jerry Lucas forty-five thousand dollars, not knowing where he was going to get the money from, and in this case it was a similar action, but instead of opening his mouth, it was the stroke of a pen. I don't think he meant anything harmful, but this was the easy way out, and if it's Friday he'll worry about covering it Monday morning. It was, 'I'm signing your name, Jim, but don't worry about it.'

"The whole family was mad. Only because of the closeness of the families was this forgiven. But obviously, it wasn't forgiven. You asked the question, 'Why wouldn't Vernon sell the Indians to George?' This has got to be one of the reasons. George's parents were terribly embarrassed by this, and many times my mother would comment that they would go to a party, and either the Steinbrenners wouldn't come because of headlines from the day before, or they would sneak in the back door, say hello, and leave. The Steinbrenner and Stouffer families were very close, and George made it very difficult for this relationship to exist.

"There are people who step on people on the way to the top, and George is one of those people."

Ben Fleiger said he had also heard that Jim Stouffer was angry because George had been "playing around" with Jim's wife. "I thought that was the main hang-up between George and Stouffer," he said.

But that wasn't it. Money was. Said Joe Bennett, "George and Jim were pretty good friends, and then the Pipers came, and then it wasn't so great. I could tell there was something between them. Jim was mad at George. It was over money, and that really was why Vernon didn't sell him the team. Vernon was really pissed, yeah. Jimmy was a good friend of mine, and he told me how mad Vernon was."

As a result, George Steinbrenner would leave Cleveland and buy a team elsewhere.

Years later Bob Sudyk of the *Cleveland Plain Dealer* asked George, "Would you have built a winning team in Cleveland the way you did in New York?"

"No doubt about it," said Steinbrenner. "The same strong group of owners that Vernon Stouffer turned down followed me to the Yankees. We had the money and Cleveland then had the biggest ballpark in the country. We could have filled it."

"Would Reggie Jackson have come to Cleveland?" asked Sudyk.

"He would have come to Cleveland in a minute," said George. "I would have had him thinking Lake Erie was the Riviera. He wouldn't have known the difference."

10 I said to myself, Okay, I have to build a new team, and I have
to build a new stadium. I don't know how I am going to do that.
—Michael Burke

Buying the CBS Yankees

T he New York Yankees began play in 1903, but they didn't
become successful until they were purchased in January
1915 by two aristocratic New Yorkers, Colonel Jacob Ruppert, a beer
baron, and Captain Tillinghast L'Hommedieu "Cap" Huston, a soldier
and an engineer. The price was $460,000.

Two men who had a ton of dough and a thirst for victory showed
what money could buy. It wouldn't be long before fans of teams
around the country would accuse them of buying pennants and of taking unfair advantage. A century of Yankee hating would begin.

When Boston Red Sox owner Harry Frazee found himself in financial difficulty, Ruppert and Huston were only too glad to take his best
players off his hands, especially in 1920 when they bought pitcher/
outfielder Babe Ruth for $100,000 and a $300,000 loan. Why baseball
commissioner Kennesaw Mountain Landis, the supposed defender of
the integrity of the game, didn't intervene is still a mystery.

It continued when Ed Barrow, the Red Sox manager, could stand it
no longer and joined the Yankees in 1920 as their general manager.
With Barrow making the deals, the Yanks picked the bones of the Red
Sox clean. The Yankees went on to win pennants in 1921, 1922, 1923,

and 1924. By 1925, the Red Sox had hit the American League cellar. In the twenty-four years Ed Barrow ran the Yankees, the team would go on to win fourteen pennants and ten world championships.

Colonel Ruppert died in 1939, and the team was sold to the threesome of baseball genius Larry MacPhail, playboy millionaire Dan Topping, and builder/developer Del Webb. MacPhail pushed Barrow out, built up the farm system, and refurbished Yankee Stadium, adding the finest lighting system in the world.

In 1945, the Yankees drew 880,000 attendees. In 1946, the number soared to 2.2 million. But MacPhail was a meddler and a drinker, and Topping and Webb bought him out at the end of the 1947 season.

Topping and Webb hired farm director George Weiss to run the team. Like Barrow, Weiss was a micromanager who possessed a brilliant business mind. In the 1930s he had copied Branch Rickey's innovative farm system and signed thousands of prospects. Between 1932, when Weiss started the farm system, and 1943, when World War II intervened, the Yankees won the American League pennant eight times (in 1932, 1936, 1937, 1938, 1939, 1941, 1942, and 1943). Every player on that team except Tommy Henrich and Joe DiMaggio was homegrown.

After Weiss took over as general manager, the Yankees won eleven pennants (in 1949, 1950, 1951, 1952, 1953, 1955, 1956, 1957, 1958, 1959, and 1960). Led by manager Casey Stengel's two adoptive sons, Billy Martin and Mickey Mantle, the Yankees were so dominating that it was said that "rooting for the Yankees was like rooting for U.S. Steel." For fans around the country, it was a continuation of a hatred for the team that began with the purchase of Babe Ruth and the other Red Sox stars in 1920.

Topping and Webb fired Stengel and Weiss after the 1960 season. Their forced retirements were, in retrospect, the beginning of the end of what had been a Yankee dynasty. Topping and Webb had decided to sell the team, and they would stop spending money on prospects. Instead they accumulated profits to make the balance sheet more attractive to the new owners.

When CBS bought the Yankees in August 1964, the farm system was virtually barren. When George Weiss was given his walking papers in November of 1960, he told reporters, "The Yankees have five more years at the most under the new management." Once CBS took over the team, William Paley discovered he had bought a shell of a team that was playing in a decrepit ballpark in a dangerous and blighted section of the Bronx.

Michael Burke, the man who stopped the New York Yankees from abandoning the Bronx and fleeing to New Jersey, was a former OSS spy who once drank bourbon with Ernest Hemingway after parachuting into Paris two weeks after D-Day. On a mission to help free the French countryside from the Nazis, the man was a true war hero and patriot.

Growing up, he was all the things George Steinbrenner as a youth wished he had been. Burke attended West Hartford's Kingswood School for Boys, where he was a star athlete and the football team's captain. He went to the University of Pennsylvania, starring at half-back and safety. Tough as nails, he gave no quarter on the football field. In his senior year against Cornell, he intercepted two passes to seal the victory. He was elected to the Sphinx Senior Honor Society.

When war broke out, he easily could have avoided service. He had a wife and a child, which made him ineligible for the draft, but unlike Steinbrenner, who pulled every string to avoid getting shot at, Burke felt a strong obligation to fight for his country against Hitler and Mussolini. His war experience in the OSS was so outstanding that the movie *Cloak and Dagger* was made based on his exploits.

He joined the OSS in April 1942. He was sent to North Africa and was instrumental in arranging to send secretly to the United States an Italian general who had invented a torpedo that would explode as it passed under a ship.

Burke was handsome, sophisticated, and urbane, and while posted in London, he made lasting friendships with such people as Ernest Hemingway and his wife and Moe Berg, the former baseball player turned OSS undercover agent.

While in California working on the script of *Cloak and Dagger*, he fell in love with and married a woman whose brother owned the Ringling Bros. circus. After failing to write for a living, Burke was broke, and he rejoined the spy agency and lived in Europe for five years during the cold war. When he returned to the States, John Ringling North, his wife's brother, hired him to run the circus, neglecting to tell him the operation was more than six million dollars in the red. Burke did what he could, firing foremen who were stealing from the company and trying to keep Jimmy Hoffa from bankrupting it, but after several years he quit suddenly to go into the television business when North hired a former circus performer he didn't like to be general manager.

Said Burke, "My five years in England taught me that manners were more important than laws and that civility is the very stuff of a decent society." It would not be the last time he would walk away because of differences with one of the other principals.

After meeting with Frank Stanton of CBS, he was hired as an assistant to the production department. After spending months learning the business, he was asked to go to Europe and develop programs from there, and was made president of CBS Europe.

In the fall of 1962, Burke returned to New York City, and he was given a new title, vice president of CBS Inc. for Diversification. Bill Paley wanted to go into new lines of business, and he wanted Burke to be in charge of the acquisitions. Under Paley's guidelines, he was to pick companies that would enhance the profits and prestige of CBS. During one meeting of Paley, Stanton, and Burke, Burke asked Paley whether CBS should buy a football team. When Stanton countered with the New York Yankees, Burke said it was a terrific idea. Burke knew that Paley was a social acquaintance of Dan Topping's, so he suggested Paley ask him to lunch. Paley did, and Topping agreed to sell.

By the late summer of 1964, Paley, Topping, and Del Webb had worked out a deal for CBS to buy 80 percent of the New York Yankees baseball club, valued at $14 million. Topping and Webb would retain 10 percent each, and CBS could buy them out in five years. Within the first year Webb sold his shares to CBS for $1 million. Within two years, Paley and Topping weren't getting along, and Paley bought out Topping as well.

On November 2, 1964, CBS took over ownership of the Yankees. The next year the team finished a dismal sixth, and by 1965 Paley and Burke knew for a fact that they had been snookered by Topping and Webb when the team played poorly and landed in the American League cellar. Paley named Burke the president of the Yankees. This mess, Burke saw, was going to be harder to fix than the Ringling Bros. circus. Burke told me, "I said to myself, Okay, I have to build a new team, and I have to build a stadium. I don't know how I am going to do that."

By 1972, the Yankees had climbed to second place, albeit fourteen games out. Burke and general manager Lee MacPhail (Larry's son) had built a representative, if not flashy, ball club, and they had every confidence that pennants would follow in another couple of years, when in the fall of 1972 Bill Paley decided he no longer wished to own the team. In a short conversation, Paley, who was unusually close to Burke, told Burke that if he made a reasonable offer, he could buy it.

Burke for whatever reason chose not to go to any of his many New York friends for backing. Instead he brought in a group from Cleveland headed by a man he knew absolutely nothing about: George Steinbrenner. Burke had done no homework in determining whether the Yankees franchise he was buying was worth the money CBS was paying, and eight years later he did no homework to attempt to learn something about the man with whom he was getting into bed. In one phone call to one of the Cleveland newspapers Burke could have learned about Steinbrenner's disturbing antics as owner of the Cleveland Pipers. Instead, he blissfully plunged ahead.

After Burke, Steinbrenner, and Paley shook hands in the winter of 1972, Burke called his right-hand man, Howard Berk, to tell him of the deal. Burke told Howard he would continue to run the team. Berk, had been asked to return to CBS, but on Michael Burke's assurances, he remained with the Yankees. Four months later, after finding out that Mike Burke was no match for George Steinbrenner, he returned to CBS. Not long afterward Burke walked away from the team he had nurtured and loved, taking over the reins of Madison Square Garden at the behest of owner Sonny Werblin.

Attorney Tom Evans remembers the day in December 1972 when Burke announced that he had signed Bobby Murcer for $100,000, making Murcer the first Yankee to receive that much money since Mickey Mantle retired in 1968. Evans, a classmate of Steinbrenner's at Williams College, was in Tampa, Florida, with Steinbrenner when Steinbrenner read the article in the *New York Times* announcing the signing.

George picked up the phone and, according to Evans, "gave Burke a tongue-lashing like a two-year-old child." Evans tried to get George's attention, wagging his finger at him to make him stop. He knew that the partnership papers had not yet been signed, and it was not too late for Burke to back out of the deal and find other partners. When Burke didn't threaten right then to take the team away from Steinbrenner, Evans knew that that was it for Burke as president of the Yankees, that George now knew Burke would never be able to stand up to him.

In the summer of 1981, I interviewed Michael Burke. It had been eight years since his short-lived partnership with George Steinbrenner had ended. He was making plans to move to Ireland, where he had bought a five-hundred-acre farm in Galway.

I asked Burke why Bill Paley decided to sell the team when he did. "I suppose it was predictable that at some point Mr. Paley would sell the Yankees," he said. "There were factors, compelling reasons. A lot of people at CBS didn't feel the Yankees fit into the whole CBS pattern. It was an appendage hanging on the end of the long horizontal structure, and though Paley himself enjoyed the Yankees and being part of them, at one point nevertheless he decided to sell.

"At first I thought of putting up my own money, but then I rejected the idea. Oh, I spoke to three or four potential buyers, but then George Steinbrenner seemed to me the most actively interested and potentially the most vigorous partner.

"The two people who called me were Vernon Stouffer, who owned the Cleveland ball club, and Gabe Paul, who was the general manager of the Cleveland ball club. Vernon didn't recommend George. He simply said they had this negotiation and it stopped. He simply said that George was interested in owning a baseball team. A simple fact.

"George rang me, and we made a date, had some initial conversations, and it ended in our agreeing to go in together as equal partners. We'd be co–general partners, and we'd have other limited partners. George had five points more stock than I did. We had a minority together, and there were a dozen other partners who had from ten to five percent. No one had more than George. But it didn't matter who owned what stock, because the way a limited partnership works, the limited partners are not involved at all in the operation. The responsibility of operating the club or any business falls to the general partners."

Burke set the price at $10 million, Paley accepted, and on January 3, 1973, the deal was announced. I asked about stories that he and George had had a violent argument at the press conference announcing the deal, and that he had been surprised that Gabe Paul was a limited partner. Burke denied both, saying, "Oh, God, no. Gabe was in it from very early on. He was one of the five percent owners from early on. Among the limited partners were Jim Nederlander, Bunker Hunt, John DeLorean, Marvin Warner, and Gabe.

"He was going to spend two or three years with the Yankees, his swan song of his baseball career. He was a very knowledgeable, experienced baseball head, a mine of knowledge. He simply wanted to be a part owner of the New York Yankees and disassociate himself from the Cleveland Indians."

Mike then explained why four months later he stepped aside. "George and I both went into this new deal with full enthusiasm, but after we had worked together for a relatively short time, it became apparent that running a small institution like the New York Yankees by yourself was one thing; running it with two people bouncing off each other day after day was another. Being with the Yankees lost some of its enchantment. And that's not an indictment of George. If it had been a huge organization it might have been different, but it was such a small organization it wasn't congenial for two people to run it.

"Any two people with strong minds, opinions, and personalities feel different. We had different approaches to life, and my instinct told me it was better not to try to force an issue, to force two feet into one shoe. It was better for me to go off. I kept my financial interest and signed a ten-year consulting agreement with the Yankees, and I decided to go do something else."

"Did you ever think of fighting him for dominance?" I asked.

"I suppose it was an option," he said, "but it didn't seem a very sensible one. Who wants to live in a hostile atmosphere, for God's sake? Life is too short to be fighting with your partner every day." He added that one reason it wasn't common to fight with George was that the rest of the limited partners were George's friends.

When Burke told George he was leaving, he said Steinbrenner tried to talk him out of it. "No," said Burke, "I think we've decided on the right course for both of us."

Burke professed to have no ill feelings toward Steinbrenner.

Freddie Bachman, one of Mike Burke's most loyal employees, joined the Yankees in March 1969. He loved working for the Mike

Burke Yankees and looked forward to coming to work every day. He watched as Burke rebuilt the team and bullied New York mayor John Lindsay into paying for the refurbishing of Yankee Stadium. He was also witness to the coming of George Steinbrenner and Gabe Paul. When Bachman left in the fall of 1973, working for the Yankees no longer was a fun job. When he quit, it was with bitterness and anger.

"When George arrived, ostensibly nothing was going to change," said Bachman. "George was going to have a little office somewhere. He had business commitments, and this was just an investment, and Mike was going to run things. And suddenly, very quickly, Gabe Paul came in, but Gabe was just going to look out for George's interests.

"Well, that lasted maybe a couple months. And all of a sudden, Gabe Paul started taking a very active day-to-day role in the club, telling Howard Berk and even Mike Burke what they were going to do, because that's what Steinbrenner wanted done.

"For example, one of George's pet peeves was the way the ushers lined up on the field after the game. George wanted them out there symmetrically like wooden soldiers so the fans wouldn't jump out of the stands onto the field. George wanted them to stand up straight, two feet apart. George was looking for an image, and the image wasn't the way he wanted it.

"George wanted to show he was in control, and there was to be no cavalier attitude. You were not supposed to enjoy your work. You are supposed to work your ass off. In the past we had been very successful through cooperation. We weren't making as much money as the guys under Steinbrenner are making, but we liked it because we enjoyed working there. After Gabe Paul came, it wasn't fun anymore.

"I recall opening day of 1973 as a not very happy occasion. Burke and Steinbrenner were fighting over who was on the invitation list, and who was coming to the party, and where the party was going to be. Mike wanted to do it the way he had traditionally done it, and Steinbrenner said, 'No, it's a waste of money. I don't like the people you're inviting.'

"Steinbrenner would argue with Burke at the drop of a hat. I think it was all premeditated. We could never tell what the arguments were about. All we knew was you could stand at the bottom of the elevator shaft on the first floor and literally hear them screaming at the top of their lungs at each other. But there was nothing that was sacred. He wanted it done his way, and that's the way it was going to be done."

In time, George Steinbrenner would become known for his penchant for firing managers. Ralph Houk was skipper when Steinbrenner bought the team. Houk, who could not abide Steinbrenner's and Gabe Paul's meddling and interference, lasted through the 1973 season and then quit.

"Ralph always had an understanding that his locker room was his kingdom," said Bachman. "If Mike wanted to say something, he checked with Ralph first. Now all of a sudden, Mike was no longer there. The sanctity of his office and the clubhouse was no longer honored. Gabe Paul was passing messages to Ralph and to the players, commenting on their abilities, their play, which was unheard of. I know that when Gabe would go into Ralph's office after a game, it wasn't pleasant.

"After George took over, Gabe made it miserable for everybody. He was a doddering old fool who for forty years had been in baseball and had never been associated with a winner. He had no tact, antiquated ideas, and he was scared of Steinbrenner. No matter what it cost him in terms of personal pride, he would espouse the Steinbrenner line. If Steinbrenner told him to go around and call someone a cocksucker, he'd do it until the guy was so fed up he quit.

"Gabe would sit back, and he'd have his glasses on the bridge of his nose, and you'd never know if he was asleep or awake. And Howard would argue with him, and then he'd go upstairs and talk with Mike. Then Mike would get involved with Gabe, and Gabe would call George, and George and Mike would argue on the phone, and it would get resolved that way, usually in Steinbrenner's direction.

"The arguments between Gabe and me became violent and vehement. I would close the door with Gabe, and we would raise the roof, and they could hear us all the way back to the ticket office. Whether the door handle was screwed on the door properly became an issue with him. As though he was busting balls just to bust balls. I don't dislike Steinbrenner. I hate Gabe Paul."

Bachman could not abide Gabe Paul, and when an exciting new job came along, he was able to call it quits. He still lives in Bronxville and is wistful about what might have been had Michael Burke been a little smarter about with whom he was getting into bed.

11

When I bought the New York Yankees in 1973, what I got wasn't what I thought I bought. There wasn't much talent there, to say the very least. The team picture of the 1973 Yankees could very well serve as a poster for birth control.

—George Steinbrenner

George Takes Charge

When Sparky Lyle reported for spring training in Fort Lauderdale to prepare for the 1973 season, he was using crutches after injuring an ankle playing basketball during the off-season. Steinbrenner saw him, and in a voice loud enough for Lyle to hear, he barked, "Is this what I paid ten million dollars for?" It was the beginning of a rocky relationship between George and Lyle, and it didn't get any better on opening day, when the Yankees played their home opener against Boston.

Before the game the teams were lined up on the foul lines for the national anthem. George saw that the hair of some of the players was sticking out from under their caps. He wrote a note to Ralph Houk and ordered him to read it to the team. It said, "I want numbers 19, 47, and 28 to cut their hair." Said Lyle, who wore number 28, "We found out early how impersonal he can be. He didn't even bother to find out our names."

"To Ralph Houk, it was the first sign that some heavy second-guessing would be coming," said catcher Thurman Munson. "To us, it made the new owner seem very out of touch with things. But Ralph read us the memo, and some of us got our hair trimmed—a little."

Rather than admit they were his rules, Steinbrenner angered the players further when he told reporters the lie that they had been made by Ralph Houk and Lee MacPhail. The players knew better.

"You can't treat baseball players like accountants or like a herd of cattle," said Lyle. "You can't tell one of your pitchers, 'Well, screw it, I don't like you, you're not going to pitch the rest of the year.' Unless he can find someone to replace him, George is going to have to put up with him. George isn't going to be able to treat the players like they're lower than life, like he does most of his employees, because if he tries it, the player will tell him to stick it."

The players noticed something else about their new owner: he didn't know all that much about the game of baseball. One time he was sitting in his box near the dugout, and with a runner on third and two outs, Roy White hit a slow ground ball. The runner on third crossed the plate before White was thrown out at first, and George began clapping and yelling, "All right. All right. We tied it up."

He was asked what he was talking about. George said, "We scored before they got the man out at first so it's tied."

"He just didn't know the game," said Sparky Lyle.

Lyle, who noticed everything, saw something else. "He would try to get involved when he didn't know anything," said Lyle. "When one of our guys would strike out or pop out in a crucial situation, George would say, 'Get rid of the son of a bitch.' If George had his way, he would have gotten rid of all of us."

Fortunately, Gabe Paul was there to stop him. In fact, the smartest move George Steinbrenner made when he bought the New York Yankees from CBS was hiring Gabe Paul to run the team. During his five years, Paul made masterly trades. His biggest asset was that he was able to save owner George Steinbrenner from himself, keeping the rash and impetuous Steinbrenner from making deals that would have badly hurt the team. Steinbrenner, Paul discovered, hated to see rookies in his lineup, and it was all Paul could do to keep him from trading away his best prospects, including a young pitcher by the name of Ron Guidry. Twice Steinbrenner sought to deal him. Twice Gabe Paul sat him down and stopped him.

When Catfish Hunter became available as a free agent in 1974, Steinbrenner showed everyone that he would stop at nothing to land a player he coveted, and once free agency became a reality in 1975, the signing of Reggie Jackson was a signal that there would be no stopping the Yankees. If Gabe Paul had not left in 1978, there's no telling how many more pennants the Yankees would have won. But once Paul departed, leaving Steinbrenner to his own self-defeating devices, the Yankees would win the pennant in 1981 and then not again until the 1990s, when for two years Steinbrenner was again suspended from baseball.

One of the first steps Gabe Paul made to improve the team was to bolster the Yankees' minor league system. "I think the major league system develops through good men in the minor leagues," Paul said. "We added a lot of scouts. We added Birdie Tebbetts. He was a very valuable scout. And after I left, George further expanded the scouting system, very expensive, very big. And it's paid off."

But it goes without saying that the resurgence of the Yankees began with a series of trades that featured the infusion of veteran talent and the expenditure of significant cash on Steinbrenner's part. Said Paul, "George had a vision. He wanted to win. He wanted to be the dominant force in New York, which is what he achieved." And he never stopped Paul from getting any player he wanted. "His favorite words were, 'Go ahead,'" said Paul.

And trade Paul did. He was able to spring lightning-fast pitcher Sam McDowell from San Francisco because Horace Stoneham, the owner of the Giants, was an alcoholic who sometimes would make a trade after drinking late into the night. Paul knew that and took advantage. Then he brought Lou Piniella in from Kansas City. His next trade was very unpopular in New York when it was made. He sent four pitchers to Cleveland for first baseman Chris Chambliss and pitchers Dick Tidrow and submariner Cecil Upshaw. The key man in the deal was Chambliss, a quiet leader who became a fixture in the field and was a steady force in the Yankee lineup for five productive years. But the trade shocked the existing players and it bothered them that the new players were coming over from Cleveland. Having seen other players come from Cleveland, they wondered if George and Gabe were bringing the entire Cleveland club to New York.

In June 1973, Paul spent $50,000 of Steinbrenner's money buying pitcher Rudy May from the California Angels. In another unpopular move, Paul traded Bobby Murcer for Bobby Bonds, even though George had promised Murcer he would be a Yankee as long as George owned the team. Paul said he hadn't known about the promise. Bonds lasted one season. Paul categorized Bonds as "desirable": "You get a lot for him. We traded him because we got Ed Figueroa and Mickey Rivers. That was a deal that helped the Yankees win the pennant."

He certainly was right about Figueroa. You could argue that for the four years between 1975 and 1978, Ed Figueroa was the best pitcher in baseball. On the same day as the Bonds trade, Gabe Paul made another blockbuster. He traded pitcher Doc Medich to Pittsburgh for Willie Randolph, Ken Brett, and Dock Ellis. Randolph would go on to be a fixture at second base for the next thirteen seasons, and Brett and Ellis would be useful pitchers for the Yankees.

The one trade Paul didn't want to make, a trade that Steinbrenner insisted on because his twelve-year-old son Hank wanted him to acquire Ken Holtzman, was sending Rudy May, Rick Dempsey, Tippy Martinez, Dave Pagan, and Scott McGregor to the Baltimore Orioles for Holtzman, Doyle Alexander, Grant Jackson, catcher Ellie Hendricks, and minor leaguer Jimmy Freeman. Holtzman and Alexander would help the Yankees win championships in 1977 and 1978, but Tippy Martinez, Scott McGregor, and Rick Dempsey helped make the Baltimore Orioles a top team for a decade. It was the first of many trades in which Steinbrenner insisted on getting rid of untested prospects in exchange for heralded veterans. Too often the veterans had limited life left in the game while the prospects went on to long, productive careers.

At one point George began involving himself more and more with trades, but Paul was able to deal with him: "Yeah, but there is one thing about George—at least I was able to—as long as you do it in private. You cannot argue with George in front of people, and that's not right—you shouldn't. But as long as you do it inside in private, you can argue all the way on anything, and he'd listen. He'd argue back and tell you, you don't know what the hell you're talking about. But when he communed with himself, he paid attention to what was said."

As a result, Paul was able twice to talk George out of trading Ron Guidry. "Much as he argued about things," said Paul, "he did pay attention when he was by himself, and I was able to talk him out of it."

For the puritanical Steinbrenner, propriety was very important. In a game against Oakland in the stadium, Sparky Lyle gave up five straight hits to lose a game. As he walked off the field, a fan screamed, "You bum, Lyle, you suck." And in front of forty thousand people Sparky raised his two hands and gave him the double-fingered salute.

Ralph Houk didn't see Lyle do it because he was standing on the mound waiting for the new pitcher, but George, who was sitting behind the dugout, saw him, and after the game he called Houk. Houk said, "Sparky wouldn't do a thing like that. He was probably giving the fan the peace sign." When Houk asked Sparky if he had done it, Sparky admitted he had. He was fined $500.

Ralph Houk, despite a lack of marquee players, thought he had enough pitching and defense to win the American League pennant in 1973. He had Thurman Munson behind the plate, Graig Nettles at third, and Bobby Murcer and Roy White in the outfield, and on the mound he had a solid staff of Mel Stottlemyre, Pat Dobson, Doc Medich, and Fritz Peterson. Sparky Lyle and Lindy McDaniel were excellent relievers. That June Steinbrenner excited his fans by bringing Sam McDowell from the San Francisco Giants for $100,000.

Best of all, the team had Ralph Houk behind the wheel, and the Major, as he was called, brilliantly directed the team into first place from mid-June until the end of July. *Sports Illustrated* was so impressed, it wrote an article proclaiming, "Pinstripes Are Back in Style." At Yankee Stadium, organist Frank Layden played "It Seems Like Old Times." And it *was* like old times. The Yankees were in first place again. The CBS Yankees were buried in the past.

Said Bobby Murcer, "I have a feeling about this team, a feeling that all the bad things are in the past, that we can win just like the Yankees are supposed to."

When the team stopped hitting and began to slide in August, the phone calls, which had begun in spring training, along with visits and memos from Steinbrenner, intensified until Houk no longer could stand it. The slump, which continued in September, saw the Yankees fall far behind the Orioles. The fans, taking a cue from Steinbrenner's criticism, began booing Houk. In the final home game, Houk came out to make a pitching change, and as he walked back to the dugout the booing was unbearable for the players to watch.

"He walked back to the dugout like a beaten man," said Thurman Munson.

The players loved Ralph Houk because he was compassionate. As far as Lyle was concerned, he was the best manager he ever played for. At one point during the 1973 season, Houk had called a meeting of his players. He told them, "This guy"—meaning Steinbrenner—"is very difficult to play for. But I'm not going to let him beat me. I promise you. I'm not going to quit. I'm going to stay right here until he fires me."

But Ralph Houk, as tough as he was, was no match for a man who had all the tools—wealth, power, authority, and a clinical psychological disorder, narcissism, which included a belief that only he could make the right decisions all of the time—to beat any employee into submission.

"He finally had to resign," said Lyle. "He told me he couldn't take any more from George, that he couldn't manage the team with George looking over his shoulder all the time. George was hollering at him continually, and it was affecting Ralph's managing. Finally Ralph said, 'Screw it, I can't stand it anymore,' and he resigned after spending thirty-five years in the organization."

Said Moss Klein of the *Newark Star-Ledger*, "In that one season he learned that his love for the Yankees, his pride in being a part of the great tradition, couldn't overpower the negative aspects of working for Steinbrenner."

Houk held a meeting before the last game of the season and told the players, "I have to get away from Steinbrenner. I can't work for him and maintain my self-respect." After thirty-five years in the organization he said he was going home to Florida to go fishing and relax.

Eleven days later Houk signed a three-year contract to manage the Detroit Tigers.

Heading into the winter meetings in 1973, the Yankees had no manager and a leadership that was in transition. General manager Lee MacPhail was about to be named American League president, and Gabe Paul was at the ready to take over for him. And Steinbrenner was waiting for the other shoe to drop. He had admitted to a felony in the Watergate case, and Bowie Kuhn was soon to rule on whether he would be suspended from baseball. Meanwhile, the team was getting ready to move to Shea Stadium from Yankee Stadium for two years while the House that Ruth Built underwent renovation.

Steinbrenner decided to go with a manager who believed in strict rules. The Yankees announced that their new manager would be Bill Virdon, who had managed the Pittsburgh Pirates for two seasons before getting fired in midseason. Virdon was a guy who rarely spoke to his players, who missed the closeness with Ralph Houk. On the plane the players hid their beers from Virdon's gaze.

A few days before the end of spring training, an article appeared in the *New York Post* in which anonymous Yankee players complained about the way Steinbrenner had interfered with Ralph Houk. He was described as a man who knew little about baseball and who constantly meddled with the team, even telling Houk whom to play and Gabe Paul whom to acquire.

The article charged that Steinbrenner's interference had undermined Houk to the point where he quit with two years left on his contract, caused chaos, doubt, and anxiety among the players, and was in part responsible for the team's fourth-place finish. The Yankee players didn't know it, but this was a man who hated to be criticized, whose anger was great whenever he was maligned in print.

When Steinbrenner entered the clubhouse and wanted to know which Yankee players were responsible for the article, Sparky Lyle fessed up. Angry because he felt he was underpaid, Lyle agreed to sit down with Steinbrenner for a heart-to-heart. An hour later Lyle was impressed more than anything else by how much George wanted to win.

The next night Steinbrenner met with the players in the clubhouse and told them, "I want you to know you have my loyalty, and I hope I have yours. I made some mistakes in the past, and I'll probably make some more in the future, but I'll try not to make the same mistakes. I want you all to know that I'm interested in one thing, and that's winning. I know that's what you're interested in, too."

"Steinbrenner's speech changed the attitude of the whole club," said Lyle. "He had everybody in a real good state of mind. When he finished speaking, he just turned and walked out of the clubhouse. And everybody got up and cheered."

One day Steinbrenner was hated by the players, and the next he was loved. Who knew what the next day would bring?

The first shock to the team came on April 26, with the trade Paul made for Chris Chambliss, Dick Tidrow, and Cecil Upshaw, sending four players to Cleveland. In the clubhouse the four traded players sat talking to reporters when Gabe Paul walked in smiling. Said Thurman Munson, it was "as though the friendships of the four men he'd traded didn't mean anything to us." When Chambliss reported to the Yankees, he felt unwelcome, and it took him a full year to adjust.

The team started well, but slumped in May and fell into the cellar in late June. Before an ugly loss to the Baltimore Orioles on May 25, Steinbrenner walked into the clubhouse and gave the players a ten-minute combination pep talk/ass chewing. He told the players he was tired of watching a player make a mistake, then play with his head down the rest of the game. He said that while errors were part of the game, if a player makes a mental mistake, he should never make that same mistake twice. Since Steinbrenner was under a cloud, with a trial coming up on charges of making illegal campaign contributions, some of the players were dubious. Another said, "It was something that had to be done."

One of the problems the veterans had was that because they were playing in Shea Stadium and not Yankee Stadium, every game seemed like a road game. Nevertheless, the Yankees finished 18–10 in August and 19–10 in September.

After the Yankees lost three straight to the Oriole trio of Jim Palmer, Mike Cuellar, and Dave McNally, George Steinbrenner ordered Virdon to play a tape recording in the clubhouse of him making a rah-rah speech. Said Thurman Munson, "It felt very high school-ish." He added, "But it was good to know he's a fan."

Under Bill Virdon, in 1974 the Yankees finished second, only two games behind Baltimore. One reason was the stellar performance of Yankee reliever Sparky Lyle, who finished the year with a 9–3 record, 15 saves, and an ERA of 1.66.

On August 23, 1974, George Steinbrenner pleaded guilty to two counts of having made illegal contributions to Richard Nixon's presidential campaign. Over the last two months of the season the cloud hung over the new owner. What would baseball commissioner Bowie Kuhn do? Would he fine him? Would he suspend him? Would he strip Steinbrenner of his ownership?

12

Jack, how did you let this happen? You're
supposed to be smarter than this.
—George Steinbrenner to his lawyer

Watergate

Perhaps the most humiliating moment in the life of George
Steinbrenner came on August 23, 1974, two weeks after the
sudden resignation of President Richard Nixon, when Steinbrenner
admitted in open court that for a year he had lied about his campaign
contributions, that he had committed a felony, conspiring with eight
of his AmShip employees to make illegal corporate contributions to
Nixon's reelection campaign in 1972 and then covering up his crime.

The way Steinbrenner did it was by the tried-and-true method of
breaking the law that barred corporate contributions to political campaigns: he wrote the eight employees checks for $5,000 each from the
American Ship checking account with the understanding that they
would pay the taxes and then funnel money into Richard Nixon's campaign by writing their own personal checks for $3,000. The $24,000
was added to the $75,000 contribution Steinbrenner made from his
personal account, giving the Republicans close to the $100,000 they
had requested from him. When the scheme was uncovered by federal
prosecutors, Steinbrenner coached his loyal men to lie about what he
and they had done, putting them in jeopardy of going to jail.

After his guilty plea, George reworked the events to put himself in a far less culpable light, contending that he did what he did because the corrupt Nixon staff had twisted his arm. In the remaking of the Watergate saga, George Steinbrenner sought to transform himself from a conniving schemer into a victim of Richard Nixon's greed.

Never mind that two years earlier he had used the same money-funneling scheme to give corporate money to the campaigns of Democratic candidates. After his guilty plea, Steinbrenner used the media to deflect his guilt onto others by contending to anyone who would listen that he never knew the scheme was illegal, but instead relied on bad advice from his lawyer, former Williams College class-mate Jack Melcher. In the retelling, it was Melcher, not he, who told his employees to lie. Neither of these claims are true, but in his need to absolve himself, George mounted a successful campaign that caused Melcher to resign from the bar, viciously ruining a decent man's career just so he would have someone else on whom to pin the blame. By doing that, he was then better able to spin his version of the Watergate story in court and avoid going to prison.

Aspects of his behavior during the Watergate ordeal bear scrutiny. The most perplexing question of all is, why did he do it? The money siphoned from the American Ship coffers was only $25,000, pea-nuts for George. He could have just as easily paid CREEP the whole $100,000 himself. Moreover, he didn't have to put himself and his faith-ful employees through the ordeal of having to testify before a grand jury. The federal prosecutor gave him the opportunity to get off on a misdemeanor and pay a small fine if only he would come and con-fess. It's what almost all of the executives from companies such as Gulf Oil, Braniff Airways, Goodyear, 3M, and American Airlines, accused of similar crimes, did. Steinbrenner wrestled with the decision on a daily basis, but because of his narcissism—it was ingrained in him to refuse to admit mistakes or misdeeds—in the end he chose to stonewall and take his chances in federal court. By doing so, he put eight of his most loyal employees in jeopardy of going to jail and made his lawyers do cartwheels to get him off—only to see him plead guilty in the end. As a result, for the first time he found himself suspended from baseball.

That Steinbrenner ended up pleading guilty to a felony in front of a federal judge happened solely because of luck, pluck, and the attention to detail brought by Jim Polk, a Pulitzer Prize–winning investigative reporter for the *Washington Star*. During the first week of January 1973, Polk became interested in a nascent scandal surrounding sizable donations to the Nixon campaign given in 1971 by the Associated Milk Producers. A public advocate attorney, financed by good-government advocate Stuart Mott, sued the Agriculture Department over the increase in the milk supports it allowed. A quid pro quo seemed obvious. With a lawsuit pending, the public advocate attorney subpoenaed bank records of all the GOP campaign committees into which money was deposited by the milk producers.

Jim Polk began looking through the records of the GOP's campaign committees that received money from the milk producers. Among the checks he discovered two written by Daniel Kissell and Roy Walker. Each was made out for $3,500. This raised Polk's eyebrows immediately because they were too large to qualify under the gift exemption. He checked their employment. Kissell was treasurer of the Great Lakes Transportation subsidiary of the American Ship Building Company, George's company.

For years Polk had heard that a good way for corporations to donate money was to give an employee a $5,000 bonus, take the top off for taxes, and give the net to the campaign. It was a foolproof way for a corporation to make a campaign contribution—which was illegal under the law.

Both Kissell and Walker had their addresses on their checks, so they weren't hard to find. Polk went to visit them both. Walker insisted he had contributed his own money, and Kissell would not comment. Polk was suspicious. He was sure Kissell couldn't afford the contribution. Polk was certain they were corporate contributions, but he had no proof. The next day he drove to the shipyard in Lorain to talk to AmShip's Robert Bartlome, another of the contributors. Bartlome, too, said it had been an individual contribution. All Jim Polk had was a pattern and a suspicion but no evidence of wrongdoing.

Around this time a source of Polk's in Washington related to him that George Steinbrenner had told some of his acquaintances he had been shaken down by Herb Kalmbach of the Nixon campaign. He had $5.4 million in cost overruns for a ship he was building for the government called the *Researcher*, and he wanted the overruns excused. For that to happen, he told his acquaintances, Kalmbach was shaking him down for big bucks.

Polk flew out to Cleveland and talked to George in his office. Steinbrenner denied giving any contributions to Nixon. He said he had had a meeting with Kalmbach, but they had talked football, not campaign contributions. Polk was sure Steinbrenner was lying to him.

"If the son of a gun hadn't tried to sell me a song and dance," said Polk, "I probably would not have followed it up."

George had just bought the New York Yankees, and in March 1973, Polk, who happened to be in New York City, decided to take another crack at him. They met at the 21 Club. Again George denied it all. Then he received a call at the table. He said, "Bad news. My kid has been in a pickup accident in Florida. The maid was driving, and I'm sure the kid will walk, but he'll never play football. I'm going to take him to Mass General Hospital to see if they can correct it."

It was another story Polk didn't quite believe, and for five weeks he called Mass General. The hospital had no patient listed under the name of Steinbrenner. "George told a lot of sob stories in the times I talked to him," said Polk. "He'd tell tales of affliction on his family for sympathy."

Polk was stymied, until he read an article by Seymour Hersh in the *New York Times* that a man by the name of Tom McBride had been named lead prosecutor to investigate illegal corporate campaign financing. The article said that among the things McBride would be looking into were cost overruns. Polk went to talk to McBride to see whether there was a story on AmShip and George Steinbrenner, and he shared what he had found. Using Polk's information as a starting point, McBride began investigating George Steinbrenner and American Ship.

In late June 1973, as the Watergate hearings were heating up about corporate campaign contributions, George Steinbrenner's name popped up on one of Nixon secretary Rosemary Woods's lists. Jim Polk went to see Herb Kalmbach, who would be known as the paymaster for the cover-up of the Watergate break-in. Kalmbach told him that Steinbrenner had made a $100,000 pledge to the Committee to Re-elect the President. He said there was no discussion of the overrun.

At the time Polk could not find out the purpose of the contribution, but it would come out later that George had wanted an ambassadorship for his brother-in-law Jacob Kamm, and he thought this was his way of getting it. But according to those close to the Nixon campaign, the going rate for ambassadorships was $250,000, so George's $100,000 wasn't even in the ballpark. Jim Polk was nevertheless convinced that the money was earmarked for the Nixon people to forgive the cost overruns of the *Researcher*.

It was July 1973, and Polk still had nothing. He flew back to Cleveland to try to salvage the story. The next day he met George in Cleveland at the Pewter Mug restaurant. When Polk told George he knew about the $100,000 donation, George's story changed. He told Polk he had given $75,000 of his personal money to the campaign, but he could not explain the $25,000 discrepancy. He said all he knew about was the $75,000. "He pleaded with me not to write anything rash, because his wife was a troubled woman, that a story like this would upset her," said Polk. George needn't have worried. Polk still didn't have enough for a story.

On September 8, 1973, federal prosecutor Tom McBride gave the eight American Ship employees immunity from prosecution in exchange for their testimony in front of a federal grand jury. They had stonewalled for months, but now they had no choice but to tell the truth. Their loyalty to Steinbrenner was strong, but their fear of going to prison was stronger. Polk recognized the names, and he wrote the story that he had inadvertently started months before. He wrote what he found, which wasn't much, and that evening he received a call from Marsh Samuels, Steinbrenner's PR man, saying George wanted to talk to him. Polk, sick of George's lies and his sob stories, refused to take the phone call. The story that came out in the *Washington Star* that day didn't affect George. Polk's going to see McBride months earlier was what hurt him.

To understand the deviousness and ruthlessness of George Steinbrenner, the best way to tell the Watergate story is through the eyes of Jack Melcher, George's lawyer through most of this ordeal, until George tossed him over the side and hired Edward Bennett Williams to lay the blame at Melcher's feet.

Melcher and George had been in the air force ROTC together at Williams College. After Williams, Melcher went on to Harvard Law School. After George led the takeover of American Ship, in 1967 he hired Melcher, his Williams classmate, to help him with some of the problems he had with the government with respect to shipping contracts. Melcher held the title of general counsel for AmShip, even though he was not yet an employee.

When George began his bonus plan—writing checks to his eight employees and having them funnel money to Democratic congressional candidates—Melcher was unaware that this was going on. Melcher, who knew nothing of the election laws, advised only that he knew you were not supposed to use corporate funds for political contributions. He told George that top executives of Republic Steel were expected to make private donations as part of their job, but that those men were making a lot of money and they could afford to do so.

Melcher, when asked why George sent CREEP $100,000, answered, "My own personal opinion that was this was something to enhance George's image and his personal prestige as a great mover and shaker. All the other big shots are putting in money, and he wanted to be one of the boys." It's as viable explanation as any.

In May 1973, Steinbrenner went to Melcher and asked him to come on board as a full-time AmShip employee as chief legal counsel. He had made the request before. Said Melcher, "He made all kinds of pie-in-the-sky promises, told me all the good things that would happen, and he finally persuaded me."

Before Melcher took the job, Steinbrenner's accounting firm of Arthur Andersen had apprised him of donations made by eight AmShip employees to the Nixon campaign. When Melcher asked George about the donations made by his eight employees, Steinbrenner told him, "These people came to me and asked me about whether or not in some way they could make a contribution because I was setting an example. Call Stan Lepkowski or Robert Bartlome. They will confirm that." Melcher did just that. Bartlome repeated what George had told him. "It all seemed perfectly reasonable," said Melcher.

When Attorney General Archibald Cox announced that any corporate officers involved in illegal campaign contributions could come see him, confess, and get off with a misdemeanor charge and a small fine, George asked Melcher what he thought of it. "What do you mean what do I think?" asked Melcher. "You told me the contributions were perfectly legal, that they were voluntary, that there were no problems with them. Were there?" George again assured him that the contributions were legit.

Melcher went and talked to each of the eight men who had made the contributions. Federal prosecutors were looking into AmShip's political contributions, and FBI investigators would be coming to see the men soon. Melcher's mission, as outlined by George, was to talk to the eight men before they met with the FBI, hold their hands, and tell them everything would be all right. Although Melcher still had some doubts, George once again reassured him.

And here's where Melcher made his fatal mistake. Meeting with each of the eight, he recounted to them the events the way George had told them to him. Later at least two of the men would go in front of the grand jury and accuse Melcher of telling them to lie. The eight employees signed affidavits that the contributions were legitimate, and in July 1973, the affidavits were sent to Arthur Andersen.

When FBI agents came to Cleveland, the first employee they interviewed was Robert Bartlome, who retold the story of how he had made the contribution personally and voluntarily. The FBI wrote down what he said, and Bartlome signed it. The next day Melcher showed the other seven what Bartlome had signed. Later, Melcher would be accused of telling the others to say what Bartlome had said.

A few days later George once again brought up to Melcher the question of whether he should go see Archibald Cox. He wanted Melcher to go down to Washington and see Cox, who had been his professor at Harvard Law School, and tell him the contributions were legal. Melcher told George he was crazy. As Melcher would understand later, they should have gone to see the attorney general.

Melcher was starting to get suspicious. He thought, *There's got to be something wrong here. Maybe I ought not to press to hard. Maybe I don't want to know.* But as a lawyer, Jack Melcher had an obligation to know. Not knowing, or not wanting to know, would lead to his downfall.

Time ran out for going to see Archibald Cox. Dozens of corporate executives had gone down and confessed, and their punishment was light, as promised. Of dozens, only two men, Tom Jones of Northrop and George Steinbrenner of American Ship, lied and stonewalled.

When the FBI showed up to talk to the employees who gave the checks to the Nixon campaign, Steinbrenner told his men in front of the agents, "Cooperate with them a hundred percent." The pronouncement came after George had met privately with each of the men. One can only guess what he instructed them to do.

Melcher sat in as the men were questioned. Their testimony was written down and taken directly to the prosecutor's office in Washington. Melcher could tell something was bothering one of the witnesses, Gordon Stafford, who was very nervous. George dismissed his concerns. After the next employee, Ian Cushanan, was interviewed, George said to Melcher, "Jack, what's this bullshit?"

"What are you talking about?" said Melcher. Cushanan looked at him, smiled, and walked off. Melcher didn't realize it, but he was about to be set up as the fall guy.

A few days before the Labor Day weekend of 1973, the eight AmShip employees were subpoenaed to testify before the grand jury about the campaign contributions. For the first time the men began to get very, very concerned. "These men were absolutely panic-stricken," said Melcher.

George, Melcher, and employee Matt Clark held a meeting in the AmShip offices. At the meeting, George gave Clark money and told him to take his wife out for dinner and relax. Later, George said that Melcher had told Clark, "Why don't you go to Europe or Japan, take two months off, disappear." Melcher said he had no memory of making such a remark.

When he tried to get prosecutor Tom McBride to postpone the hearing, McBride said, "We will only postpone the grand jury hearing if Steinbrenner comes to Washington to our offices and tells us the honest-to-God truth."

As the testimony date approached, George again lied to Melcher. "Jack," he said, "I don't know what's going on. They're persecuting me. The Republicans have been persecuting me. They know I've been active with the Democrats. The damn Republicans are persecuting me." George and Melcher went to meet with some of the contributors. While George met with Bartlome and another contributor in the cafeteria of American Ship, Melcher sat and waited. When Steinbrenner returned, he had a hangdog look, as though he had been stabbed in the back. George said, "I can't believe what happened. Bartlome just told me the story. I can't believe it."

According to George, it was at that point that Robert Bartlome laid out the whole program to him, how on their own Bartlome and Stan Lepkowski had turned corporate funds into private contributions. George held his head in his hands. He said to Melcher, "Bartlome said he thought he was doing me a favor. I can't believe it. I'm ruined. I'm absolutely ruined." He added for dramatic effect, "Find me a bridge to jump off."

As Melcher watched, he was thinking, *Good Lord, George, this is incredible.* Then under his breath he uttered the word "bullshit." He pondered what would account for the blind loyalty of these employees.

Said Melcher, "You have to remember that anyone who works for George is reminded daily, constantly, of what a privilege it is, and he damn well better perform and do what George wants, or he's out on his ear. Induced terror, if you will. That's the atmosphere, so you can understand how these guys, who had achieved some modest success in life, were literally just scared to death."

At that point Melcher decided that to better protect themselves, the eight men ought to have independent counsel if they were going to testify. He thought, *God knows what's going to happen to these men and to the company.* He began to think somebody might go to jail.

At a meeting the next day Melcher recommended to Steinbrenner that the men hire their own lawyers. George agreed.

It was now mid-September, and as late as two days before their scheduled grand jury appearance Steinbrenner was telling them, "Don't worry about it, guys. I'll take care of it. I'll go down and talk to McBride."

The evening before, Steinbrenner told Melcher to stay in his hotel room in Washington, that he would contact him about going to see McBride. By this time, Melcher had been replaced as chief legal counsel by Edward Bennett Williams, one of the most famed criminal defense attorneys in American history. During his career, he had defended the rich, the famous, and the powerful, including Frank Sinatra; mobsters Jimmy Hoffa and Frank Costello; politicians Joe McCarthy, John Connally, and Adam Clayton Powell; and wealthy financiers Robert Vesco and Michael Milken. His record of success was uncanny. While Steinbrenner was meeting with Williams, Melcher sat in his hotel room, waiting for George's call, which came early in the evening.

"I really want to see McBride and tell him everything," Steinbrenner told Melcher. "Even though my lawyers won't let me do it, I'm going to do it anyway."

Later in the evening Steinbrenner called Melcher again. He said he was with Edward Bennett Williams and other lawyers, and it hadn't yet been arranged. Left in the dark, Melcher was given the impression by Steinbrenner that Williams and McBride were trying to work something out.

Time was running short. The eight employees were to appear before the grand jury at nine fifteen the next morning. Melcher began getting nervous phone calls from the men starting around six in the morning. He kept calling George to see what he was going to do, but couldn't get hold of him.

The employees asked Melcher, "What's the matter with this guy? He told us all along he was going in. I don't want to go in and say these things, but I have to. My lawyer says I have to tell the truth. Can't you do anything with him, Jack?"

Melcher realized at that point there was nothing he could do. The men were faced with an untenable situation. If they told the truth, they would indict their boss. Their loyalty to him made that choice unbearable. They were holding down $15,000-a-year jobs, and they were afraid to lose them. They were saying, "How can George do this?" In the minds of these men, George had built himself up as one of the most powerful people in the United States. They felt he could do anything. They were incredulous he couldn't get this stopped, and there was a great deal of unhappiness among the men that he was unwilling to do anything.

Said Melcher, "George's motto is, Promise them anything."

But apparently Edward Bennett Williams told his client, "I'm not going to let you go and talk to McBride. We're in for a legal battle." At this point Jack Melcher found himself almost entirely cut off from the proceedings. Edward Bennett Williams was in charge. Jack Melcher was ancient history.

The Ervin Committee subpoenaed a pile of documents, and Melcher was the one chosen to deliver them. He acted as a courier, and he was never called upon to testify. When the eight employees were called to testify under oath, it became clear who was behind the entire scheme: Jack Melcher. When Matt Clark was asked, "Why did you tell these lies to the FBI?" his answer was, "Jack Melcher told me to."

Said Melcher, "That was unbelievable. No way did I tell him to say that."

It wasn't long before Bill Lawless, one of George's other lawyers, told Melcher to get a lawyer.

"For what?" Melcher wanted to know. "What the hell do I need a lawyer for?"

Lawless, a friend, understood what was happening. "Just do it," he said.

At the end of the week Melcher returned to Cleveland to meet with George, who treated him roughly. "Jack, how did you let this happen?" George asked. "You're supposed to be smarter than this. Why didn't you read the warning signs?" Melcher didn't know what to say. There were no warning signs, because George had lied about what he had done and stonewalled to keep his own attorney from learning the truth about his role in what had turned into a national scandal.

Based on the false testimony against Melcher, in January 1974 the prosecutor's office decided to convene a grand jury and proceed against George and also against Jack Melcher, charging him with being involved in the cover-up of Steinbrenner's scheme.

Melcher had a tough decision to face. He not only would have to battle the government, but he would also have to go up against the powerful duo of George Steinbrenner and Edward Bennett Williams. In 1971, he had had a rather serious heart attack, and the tension and pressure brought by the indictment wasn't doing his health much good.

Melcher was sure if he went to the mat and defended himself, he would win. What he didn't know was whether he'd live to survive the trial. He decided he would plead guilty to a misdemeanor—being an accessory after the fact to Steinbrenner's contributions. He appeared in court and was fined. He had to admit he had doubts about whether the story Steinbrenner was telling him was true.

Said Melcher, looking back, "Basically, I didn't know and I didn't want to know. When you're working with George Steinbrenner, he's pulling the strings and you go along. George was stonewalling and doing it rather convincingly, but in my mind I knew something was wrong. It was a serious mistake for me to go along."

After Melcher's guilty plea, the publicized agreement of his cooperation with the federal prosecutor made it impossible for him to continue with the company. George effectively cut him off from having anything more to do with AmShip. Melcher took a leave of absence with pay.

In September 1974, George was indicted and made a grandstand comment on the steps of the courthouse that he would be vindicated. Then, later that fall, he abruptly pleaded guilty in front of Judge Leroy Contie.

In October, Melcher was asked to resign from American Ship. He refused and said, "If he wants me out, he can pay off my contract, and I will leave."

Melcher was due approximately $75,000 a year for three more years. George sent him a check for $300 that paid "any and all obligations owed by the company." His note concluded, "I personally wish you well in all your endeavors." (Melcher never sued, and he never received another dime.)

Shortly after the story about Melcher's misdemeanor guilty plea appeared in the Cleveland newspapers, the *Lorain Journal* on November 28, 1973, ran an editorial calling for Jack Melcher to be disbarred. The editorial headline read, "A Question of Perjury." The paper's editor in chief, Irving Lebowitz, wrote the editorial. It was the first salvo in George Steinbrenner's campaign to have Jack Melcher disbarred.

Months later Melcher received a letter from the Cleveland Bar Association saying they were going to investigate him, but it came to nothing. That should have been the end of it. In the great majority of cases, once someone is cleared by one bar association, that's the end of the investigation. Not this time, though. In this case, George Steinbrenner needed Melcher to be disbarred so he would have someone to blame.

In late January 1975, Melcher received notification that the Ohio Bar Association was going to investigate him. This was so highly unusual that Melcher hired a private investigator to determine why there was a second round of hearings. The investigator let Melcher know that Steinbrenner was behind it. "George has an insidious way of doing things through other people," said Melcher.

As the investigation continued, Melcher began to have heart problems. His chest pains were becoming serious. He said, "They were going to set up a hearing in Cleveland, and finally I said to myself, The hell with it. I've had it. I'm not going to go through with this anymore."

In November 1975, Jack Melcher resigned from the Ohio State Bar, the ultimate victim of George's vengeful ways. Melcher died in 1999. He never practiced law again.

When George Steinbrenner stood before federal judge Leroy Contie in a Cleveland courthouse, he was facing a maximum of fifty-five years in jail. As he waited to hear his fate, he stood beside attorney Edward Bennett Williams wearing a double-breasted blue sport coat with brass buttons and gray pants. He looked serious but not overly concerned.

Inside the courtroom the sounds of nearby traffic could be heard. On the pew benches were U.S. attorneys, court reporters, and curious bystanders. The courtroom was full but not packed.

In front of Judge Contie, George pleaded to two felony counts. Contie then announced that he was fining Steinbrenner $15,000 and fining American Shipbuilding $20,000. He banged his gavel, and it was over. No jail time for George Steinbrenner. He and Edward Bennett Williams shook hands, and everyone was smiling.

Later it would come out that almost a hundred of Cleveland's most respected citizens had sent letters to the court saying how much Steinbrenner meant to Cleveland and how much good he had done for the city. The fine also was an indication that the government didn't have much interest in punishing those convicted of violating the campaign contribution laws.

Tom McBride, who prosecuted the case, was furious at how easily George got off, considering the nature of what he had done. "The story the American Ship employees told was patently false from the beginning," said McBride. "The story that they were such staunch Republicans and loyal Nixon devotees that they would give three thousand dollars, when some of them were making an annual salary of fourteen thousand dollars, wasn't believable on its face."

More than anything else, he felt that Steinbrenner had badly used his employees. "Characteristic of this whole case were the witnesses, these poor, sorry employees," he said. "And here Steinbrenner is living in a dream world, bending reality to his vision of it, trying to make these guys view it the same way. And it was just crazy. It was bizarre. He had such an economic hold over these people. They couldn't do anything. They were absolutely petrified. They all lied at first. Basically, they all came around and told the truth. I'm used to organized crime cases. This was a pushover."

McBride said that if he had to do it all over again, he would not have done anything differently. "The real issue was whether he would plead to the obstructive acts. Those were the ones that were really serious. It wasn't so bad that he gave money, it was that he tried to get these guys to lie and cover it up. He pleaded to that as well. If Judge Contie had wanted to send him to jail, he certainly had the admissions of criminal acts to do so. After Contie's decision to fine him, there was a lot of disappointment in our office."

13 Pete, I gotta tell you, I'm going to get Jackson, and I'm going to get Billy Martin.

—George Steinbrenner to Pete Callahan

George's Short Exile

On November 27, the day before Thanksgiving 1974, George Steinbrenner was suspended for two years from running the New York Yankees by baseball commissioner Bowie Kuhn, who forbade him from having any association with the team or its personnel. If George could force his AmShip employees to give to Nixon's campaign, Kuhn argued, he could force his players to fix a game.

Bowie Kuhn was the baseball commissioner because he wasn't much of a lawyer. But he was unusual as commissioner in that he slapped down several owners when they misbehaved, fining Ray Kroc of San Diego and Ted Turner for tampering with players on other teams, and preventing Charlie Finley of Oakland from selling off three of his most valued players for cash.

Kuhn could have forced Steinbrenner to sell his interests in the Yankees. Only two other owners, William Cox and Fred Saigh, had ever been so disciplined by a commissioner. Critics of Bowie Kuhn and supporters of Steinbrenner argued that George had been punished enough, that there was no good reason for baseball to penalize him further, and they may have been right about that. Others argued that the punishment had no teeth. Wrote Red Smith in the *New York Times*, "Giving him a two-year 'suspension' that costs him nothing is like sending a naughty boy home from school for the Christmas holidays."

Steinbrenner's initial reaction was to say he would seek an injunction, but after talking with his lawyers, in the end he decided to go along with the ruling, saying, "Winning the pennant is my immediate goal, and I don't want anything to stand in the way of that." George correctly figured if he made nice with Kuhn, he could get his sentence reduced, which is exactly what happened. He was ostensibly barred from signing players or discussing deals, but how Kuhn could stop him from talking to Gabe Paul on the telephone was another story. Most important, Steinbrenner was allowed to keep his stock in the team. In the end, Paul had carte blanche to rebuild the Yankees with a series of excellent trades, but it's doubtful things would have been different without the suspension. One thing the suspension did was to keep George off the backs of his managers and players in 1975. Other than that, Kuhn's suspension was toothless. It didn't cost Steinbrenner any money, and he still was involved in making trades, in that Gabe Paul told me he always talked to George first before making a deal.

"I wasn't going to spend his money without talking to him first," said Paul.

The experts wondered whether Steinbrenner's suspension would cost Kuhn his job, but it didn't. Kuhn was reelected on July 16, 1975, for another seven years. Supported by Steinbrenner and the Yankees, he cut George's sentence from two years to fifteen months. George would be back in charge of the Yankees by the end of spring training 1976.

On February 21, 1975, Patrick Cunningham, who for the past year had served as the Yankees' legal counsel, was named acting general partner of the Yankees, but when the players arrived at spring training George Steinbrenner was sitting in his usual seat near the dugout. Though ostensibly barred from making decisions, he was allowed to come to the games as a fan.

Gabe Paul had made headlines for the Yankees in October the year before when he traded talented, dependable Bobby Murcer for the exciting fan-attractor Bobby Bonds. On the same day, he traded the quiet, dependable pitcher Doc Medich for three Pittsburgh

Pirates: Willie Randolph, a future All-Star second baseman; relief pitcher Ken Brett, George's big brother; and Dock Ellis, who gained fame for pitching a no-hitter for the Pirates while on LSD. Dock would later cause his teammates to crack up when he issued the lines, "I love it when George Steinbrenner flies. The more he flies, the greater the odds his plane will crash." Dock, who was never dull, was not a Yankee for long.

Perhaps the most important signing of the entire George Steinbrenner era came on New Year's Eve of 1974. Jim "Catfish" Hunter, who had led the Oakland A's to three World Series championships in a row, in 1972, 1973, and 1974, suddenly was declared a free agent. A's owner Charles Finley had signed Hunter to a contract that provided for Finley to pay into an annuity fund for Hunter each year. In 1974, Finley refused to do it, and when Hunter took him to arbitration, he was declared a free agent.

A signing frenzy ensued, and rightly so. Hunter had won twenty games a season four seasons in a row. He was only the fourth pitcher to win two hundred games by his thirty-first birthday. The other three were fellows named Cy Young, Christy Mathewson, and Walter Johnson. Here was the chance to sign one of the premier pitchers in the game, and everyone was interested. The only question was how much it would cost.

The two teams left at the end of the bidding were the San Diego Padres, owned by McDonald's magnate Ray Kroc, and the Yankees. Croc offered a little more money, but the Yankees were offering seventy-five years of tradition in addition to $3.75 million for the next five years.

When Hunter chose the Yankees, it meant the end of the financial structure of baseball as we knew it. Steinbrenner, who owned the team in the biggest market with the biggest upside, could most afford to spend what at that time seemed like a king's ransom for a baseball player. Steinbrenner correctly foresaw that the Yankee fans were hungry for an exciting, talented team and would flock to the stadium to see it. A win-at-all-cost guy, he saw baseball not as a game but as an entertainment, and he vowed to spend whatever it would take to bring a championship back to New York. The signing of Catfish Hunter made believers of every Yankee fan.

Hunter, who passed away in 1998 at the age of fifty-three, talked to me in 1981 about signing with George Steinbrenner and the Yankees. "The first team I talked to was Cleveland, and they offered me a million dollars, and I came home and told my wife, Helen, 'They're crazy.' It was for five years. A million dollars. I couldn't believe it. And we kept talking to every club, and I talked with the Yankees. Clyde Klutz, who signed me with Kansas City, was living nearby, and he was with the Yankees, and he and Gabe Paul came down to Ahoskie, where my lawyers were, and talked to me. Clyde said he was going to stay over, and I said, 'I'll eat breakfast with you the next morning.' When I left home that morning, I told my wife, 'I'm going to sign with somebody. I can't keep dragging it out. I'm getting tired of going over there so many times.'" In a few hours, he made his decision to go with the Yankees.

"I picked the Yankees [over San Diego]," Hunter continued, "because they were closer to home. It wasn't strictly the money because San Diego offered me more than they did. It was close to home, and the main trigger to the whole thing was Clyde Klutz, the scout who signed me to start with Kansas City."

The Yankees, with everyone's hopes high, began the 1975 season a dismal 2–7. Catfish Hunter was winless after his first three starts. On April 23, the team dropped into last place. Hunter was getting frustrated, and so was Steinbrenner, who by April was back at the helm of the team after his fifteen-month suspension. Steinbrenner, who played the press like Heifetz played the violin, gave reporter Maury Allen of the *New York Post* an exclusive.

Said Allen, "The first year Catfish Hunter was doing a tobacco commercial on the field at nine in the morning. Steinbrenner had been in his office for two hours. He looks out onto the field and sees Catfish, who is zero and three, and he goes insane. That night Catfish lost, making his record zero for four.

"This was a Friday night, and I'm working the game, and George comes over to me, and he says, 'Come to my office when the game is over.' I go to his office, and as soon as I sit down, he says, 'Can you believe that goddamn Catfish Hunter? He's filming a commercial. He's horseshit. He's going bad,' and he started ranting and raving. This was a player to whom he had paid three million dollars, a very significant purchase.

He goes off for twenty minutes, and he says to me, 'That should give you a front-page story, right?'

"I said, 'Right.'

"'Make sure you don't put my name in the story,' he said.

"He wanted to nail the guy, but he didn't want to be quoted. The gag line always was, 'A source close to the Yankees.' George was the source close to the Yankees.

"As soon as the story appeared the next day, Catfish Hunter catches me in the clubhouse. He screamed, 'That no-good cocksucker. Why didn't he say it to my face?'

"The one thing that was significant: George wasn't seeking personal glory, though no question, he wanted his name in the paper. No question he wanted to be important, but deep down his motivation was to shake up these guys. I think deep down he also thought by abusing them, they would play harder.

"And immediately Hunter went on a winning streak. Of course Steinbrenner came over to me and said, 'See, Maury? See what we did?'"

The Yankees moved into first place in June, stayed there for five days, dropped to second, and never returned. A twenty-three-win season for Hunter wasn't enough to give the Yankees the pennant. Too many injuries hampered their efforts. Bobby Bonds injured his knee after he crashed into a wall in Chicago. A week later Elliott Maddox wrecked his knee, and a month after that Ron Blomberg tore up his shoulder. An ear problem brought down Lou Piniella.

On August 1, 1975, Hunter beat the Indians. When the players got to the clubhouse, the TV lights shone from Bill Virdon's office. Reporters asked him if he had been fired, but he said he had no idea. After the reporters left, Gabe Paul called Virdon to tell him he was through. The Yankee players never saw him again.

Virdon hadn't done a bad job. That wasn't why he was fired. Virdon, it turned out, had been an interim manager all along. George Steinbrenner had been waiting for the manager he really wanted to become available. In the spring of 1973, during a one-sided loss to Oakland and their slugging outfielder Reggie Jackson, he had told his Williams classmate Pete Callahan, "Pete, I gotta tell you, I'm going to get Jackson, and I'm going to get Billy Martin."

When Texas fired Martin not long after he got into a ruckus with traveling secretary Bert Hawkins, George pounced. Reggie Jackson would not come aboard for another two years.

The day after Bill Virdon's firing was Old-Timers' Day at Yankee Stadium. Billy Martin was in town. The players put two and two together. The long, excruciating psychodrama played out between George Steinbrenner and Billy Martin was about to begin.

14 George and Billy were attracted to each other as surely as a moth to a blowtorch.

Wooing Billy

All his life, Alfred Manuel "Billy" Martin was a fighter. His mother taught him from childhood. She repeatedly admonished him, "Never take shit from nobody." She didn't, and he didn't either. As wealthy as George Steinbrenner grew up, that's how poor Billy was. Times were hard in the San Francisco suburb of West Berkeley once the country was gripped by the Depression. Billy always had a roof over his head and food on the table, but little else. His clothes were ragged, something he didn't realize until junior high school, when he was thrown in with the rich kids of Berkeley's upper-crust society. Because they came from the top of the hill along University Avenue, Billy and his friends called them "the Goats."

"They just wouldn't have anything to do with us," said his friend Ruben DeAlba. "To the Goats, we were garbage."

But Billy had James Kenney Park, a long block from his home, and he played baseball with his older brother Tudo and Tudo's friend Augie Galan, who played with the Chicago Cubs. What Billy learned from them was aggressiveness. At age thirteen he was playing with men in their twenties and thirties, and by high school he was an all-star in his junior and senior years, even though he missed the last two weeks of his senior season after he punched out a heckler in the stands, then punched out the umpire who tried to break them up.

All through high school Billy Martin told his friends he was going to be a New York Yankee, a member of a team that boasted four Italian American players: Phil Rizzuto and the three San Francisco Bay Area stars, Joe DiMaggio, Tony Lazzeri, and Frank Crosetti.

It's a wonder Billy made it past high school. He was a hoodlum who went into bars and beat up patrons. But Red Adams, a savvy baseball man, watched him play and recommended him to Casey Stengel, the manager of the Oakland Oaks. Stengel loved Billy's enthusiasm and adopted him. The two men, a punk kid and an old-time ballplayer, developed a bond that wouldn't be broken for a decade. Binding them was their deep love for the game of baseball.

Billy starred at second base for Oakland in 1948, and when Stengel was hired as Yankees manager in '49, he promised to bring Billy with him in '50. Stengel kept his word, and in spring training in 1950 the veterans noticed that Stengel and the kid had a special relationship. Stengel told reporters, "That fresh kid, how I love him."

Billy played for Stengel from 1950 through June 1957. He starred in the 1952 and 1953 World Series against the Brooklyn Dodgers. He was in the service in 1954, the one year the Yankees didn't win the pennant between 1949 and 1959. When he returned in August 1955, the Yankees trailed Cleveland. He told his teammates, "I'm broke, and you're playing as though you're trying to lose. We gotta get to the series. We gotta."

They did, and they did again in 1956. Then, in June 1957, Billy, Mickey Mantle, Whitey Ford, Hank Bauer, and John Kucks went to the Copacabana to celebrate Billy's birthday. Bauer punched out a drunk, and the Yankees made headlines. Billy was traded not long afterward, breaking his and Stengel's hearts.

From that day on all Billy ever wanted was to return to the Yankees. It would be another nineteen years before his dream would be realized.

After he was traded away by the Yankees, he knocked around baseball for another four years, going from team to team, playing as though he was in a daze. He went to Kansas City, Detroit, Cleveland, Cincinnati, Milwaukee, and finally to Minnesota, where in the spring of 1962 he was released.

Heartbroken, Billy was hired by Twins owner Calvin Griffith to be a scout at $10,000 a year. He kept his drinking under control in order to survive in baseball. After three years Griffith hired him to be third base coach. He tutored the infielders and was especially helpful to the Latin players, especially shortstop Zoilo Versailles and outfielders Tony Olivo and César Tovar. In 1965, Versailles, the league MVP, led the Twins to the American League pennant. Billy was a great coach. Casey had taught him well.

He wasn't so good at the politics. As a coach he couldn't get along with the traveling secretary and a couple of the other coaches. He won the pennant managing in Triple A Denver, but when he returned to manage the Twins in 1968, he fought with farm director Sherry Robertson, Griffith's stepbrother, and then he offended Griffith when he barred vice presidential candidate Hubert Humphrey from his club-house. Later that year he punched out Dave Boswell, one of his pitchers. Even after the Twins won the American League Western Division title, Griffith had had enough of Billy.

After sitting out all of 1970, he was hired to manage Detroit, but after taking the Tigers to a division title, Billy alienated general manager Jim Campbell, and he was fired after his third season.

Experts wondered if two firings meant the end of Billy as a manager, but he won too often not to return, and in 1974 he was hired by Bob Short, owner of the Texas Rangers, one of baseball's laughingstocks. Short, needing a manager who could straighten out the franchise, gave Billy complete control. Billy turned the club upside down, bringing in new blood from the farm system, and he led the ragtag Rangers to an unexpected second-place finish, only five games behind powerful Oakland. As late as July 30, the surprising Rangers were tied for first place. If one wanted proof of Billy Martin's genius as a manager, that was it.

Said Texas third baseman Roy Howell, "Billy was the best there was at showing you how to beat somebody."

But Billy's Texas honeymoon ended when Bob Short ran out of money and sold the team to Brad Corbett, the owner of a company that made PVC pipe. Billy assumed Corbett would allow him to run the team as before, but he was naïve. Corbett was the more traditional owner, a wealthy man who buys a team and immediately considers himself an expert. Corbett didn't let Billy make any decisions.

He hired his own people and listened to them, not Billy. Martin's days were numbered when he slapped traveling secretary Bert Hawkins on a plane flight. Hawkins's wife had wanted to form a wives' club. Billy was taking a girlfriend, not his wife, on the team plane and didn't want any part of any wives' club. By the summer of 1974, Billy was complaining of interference from Corbett and the front office.

Billy drank, and he talked to reporters when he should have kept quiet. All he did was alienate himself further from the Texas owner. On the morning of July 21, 1974, he went on a daily radio show and criticized Corbett. He predicted Corbett would fire him, and that afternoon he did. With Billy gone, the Rangers returned to their inept ways, once again becoming the graveyard of baseball. Said Roy Howell, "When Billy was fired, we knew we were in trouble." Frank Lucchesi took over, and the team finished dead last.

After Billy was fired by Texas, he took off to go fishing on a secluded lake in Colorado. He wanted absolute privacy, wanted to cleanse himself from the layer of disgust that had covered him in Texas. Billy knew the firing would cause the players and the Rangers fans to become losers, which bothered him deeply. He swore he would never put himself in such a subservient position again. Ironically, that's when George Steinbrenner came a-calling. If George could sign Billy, he would fire Yankees manager Bill Virdon and bring in the manager he had vowed to get and wanted all along.

One of the other ironies about George's firing Bill Virdon and hiring Billy Martin was that Bill Virdon was close to the perfect manager for George. During the year he managed the Yankees, Virdon resented George's many phone calls and intrusions and second-guessing like every one of George's many managers, but he was a good soldier, swallowing his pride, taking the abuse, and doing whatever George wanted with a "Yes, sir."

George was still under suspension, and he wasn't allowed near the clubhouse. After a game in which the Red Sox beat the Yankees soundly, Virdon called a meeting to chew them out. He was holding a tape recorder, which the players thought strange.

"Gather round here and listen," said Virdon. He played the tape and on it was George:

"I'll be a son of a bitch if I'm going to sit up here and sign these paychecks and watch us get our asses kicked by a bunch of rummies. Now, goddammit, like they say down on the docks, 'You have to have balls.'"

The players thought it hilarious. For weeks they went around grabbing their balls, saying to one another, "You have to have balls." They had to admit they admired Steinbrenner's competitiveness.

Unfortunately for the Yankees, while he may have been the right manager for Steinbrenner, Bill Virdon was the very wrong guy for the job. The players certainly liked him—he was so nice they called him "Mr. Milk Shake," because everyone thought he was a health nut—and he enjoyed their antics, but to be successful, he had to be able to stand up to George and let his players know that he wasn't a puppet or a lackey. His other problem was that he played for the three-run home run on a team that needed to play small ball.

He didn't bunt, hit and run, or move the runners, and the Yankees would lose games by a run or two. For weeks the players were saying to one another, "Let's do something," and then finally a group of players met secretly in Sparky Lyle's hotel room in Texas. He, Graig Nettles, Dick Tidrow, Chris Chambliss, Lou Piniella, Roy White, and Bobby Murcer all agreed that when a bunt situation arose, they would bunt, sign or no sign. Once Virdon figured out what they were doing, he never said a word, averting what could have been an ugly scene.

The truth was that Billy Martin was probably the worst possible choice to be the Yankee manager considering George's meddling, abusive behavior and Billy's unstable personality and volatile nature. Billy's friends contend that George's tough-love treatment of him exacerbated his alcoholism and fueled his erratic behavior at the end of his life, contributing to his tragic death when, inebriated, he broke his neck after he crashed his truck head-on into a culvert near his home on Christmas Day 1989.

George and Billy were attracted to each other as surely as a moth to a blowtorch. When living in Cleveland, George had always admired the way Billy played ball as the on-field spark plug of the Yankees. Often he would go to Municipal Stadium to watch the Indians play the New Yorkers. For the better part of a decade, except for 1954, when the Indians won 111 games and the American League pennant, Billy's Yankees inevitably would finish the season in first place.

When Billy was fired as manager by Texas, George Steinbrenner called Gabe Paul and told him he wanted to hire him. George was aware of Billy's success wherever he went, and he also saw that he was an attraction who brought fans into the ballpark. Under the stoic, traditional Bill Virdon the Yankees were boring. Steinbrenner was looking for pizzazz, box-office boffo. He wanted a manager and a team that would make things happen.

Gabe, who knew Billy, wasn't so sure hiring him was a smart idea. Gabe was fully aware that Billy liked to be in charge, and knew his boss was just as adamant about who steered the ship. Gabe presciently feared the combustibility of the two egos' clashing. He also saw himself as the peacemaker between the two—a chilling thought.

Gabe told George he was afraid of the chemistry with Billy, but George, as Paul recalled, said, "I still want him." Gabe Paul swore he would not allow Billy the leeway that Bob Short had given him in Texas. He worried that Billy would start second-guessing his player moves. He worried that Billy wouldn't be a team management player, wouldn't meet or consult with him. In short, he worried that Billy would be Billy.

Steinbrenner's worries were about Billy's morality, which was pretty ironic considering he was under suspension from baseball for his own illegal acts. George knew of Billy's reputation and feared that he would get drunk and punch somebody, embarrassing the Yankees.

When Paul called him, Billy had reservations about signing with another team. He could sit out the rest of the season and the next season as well and still collect the rest of his $72,000 salary from the Rangers. He felt he should have time to heal his wounds.

But the pull of managing the Yankees was too strong for Billy to resist. Billy had always considered himself the one true Yankee, and when as a player he was traded by the team in the spring of 1957, he was traumatized in a way that would color the rest of his life. Even after he began his managing career, he had but one objective: to return as manager of the Yankees, where he could then work to beat his mentor Casey Stengel's record of ten pennants.

"It was the only job I ever wanted," Billy told me. He also told me, "I never should have agreed to manage the Yankees when I did in 1975."

He never should have. The contract Steinbrenner and Gabe wanted him to sign was an insult. The salary was okay. It was the same $72,000 he was making in Texas, but Gabe and George inserted behavior clauses that alienated him from the start. One clause said he was to "personally conduct himself at all times so as to represent the best interests of the New York Yankees and to adhere to all club policies." Another forbade him from criticizing management in any way. Also he had to make himself available for consultations with management. If he didn't conform, said another paragraph in the contract, he could be fired and he no longer would be paid.

Said Billy later, "Why should I put myself in a weak position? I didn't like the trap that I was being set into. I just didn't like the whole thing. It smelled. I was putting myself in a position where this George Steinbrenner could handcuff me, and I didn't know him very well. I had heard he was wild and erratic, but I had only met him one time in a restaurant for a quick hello, and I really didn't know anything about him."

When Paul persisted, Billy turned down the job a second time. Paul then called George and put the two of them on the phone. George said, "Billy, I would like to have you as our manager."

"I'd like to be the manager of the Yankees," said Billy, but then reiterated that he didn't like the offer.

George, who could spot a person's weakness in a heartbeat, played hardball. He said, "If you don't take the offer now, you will never get it again. C'mon, Billy, be the manager. Here's your big chance to manage the Yankees, something you've wanted to do."

Billy said, "I'm not going to take it now."

"You go home and think about it," said George.

Then George got Bob Short, the man who had hired Billy in Texas, a man Billy loved and trusted, to call him. Short, who worried that Billy had so outworn his welcome that other offers wouldn't come, told him it would work out. Of all of Billy's friends, George knew just whom to call to get Billy to cave in.

But in this case, Short was wrong about it all working out.

Short kept on. He asked to speak to Billy's wife, Gretchen, and the two talked for about a half hour. After she hung up, Billy asked for her opinion.

"I think you should take the job," she said. "You always wanted to go back to the Yankees." Gretchen also was worried that Billy wouldn't get another job. After all, he had been fired in Minnesota, Detroit, and now Texas. His reputation as a troublemaker was growing.

When he went to bed that night, Billy still was undecided, but the pull of being Yankees manager was just too strong, and he agreed, clauses or no clauses.

The next day Billy and his wife flew to New York, where George hid them in a hotel to keep the media away from Billy. The following day, August 14, 1975, was Old-Timers' Day, and George, who grew up rooting for the Indians of Bill Veeck, had a surprise for the fans almost as good as Bill Veeck's surprise of a midget jumping out of a cake and going to bat in a game.

Before a packed house at Shea Stadium, PA announcer Bob Sheppard intoned the names of some of the greatest players in Yankees history: Whitey Ford, Yogi Berra, Mickey Mantle, and Joe DiMaggio. Each received a roaring reception. DiMaggio normally was the last player to be introduced, but on this day tradition went by the boards. One player remained to be announced.

Announced Bob Sheppard, "Number 1, the new manager of the New York Yankees . . . Billy Martin."

Yankees fans were stunned. Billy ran onto the field wearing a cowboy jacket, pants, and boots, and was greeted with a raucous standing ovation. There was scattered booing, and it was just like Billy to hear the boobirds amid the din of worshipful adulation.

Billy told himself, *They're booing right now, but before I'm through everyone will be cheering.*

Billy the Kid was back in pinstripes, eighteen years and two months after that June day in 1957 when Yankee GM George Weiss broke his heart by trading him to Kansas City.

When Billy began as Yankees manager in August 1975, he decided to focus his energy on getting the team ready to win the pennant in 1976. The best thing to do then, he felt, was change very little. He wanted to observe who were the clubhouse lawyers, alibiers, and complainers and get rid of them. When Pat Dobson expressed doubts about him, Martin made a mental note. When Doc Medich one day blamed one of his outfielders for losing a game, he made another.

During the last week of the season, the team had been winning, and before a game, outfielder Bobby Bonds told Billy his legs were hurting and he wasn't going to play that day. Bye-bye, Bobby Bonds.

Billy's second task was to change the attitude of the ball club. When he arrived, the players brought their friends and relatives into the clubhouse. Pitchers were playing cards and eating sandwiches in the bullpen.

"They were acting like it was a country club," said Billy. "When I'm managing, you'd better take your job seriously, or you won't be around long. If you play for me, you play the game like you play life. You play it to be successful, you play it with dignity, you play it with pride, and you play it aggressively. Life is a very serious thing, and baseball has been my life. What else has life been? That's why when I lose a ball game I can't eat after a game. Sometimes I can hardly sleep. If you're in love with the game, you can't turn it on and off like a light. It's something that runs so deep it takes you over. If I lose, I say to myself, What if I'd have done this or that?" Under Billy the last part of the 1975 season, the Yankees' record was 30–26, and the team finished twelve games behind the Boston Red Sox. After the season, Dobson, Medich, and Bonds were all traded. Gabe Paul, knowing how much Billy liked to take advantage of speed, traded them for two outstanding base runners, Mickey Rivers and Willie Randolph. Three of the new acquisitions, Rivers, Oscar Gamble, and Dock Ellis, had reputations for being rebellious and hardheaded. Billy didn't care about that, and neither did Gabe Paul. Billy's favorite line was he'd play Hitler, Mussolini, and Stalin if they had ability.

As 1976 began, twelve years since they had won a pennant, Billy and Gabe worked closely together to help build the Yankees into a powerhouse. At the beginning of spring training Billy wrote a letter to each of his players saying that the days of Yankee mediocrity were over. He stressed pride, desire, and the will to win. "I have never been with a loser, and I'm not going to start now," he wrote.

Everything in Yankeeland seemed peaceful. George Steinbrenner was under suspension the entire 1975 season, allowing Gabe and Billy, who respected each other's abilities, to work their magic together. George was scheduled to sit out the whole of 1976 as well, but on March 1, 1976, baseball commissioner Bowie Kuhn announced he was shortening Steinbrenner's ban and allowing him to return as the active head of the Yankees.

When the players heard in March 1976 that Steinbrenner had been cleared to resume involvement with the team, they braced themselves for an onslaught of what they called "George's petty shit," but during spring training of 1976, George rarely interfered with Billy or the players. Part of the reason may have been that Steinbrenner didn't think he had a very good team and felt he would hurt his reputation by being involved with it.

Before the 1976 season, George bet Billy one of his tugboats that the Yankees would not win the pennant. It happened one evening during a baseball clinic in Curaçao when Billy and George sat down to discuss the coming season. When Billy predicted that the Yankees would win the 1976 pennant, George thought Billy was being too optimistic. "You know," said George, "we have a lot of holes." Then he thought about what Billy had said and replied, "You are like heck."

Billy, feeling flush, asked him, "What do you want to bet?"

Steinbrenner said, "Tell you what. I own some tugboats. If you win the pennant, I'll give you a tugboat."

Billy said, "A tugboat is worth about three hundred thousand dollars, right?"

George said, "You win, you got it."

Billy took George at his word. He was looking forward to winning that tugboat from George.

On July 10, 1962, George (second from left) was photographed with NBA owners (from left to right) Dan Biasone, Walter Brown, Ned Irish, Ben Kerner, and an unidentified man after George's Cleveland Pipers were voted into the NBA. When it turned out he couldn't raise the entry fee, the offer was rescinded.

George sits in the stands, surveying his domain, in the early 1970s.

Michael Burke and George attend the reopening of Yankee Stadium on April 13, 1976. A couple of months later, Burke would disappear.

George and Billy Martin celebrate winning the 1977 American League pennant after the Yankees defeat the Kansas City Royals.

George with Billy Martin and Lou Piniella. In February 1988, Martin was the manager and Piniella the general manager. Neither lasted for long.

Reggie Jackson and George. George offered Reggie a bonus equal to the cost of a Rolls-Royce to get him to sign with the Yankees.

George and Dave Winfield. First George called him "Mr. May," and then he tried
to ruin his life.

George and Yogi Berra in the Yankees' dugout in 1984 Yogi was the Yankees'
manager in 1984. The next year George fired him after sixteen games.

In a spring training game against the Red Sox in March 2002, George let everyone know how disgusted he was with the way the Yankees were playing.

On September 15, 1989, in a game against Seattle, Yankees fans let it be known how they felt about George's stewardship.

After the Yankees swept San Diego to win the 1998 World Series, George and Joe Torre shed tears of joy.

George, wearing his aviator shades, watches a game at Legends Field in March 2006.

(From left to right) Daughter Jessica, son-in-law Felix Lopez, an unidentified woman, George, son Hank, and former GM Clyde King watch a spring training game in February 2008.

Daughter Jennifer (left), George, and wife Joan, at the dedication of Steinbrenner Field in Tampa.

Joe Torre, George, and Brian Cashman watch batting practice before a game in February 2006. Cashman outlasted them both.

George and George Costanza (played by Jason Alexander) on an unaired episode of *Seinfeld* in the mid-1990s.

What George Steinbrenner hath wrought.

15

I just couldn't make him understand that he was hurting the club doing things like that. What does George know about Yankee pride? When did he ever play for the Yankees?
—Billy Martin

George's First Pennant

With Gabe Paul acting as a buffer between George and Billy Martin, Billy's problems with the Yankee management in 1976 were few and far between. During spring training Billy's practices went from ten in the morning until one in the afternoon. They were structured, and players wasted little time while practicing myriad skills. Every day the players worked on fundamentals, including bunting, relays, rundowns, and pickoff plays. The pitchers practiced covering first base. By the time the season started, the players were versed in the fundamentals.

During practice one day George came over and suggested to Billy that he hold double sessions, also practicing in the afternoon as they did in football. Billy said no, that he didn't want to burn out his players, leaving them with no gas in their tank at the end of the season. Gabe felt the same way. When Billy held his ground, he wasn't challenged again.

Early in the season Gabe came to Billy and asked if he would play a tape recording for the players that George had made. Gabe said, "George wants to motivate the players." Billy said no, that he didn't need George's tapes to motivate the players, that he could do it himself. Gabe also insisted that Billy come to his office every day at three for a meeting. Billy told him, "My time should be spent with the players, not with you."

The Yankees were a very happy ball club that season. The players got along, and when the regular season began, the Yankees won fifteen of their first twenty games and held the American League East lead from beginning to end. It was the happiest ball club Billy ever managed.

Pitcher Sparky Lyle explained why Billy was so popular with most of his players. "Billy, see, is different from most managers. He fights with the ballplayers, drinks with them, and he gets closer to them than most managers. Billy is really easy to play for because he treats his players like men, whereas many managers treat you like kindergartners. Billy doesn't have a curfew check, and if I want to stay out until the bar closes, all I have to do is ask him, and he'll say yeah. He still remembers what it's like to be a player. Other assholes, as soon as they switch from player to manager or coach, they immediately forget they were ever a player.

"When Billy took over the Yankees, everybody on the team really loved him. We were excited about having him as a manager, because he'd make a move, pinch-hit or steal or bunt, and he'd walk up and down the dugout and explain why he did what he did. The guys liked that."

By July the Yankees were fifteen games in front and running away with it. Then in August they lost six of seven, and George showed signs of panicking. He asked to come into the clubhouse and talk to the pitching staff, and Billy uncharacteristically agreed. Said Billy, "I listened while he chewed them out like he was talking to a high school football team. He was giving them the rah-rah talk. 'You guys don't want it bad enough. You're not giving a hundred percent. You guys are Yankees and have to play like Yankees.' It went on like that. It was ridiculous, but it's his ball club, and he's entitled to do what he wants."

After George left, said Billy, the pitchers were all making fun of George. "I just couldn't make him understand that he was hurting the club doing things like that. What does George know about Yankee pride? When did he ever play for the Yankees? What does he know about major league players' feelings? He doesn't. He'd call me on the phone and yell at me to 'chew this guy's ass out.' Or he'd say, 'Bat this guy lower in the order, that'll show him.' You don't do that. Children do things like that. You have to get your point across without humiliating the player, without embarrassing him. That's the worst thing you can do to a player."

Billy also got upset when George was caught on TV making a face that expressed his displeasure when a Yankee player did something he didn't like. Martin wanted George to mask his feelings, so the reporters wouldn't notice his reactions and write about it.

Then in June George did something that infuriated Billy. Billy was negotiating for a long-term contract, and George brought manager Dick Williams to sit with him in his box. George was letting Billy know that if he didn't like the money he was being offered, George had someone else waiting in the wings. Said Billy, "It didn't intimidate me, but it made me madder'n hell."

One of the reasons George and Billy were getting along as well as they did was that Billy desperately wanted George to like him as a person. "I bent over backwards to show him I was with him," said Billy. "I was overtrying to get him to like me, and sometimes I'd go up to his office and he'd be so nice to me that I'd leave there just happy as heck. It was so important to me that he liked me, and everything was really great—until it began to look like the team was going to win the pennant, and at that point I began to feel that George was acting jealous of me. He seemed to resent that he didn't have a big enough hand in it, seemed to feel that he wasn't going to get enough credit, and it bothered him that I was getting so much publicity. Hell, everyone knew it was George who put the team out there, that it was his money, and it was George who did all those wonderful things to bring the Yankees back, and there was no reason for him to resent me or feel jealous of me, none whatsoever."

But Billy could not comprehend that because George was a narcissist with an ego so big (or so fragile) that it was important for him to take all the credit for the success of his ball club. George wanted everyone to know that it wasn't Billy Martin who made the Yankees winners again, nor was it Gabe Paul who had structured the deals, nor was it the twenty-four players who won the games—it was George Steinbrenner who had saved the Yankees. George Steinbrenner had done it.

The Yankees won the 1976 American League pennant when they defeated the Kansas City Royals in a hard-fought five-game series. It was a tight series, won in the bottom of the ninth of the final game when Royals reliever Mark Littell threw Chris Chambliss, the first batter, a fastball that Chambliss lined into the right-field stands for the victory. For Yankees fans who had suffered through the last ten years, it was a moment that would never be forgotten as long as they lived. For the first time since 1964, the Yankees were back in the World Series.

When Billy asked George for his tugboat, George reneged and changed the bet. "You have to win the World Series to get the tug-boat," he said.

The sadistic schedule makers forced the Yankees to start the World Series the very next day against the Cincinnati Reds, and the Yankees pitching staff wasn't ready. Doyle Alexander, Billy's fifth starter, pitched the first game, and he didn't pitch badly, but Reds ace Don Gullett was magnificent, allowing five hits in a 5–1 win.

In the second game, the Yankees were tied 3–3 in the ninth when shortstop Fred Stanley picked up a ground ball hit by Ken Griffey and threw it into the Yankees' dugout. In game three, Dock Ellis was KO'ed early, and the Yankees lost, and Ed Figueroa wasn't much better in the finale, a 7–2 pasting.

After the game, Billy sat on the floor of the trainer's room, a picture of dejection. George came in and looked at Billy. "If daggers could have come out of the man's eyes, they would have," said Billy. "He was looking at me like, 'How can you do this to me?' as if I had lost the series in four straight on purpose, like he was embarrassed. It was then that George decided he was going to make some changes, that he was really going to get into things, because he wasn't going to be embarrassed like that again."

16

If you want to fire me, go ahead and fire me right
goddamned now.

—Billy Martin

The Bronx Zoo

Baseball was dumped on its head in 1976 with the end of the reserve clause. Since the dawn of time if a major league player signed a contract, the reserve clause allowed his team to automatically renew him at the end of the season. Simply stated, clubs had the right to renew a player's contract year after year in perpetuity, leaving the player with the choice of signing his contract for what he was offered or quitting the game entirely.

That changed after pitchers Andy Messersmith and Dave McNally played the 1975 season unsigned and filed for free agency. Messersmith would have signed had Los Angeles Dodgers owner Walter O'Malley given him a no-trade clause in the contract, but O'Malley refused. He told the pitcher, "The league would not approve the contract," which was as true as his statement that the Dodgers would never leave Brooklyn.

Company man Walter Alston, the Dodgers manager, proclaimed, "If Messersmith is declared a free agent, then baseball is dead." To that Marvin Miller, the head of the Players' Association, responded sarcastically, "I half expected him to claim that Los Angeles would fall into the Pacific."

An arrogant Bowie Kuhn contemptuously told the players to go ahead and file their grievance. Meanwhile, the Player Relations Committee—the group representing the owners—filed an injunction asking a court in Kansas City to enjoin the arbitrator from hearing the grievance. A federal judge denied the injunction.

After the denial, the owners began to panic. Montreal offered McNally a $125,000 contract, plus a $25,000 bonus. He was told he could keep the bonus money even if he didn't make the team. Had McNally accepted the offer, Walter O'Malley surely would have let Messersmith have his no-trade clause. But McNally said no. "It wouldn't be right taking the money," he said.

The hearing was held on November 21, 1975, in front of arbitrator Peter Seitz, who begged Kuhn to negotiate with the players. Kuhn arrogantly refused to budge.

John Gaherin, the negotiator representing the owners, also pleaded for a compromise. Kuhn, who either wouldn't or couldn't take the hint, stood firm.

On December 23, 1975, Seitz made his decision. Messersmith and McNally were free to sign with any other team. There was nothing, he ruled, that said a contract could be renewed for more than one year. It was one of the most important decisions in the history of American sports.

The owners went to court to try to overturn the ruling but lost. The owners made the players an insulting offer of free agency after nine years, which the players easily rejected. The owners then tried to stall, appealing to an appellate court. When they lost, the owners dug in their heels, locking out the players, but the ploy lasted only seventeen days before Walter O'Malley ordered Commissioner Kuhn to reopen the camps.

In the end the owners capitulated. They agreed that any player could be a free agent after six years, and after five years of service a player could demand a trade. A player could choose six teams he wouldn't go to. If the club failed to trade him, he'd become a free agent. At the end of the 1976 season there would be a reentry draft. Each team could sign two free agents, or if a team lost players, it could sign as many players as it lost. Each team could draft as many players as it wanted so long as the player had not been drafted by twelve other teams.

The Yankees selected nine players, in the following order: Bobby Grich, Don Baylor, Don Gullett, Gary Matthews, Wayne Garland, Reggie Jackson, Berto Campaneris, Dave Cash, and Billy Smith. George announced, "Grich, Gullett, Baylor, and Jackson are the players we're most interested in."

On November 17, 1976, the Yankees signed pitcher Don Gullett, who had starred for the Cincinnati Reds. George had promised Billy Martin another arm and a big bat. Gullett surely would be the arm.

As for the big bat, Gabe Paul most wanted to sign Grich, Baltimore's star second baseman. Don Baylor was Gabe's second pick. Billy wanted to sign Joe Rudi, like Grich a right-handed bat and a player Billy felt would provide solid defense in left field. But Rudi was thirty-one and slow afoot, and Gabe thought the Yankees should get someone younger.

George would have gone along with signing Grich or Baylor, but both signed with California. Rudi also signed with California, and George was beginning to panic. The legend is that George wanted Reggie Jackson first and foremost because he was a guy who would put asses in the seats, but history doesn't back up the legend. Once Grich, Baylor, and Rudi signed, there was one impact player left: Reggie Jackson. If George didn't act fast, he was going to be left without improving the offense. What would the fans think?

Gabe Paul was against it, because he knew sticking the egotistical Jackson in the middle of a team that had won the pennant would result in bad chemistry. Moreover, giving Reggie $3 million meant that the veteran Yankees would feel underpaid and underappreciated. Paul was a hard-ass, but he was sensitive to the moods of his players.

George didn't care. Since he rarely cared about anyone's feelings, why should the players be any different? Billy, left out of the decision-making process, was furious when he learned of George's plans. "As the manager, don't I have anything to say about it?" he asked.

No, he didn't. As an opposing manager, Billy saw the way Reggie put himself ahead of the team wherever he went, taking to the press like they were old buddies, sucking up to the media to make himself the story. Billy, who was nasty to many of the writers covering his teams, could not fathom why Reggie—or anyone else—would be cooperative with the writers covering him. Several times in games

Billy had his pitchers throw at Reggie deliberately, in part because he thought Reggie was gutless but also because he disliked Reggie enough to want to hurt him.

But George understood Reggie's value to the Yankees. More than any of the other free agents, Reggie Jackson would help fill Yankee Stadium. Reggie was a Bill Veeck kind of player. He was a player who hit long home runs, created controversy, and provided headlines and drama on and off the field.

George was determined to get Reggie at any price. This was the one aspect of George Steinbrenner's character that set him apart from every other owner. Most owners kept their eye on the bottom line. Rarely did those teams win, but they were profitable. George didn't care about the bottom line. All he cared about was winning, and if getting Reggie Jackson improved his chances of winning, then damn the torpedoes—full speed ahead.

Yankees fans may have disdained George as a bigmouthed stranger from Cleveland when he first took over the team, but when they saw his willingness to spend big bucks on exciting, expensive free agents like Catfish Hunter, Don Gullett, and Reggie Jackson, the hard-bitten Yankees fans became rabid George Steinbrenner fans.

The arrival of Reggie Jackson in New York on the same team as George Steinbrenner and Billy Martin ensured that the New York Yankees would become the most dysfunctional baseball team of all time. When Sparky Lyle wrote his diary of the 1978 season, the book's editor, Larry Freundlich, had a brainstorm. He suggested calling it *The Bronx Zoo*, and never was there a more apt title for a sports book. Yankee baseball, which for too many years had been decried as staid and boring suddenly was turned into such a daily soap opera that Lyle's book could have been called *As the Clubhouse Turns*, the title that got edged out at the last minute by Freundlich's inspiration. Sparky had wanted to call it *From Cy Young to Sayonara*, apt for him but not far-reaching enough. *The Bronx Zoo* said it all.

The best baseball teams usually are the ones with players who are talented and who mesh as a team, both on the field and off. In baseball history there have been very few exceptions. There have been feuds between teammates—it was said that Babe Ruth and Lou Gehrig didn't talk to each other for five years during the middle of their reign with the Yankees, but it wasn't reported and only their teammates knew about it.

Sometimes a key player doesn't get along with a manager—Miller Huggins and Babe Ruth did not get along. And sometimes a star player doesn't get along with a teammate—witness Carl Yastrzemski and Tony Conigliaro on the Red Sox of the 1970s. But never before had there been a daily drama that involved constant feuding, fussing, and fighting among the owner, the manager, and a star player.

In sports history there have never been two years of craziness such as there were with the New York Yankees in 1977 and the first half of 1978, when Billy Martin self-destructed, saying of Reggie Jackson and George Steinbrenner, "They were meant for each other. One's a born liar, and the other's convicted."

That year and a half was also a living hell for Jackson, as Billy did all he could to make the big slugger become just one of the guys. Billy deeply resented Jackson's favorite-son status, and time after time he tried to knock him down a peg or two. Billy said it was for the good of the team, and it may have been, but the effect on Jackson was devastating. It's remarkable that Jackson survived the year and half playing under Billy.

Not long after the Yankees signed Jackson, George made Billy crazy by bragging in the papers about how he had romanced Reggie like a woman, inviting him to the 21 Club, offering him a big enough bonus that Jackson was able to buy himself a Rolls-Royce Corniche, and telling the world how close he and Jackson had become. When Billy read about it in the papers, he couldn't contain his rage.

I'm the manager, Billy told himself, *and George has never even taken me to lunch.* Nor would he ever. Like other owners before him, George was more than a little afraid of Billy and never once thought of him as anything but a thug.

From the first day of spring training Reggie would stand by his locker surrounded by newspaper reporters. Reggie loved the attention and enjoyed being quoted as much as George did. Billy, however, was repulsed. "He was out to let everybody know he was going to be the leader, that the other guys better move over because Reggie was here."

Shortly after the start of spring training, Billy called Reggie into his office. The gist of the conversation was that a "real leader" does his leading in the field, not in the clubhouse. And he specifically told

Reggie he hoped there wouldn't be any friction between him and Thurman Munson, who according to Billy was getting bad vibes from Reggie telling the reporters what a big man he was going to be on the Yankees.

Considering the cast of characters, the spring went rather smoothly. Reggie did everything Billy asked him to do, and if there was friction, Reggie would sit with Billy and they would talk it out.

Gabe Paul had been afraid that Reggie's mega-salary would inflame his regulars, and that in fact was the case. George had promised Thurman Munson he would have the highest salary on the Yankees, and as far as straight salary was concerned, he was making more than Reggie. But when Thurman found out George was giving Reggie several hundred thousand dollars in deferred payments, he blew his stack. He felt that Steinbrenner had lied to him. Graig Nettles also complained about his contract, as did Mickey Rivers and Dock Ellis. The outspoken Dock got into it with George in the press, and by the end of April he was gone.

The greatest stress on Billy during spring training came over the fact that he didn't care whether the Yankees won the exhibition games or not, and George wanted to win every one. They argued constantly. Billy told him he was so wrong it was "ridiculous." George would say, "Gotta have that momentum, that drive going into the season." Billy's response: "George, forget about that."

Billy, who felt he knew best, refused to give in to George's wishes and threats. "The man was driving me crazy," he said. "He wanted me to do all these things, and I knew they were wrong, and yet he was the owner of the team. It was a very uncomfortable spot to be in, but I felt that the team came before anything or anyone, including him, and I was going to do what was right, no matter what."

But if George's basic philosophies drove Billy crazy, his micromanaging was making him furious. If a player made a mistake during a spring training game, George would call Billy on the phone during the game and say, "You get him into your office and fine the son of a bitch."

"Sure," Billy would say, then he'd hang up and ignore the directive.

Said Billy, "I would never call the player in and humiliate him like he wanted me to do. George didn't care who the guy was, whether it was Munson or Nettles or a minor league kid. If you do that, you end

up losing your players. They're not going to bust their butt for someone who's fining them all the time. You want players to be relaxed and
respect you and give you their best. What good is fining them?"

But George's worst trait was the constant second-guessing. If a
player made a mistake, George would throw up his hands and make
a face, actions that were caught by the TV cameras. When he started
sending notes down to Billy in the middle of the game, telling him
whom to play or what to do, that's when Billy lost it. Asked Billy,
"Why the hell had George hired me? What did he need a manager
for? If he was so smart, why wasn't he managing the team himself?"
These were questions Billy would ask himself constantly.

One time George sent assistant general manager Cedric Tallis down
to the dugout during a game with one of his notes filled with statistics.
Billy told Tallis, "No more notes. Don't come down here anymore."

Said Tallis, who was cowed by Steinbrenner, "I gotta, he's going
crazy up there."

Said Billy, "Let him go crazy." Cedric would leave, and Billy would
take George's statistics and dump them right into the wastebasket.

There was one other issue between Billy and George. In 1976, before
Reggie's arrival, Chris Chambliss, a batter who made excellent contact,
who struck out rarely, had hit fourth in the batting order, and he had
helped lead the Yankees to a pennant. With Reggie on the team, George
wanted his new slugger batting fourth, not the reticent Chambliss.

Said Billy, "I had no dislike for Reggie Jackson. It wasn't anything
personal at all, and if George would have kept his nose out of it, everything would have worked out just fine. It's just that Reggie had it in
his head that he was more important than the ball club, and I felt the
other way."

If Billy wanted Reggie batting fifth, he'd bat fifth. If Billy wanted
Reggie to DH, he'd DH. Neither Reggie nor George was going to
dictate to him how he should play one of his players.

The second-guessing wasn't limited to the offense. If Billy took out
a pitcher or left a pitcher in and George thought he should have done
the opposite, he'd call the dugout.

Said Billy, "What had he ever won? What had he ever done, except to
sit up in the stands and second-guess? I don't want to be listening to a guy
who's a born second-guesser, somebody who doesn't know much about
the game, somebody who knows just enough to make himself dangerous.

You know, it's much easier to second-guess. The world is full of second-guessers. How would he like it if I was making judgments on every single thing he was doing?"

March hadn't ended when Billy and George had an ugly blowup over whether Billy should take the bus with the players to the spring training games. Billy wanted to ride with his coaches in his car so they could talk strategy away from the ears of their players. George wanted him on the bus. During a phone conversation, Billy promised George he would take the bus, and as the conversation dragged on, the bus left without Billy because under Billy's rules the bus was to leave on time no matter who wasn't on it, and he had no choice but to drive himself. The game was against the Mets, and after the Yankees lost and George found out Billy had driven his own car, he came storming into the dugout with Gabe and in front of his players accused Billy of lying to him. Billy didn't have the chance to tell George he had missed the bus because he was talking on the phone with him and the bus had left him.

"I don't know what to do," George bellowed. "I'm fed up with all of this."

Billy said, "I'm the manager of the team, and don't you be coming into my clubhouse again for any reason, coming and telling me what I should or shouldn't do and calling me a liar. You get your ass out right now. If you want to fire me, go ahead and fire me right goddamned now." Billy took his fist and slammed it into an ice bucket, sending ice into George's clothes and hair.

After George and Gabe left, Billy was sure he was gone.

By the next morning George had calmed down, surely with Gabe's coaxing. According to Billy, George apologized, and Billy promised to take the bus with the players. Said Billy, "We left on friendly terms. If he would only think before blowing up and acting like a little kid, it would be easier on everyone. He's like a little kid who keeps kicking on the door until he gets his way."

The rest of spring training went rather smoothly for Billy, until Reggie did something to really piss him off. Reggie had come to him and asked him if he could play a lot of innings so he could play himself into shape, and Billy obliged him. Then in the papers Reggie complained that Billy was playing him so much. It made Billy wonder about Reggie. What motivates the guy, what moves him? Billy wondered. Billy saw there were two Reggies: the good Reggie and the bad Reggie.

"Every once in a while the other Reggie would come out," said Billy, "and that's when there'd be trouble."

May was relatively peaceful until the last week, when Reggie's interview in *SPORT* magazine hit the streets. During spring training, he had foolishly opened up his heart and revealed his insecurities and jealousies in a wide-ranging interview with journalist Robert Ward. Reggie had come to camp overweight, his elbow was killing him, and he was expected to step into the lineup and be the catalyst to a world championship. That's a lot of pressure for anyone, and Reggie was suffering from doubt and apprehension. He finished a long monologue by saying, "The way the Yankees were humiliated by the Reds, you think that doesn't bother Billy Martin? He's no fool. He's smart. Very smart. And he's a winner. Munson's tough, too. He is a winner, but there is just nobody who can do for a club what I can do. That's just the way it is. Munson thinks he can be the straw that stirs the drink, but he can only stir it bad."

If Reggie had wanted to alienate Billy and his cadre of fiercely loyal players, including Graig Nettles, Sparky Lyle, Chris Chambliss, Lou Piniella, Mickey Rivers, and of course, Munson, he could not have chosen a better way. Munson, who had his own insecurities, couldn't figure out for the life of him why Jackson was attacking him, and he never forgave him for doing so. Neither did most of his teammates. Soon after the article came out, Reggie hit a home run, and when he crossed home plate, he refused to shake his teammates' hands. Making things worse, Reggie would sit in front of his locker and count the money in his wallet, a stack of hundred-dollar bills, even while he was being interviewed or while he was talking to teammates. He would do this all year long.

As a result, Jackson had no friends and only two allies, backup catcher Fran Healy and the guy who signed him—George Steinbrenner.

The most memorable blowup between Reggie Jackson and Billy Martin came during a three-game series in Boston in mid-June. After the Yankees lost badly in a Friday night game, on Saturday Jim Rice of the Red Sox hit a ground ball to right field, and Reggie, who wasn't the smoothest of fielders, tentatively moved toward the ball. Intending to show Reggie up, Billy sent Paul Blair out to replace him in mid-inning. Reggie clearly was surprised to see Blair, who had the distasteful task of telling Reggie he was out of the game. Even as Reggie trotted into the dugout, he had no idea why he had been taken out.

Eventually, Reggie understood, and when he did, he was livid. He said to Billy, "Don't you dare ever show me up again, you motherfucker." For Billy, "motherfucker" was the magic word that set his blood to boiling.

Billy charged through a group of players and coaches with the intent to hit Reggie upside the head. The scene was caught on national television. Billy was able to blow past Ellie Howard, but he couldn't navigate past Yogi Berra, who had grabbed him by the crotch and wouldn't let go. Billy swears he would have beat the hell out of Reggie. Reggie, who had seventy pounds on Billy and was eighteen years younger, swears he would have been the victor. Meanwhile, back in Cleveland, George Steinbrenner was watching the game on TV, and when he saw Billy go after Reggie, his first impulse was to fire him. With Billy, George's biggest problem was the fans, who loved his manager's tenacious style and personality. When Billy Martin was managing the Yankees, they were clearly Billy's Yankees, and George was keenly aware that firing him was a very risky proposition. Billy would have to do something a lot more outrageous than try to punch one of his players in the dugout during a game to get fired.

Gabe Paul met with Billy and Reggie the next day. As far as Billy was concerned, when the meeting was over, the incident was over.

Not for George, however. When George talked to Billy, Billy said he was merely doing what he often did, punish a player for not hustling. But George sided with Reggie, and he used the incident to push his favorite position: "Billy, I want you to use my statistics more." Then George told him, "As far as I'm concerned, you're gone, but I'll leave it up to Gabe."

Billy said, "You're the boss. You own the ball club. If you want to fire me, I'm not going to argue with you, but I would appreciate it if you would pay my salary because I need the money to support my family." George said he would.

When Billy left the meeting, he didn't know whether he'd be fired or not. Ironically, it was Reggie Jackson who may have saved Billy's job. Reggie knew he would be blamed for the firing by the fans, and he pleaded with George not to do it. Billy also remained because of

Gabe Paul's level head. Firing Billy in the middle of the season, Gabe knew, would only make the situation worse.

But for the rest of his days as Yankees manager—and Billy was Yankees manager five times—every day the axe hung over his head. Anytime he made the slightest controversial move, there would be headlines in the *Daily News* and the *Post* and stories speculating whether Billy's days as manager were coming to an end. Since most of the reporters hated Billy's guts, this was payback for them, who were looking forward to the day when he'd be gone. It was pressure no man, never mind a demon-plagued alcoholic like Billy, could possibly endure.

By July, the Yankees were back in first place. Nevertheless, George continued to second-guess Billy every day, because that's what George did. Because he knows best, the narcissist never rests. Any day Billy rested Lou Piniella, Billy heard about it. Anytime Billy played Carlos Lee, whom George hated, he heard about it. Making things harder for him, Billy knew, was that the disgruntled players—and there were always disgruntled players on a ball club—would go to George to complain, and instead of kicking them out of his office, George would sit and listen and backbite Billy.

One time in Chicago, George called Billy in the dugout during a game. Billy, pretending he didn't know who it was, shouted, "Don't be calling me during the game, you asshole." And he hung up.

As the season wore on, Billy became angrier and angrier. According to Billy, the players, including Reggie, pleaded with George to leave him alone, but George wouldn't. And because a player knew he could go directly to George with his complaints, Billy was losing control over some team members.

All the while, the press was having a field day. Reporters couldn't afford to go to sleep for fear of missing a scoop. It was player against player, player against manager, manager against owner, and every day the headlines mirrored the craziness of the Yankees clubhouse.

At this point, Billy was so paranoid, he was convinced George was listening in on his phone conversations in order to build a case to get him fired. George denied this vehemently, even threatened to sue Billy after his autobiography, *Number 1*, was published, but Billy was sure it was so. According to Billy, one of the secretaries told him, "Watch out for George. He's keeping a file on you, every word you say, everything you do." Billy may have been paranoid, but he knew very well whom he was dealing with.

In July, the Yankees slipped out of first place, and George's drum-beat of criticisms intensified. When team captain Thurman Munson complained in the papers about George's interference, George called Billy and ordered him to call a press conference to say that he wasn't interfering at all. Billy, fearing dismissal, did it, but everyone under-stood he didn't mean it.

It wasn't too long after that when Billy happened upon Munson and Lou Piniella huddling with George in George's hotel room. Billy thought the three were ganging up on him, until the players explained that they were there to try to get George to leave him alone. They said they told George, "If a manager is worried about whether or not he's going to get fired, he's not going to be able to do his job." They pleaded with him to take out the behavior clauses in Billy's con-tract and let him manage unfettered. George promised the players he would. The promise was an empty one.

In his hotel room there was a blackboard, and on the board was the lineup of the Boston Red Sox next to the lineup of the Yankees. George had been trying to compare the two.

"What's wrong with the team?" George asked Billy.

"You, George," was Billy's answer. "You're what's wrong with the team. You're meddling all the time; you're creating problems leak-ing out stories in the newspapers. When you get mad at a player, you call the newspapers and leak out a story on him. You're the problem."

George was constitutionally unable to just take out his clauses and leave Billy alone. He felt a need to squeeze one little concession from him. If Billy would use George's lineup—the one with Reggie batting fourth—just once, he'd take out the clauses. And Billy used George's lineup just once, and then he went back to what he was doing.

Not ten days later after the meeting at which he promised not to interfere with Billy, George was on the phone asking around to see whether Walter Alston would make a good manager for the Yankees. And George made sure the press knew about the phone call. Then he asked Coach Dick Howser if he would take over for Billy. Howser, a loyal soldier, said no. Then the rumors surfaced that George had talked to Dick Williams about becoming the manager.

All of these rumors were just making the fans furious with George. The negativity became so obvious that George called a press conference to defend himself against the charges that he was interfering and treating Billy badly. Again he said it would be up to Gabe Paul whether Billy was fired or not. No one believed him. Though George had promised Billy he would take out the behavior clauses, at the press conference he threw up seven rules Billy would have to follow if he wanted to stay the manager, the rules Gabe had written out when Billy was signed. Among them: Does he work hard enough? Is he emotionally equipped to lead the men under him? Is he organized? Is he prepared? Does he understand human nature? Is he honorable? To those George added, Does he win?

Said Billy, "At this point in the season we were only about three games out. What was so terrible about that? I dare anyone in the world to work under those conditions. Here was a felon [referring to George's Watergate conviction] setting himself up as judge and jury to decide whether I was good enough, moral enough, and a good enough student of human nature to manage his team."

Looking at Billy's situation objectively, it was absurd. Billy was working for an egotist who needed psychiatric counseling surely as badly as his alcoholic manager did. But since George was wealthy and owned the team, everyone just pretended he wasn't the ego-driven sadist that he was.

In late July, Thurman Munson was the one who took a stand. Thurman had hit his hundredth home run, and George sent champagne. Billy handed him a beer. Thurman drank the beer. Thurman then grew a beard in direct defiance of George's "no facial hair" edict. When Thurman made it clear he wasn't going to shave it off, George countered by telling reporters he was holding Billy responsible for Thurman's beard. At the same time rumors were afloat that George was talking to Frank Robinson about managing the Yankees. Billy's nerves were frayed. Thurman finally shaved when he saw the toll it was taking on Billy.

Perhaps Thurman's protest had an effect, because the next day, unexpectedly, George agreed to give Billy a two-year extension of his contract. George said, "Billy, you're doing a great job, and I'm going to give you a nice raise." The contract was blank. Billy told George to fill in the numbers. George gave him a hike from $72,000 to $90,000 a year. Immediately, there was détente, even a love fest. Billy was so grateful that George had finally showed him some respect that he agreed to bat Reggie fourth every day and play Lou Piniella regularly in right field. Billy in turn asked George to hire his old pitching coach, Art Fowler, whom Gabe had refused to allow to come to the team in the spring. George said yes. And from the day Art Fowler arrived on board, the Yankees won forty of their next fifty games. Ron Guidry, Mike Torrez, and Don Gullett were the mainstays of the pitching staff. Meanwhile, the Red Sox folded.

George's two star acquisitions won the pennant clincher for the Yankees: Don Gullett pitched a shutout and Reggie had a grand slam home run.

After the season, Billy made it clear that the biggest obstacle to winning the pennant had not been the Red Sox but the Yankees' owner. He saw what happened when George was feeling he wasn't getting enough credit for the success of the Yankees: George would try to sabotage him.

Said Billy, "We had won against all odds. George had done everything he could to keep us from winning, but he had failed. During the stretch run he wasn't completely silent. Every chance he got he was telling people how he had won it for New York, and he downplayed the role Gabe and I played whenever he could."

George was asked by a reporter whether Billy would be fired after the playoffs and the World Series. Ordinarily it would be a ludicrous question. And any other owner would have dismissed the question out of hand. George's answer: "We'll have to wait and see."

Billy thought, *In two years, we've come in first two times. How much better could I possibly do? What does the man want from me?*

Indeed.

The playoff against the George Brett–led Kansas City Royals went the full five games, and in game five against lefty ace Paul Splittorff, Billy put his job on the line and benched lefty Reggie Jackson, who rarely hit Splittorff. (It should be noted that Reggie Jackson, despite the distractions and the discord, managed to finish the regular season hitting .286 with 32 home runs and 110 RBIs.)

Billy replaced him with the right-handed Paul Blair, who had had a long, distinguished career with the Baltimore Orioles and was a premier defensive outfielder but wasn't in Reggie's league as a hitter.

Jackson's jaded reaction: "This was simply get-even day for Martin with Jackson, and fuck the consequences."

When Martin told Steinbrenner what he intended to do, George made it clear that if the Yankees lost the game, Billy would be fired.

Kansas City led by the score of 3–1 in the eighth inning. With runners on, and a righty reliever in the game, Billy sent Reggie up to pinch-hit. Jackson came through, singling in the Yankees' second run. Reggie derisively labeled himself Mr. Pinch Hitter. In the ninth, the Royals relieved with Dennis Leonard, their twenty-game winner.

Paul Blair blooped a single to center. Light-hitting shortstop Bucky Dent was the batter, and Billy sent Roy White to pinch-hit for him. Royals manager Whitey Herzog countered with lefty pitcher Larry Gura, a pitcher whom Billy denigrated because he threw so softly.

White walked, moving Blair to second, and then Mickey Rivers singled sharply over second to put the Yankees ahead.

Yankees closer Sparky Lyle, who would win the American League Cy Young Award after appearing in seventy-two games, winning thirteen and saving twenty-six others, shut down the A's in the ninth, and the Yankees were American League champions for the second year in a row. Reggie, who hit two for sixteen in the playoffs, was relieved he would have a chance to redeem himself in the World Series. After the game, Billy opened a bottle of champagne and poured it over George Steinbrenner's head.

"That's for trying to fire me," said Billy, still trying to ingratiate himself with a man who refused to be ingratiated.

"What do you mean try?" said George. "If I want to fire you, I'll fire you."

The 1977 World Series, one the Yankees were to win, went six games. Before the final game, Gabe Paul called Billy into his office and told him George was giving him a big bonus, including a Lincoln Continental, and he was going to pay the rent for his apartment. He also told Billy he'd be back for sure in 1978.

Billy should have been pleased, but anger overcame any positive emotions. Thought Billy, *That was nice of him. I only won them two pennants in two tries.*

The sixth and final game of the 1977 World Series was one of the most memorable in Yankee and baseball history, thanks to Reggie

Jackson, who hit three long home runs on three consecutive pitches off three different pitchers, Burt Hooten, Elias Sosa, and Charlie Hough. The third home run went more than five hundred feet into the blackness of the empty seats in dead centerfield. Once, a long time before, Frank Howard had hit a ball there. Reggie became only the second player ever to accomplish that feat. When he ran back onto the field for the ninth, the raucous Yankee Stadium crowd paid him the highest compliment, stomping and yelling and throwing paper and anything else they could throw, all the while chanting, "Reg-gie, Reg-gie, Reggie." After Lou Gehrig's "luckiest man on the face of the earth" speech and Don Larsen's perfect game in the 1956 World Series, it was arguably the greatest day in Yankee Stadium history.

Billy sat in his office after winning it all at the end of a long, hard season. He thought about how George's treatment of him was affecting him. He commented, "It was tearing me up, making me sick, and it was a miracle I didn't have a stroke or a nervous breakdown. If I had been an older man or if I hadn't had a strong constitution, I might have had one, because of all the hassle and bullshit from him, petty bullshit, harassment. Not every once in a while. Constant harassment. Every day, whether or not he was in town, he'd call and cause problems. Somebody was on the field without a hat. Make him put his hat on. One player was wearing a red shirt under his uniform. Make him take it off and put a blue one on. A player was sitting on the railing talking to the fans. Billy, go down and get him away from there. He'd ask me why I wasn't on the field. I was talking to a player in the clubhouse. Oh. One day he sent two of his goons down to run my kid off the field. We got no insurance to cover it, they said. Petty shit, every day, every single day."

At the same time, Billy was happy for Gabe Paul and for George, "because George wanted it so bad." Thought Billy, *Now he can really have fun at the 21 Club. He'll go around and give rings out to his friends, and he'll be able to talk about this one as long as he lives.*

After the game, Reggie went into Billy's office, put his arm around him, and shared champagne. And irony of ironies, *SPORT* magazine, the cause of most of Reggie's problems all season long, gave Reggie its MVP award for the series. He had gone nine for twenty with five home runs and eight RBIs. And earned a new nickname: Mr. October.

So in the end George Steinbrenner was proven right to take Jackson over either Joe Rudi or Bobby Grich. George wanted the guy who would put asses in the seats, and by doing so, Reggie turned the Yankees into the premier attraction in all of sports. The by-product was emotional trauma suffered by everyone else on the team who had to watch the painful psychodrama, but as far as the rejuvenated fans were concerned, with that one move, George Steinbrenner looked like a genius.

After the Yankees won the pennant in 1977, Gabe Paul paid for a pair of tickets for the World Series for his brother, but George took into his possession all the tickets designated for the Yankees front office, including Gabe's. When Gabe, and a lot of other Yankees executives, called George to ask for their tickets, George stonewalled. He wanted them for his powerful friends. Gabe had so much difficulty getting George to give up the tickets that he was in tears. He finally got them, and his brother went to the games, but it was a deciding factor when in the winter after the 1977 season Gabe Paul decided to leave the Yankees and return to Cleveland to help his friend Steve O'Neill run the Indians.

Pearl Davis, one of the very few African American employees working for the Yankees, recalled what Gabe had gone through working for Steinbrenner. She had been there since 1968, working first under Howard Berk, who was vice president in the charge of special projects during the CBS era. She had come to work for Gabe when Berk left soon after Steinbrenner bought the team. She and Gabe were very close, and she witnessed firsthand how Steinbrenner operated, and especially how he treated Gabe Paul.

Steinbrenner took an instant dislike to the independent and proud Davis, who was a valued and adored employee, and his ill will grew after she tried to organize a union of the secretaries, whom she felt needed protection from George. "In *The Bronx Zoo* you wrote about the secretary who was fired because she didn't bring Steinbrenner a tuna fish sandwich fast enough," Davis said. "Her name was Rae Shmerler. What happened, he ordered a tuna fish sandwich on whole wheat, and she did order it, and it was brought up to her office, but that office was so hectic, with ticket requests and all, and it was on her desk, but she forgot to bring it to him, and he fired her.

"'Get the hell out of here,' he screamed. That was it.

"Steinbrenner had so many people who came out of there crying. One sued him because he wanted to go to bed with her. She wasn't going to stand for it. She sued him, and she won ten thousand dollars out of court. They hushed that one up."

Billy Martin and Pearl Davis were witnesses to the shabby way Steinbrenner treated Gabe Paul. After the Billy-Reggie almost fight in the Boston dugout in 1977, Gabe had used his influence with Steinbrenner to make sure Billy would stay. George, who resented that he badly needed Gabe, then did something so despicable that Gabe quit. Behind Gabe's back he told anyone who would listen that Gabe was just a figurehead, that he—George—was the one who'd really made the decision about Billy. When Gabe heard that, he packed his bags and quit.

Said Billy Martin, "George was always telling me, 'I gotta get rid of Gabe. Gotta get rid of him.' George told me Gabe was getting senile.

"All Gabe was trying to do was help George. Gabe was the one who had made those great trades that allowed the Yankees to win pennants and make money for George, but George was so jealous of Gabe, just the way he was jealous of me. He didn't want anyone else getting the credit. Gabe, however, would never knock George behind his back. Gabe would say, 'But this is the way George wants it, Billy. You have to do what George wants.' Gabe came back after George flew to see him and pleaded with him to come back. He told Gabe, 'I'll never do it again, Gabe, I promise.' He kept his promise about a day."

The same tactic George employed to punish his managers by threatening to fire their coaches, he used with Gabe, threatening to fire Pearl Davis. Fortunately for Pearl, Paul wouldn't allow that to happen.

Gabe, fearing George's retribution toward Davis once he left, pleaded with her to join him in Cleveland, but she had family obligations in New York she couldn't shirk. Gabe advised her to find another job, but like so many Yankees employees, she felt she was a true-blue Yankee, and she couldn't bring herself to leave a job she truly loved. But as Paul feared, once he left, Pearl Davis was at Steinbrenner's mercy. It wouldn't be a pretty ending.

Once Gabe Paul departed, Davis was assigned to work for Pat Kelly, the Yankee Stadium manager and George's hatchet, a man she despised and others feared. There had been a meeting of the staff.

Steinbrenner said, "We have to get rid of Pearl Davis." And within year she was out, the victim of a false accusation manufactured by Kelly.

Thought Davis, *How could this black girl form 148th Street and Seventh Avenue stand up to George Steinbrenner?*

With Gabe Paul no longer around to keep Steinbrenner from making snap, unwise personnel decisions, beginning in 1978 the Yankee ship was taken over by the Yankees' Captain Queeg, a blustery, irrational, ego-driven neurotic capable of shouting, "Off with his head" or, more often, "You're fired" or "You're through" at the drop of a fly ball.

With Gabe Paul no longer there to moderate the owner's excesses, Billy Martin and the players began the 1978 season at George Steinbrenner's mercy. George wasn't able to undo in one year all that Gabe and Billy had accomplished in 1977, but he came within a Bucky Dent home run of doing so. With Gabe no longer in the picture, the mano a mano between George Steinbrenner and Billy Martin became a battle to the death. Given who had the upper hand, the end result was not surprising. By summer Billy would be out, leaving George as the focus of the media and the fans.

With George steering the ship, from 1979 through 1995, a period of seventeen years, the Yankees ran aground, except for the one American League championship gained through the fluke of a strike-torn season. It would take a truly despicable act on George Steinbrenner's part to get him removed from the top spot on the Yankees, a two-year period when talented baseball men repaired the damage caused by the Boss and returned the Yankees to championship form. But until then, it would be seventeen long, agonizing years of the George Steinbrenner Freak Show.

17

Get Beattie out of here, he isn't ready. I want him
on a plane to Tacoma.

—George Steinbrenner

"One's a Born Liar ..."

The man George chose to replace Gabe Paul was another of his Cleveland Indian heroes, Al Rosen, once the Indians' star third baseman. Rosen was working in a casino in Las Vegas when George "rescued" him. Rosen had had some hard years before coming to the Yankees, involving a fraudulent real estate scam called the Hill Properties. Rosen had a big following in the Jewish community in Cleveland, and he sold stock in this land deal, which turned out to be a fraud. It wasn't Rosen's fault, but his standing in the community was hurt badly. He moved to Las Vegas at the behest of an old Cleveland buddy by the name of Mo Dalitz. Adding to Rosen's woes was the suicide of his first wife.

Like with Howard "Hopalong" Cassady, it was an opportunity for George to give one of his hero-buddies a job. The problem for Billy was that Rosen felt a strong loyalty to the man who hired him, and when George wanted to do the things that George wanted to do—make a really bad trade or micromanage—Al Rosen, unlike his predecessor Gabe Paul, who usually could talk George out of a bad move, would go along. The damage to the Yankees would be costly.

George continued his practice of buying talented free agents for large sums of money, but again, he didn't have Gabe Paul to advise him, warn him, and talk him out of making deals that would hurt the team. Despite the fact that Sparky Lyle, who was in the prime of his career at age thirty-three, had won the Cy Young Award the year before, officially designating him as the best pitcher in the American League in 1977, George paid free agent relief pitcher Rich "Goose" Gossage a six-year contract worth $2.75 million to leave Pittsburgh and come to the Yankees. He paid Cincinnati Reds relief specialist Rawley Eastwick a cool million, and he signed free agent Andy Messersmith, who was coming off a sore arm, for three years at $333,000 a year. The problem with George buying pitchers was that he was so impulsive he didn't believe in due diligence. Most prudent team executives have pitchers whom they wish to acquire get checked out first by their doctors. As a result of his not doing this, too often pitchers George bought for inflated salaries arrived in less than peak health.

When spring training began, Billy saw immediately that Eastwick had a bum arm and that Messersmith no longer possessed the velocity that had made him a solid starter with the Los Angeles Dodgers. Billy didn't make nice with George and Rosen when they asked him how the two new acquisitions were doing. Said Billy, "Just because you got these guys, don't compound your mistake by keeping them. Admit you made a mistake. Trade them."

George also signed players because of his belief that two good first basemen were twice as good as one, though rarely did it work out that way. When George signed left-handed first baseman Jim Spencer, he angered Billy because he already had an excellent first baseman in Chris Chambliss, and when spring began, Billy couldn't figure out for the life of him how Spencer was going to get any playing time.

When George traded Eastwick to the Philadelphia Phillies, in exchange he received outfielder Jay Johnstone, another left-handed bat. Billy saw no use for Johnstone except as a designated hitter. Steinbrenner was collecting DHs, and Billy would complain that the team was two or three players short because the players George was acquiring didn't measure up or had no place to play.

Billy was perplexed and outraged by Steinbrenner's player moves. "I never knew what George was going to do," he said.

According to Billy, George was going to trade Thurman Munson to the Pirates for slugger Dave Parker. Billy told him, "George, no way you can part with Munson." Billy was convinced George was getting rid of the players Billy liked. That wasn't as far-fetched as it sounds. Among Billy's favorites were utility infielder Mickey Kluttz, catcher Mike Heath, and Paul Blair. George traded all of them away. He was becoming the incarnation of Frank "Trader" Lane.

Said Billy, "His trades were driving me crazy, and I knew with Gabe gone, here was this unknowledgeable man making these deals, and I'd be the one who had to keep all these guys happy."

Billy, who couldn't keep his feelings to himself, made the mistake of referring to George's new acquisitions as "George's boys" to *New York Times* reporter Murray Chass. Once again, George threatened to fire him. He told Doug Newton, Billy's agent, "If Billy made those comments about me, he's gone. And if Chass wrote these comments out of context just to antagonize me, we're going to ban him from the clubhouse." Newton told George that Billy had made the comments in spring training, and they had been made in jest.

George ordered Billy to talk to Al Rosen about it, which was a large part of Billy's problem with George. Instead of confronting Billy, George often had a middleman work it out. When Rosen showed Billy the article, Billy became infuriated. He told Rosen he had made the statements four months earlier in spring training. Billy said, "Why don't you get your facts straight before making such a big deal over nothing?" He told Rosen to ask Chass.

Rosen told Billy that George had ordered him to give Billy a lecture. Billy's blood boiled over. He said, "Listen, pal, if you or George want to fire me, just do it, get it over with, let's not go into any of this Mickey Mouse stuff." The Yankees were getting ready to go on a road trip, and Billy told Rosen he was going to go and change out of his uniform to get ready for the trip. He said, "Let me know if I ought to take the bus or not." Then he walked out and slammed the door behind him.

Fifteen minutes later Billy called Rosen on the phone. He wanted to know whether he should be on the bus. Rosen told him to go. But Billy's stomach was churning. Two World Series appearances or not, Billy was on trial every day for his job.

Injuries complicated things. From his pitching staff, Catfish Hunter, Ron Guidry, and Ed Figueroa all were hurting, and so were Andy Messersmith and Don Gullett.

By mid-May, the Yankees trailed the Red Sox by two games. As Billy feared, George never left him alone, second-guessing his lineups, leaking information to reporters about him, making Billy look bad to his players, undercutting his manager's authority whenever he could. Several of the players were furious over their low-paying contracts compared to those of the group of free agent signees. Mickey Rivers was angry and stopped playing hard. Sparky Lyle was angry because he had been the Cy Young Award winner and was making $140,000 a year while Gossage had signed a contract for millions. Nobody knew it, but Sparky was writing a diary of the season. When the resulting book, *The Bronx Zoo*, appeared during spring training of 1979, it hit like a bomb going off. George didn't know it, but Sparky's reportorial skills were as sharp as his slider.

By mid-June, George was burning up the phones, calling players to complain about their performances. After a losing game against the red-hot Red Sox, George called young pitcher Ken Clay and told him he hadn't tried hard enough. Two days later rookie Jim Beattie started and was hit for five runs in only two innings. Watching from his seat near the dugout, George subjected Al Rosen and Cedric Tallis to a string of expletives directed at Beattie, Billy, and Fowler. He told Rosen, "Something has to be done. Martin and Fowler are messing up our pitching." By the fourth inning the score was 7–0 in Boston's favor. George barked at Rosen, "Get Beattie out of here, he isn't ready. I want him on a plane to Tacoma." Before the game was over Billy learned that George had sent his kid pitcher to the minors.

Said Billy, "He didn't even tell me, let me talk to the kid. I felt really bad. You don't do that to a young pitcher. It's the greatest way in the world to break a guy's morale. My job with the pitchers is to build their confidence. Pitchers get to a certain point, and you have to go with them to get them over that hump. But if you break them down and keep breaking them down, they're never going to get their confidence. The whole thing to managing is building up the ego, making a player feel he can do it. But you have to have patience, especially with a young kid.

"George gets mad, gets rid of him, sends him down. When he comes back up, do you think he'll give you his loyalty, give you his best?"

A couple of days later there was an article in the papers from a "reliable source" saying the Yankees were crumbling because of the manager. As far as Billy was concerned, the real problem was that what with injuries to key players, George was beginning to panic. Billy kept telling him, "Wait till Dent and Randolph and Rivers and Munson and Hunter all get healthy." But George wasn't listening. Instead, he wanted to fire the team trainer. Billy talked him out of it. George then switched his scapegoats. He decided to fire pitching coach Art Fowler instead, blaming Fowler for the injuries. Billy told him if he did that, he would have to get rid of him as well.

Rosen told Billy he would get Art a job in the minor leagues. Billy, aware that George had sent Rosen to do his dirty work, told him no under any circumstances. George backed off—this time. According to Billy, on the bus from the ballpark to the hotel Art Fowler cried "like a baby."

By mid-July, the pressure George was putting on Billy was becoming unbearable. George was spreading rumors in the papers, saying Billy was suffering from ill health, that he had offered him a chance to quit to save his health, that he had offered Billy a consultant's job so Billy could set up a camp for boys. When Billy read those stories he had to laugh, because as far as he was concerned, George really didn't give a shit about his health or his welfare.

Said Billy, "If he had been so concerned about me, you'd have thought all the time I was in my New Jersey apartment all by myself he would have just once called me up and invited me out to dinner. Not once did he call me. In all the years I worked for him. If he had been concerned about me, he would have been my friend, and I never saw that in him. If he was interested in my health, he would have quit second-guessing me, quit telling me how to manage."

On July 17, 1978, during a year in which Billy and Reggie Jackson were getting along just fine, Billy was told to give Reggie the message that George wanted to see him. Billy noted that Reggie was in a fine mood when he arrived at the park, but that after he returned from his meeting with George, he was scowling. When Reggie looked at Billy, anger radiated from his whole being. Jackson told third base coach Dick Howser, "Tell Martin I don't want to talk to him anymore, and tell him I don't want him giving me any more signs."

When Howser told Billy what Reggie had said, Billy couldn't figure out why Reggie was so angry. He asked George, and said George told him, "Somebody said that Jeff Burroughs's wife said that you had said something about Reggie, and it got back to Reggie." Billy had no idea what he was talking about.

What one couldn't imagine was why George would reveal such a thing to Reggie, especially considering the ramifications that night.

In the bottom of the tenth inning, with the score tied, the Yankees had Thurman Munson on first. Even though Reggie had specifically told him not to give him any more signs, Billy gave a sign for Reggie to bunt. Reggie fouled the ball back for a strike. Billy gave Howser the sign to swing away. Reggie bunted a second time, against orders. And then he bunted a third time, fouling the ball off for a strikeout. The Yankees ended up losing the game, and the détente between Reggie and Billy was over.

Billy very badly wanted to punch Reggie in the face, but he didn't. After the game, he was so angry he took his clock radio and threw it against the office wall. It smashed into pieces. Yogi Berra kept telling him, "Don't hit him. Don't do anything."

Billy got on the phone to Al Rosen and told him if he didn't fine and suspend Jackson, he was going to quit. He said, "Let him get away with that, and you might as well forget the ball club. Might as well make Reggie the manager."

Billy wanted Reggie suspended the rest of the year, but that wasn't about to happen. Billy was sure the Yankees were a better team without him. Rosen suggested a five-day suspension. Billy went along.

In the same game, Sparky Lyle, who was having a contract squabble with Steinbrenner, pitched the fourth and fifth innings, but after Billy asked him to go out for the sixth, Sparky told Billy he was done for the day, that he would not pitch any more. Because his job as closer had been taken over that season by Goose Gossage, and Sparky was now having to pitch in long relief, he was justly furious about his loss of status. Billy fully understood what Lyle was going through, and since he had enough time to warm up another pitcher, he cut him some slack and let him leave the game.

The next day Billy was accused of bigotry, because he had excused Sparky and hadn't excused Reggie. Said Billy, "If Reggie was green he was going to be suspended. Color had nothing to do with it."

The Yankees won all five games they played during Reggie's suspension, gaining on the Red Sox, who were starting to have injury problems of their own. With Reggie gone, Billy felt his job was a lot easier. "The carnival, the sideshow, was missing," he said. He would have been just as happy if Reggie had never come back.

The sideshow returned the day Reggie did. George called Billy on the phone and said, "You play that boy. He's been working out." When Coach Dick Howser asked Reggie if that was true, Reggie said he hadn't touched a ball or a bat. Billy, disobeying George's orders, didn't put him in the lineup in the game against the Chicago White Sox.

In front of a group of reporters, Reggie told them, "The magnitude of me, it's uncomfortable. I'm not the story. What have I done? Nothing. The magnitude of me is overemphasized." When asked if he would apologize to Martin, he said, "I dunno, perhaps yes because of the way they interpreted events. But I didn't feel I did anything wrong." Just seeing the crowd of reporters enraged Martin, and when he heard Jackson say he hadn't done anything wrong, well, if Billy had been carrying a gun, Reggie would have been a dead man.

After the game, which the Yankees won, Billy ran into Bill Veeck, the owner of the White Sox. During their conversation, Veeck told Billy that George had talked to him about trading Billy to the Sox for their manager, Bob Lemon.

"You're not kidding me, are you, Bill?" Billy asked.

"No Billy," Veeck said. "George wanted to trade you for Lemon."

This was the final indignity for Billy Martin. He could stand it no longer. Said Billy, "To think I had busted my tail to bring the Yankees to their former glory and fame, and here the owner behind my back was trying to make a trade to get rid of me! Here he was going around telling people how he's always looking out for Billy Martin! How could he tell everybody that when the truth was he was secretly trying to get rid of me?"

This was not a rhetorical question. You would think if a team owner hired a manager and that manager brought home two pennants and a world championship, you would leave him alone and let him do it again. But not George Steinbrenner. As far as the fans were concerned,

Billy Martin had become the man who returned the Yankees to glory, and as far as George was concerned, this wasn't acceptable. George had done it, not Billy. And to prove it, he would get another manager to take Billy's place, and he'd win anyway.

Billy advised Murray Chass of the *New York Times*, "When we get to the airport, I want to see you." When the Yankees arrived at O'Hare Airport in Chicago for their trip to Kansas City, Billy was in a foul mood. Reggie had told the reporters that Billy hadn't spoken to him in a year and a half, a blatant exaggeration. Thought Billy, *How could he have said that? Why did he say that?* He knew it wasn't true.

Billy was walking down the corridor of the airport with Chass and Henry Hecht of the *New York Post*. Running through his brain were the twin statements that he hadn't talked to Reggie in a year and a half and that George had considered trading him to Chicago for White Sox manager Bob Lemon.

During his conversation with Chass and Hecht, Billy said, "Shut up, Reggie Jackson. We don't need any of your shit. We've been winning without you, and we don't need you coming in and making all these comments. If he doesn't shut his mouth, he won't play, and I don't care what George says. He can replace me right now if he doesn't like it."

Martin left the reporters, and when he returned to the gate, he said to Chass, "Did you get all that stuff in the paper?" Then he unleashed his famous line: "The two of them deserve each other. One's a born liar, and the other's convicted." Billy liked the sound of the sentence, and he said to the two reporters, "It's on the record. Did you get it?" He wanted everyone to know how he was feeling.

He had to know he was committing job suicide—Hecht hated Billy's guts and would have gladly written the words to get him fired—but at this point Billy didn't care. Chass wrote that "only an irrational man would say what he was saying," but the truth was the opposite. Billy couldn't hold his feelings in any longer. He couldn't work under those conditions anymore.

Once the headlines came out in the papers the next day, Billy decided he wasn't going to give George the satisfaction of firing him. He was going to quit, but George made it clear that if Billy didn't lie and say he was quitting for health reasons, he wasn't going to pay him the rest of his salary. George was going to make sure Billy didn't blame his resignation on his constant interference. He knew how the fans would react if he did.

Billy held a press conference in the lobby of a Chicago hotel and resigned. At the end he broke down and cried. As he thanked the Yankee fans for their support, he was sobbing so badly he barely could get the last words out. Yankees broadcaster Phil Rizzuto put his arms around his old teammate, and the two exited the hotel.

It was at this point that Billy Martin should have been disgusted enough to walk away from George Steinbrenner forever. He needed to work for someone who respected his ability and gave him the authority to work his magic. He also needed to work for someone who didn't cause him to drink so heavily. When he was under the normal stress of the job, he drank, and with the Yankees he had to manage his players half the time and combat George the other half. George drove him crazy, and as his temperature rose and the anger within him took over, he drank and drank and drank, and that's when he became a walking bomb waiting to detonate. Alcoholism is a disease like cancer. It can be treated, but the victim has to be willing to go for treatment. If someone could have reached him, that person could have—should have—convinced Billy to go to the Betty Ford clinic and become sober. Short of that, that person alternatively should have made Billy see that working for George Steinbrenner was literally poison to his physical and mental health. But managing the Yankees was the one and only job Billy ever really wanted, and that yearning didn't end even after he resigned.

Not for the last time, George had "you're fired" remorse. As soon as Billy was let go, George immediately feared his former manager's being hired by a rival team and thus being in a position to beat his brains in. In fact, Billy learned from agent Doug Newton that several teams had called wanting to know if he would manage. To avoid that possibility, George Steinbrenner came up with an ingenious solution, one that combined practicality with a touch worthy of P. T. Barnum and his buddy Bill Veeck.

Billy was fired on a Tuesday, and Yankees Old-Timers' Day was coming up that Saturday. George had told Doug Newton that he wanted Billy to come back in 1979. "He'll take care of Lemon and bring you back in the spring," said Newton. Billy couldn't believe

George had made such an offer. Even to him, it sounded far-fetched. This was a rarity in sports history. Who fires somebody and hires him back a few days later? (Remember Trader Lane and Joe Gordon?)

"Do you think he's serious?" asked Billy.

"George is just crazy enough to be serious," said Newton.

Billy told Newton he didn't think he and Steinbrenner could ever work together, but decided it wouldn't hurt to hear what he had to say.

George told Billy, "I woke up, and I felt in my gut that it wasn't right not having you as manager of the Yankees." Billy said he felt the same way. George asked Billy if he'd come back in 1979. Billy said he would if things changed between them. Here's where George had Billy by the short hairs. Billy wanted very badly to be George's friend, and George used his considerable charm to let him know that if he came back to manage the Yankees, not only would he be manager, but this time they'd be buddies. It was what George knew he needed to say to get Billy to say yes, and Billy declared himself convinced.

George told Billy that one of his weaknesses was that he liked to have his nose in everything and one of Billy's weaknesses was that he wasn't as disciplined as George would have liked him to be. George cooed, "If we both could give a little, I don't think we'll have any problem at all."

Billy fell for it. George said if Billy agreed to come back, he wouldn't interfere as much, wouldn't run Billy down in the papers, and wouldn't make the player personnel decisions. In exchange, Billy promised to prepare reports on different players and to teach George the game of baseball as he knew it. Billy asked George if he'd teach him about the general manager side of the game. "Sure I will," said George, who also agreed to go to Billy directly with problems and not send intermediaries. When George asked Billy if he would work with him freely, Billy said he would.

"It sounded so terrific," said Billy.

It was supposed to. When Billy "quit," Yankees fans were ready to burn down the stadium. Billy Martin was by far the most popular Yankee since Mickey Mantle had retired in 1967, and with him thrown under the bus, the fans were ready to hang George from the center-field flagpole. George needed to rope Billy into his neck-saving solution, and Billy was a sucker for his come-on.

"It's Old-Timers' Day Saturday," said George, "and I'd like to make the announcement that you're coming back in 1979 then. The fans'll go wild, and it will be tremendous."

And it was, though it almost didn't happen, because a few days before the big day George in a conversation with Doug Newton accused Billy of leaking the story. So much for George's promise to call Billy directly if he had an issue with him. In response, Billy told George to forget the comeback. George tried to mollify Billy, telling him to "forget the leaking-out thing." Billy's appropriate response: "Tell George he can stick his job up his ass—again."

Another glitch arose. Yankees general manager Al Rosen said he'd resign if his close friend Bob Lemon wasn't given the opportunity to finish 1978 and complete 1979 as well. Billy would have to wait until 1980. Billy agreed.

Old-Timers' Day that Saturday at Yankee Stadium was festive and packed. In front of a full house, public address announcer Bob Sheppard read out the names of the former Yankees who had returned for the occasion. Among the players named last in order of greatest importance to the fans were Whitey Ford, Yogi Berra, Mickey Mantle, and Joe DiMaggio. But on this day once again DiMaggio was the second-to-last old-timer announced, because after the Yankee Clipper received his applause, Sheppard intoned, "The manager for 1980, and hopefully for many years to come, Number 1, Billy Martin." A shock wave went through the stadium. The fans cheered for what must have been a full ten minutes. Billy, wearing his pinstriped number 1, stood in the middle of the field and waved and waved. George Steinbrenner had converted what surely would have been one of his grossest errors, pushing this feisty Yankee great to quit as manager, into the year's greatest public relations coup.

With the resignation of Billy Martin, the Bronx Zoo went into hibernation. With the phlegmatic Bob Lemon at the controls, there were no more daily stories discussing whether the manager would be fired. In fact, the New York metropolitan newspapers went on strike on August 10. Without the gang of reporters pestering and second-guessing the manager and the players, it was one of the calmest periods of the Steinbrenner era. Under Bob Lemon, the Yankees finished the year 48–20 as the players got healthy, and under Lemon's steady hand, the team made up a fourteen-game deficit to the Boston Red Sox, finishing in a tie with the Sox at season's end. The playoff game is what everyone remembers about the 1978 season, but the more remarkable achievement was catching the Red Sox after being fourteen games back. The Giants had caught up to the Dodgers in 1951 from thirteen games back, and that has been remembered as well as the Bobby Thomson home run to win the pennant. What the Yankees did was just as remarkable. Ron Guidry completed a sterling 25–3 season with a 1.74 ERA. He won ten of his last eleven games. Catfish Hunter, after returning from the disabled list in July, went 10–3 down the stretch. Goose Gossage was lights out as Sparky Lyle stewed on the bench.

In the one-game playoff, Yankee shortstop Bucky Dent, the lightest-hitting player in the lineup, attained immortality when he hit a three-run home run off Mike Torrez, a Yankee the year before, in a 5–4 victory. Lemon allowed Dent to hit because Willie Randolph had hurt himself, and if Dent came out, he didn't have a replacement. Before Dent hit his historic home run, he had hit exactly five all season long. So much for statistics and tendencies. It's no wonder Boston fans spent the next twenty-five years in therapy complaining about Bucky Fucking Dent.

Goose Gossage got the final out, as Carl Yastrzemski popped out to third baseman Graig Nettles to end the game and give the Yankees the division title. They defeated Kansas City for the pennant and then ran through the Los Angeles Dodgers in six games to win their second World Series in a row.

Reggie Jackson hit .400 for the series with four home runs and fourteen RBIs, and he was again the star of the series. Commented Reggie, "I was a lousy bunter and a born liar, but I had ten Yankee home runs in two Yankee Octobers. And I had two more World Series rings, which made it five for all of you at home keeping score."

For an entire winter Billy Martin wondered whether the announcement about his rehiring had been a brilliant publicity stunt or whether it was for real. Reggie Jackson, when he heard the announcement that Billy was coming back, said, "I felt like I'd been hit with a Frazier left hook." Reggie's reaction was that he had been sold out by Steinbrenner for the sake of public relations. He wondered, *If George could hire him back, obviously they had kissed and made up. But what about me?*

Said Jackson, "For the first time, for the very first time, I understood that deep down Steinbrenner was a man with few principles, a man who would sell you out in a second, a man to whom real loyalty could never be very meaningful." That evening Reggie told his father he would never trust George Steinbrenner as long as he lived.

18

We don't need to apologize. We have nothing
to be ashamed of.

—Reggie Jackson

George in Charge

That World Series win in 1978 would be the last one the
New York Yankees would participate in for a period of
eighteen long years under owner George Steinbrenner's emotional,
egotistical, absurd, grandiose, self-destructive, and at times sadistic leadership. During this period, he would fire twenty managers,
including Billy Martin four more times, have a swinging door for
pitching coaches and players, be fined large sums for publicly criticizing umpires, and infuriate fans so badly that at games they would
chant, "Steinbrenner sucks." All the while George showed a willingness to spend millions on free agent ballplayers, a trait that might
have won him many more pennants had he allowed someone with
some knowledge of professional baseball make the personnel decisions. The problem was that George, who thought as a fan, wasn't
competent to serve as an evaluator of baseball talent. You measure the
skill of a player on his performance over months, if not years. George's
test too often rested on how he felt about a player on any given day.
It was this trait more than any other that would consign the George
Steinbrenner Yankees to also-ran status.

Following the series win, in spring 1979, Sparky Lyle, who was the odd man out in 1978 after George signed Goose Gossage, got even with Steinbrenner with the publication of his tell-all diary of the 1978 season, *The Bronx Zoo*. George thought he could keep his misdeeds and peccadilloes secret through an effective combination of bluster, power, and the massaging of the journalists covering the Yankees, but he couldn't anticipate how angry the prideful Lyle was over losing his closer's role to Gossage. Lyle exposed George in detail as the strange, bullying egomaniac that he was. *The Bronx Zoo* catapulted onto the *New York Times* best-seller list, reaching number two behind *The Scarsdale Diet*, and it remained there for twenty-nine weeks.

Former Yankees pitcher Jim Bouton, who was banned from attending Yankees functions because of his authorship of the groundbreaking book *Ball Four*, was working as a TV reporter at ABC-TV in New York City at the time. Ironically, it was Bouton to whom Steinbrenner turned for support as the *Bronx Zoo* maelstrom swirled around him. "After the publication of *The Bronx Zoo*, he was sweet as sugar with me," said Bouton. "I was in spring training trying to get interviews with the Yankees, and he invited me up to his penthouse suite. He made a lot of funny jokes about the book, and he came off terrific. He was a master.

"We went on the air, and the cameras started to roll, and he said, 'It wasn't a tuna fish sandwich that I fired a secretary for, it was peanut butter and jelly.' He said a lot of wise and funny things that made him look terrific.

"My feeling was, It's a good thing this guy owns the New York Yankees, because imagine if he was the secretary of Health, Education, and Welfare. As president of the Yankees, as opposed to president of the United States, he only blows the World Series, not start World War III."

The Bronx Zoo went on to sell 210,000 copies in hardcover. In the end, both Lyle and Steinbrenner got what they wished for: Lyle was traded to the Texas Rangers before the spring was out.

Readers of *The Bronx Zoo* were titillated by Lyle's revelations about Steinbrenner, and they laughed at Sparky's antics, sitting on birthday cakes nude and playing practical jokes on his teammates. But Lyle, like most baseball players who make it to the major leagues, knew a thing or two about the game, and among his discussions was a stinging criticism of the way Steinbrenner ran the team. For Lyle, George's signing Goose Gossage when he already had the Cy Young Award winner on his roster was wrong for a number of reasons. His analysis of how badly Steinbrenner's philosophy of acquiring stars from other teams would hurt the Yankees would turn out to be prophetic.

"George doesn't learn, and before long he ain't gonna be winning either," wrote Lyle. "Every year he gets rid of people who have helped him win the year before, and he gets somebody who's never been through a pennant race before, a guy who was never on a winner. And if he isn't careful, he's gonna have a whole club of these guys. He'd have gotten rid of all his winners, and he'll be left with a team of good ballplayers who have never been on winners. He'll have a hell of a second-place club. He'll end up having a club like Boston, a team that wins ninety-nine games but no bananas. I don't know whether Rosen knows talent, and I don't know whether Rosen will be able to argue with George and make George see when a trade he wants to make is a bad mistake, like Gabe did."

It turned out that Al Rosen had zero influence on Steinbrenner. The despotic reign of King George had begun. Without Gabe Paul to sit him down and quietly explain why what he wanted to do was not in the best interests of the Yankees, the club was at the mercy of his every whim. Some of those whims would cost the Yankees dearly, both on the field and off. When George made a move, he never took into account how that move affected those on his staff or on his team. Because he had fired Billy Martin in the middle of the 1978 season, replacing him with Bob Lemon, and then announced that Billy would be coming back in 1980, Bob Lemon would have to manage in 1979 with the specter of Billy looming behind him. Then in November 1978, Lemon's son Jerry was killed in a car accident, and when Lem reported for spring training in 1979 it was clear that he was only a shadow of himself.

Rosen was loyal to people—like Lemon, a former teammate whom he appreciated for his calm and decency—and it didn't take him long to resent Steinbrenner's bullying tactics and his penchant for disrupting people's lives. He also resented being forced to be Steinbrenner's hatchet man.

On May 23, 1979, Dick Tidrow, who had been an important part of the Yankees championship bullpen, had an ineffective outing. Every pitcher has them. But there was a reason Tidrow wasn't pitching well.

Goose Gossage had damaged ligaments in the thumb of his pitching hand after a brawl with teammate Cliff Johnson, and after surgery he missed the first three months of the season. Lem had to use Tidrow to close, and he was being overworked. As Tidrow, whom his teammates nicknamed "Dirt" for his scrappy nature, was walking off the mound, George from his box ordered Rosen to "get rid of Tidrow." Rosen, tired of arguing, called one of his many friends in baseball, Chicago Cubs general manager Bob Kennedy, and dutifully traded Tidrow to the Cubs for pitcher Ray Burris. Had Billy Martin been the manager, he might have stopped Rosen and George from trading Tidrow, but Billy wasn't there either, and the Yankees were the losers. Tidrow finished the 1979 season 11–5 with a 2.71 ERA for the Cubs, while Burris was 1–3 with a 6.11 ERA for the Yankees. When the deal went bad, Steinbrenner blamed Rosen.

Then on June 18, George, panicking because the Yankees weren't in first place, decided he needed his pepper-pot motivator back at the helm. George met Billy, who was scouting for the Yankees, in Columbus, Ohio, and he told him, "Billy, Lemon is doing a terrible job, just terrible. He has no control over the players, he's not doing anything, the poor guy can't do it."

Lemon gave Billy the choice of taking over right then and there instead of waiting until 1980, the original plan. Billy decided to take over right then and there, because he had no patience and he was afraid that if someone else took the team and succeeded, he might not get the offer again. Billy asked for the same money Earl Weaver was making in Baltimore, and after George fired Bob Lemon, he gave Billy a three-year contract worth $125,000 a year.

The move had consequences. Reggie Jackson's betrayal was complete, and Al Rosen was disgusted at the way his friend Lem had been treated.

Rosen then became the target of George's ire after Rosen routinely approved a change in the schedule to allow a game in Anaheim to begin at 5:30 rather than 7:10 so it could be televised nationally. George became outraged because Nolan Ryan was pitching for the Angels, and he felt the new time gave Ryan an advantage because the sun was in the batters' eyes. In a call to baseball commissioner Bowie Kuhn, Steinbrenner ripped into Rosen for agreeing to the change.

The day after the All-Star Game, Al Rosen resigned as general manager and returned to California. Later he told George, "I love you as a friend. I just can't work for you."

The 1979 season was jeopardized early on when Goose Gossage went down and Ron Guidry hurt his back and won only six games. The team's fate was sealed on September 1, when Thurman Munson crashed his plane and died as he was practicing touch-and-gos at a small airport in Canton, Ohio, his hometown.

For Billy Martin the season wasn't a complete loss, however, because of his improved relationship with George. Billy sounded like an abused child who was happy because his father didn't beat him as much as he had in the past.

"Instead of calling down in the middle of the game and being real mad, he would have somebody call down after the game and ask me to come up and talk with him. I'd go up, he'd ask if I'd like a beer or a drink, and we'd go over personnel together. I was amazed, because he was so pleasant to get along with. I couldn't believe it. And he was that way all through the season. He was just great."

Even Billy and Reggie got along in 1979. Said Billy, "I couldn't have asked for more. He played terrifically, and he played hurt, and a few times when I benched him he didn't complain, and he and I got along great. Reggie's a good person. He did everything I asked him to do. We really got to know each other, and we became friends [a slight exaggeration]."

After the season, Billy and George were planning for the next season. Billy wanted his pal Mickey Mantle to join him as a first base coach. George was evasive. Billy told George he was sure the Yankees would win the pennant in 1980.

That winter Billy Martin went hunting in Minnesota with his friend Howard Wong, a Minneapolis restaurateur. He was scheduled to fly that afternoon to Dallas to hang out with Mantle, but he got back late and missed the plane. Careers can turn on such missed planes. Billy's sure did. He went into the bar at his hotel and got into a loud argument with a man who claimed to be the Marshmallow King.

When the anger escalated, Billy bet him three hundred dollars to a penny the man couldn't lick him. The two men took two steps outside the bar, and Billy coldcocked him as flat as a marshmallow in a s'more.

When the *New York Post* screamed about the incident in a thirty-two-point headline, Steinbrenner, who didn't care whose fault it was only that Billy had been in another fight, fired Billy—again. To make his case stronger with Yankees fans, he publicly discredited Billy by telling commissioner Bowie Kuhn and reporters that Billy had drinking and financial problems. He also mentioned that Billy was a serial brawler. "It's his pattern of behavior," said George.

To keep Billy from managing elsewhere, George offered Billy the job of TV color commentator. But the job would require that Billy travel with the team from which he had just been fired, and he declined. Billy was then contacted by Charlie Finley to manage the Oakland A's, and he took the job. Though Finley was a difficult owner, for Billy, managing the A's would be a perfect fit, his dream job, even if he didn't recognize it.

George replaced Billy with Dick Howser, who in 1980 did a superb job using his personnel, platooning Bob Watson, Jim Spencer, Oscar Gamble, Lou Piniella, Bobby Murcer, and rookie Joe Lefebvre to effective use. Howser, who proved to be a steady leader, led the Yankees to 103 victories. But he was plagued by the same criticisms and second-guessing that George rained on all his managers.

Life in Yankeeland was relatively peaceful until August, when the team lost three of five games to the Orioles. Steinbrenner, panicking, blasted Howser and the players in the press. Among Howser's failures, according to George, was not sacrificing over a runner during a game, costing the Yankees a run and the game.

Howser, a proud man, was genuinely hurt and annoyed and angry. In an interview that he gave a short time later, he made a subtle dig at Steinbrenner. He said, "If I can't be manager of the year, maybe at least I can be rookie manager of the year. Hell, that would be something to win—especially in my first year."

Steinbrenner, who insisted on loyalty even if he himself didn't know the meaning of the word, saw Howser's words as a direct challenge, and worked to get revenge. First he made a number of roster moves without consulting Howser. When he brought Clyde King in as a pitching coach to work with Ron Guidry, Howser had no input in the decision. Steinbrenner ordered Guidry, who was struggling, sent to the bullpen. Again, Howser wasn't consulted. George delivered a first baseman's glove for Bobby Murcer to use, angering first baseman Jim Spencer. When a reporter asked Howser if Murcer could help the Yankees at first base, he just smiled wryly. Steinbrenner then put infielder Fred Stanley on the disabled list even though Stanley wasn't hurt and replaced him with Brian Doyle. Howser couldn't help but feel that Steinbrenner was doing everything he could to keep him from winning a pennant.

Howser's undoing came in the playoffs, which the Yankees lost to the Kansas City Royals. In the crucial game, Willie Randolph was thrown out at home plate on a perfect relay from Willie Wilson to George Brett to Darrell Porter, after Wilson overthrew the cutoff man. Steinbrenner, blaming third base coach Mike Ferraro, decreed Ferraro would never man the position again and that Don Zimmer would be the Yankees' new third base coach.

Howser was understandably furious. He told reporters he should have been consulted. The way Steinbrenner saw it, Howser again was challenging him. He said in rebuttal, "I'm very disappointed in him. My staff is in agreement with everything I have projected, and we're not quite ready to have Dick Howser start running the New York Yankees totally yet."

Howser and general manager Gene Michael were summoned for a meeting at George's offices in Tampa. According to the story spun by Steinbrenner, it was "agreed" that Howser would not return and that Michael would take his place. As part of the deal, Steinbrenner agreed to pay off Howser's mortgage on his new house in Tallahassee. The reaction from Yankees fans was fierce.

Then, as he did after he fired Billy the first time, Steinbrenner changed his mind. He called Michael to tell him so. Michael, who liked being the general manager, was delighted. But when Michael told Howser, the once-burned skipper told him, "I'd rather leave it this way. I don't want to go through it again. The last few weeks, my stomach has been upset, and I just haven't felt good. No, let's leave it as is." Howser was too sane a man to return.

When he saw that getting Howser back wasn't an option, the next day Steinbrenner announced that Howser was "resigning" because of a lucrative real estate deal (Steinbrenner paying off his mortgage). Steinbrenner told reporters the door had been opened for him to return, but he chose not to. (This was a true statement.) George then said that Howser wanted to be a Florida resident all year-round. (This was not a true statement.)

Eight months later, Howser accepted a job managing the Kansas City Royals, and four years after that, he led Kansas City to a World Series victory. In July 1986, it was discovered that Howser had a malignant brain tumor. On June 17, 1987, he died at age fifty-one.

In December 1980, Steinbrenner made headlines with another one of his free agent buys. He infuriated the other team owners, who were trying to keep costs down, when he gave San Diego outfielder Dave Winfield a ten-year, $16 million deal, which included a bonus clause that would inflate the contract to $23 million for the life of the contract. Old-time baseball fans like journalist Joe Flaherty, who had been a fan of the New York Giants before they broke his heart and moved to San Francisco, thought the sum obscene.

"I know of no business with the insanity of what's happening," said Flaherty. "This is wrecking the industry. Only these fools with their greed. These are businesspeople who spend the younger part of their lives as jock sniffers, and they don't care what they spend as long as they can end up on national television with their hair doused with champagne and twenty jocks rumpling their hair.

"New York is at an advantage. But why bring a right-handed power hitter and put him in the worst-hitting ballpark for a right-handed hitter? There's no logic at work. He came to the Yankees with a lot of talk that he didn't perform well in his last year at San Diego because he had a lot of pressure on him before he became a free agent. I believe he's a pitchable hitter. Maybe the pitchers had his number and it had nothing to do with pressure. Lou Piniella's numbers are better than Winfield's.

"Let's say George has 2.5 million attendance, and he gets five million from WPIX. He says, 'I can be exorbitant.' But where does it end? What do you pay Mike Schmidt at the end of next year? He's an MVP two times running. What do you think he could ask for?

"These owners don't know the holes they are digging. The reason the players beat them all the time is the owners do not trust Steinbrenner or Ted Turner, because they know they will break any lines they lay down for self-glorification. Finally, who gives a shit? Do you really get a sense this is the New York Yankees winning, or do you feel like you have a mercenary army going out there? That's the madness we are dealing with."

The year 1981 was a bizarre one, even for George Steinbrenner. It began with the Case of the Red Lips, and it ended with Steinbrenner's imaginary KO of two men in an elevator in Los Angeles and an apology to the city of New York and to Yankee fans everywhere. In between he threatened to sue Billy Martin if he didn't take out several allegations in his book, *Number 1*, screwed around with the roster in order to take publicity away from the crosstown Mets, and tortured manager Gene Michael before firing him and bringing back Bob Lemon. He also humiliated Reggie Jackson for having the audacity to be in a batting slump. This was the year the reporters began referring to George as "Mr. L. Toons" (the L, of course, stood for Looney). It was also a year to remember, in part because the strike-shortened season allowed the Yankees to sneak into the World Series.

The Case of the Red Lips jeopardized the job of public relations head Larry Wahl. The theme of the yearbook was the Big Apple, and on each player page the designer placed a red apple with the player's number inside. The printer wanted to make sure the red color was the same throughout the book, and he focused on the apples, not the other pictures. George had chosen a black-and-white photo of himself that had been colorized, and when the yearbook was printed, his lips were a tad more red than normal. At first, George was satisfied with the way it came out, until a secretary said to him, "Oh, it looks like you have lipstick on." Said an employee who was there, "That's how it usually goes with George. Someone will push a button and send him over the edge."

When George heard the criticism, he freaked. He bellowed that the photo made him look like he was wearing lipstick, and he ordered all ten thousand copies destroyed. When ESPN reporter Keith Olbermann took the story national, George blew up at Wahl again. The genial Wahl, who was newly married, resigned in June and took a better-paying job at ABC.

After Billy Martin punched out the marshmallow salesman and was fired, he had time to sit down and work with me on his autobiography, which was titled *Number 1*. I would travel to his home two or three times a week, or we would go to a restaurant or a bar, where he would drink club soda and lime. After losing his job, I guess he figured it was a good idea to stop drinking, and he abstained the whole eight months we worked together.

Before the book came out, it was excerpted in the *Daily News*, which bulleted the five things their editors found most interesting/outrageous. Right around publication in the spring, Billy and I both got letters from Steinbrenner insisting that the five bulleted items be taken out of the book. Among those items were the tugboat incident and Billy's charge that George had his phones in the stadium tapped. Billy insisted that what he had said was true and initially refused to back down.

Once the book was published, it quickly hit the *New York Times* best-seller list, racing to number five. It was on the *Times* list for fifteen weeks. George then put pressure on Billy to take out those bulleted items, knowing that if Billy did his credibility would be questioned and book sales would drop precipitously. Which is exactly what happened. We sold 110,000 copies before it was announced in the *Daily News* that Billy was taking out the bulleted items in the next edition of the book.

It was around this time that I interviewed George for a biography of him that I was in the process of researching. George did what he often did. He tried to pit Billy against me. Billy had told me he tried to do that often with his players, especially Reggie Jackson, and here he was, doing it to me. He told me that Billy had nothing good to say about me and denied that what Billy had said about tapping his phone, a federal offense, and the other stuff Billy said in the book was true. Without saying so directly he was able to let me know that if I didn't watch my step in writing my book on him, a lawsuit was not out of the question.

During spring training of 1981, George and New York Mets general manager Frank Cashen had a contretemps. Cashen made a joke about the area around Yankee Stadium being so dangerous that it was like Fort Apache the Bronx. A reporter put it in the paper and it made back-page headlines in the *Daily News*. Steinbrenner wanted Cashen fined or at the least made to give an apology. Cashen refused.

The Mets beat the Yankees that day on two long home runs. Rookie pitcher Mike Griffin gave up five runs to lose it. Steinbrenner's anger was monumental. Reporters couldn't wait to hear what he had to say. He didn't disappoint. He blasted catcher Rick Cerrone for striking out with the bases loaded, making a throwing error, and calling the two pitches the Mets hit for homers. He blasted other Yankee players as well. He finished by saying, "The team was embarrassing. Now's the time to screw down the hatches. I want to see some improvement." Then he said, "And Mike Griffin won't be pitching for us any longer." It was not an idle boast. Griffin was sent to Columbus and traded to the Chicago Cubs a few weeks later.

Oh, did Steinbrenner resent the Mets, who had a rookie making headlines by the name of Tim Leary. What caught the eye of the newspapermen was the skill of this kid, who had pitched only in Class A ball the year before. Steinbrenner became insanely jealous when the Mets stole headlines from him, and so to compete with the Mets for the back-page headline, he picked a twenty-year-old pitcher by the name of Gene Nelson, with a 20–3 record in Class A Fort Lauderdale the year before, to be the Yankees' answer to Tim Leary. When George put Nelson on the roster, another pitcher had to go, and so he sent down twenty-two-year-old Dave Righetti, a young player who had pitched well enough to make the team and deserved to be there.

Steinbrenner got his headlines. He talked about how Nelson was a real-life Frank Merriwell story. "People will come and see him pitch," he said. "He'll put fans in the stands."

But this was just wishful thinking on Steinbrenner's part. Nelson wasn't ready, and while Righetti was wasting away at Columbus, he compiled a 5–0 record. When he returned, he won his first three starts, helping the Yankees to the lead when the players went on a seven-week strike that began on June 12, 1981.

The players set the strike deadline for June 1, and in response Steinbrenner said that the owners were never more "unified and prepared for a strike." He predicted that players' union head Marvin Miller would meet his Waterloo. The owners contributed $15 million to a strike fund, and they took out insurance. The issue was free agency. Some owners wanted to be compensated with a player if they lost a free agent. The players dug in their heels. By July 12, 392 games had been lost and the All-Star Game canceled. The strike dragged on. Even Secretary of Labor Robert Donovan couldn't resolve it.

A private meeting between Miller and American League president Lee MacPhail finally brought the fifty-day strike to an end. More than a third of the season was lost. The status stayed pretty much quo. Both sides lost a lot of money. Fortunately, the fans didn't become bitter, and baseball had record attendance in 1982.

One of the biggest beneficiaries of the strike was the Yankees, because when the players returned, it was decided that the season would be split in half and the teams in first place at the time of the strike would automatically make the playoffs. Under manager Gene Michael, the Yankees had finished the first half with a 34–22 record, finishing two games ahead of the Orioles. For the second half, the Yankees played only .500 ball, and George was fuming. He blamed Reggie Jackson, who was in a slump, and he blamed Gene Michael.

George had made life miserable for both of them when Reggie reported late for spring training. He ordered Michael to "rip Reggie" in the newspapers. Once again, George was putting his manager in a no-win situation. And he was letting Reggie know the slugger wasn't the pal he thought he was.

The low point of George's behavior came in August 1981. With Reggie slumping, George ordered Michael to bench him one night, and another night he ordered Michael to pinch-hit the light-hitting Aurelio Rodriguez for him. George then publicly ordered Jackson to undergo not only an eye exam but a complete psychological test as well. Reggie felt humiliated and angry.

The Yankees were in Detroit when Reggie returned from having taken the tests. In was early in the afternoon, and he asked Jeff Torborg to grab a couple of buckets of balls and throw batting practice. Reggie asked pitcher George Frazier if he'd shag. Frazier said yeah.

"Then go sit in the upper deck," Reggie said.

Torborg threw a couple dozen balls, all but a couple of which Reggie hit out of the park, most into the upper deck. When he was done, he said to Frazier, "Go tell the man what you think of my eyesight."

Steinbrenner's treatment of Michael bordered on abuse. He kept bringing him in for meetings, telling him to "wake up the team," and he threatened to fire him often, sometimes publicly. On the day Reggie returned from his tests, Michael had a surprise for the reporters. He had written some notes on a legal pad, and he wanted the reporters to know how he was feeling. He said he was tired of George's phone calls after games and being told it was his fault when they lost. "I don't want to manage under these circumstances," he said. "Fire me and get it over with or stop threatening me. I can't manage this way. I've had enough."

Over the next eight days Steinbrenner kept him hanging. General manager Bill Bergesch and other Yankee front office members were ordered by Steinbrenner not to talk to Michael while Steinbrenner called Bob Lemon, living in California, to come back and manage.

After Michael was fired, George said he regarded him as "a son" and asked him to resume his duties as general manager. Michael told George he was a good manager. "Sure you are," said Steinbrenner. "But why would you want to stay manager and be second-guessed by me when you can come up into the front office and be one of the second-guessers?"

George's bizarre logic made sense to Michael, who took the job.

Under Bob Lemon, the team continued to play .500 ball. The Yankees finished the second half of the 1981 season with a 25–26 record. Turns out, Gene Michael didn't do so bad a job after all.

The Yankees met the Milwaukee Brewers in the playoffs. After winning the first two games, the Yankees lost the next two. After the fourth game Steinbrenner stormed into the clubhouse uninvited and unannounced and began chastising the team. Rick Cerrone had made a baserunning mistake in the 2–1 loss and George said something about it. Cerrone had been a whipping boy all year. It started when the catcher, whom George got in a trade from a terrible Toronto Blue Jays team, became dissatisfied with George's contract offer and took the Yankees to arbitration. As a Blue Jay, Cerrone had earned $50,000 in 1980. George upped the offer to $110,000. For 1981 he offered $350,000. Cerrone felt he was worth $440,000 because he had replaced Thurman Munson and had handled the pitching staff superbly. He had also batted .277 with fourteen home runs and eighty-five runs batted in.

When the arbitrator ruled that Cerrone deserved the $440,000, George became furious, charging the catcher with disloyalty to the Yankees, their players, their fans, and to George himself. George expressed his disappointment in Cerrone and then went after the arbitrator, whose verdict he called "senseless." He added, "The poor soul."

Cerrone blew up and responded like the enraged TV broadcaster Peter Finch played in *Broadcast News*. "I'm sick and tired and I'm not gonna take it anymore," he said. "Fuck you, you fat son of a bitch. You never played the game. You don't know what you're talking about."

"And you won't be playing the game as a Yankee next year," Steinbrenner replied. Then he said, "And we'll find out what you're made of tomorrow." And he stalked out. Teammates congratulated Cerrone for saying what many of them had been thinking but didn't dare verbalize.

Steinbrenner's reaction could not have been anticipated. Cerrone had embarrassed him in front of all the players, a cardinal sin, but somehow he got away with it. The next day George left a card in Cerrone's locker saying the incident should be forgotten. He warned him not to screw up on the base paths again.

The Yankees won the pivotal game against the Brewers and went on to defeat Billy Martin's Oakland A's to win the American League pennant. Their opponent would be the Los Angeles Dodgers.

The Yankees won the first two games, then lost four in a row.

Reporters and fans were particularly critical of Lemon's managerial moves in game three. George had ordered Lemon to bench Reggie Jackson, the team's best hitter, because they were facing the Dodgers' left-hander Fernando Valenzuela. The Dodger ace was leading by a run in the eighth inning when the first two Yankees singled, and Lemon pinch-hit Bobby Murcer for pitcher Rudy May and had Murcer bunt, something critics were sure May could have done. Murcer ended up bunting into a double play.

Immediately after the game, Steinbrenner, flanked by two security guards, pushed his way into the Yankees' clubhouse. Five minutes later, when the reporters were allowed to enter, Steinbrenner told them, "I didn't say anything."

But when reporters started asking questions, they learned that George had said plenty, criticizing "foolish mistakes." The most foolish mistake was Lemon's ordering Murcer to bunt. George had also ripped into players Jerry Mumphrey and Dave Winfield.

Said George, "There'll be changes tomorrow." The real Yankees manager had spoken.

In game four, Mumphrey was benched, and Reggie returned. Despite a batting slump, Winfield remained the number three hitter. It has been suggested that Steinbrenner ordered Mumphrey benched not because he was 2–10 in the series, but because he was scheduled to be a free agent, and his agent, Tom Reich, had taken a hard line in the bargaining.

The Yankees lost the game 8–7. Reggie had two walks and two singles, and hit his tenth home run of his World Series career. Meanwhile, as Mumphrey stewed on the bench, in the seventh inning he watched his replacement, Bobby Brown, George's pet project, misplay a routine line drive into a double. The runner ultimately scored from second with the winning run for the Dodgers. George's strategy cost the Yankees the game. Mused Mike Lupica in the *New York Daily News*, "Why can't the Fat Man ever leave well enough alone?"

After the game, Lemon tried to cover up the fact that George had ordered him to bench Mumphrey. He said he had been "saving" him, though he didn't say what he was saving him for.

After the 2–1 loss in game five, Steinbrenner left the press box and headed for Bob Lemon's office in the clubhouse. He wasn't seen again until 11:30 that night, when he called a press conference at the LA Wilshire Hotel. George's left hand was in a bandage—he said he had broken a knuckle—and he had a bruise on his forehead. He began telling reporters how in the hotel elevator he had fought with two men who had been bad-mouthing the Yankees and the city of New York.

Almost no one believed him. The way George told the story, one of the guys got on the elevator with a beer bottle in his hand and the other was wearing a Dodgers cap. The guy with the beer bottle said, "Steinbrenner, right?" George said he said, "Yeah, that's right." The guy with the beer replied, "Why don't you go back to those fucking animals in New York and take your choke-ass players with you."

Steinbrenner said he cursed at the guy, and there was a brawl. "He hit me in the side of the head with a bottle, and I reacted. I clocked him with my left hand. He fell—I think he was drunk to begin with—and the other guy hit me in the mouth. I slugged him too. The elevator door opened, and I got off. I left them there, one guy on the floor and the other guy kneeling over him. Then I went to the washroom, washed the blood off my mouth, and went to dinner." When his left hand began to throb, he called the team doctor, John Bonamo, who wrapped it. Then George called the press conference to announce the fight. If George was trying to bring the spirit of Billy Martin to the festivities, he was doing a fine job. All that was missing was the information that the guy he'd KO'ed sold marshmallows.

A Yankees employee who was in LA at the time and who requested anonymity insists there had been a fight in the elevator, though what happened wasn't anything like what George said had happened. The employee knows it happened, he said, because he was listening to a local Los Angeles radio station when the two Dodgers fans who were involved gave a recitation of what happened to the host of the show.

Said the employee, "The way they described it, they had to have been there to know the details they knew. What happened was, George was going down in the elevator, and whatever floor the two guys were on, one guy was at the elevator and the other guy was in his room when the door opened. The guy at the elevator stuck his foot in the door to hold the elevator for his buddy, and George, being George, said to him, 'Either get in or get out.'

"The guy turned to look who said that, and he recognized George. He called down to his buddy, 'Look who's here.' Once again George barked, 'In or out,' and the guy turned around and clocked him.

"My guess is that after George was hit, he pushed the guy out of the elevator. The door closed, and George went down in the elevator." The suspicion was that George hurt his hand when he punched the door of the elevator in anger after the fan left the car. A lot of people didn't believe *any* of George's story.

The night before the sixth game, which was scheduled to be played at Yankee Stadium and was rained out, Commissioner Bowie Kuhn hosted a party at the Sheraton Hotel in New York. The press was invited. Among the invitees was Burt Sugar, the editor of *Ring* magazine and an aficionado of all sports. Sugar was one of those skeptics who didn't believe for a second that Steinbrenner had been in a fight. George was a berater. He wasn't a fighter. Sugar expressed his opinion and got thrown out of the party for it.

There was one more great George moment in 1981. After the Yankees lost to the Dodgers in the World Series, George publicly apologized to the citizens of New York. It was a moment of madness and levity. Among the Yankee players, Reggie Jackson reacted most strongly. "We don't need to apologize," he said. "We lost in the World Series. We have nothing to be ashamed of. We have nothing to apologize to the city of New York about."

Baseball fans everywhere reacted contemptuously. Joe Flaherty, who also resented that Steinbrenner was a proponent of a tiered playoff system, was one of them. "We've come to a juncture when we apologize for winning a pennant," said Flaherty. "That's the insanity of the times. Another moral lesson: does it mean that unless we are number one, our life is a failure? Well then, why don't we all sit down and read *Hamlet, Othello, The Tempest*, and throw our typewriters out the window, because no way as writers we're going to be number one. All is failure.

"Publishers no longer are looking for intellectual breakthroughs. They are looking for the next Judith Krantz or the next Harold Robbins. Hollywood only wants to make a $25 million movie if it makes $150 million. We have come to that juncture. George is the perfect man for our times, and he has seized on it.

"Everything is going out the window—loyalty, sanity, quality, judgment—and this is being wrought with this mentality.

"Steinbrenner is a nouveau, a vulgar rich man from a small burg, and he has the Big Apple to play in. It's really for the enshrinement of Steinbrenner, not for baseball. It he had any love or smarts for baseball, how could the man sit down and say that he's in favor of mini-playoffs or a split season because television wants it? It's a television mentality. The strength of baseball is that in a country that has begun to insist from Calvin Klein jeans that we've lost the basis of making honest products, the nuts and bolts that made us a country, baseball was honest. You had to be the best over a hundred sixty-two games, and this guy can't see this. It will signal the death knell of baseball. Once baseball becomes bogus, watch the attendance drop. I don't care who's playing the outfield for you.

"George is very similar to Tom Buchanan in F. Scott Fitzgerald's *The Great Gatsby*. There is a quote in there where he talks about 'the rich being very different from you and me,' where they come in and play with lives and walk away leaving a mess. Steinbrenner is Tom Buchanan."

19

He couldn't accept the notion that he wasn't the
baseball genius he thought he was.
—Graig Nettles

The Fans Chant

If George was self-destructive in 1981, his behavior the next
season was even more bizarre. In 1982, he had three different
managers, firing Bob Lemon and Gene Michael a second time each,
and five different pitching coaches (Jeff Torborg, Jerry Walker, Stan
Williams, Clyde King, and Sammy Ellis). He churned players like
never before, using forty-seven of them; he wasted millions of dollars
buying players who were either over the hill or had no place to play.
The New York fans, the hippest in the world, completely understood
Steinbrenner's role in all of this. By the end of April, they were chanting, "Steinbrenner sucks, Steinbrenner sucks" at the top of their lungs.
Which only made George act crazier.

After fighting with Reggie Jackson in 1981, Steinbrenner decided
he was fed up with his outspoken slugger and let him leave, but not
before making derogatory comments about him and his ability in
the papers. Reggie signed with the California Angels. On the day
George apologized to the city of New York after losing the World
Series, he decided the way to go was to transform his Yankees into
a team of speed merchants. He signed outfielder Ken Griffey to a
multimillion-dollar long-term contract and signed the speedy Dave

Collins, also an outfielder, for three years for $2,475,000. His plan was for them to bat one and two in the lineup, and for them to run, run, run. The only problem was that the Yankees outfield already had Dave Winfield, Jerry Mumphrey, Steve Kemp, Oscar Gamble, Lou Piniella, and Bobby Murcer, and Bob Watson was a talented first baseman. There really was no place for Collins to play.

It was the year of George's speed-team experiment that would fail so miserably George would become a laughingstock with the team and with the fans. When George brought Olympic hurdler Harrison Dillard to spring training to teach the players the fundamentals of running, the derision rose. The press began making fun of George's new philosophy, and they derisively began calling the team the "Bronx Burners." Graig Nettles began calling the team the "South Bronx Striders." One problem with the Bronx Burners philosophy was that it didn't match that of the manager, Bob Lemon, who was not an aggressive man. When the season began, the Yankees hardly ever stole a base.

Adding to the instability, George was in a panic all season long. He made spring training a nightmare for everyone. He made the players "volunteer" to arrive at camp two weeks early. Most of them became resentful. And tired. Steinbrenner met with Bob Lemon and the coaches every day, berating them, calling Lemon on the phone with suggestions, driving his manager so crazy that before the start of the season he was ready to quit.

After the Yankees won only two of their first six exhibition games, twenty-two-year-old Dave Righetti took the mound and pitched poorly against Baltimore. After the game, George held a team meeting in which he blasted the young pitcher. "Maybe he's reading his press clippings too much," George said. "He'd better not come down with sophomore-itis."

When the reporters talked to Righetti, the talented young pitcher expressed confidence in himself. He said he was sure he would make the team. "They know what I can do," he said. After all, Righetti had just been named the American League Rookie of the Year.

A day later George spitefully shipped Righetti to Columbus. Steinbrenner went out of his way to say that the kid wasn't being punished for sticking up for himself, but no one believed him.

Lemon, who had been promised by George that he would manage all year long no matter what, lasted exactly fourteen games. With the team record 6–8, he was fired. George promised Lemon he would be a West Coast scout for life, until 1988, when he cut him out of the budget.

When Lemon was fired, Goose Gossage talked about the terrible morale on the team caused by Steinbrenner's constant criticism and his inept leadership. He said, "I'm depressed. It's no fun anymore. I think things have gone a little too far. It's getting worse. I've never faced anything like this before."

Then at a game at the stadium against Reggie Jackson and the California Angels, Reggie hit a long home run off Ron Guidry, and as he circled the bases, the 35,458 fans jumped to their feet and began chanting, "Steinbrenner sucks, Steinbrenner sucks, Steinbrenner sucks."

The Yankees players thought it hilarious.

While the fans were chanting, on the bench catcher Rick Cerrone playfully asked manager Gene Michael, "What are they saying? I can't quite make it out."

Ten minutes after the game, an apoplectic Steinbrenner called a team meeting of the manager and the coaches. He said to them, "This is the worst thing that ever happened to me. How could this happen? How could the fans do this after all I've done for them and this team? I was humiliated. My family was humiliated. I can't believe this."

While Steinbrenner was sputtering, Michael and the coaches were trying not to laugh. At one point Steinbrenner spotted Jeff Torborg biting his tongue and smiling.

"Do you think this is funny?" he screamed at Torborg. "You think this is a goddamned joke? Didn't you hear what they were saying? 'Steinbrenner sucks! Steinbrenner sucks!' You think that's funny? How would you like it if they were chanting, 'Torborg sucks, Torborg sucks'?"

As the meeting broke up, everyone was shaking his head and laughing inside. The next day there was another game against the Angels at the stadium. Steinbrenner was absent. He had flown back to Tampa "on business." Some of the players, including Dave Winfield, saw his departure as an act of cowardice. The player with the ironclad ten-year contract told reporters, "I'll be here long after everybody else anyway. I might as well take my swings." And swing he did.

Winfield accused Steinbrenner of taking credit for the victories and letting the players take the blame for the defeats. "He surrounds himself with baseball people, listens to their opinions, and then repeats them as though he is the expert," Winfield said. And then he called Steinbrenner a coward for leaving New York and going back to Tampa after Yankees fans bellowed, "Steinbrenner sucks."

Winfield chided Steinbrenner for not wanting to pay Reggie Jackson and letting him go to the Angels. He said, "Tell George I thank him for getting me the big contract. And tell him I have to laugh that he didn't want to pay Reggie a million dollars at age thirty-nine. But he'll be paying Dave Winfield three million at age thirty-nine." It would take a few years for Steinbrenner to get his revenge on Winfield, but get revenge he surely would.

On May 4, 1982, the Yankees lost an extra-inning game to Oakland at the stadium. The next day the team was to fly to Seattle to start a two-week road trip. Their record was 9–13, and it had become clear that George's speed team concept had failed miserably. And in twenty-two games, the team had hit but ten home runs.

George held one of his team meetings, and he told the players that they were making *him* look bad. He ordered Gene Michael to hold a practice the next day. The game had ended after midnight, and every-one was exhausted. George didn't care. "These guys have to pay a pen-alty for the way they've played," he said.

The workout, ordered as a punishment, lasted fifty minutes. The players then showered, dressed, and headed for the airport, steaming.

When George finally realized his revolutionary concept had failed, the days of the Bronx Burners were at an end. Desperate for more power, in a panic he traded for John Mayberry, once a talented slug-ger for the Kansas City Royals and Toronto Blue Jays, but at this point over the hill. Mayberry was being paid $3.2 million for four years, but at age thirty-two he was done. George took on the rest of his contract, and in 1982 Mayberry hit .209 for the Yankees with eight homers and twenty-seven RBIs. He was released the next year. The deal was so wasteful that the Yankees had to pay Mayberry half a mil-lion dollars *after* he retired.

John Mayberry wasn't the only player George bought who didn't fit in. Three other expensive investments in Roy Smalley, Steve Kemp, and Doyle Alexander turned out almost as badly.

No one could figure out why George wanted Smalley when he already had Bucky Dent, except that Smalley had made the All-Star team, and George liked to collect former All-Stars. When Smalley arrived, it was clear he wasn't nearly as good defensively at shortstop as Dent. Smalley, who had limited range, should have been at third, but Graig Nettles was there. Dent was traded to Texas, and Smalley played in ninety-one games, hitting eighteen home runs and driving in sixty-two runs. He was traded to the Chicago White Sox the next year.

Steve Kemp signed for a huge contract, $5.5 million for five years. This was another ludicrous overpayment by George that made the other team owners crazy. Edward Bennett Williams, the lawyer who had kept Steinbrenner out of jail in the Watergate case, owned the Baltimore Orioles. "George," said Williams, "stockpiles hitters like nuclear weapons."

In the fourth game of the season, Kemp collided with Jerry Mumphrey and Willie Randolph, and he heard something pop in his shoulder. He kept playing, but he was never the same hitter again. By the end of 1984, George had given up on him. Steve Kemp was only thirty-three when he retired.

Pitcher Doyle Alexander, who received $2.2 million for four years, was another of George's expensive signings. When he signed him for the 1982 season, George bragged that Alexander would win fifteen games. When Alexander had signed for four years, Graig Nettles told one reporter he figured it would take Alexander all four years to win those fifteen games. Nettles knew something George didn't: it took a special kind of player to make it in New York. It's one thing to play in a city where the team is out of contention and there is no pressure. It's another to play on a team where the owner and the fans expect you to win every day.

Doyle Alexander was a finesse pitcher who needed to feel comfortable to find his control and pitch well. He had won seventeen games pitching for Baltimore and Texas, and he had had a nice fourteen-win season in Atlanta in 1980. After winning eleven games for the San Francisco Giants in 1981, he became a free agent and signed with the Yankees.

Alexander came late to spring training, had two fair starts, and then was pounded by the Seattle Mariners. When Bob Lemon took him out, he came into the dugout and punched the wall, breaking a knuckle in his pitching hand. Alexander was out for six weeks. He was fined $12,500. He was sent to Columbus to rehab, and when asked to make a couple more starts there, he refused.

George brought him up June 9, 1982, and he ordered Gene Michael to pitch him. Against Oakland he allowed five runs and lost. After the game, general manager Bill Bergesch read a prepared statement written by Steinbrenner: "George said he is sorry he signed Alexander off the recent series of events. If we could trade him tomorrow, he said he would authorize me to do it. What Doyle Alexander did tonight was disgraceful, but typical of the selfishness of the modern-day ballplayers."

On August 6, Alexander started against Detroit and allowed six runs. From Tampa, Steinbrenner issued his most outrageous statement of all: "After what happened tonight, I'm having Doyle Alexander flown back to New York to undergo a physical. I'm afraid some of our players might get hurt playing behind him. He steadfastly refused to go back to Columbus another time to pitch his way back in shape. That's okay if you back it up with solid performance. But Alexander has given up eight homers in 38 innings, and his last two starts he's given up 11 runs in five innings. Obviously something is wrong and we intend to find out."

Commented an outraged Goose Gossage, "Doyle is getting a physical, but George needs a mental."

Alexander won one game that year, finishing 1–7 with a 6.08 ERA. After a year and two months he was released. He had no value on the market. At the time of his release, Steinbrenner still owed him $1.5 million on his contract. Of the twenty-four games in which he appeared as a Yankee, the team lost twenty-one. Three weeks later Alexander signed with Toronto and became a solid starter again. Without an owner hounding his every step, the big pitcher won seventeen games in 1984 and 1985. Steinbrenner paid his salary while he did it, too.

Gene Michael as manager lasted exactly eighty-six games in 1982. He was fired on August 4 after his Yankees finished 44–42 under him. He had done a terrific job managing a team with no chemistry, no direction, and, worst of all, no Reggie Jackson. Clyde King, George's at-the-ready jack of all trades, took over the team from Michael.

Two weeks later the Yankees took both games of a doubleheader from the Kansas City Royals. After the game, Goose Gossage, who had watched with mounting disgust while Steinbrenner with the help of the press kept the team in a constant state of turmoil, was asked by a radio reporter whether a newspaper headline in the *New York Post* from the day before, "Wild Goose Whipped," had upset him.

Gossage replied by launching into a profane tirade against the reporters, the fans, and Steinbrenner, whom he referred to as "the Fat Man." He called the fans "fickle and fair-weathered." He went on, "We're out there busting our asses. The results haven't been great. They were in the past. They must think because of all the money we make that we don't have pride to go out there and bust our butts."

Gossage complained about the constant turnover. "Every guy comes in here and looks at the lineup to see who's in there," he said. "What kind of crap is that? It just makes it a hell of a lot tougher to play here than it should."

Uncharacteristically, Steinbrenner didn't respond except to say, "Tell Goose I've been on a diet, and I've lost eleven pounds since June."

In the same August 17 edition of the *New York Post*, George and Reggie Jackson, who was playing for the California Angels, engaged in a nasty war of words. Steinbrenner had started it when he questioned whether the Angels were corking their bats. Reggie responded by referring to George's Watergate conviction Billy Martin–like by saying, "Steinbrenner doesn't speak the truth. It's been proven. He's been hauled into federal court in Washington and they proved there that he doesn't speak the truth." He suggested that George mind his own business. Reggie then accused Steinbrenner of making late payments to other teams. Steinbrenner, furious, lashed back. He said that nowhere in his statements did Jackson refute the charge that he had illegal bats. He then took direct aim at the former star player he said he once romanced like a woman. "If anyone has a financial problem, it might well be Reggie because several New York restaurant owners have told me that Reggie has an awful lot of unpaid checks in their restaurants."

Adding to the insanity, Reggie's Angels were playing Billy Martin's Oakland A's, and the previous day Martin had asked the umpires to check Reggie's bat. He said he did it in retaliation for the Angels' always asking the umpires to check the baseballs for scuff marks made by A's pitchers. Reggie saw a darker motive. In his paranoia, he accused Martin of doing it on George's orders. "You know who started this? George, that's who. I have four hundred and seventy homers, man. I don't need any of that stuff."

George said that anything more he had to say would be said to commissioner Bowie Kuhn. For a day, George, Reggie, and Billy were bringing back the good old days. Ah, nostalgia!

In 1982, the Yankees finished 79–83. Dave Winfield hit 37 home runs and drove in 106 runs. No other Yankee drove in 70. The team finished fifth, sixteen games behind Milwaukee Brewers manager Harvey Kuenn and his Harvey's Wallbangers.

Bill Bergesch, whom George hired in 1982, was the perfect general manager for George. He yes-sirred him and didn't argue with him. Bergesch also acted like a secretary. He would bring with him pads of paper, and when George talked, he would write down everything he said.

Said one Yankees employee, "I have never seen anyone take as many notes as Bill did. Every time Bill got called up to George's office, he had these two big briefcases, catalog cases, six inches wide, with notebooks and pads inside. If George would ask him a question about a player, whether on the Yankees or another team, Bill would have information from somewhere. It was never Bill's opinion. It was what so-and-so scout had to say about him. In a way, George was general manager using Bill Bergesch's information. I'm sure he had Bill calling people for trades, but it wasn't like Bill was a talent evaluator like Gene Michael."

Maybe so, but Bergesch was a better talent evaluator than George was. In December 1982, he coveted lefty Floyd Bannister, who during the 1982 season struck out a league-leading 209 batters for the mediocre Seattle Mariners. In discussions with agent Tony Attanasio, George convinced himself that Attanasio's client Bob Shirley could pitch as well as Bannister. George signed Shirley to a three-year, $2.4 million contract. Shirley, who threw junk, had compiled a 53–74 record in six seasons in the National League. Though George was wishing and hoping Shirley would become Bannister, it wasn't to be. His record with the Yankees was 13–20. In his four years with the Yankees he won five, three, five, and zero games. Bannister, who signed with the Chicago White Sox, won sixteen, fourteen, ten, and ten in the same period.

Clyde King, Steinbrenner's third manager in 1982, was desperately hoping George would bring him back for 1983. But the team was in such bad shape that George decided he once again needed the one man who could whip the Yankees back to respectability: Billy Martin. George had called Billy during the middle of the season and told him if he could get himself out from under his contract in Oakland, he would be the Yankees manager in 1983.

Like a butterfly to a beach sunflower, Billy got himself fired and returned to New York, sure that he could win it all again and fortified by the mistaken belief that George would change.

Graig Nettles had the last word on George and the 1982 season. He knew exactly George's motivation when he got rid of Reggie Jackson. Now it was George's team, his and his alone, said Nettles. He made it clear in the spring that he was in charge. He was the decision maker. The fate of the team was all up to him. Nettles watched as the Yankees floundered with George taking charge.

"George may pride himself on being a hotshot shipbuilder, but when the Yankee ship began going down, George just ran for the lifeboats," said Nettles. "He couldn't accept that things had not worked out the way he wanted them to. He couldn't accept the notion that he wasn't the baseball genius he thought he was. His reaction was to blast all his players in the papers.

"Last year the fans finally got wise to what George is all about. The 'bottom line' finally caught up with him.

"George got rid of the powerful personalities on the team. But when he did that, he was taking a big chance. In the past he always allowed himself a buffer, someone to take the heat or the blame if things didn't work out. He had Al Rosen and then Cedric Tallis. But then he let everyone know he was the one calling the shots, making the deals. He figured that when the Yankees won, he would get all the credit. Unfortunately, it didn't quite work out that way, and the fans knew where to point the finger of blame. The result was 'Steinbrenner sucks.' He underestimated them. He always does. He doesn't give them enough credit for being knowledgeable. They understood exactly where it was at."

20 | This isn't my fucking team, it's your fucking team.
—Yogi Berra

Hello, I Must Be Going

George brought Billy Martin back for a third time in 1983, giving him a four-year contract at $400,000 a year plus a signing bonus and $100,000 in expenses. He then proceeded to torture him anew. George had promised Billy he wouldn't second-guess him, wouldn't call him in the dugout or at home, and wouldn't send him helpful notes, but George's behavior was something he couldn't help. He was both a pathological liar and a control freak. To get what he wanted—in this case Billy's name on a contract—he would say anything, and Billy was foolish enough to believe him.

Said Graig Nettles at the time Billy was rehired in 1983, "George and Billy are like Richard Burton and Liz Taylor. They are attracted to each other. They enjoy the glamour of having each other around. Each respects the other for what he does for the team. Billy likes how George isn't afraid to spend money for players. George respects Billy's ability to walk into a chaotic situation, shake things up, and turn a team into a winner.

"The only question Billy's hiring brings up is the same question that has come up every time Billy manages for George: will George leave Billy alone so he can do his job? He never has in the past. I really don't see any reason why he should in the future."

Since George had fired Billy twice, the reporters, many of whom despised Billy, would write articles at the slightest provocation about the chances of his being fired. The continuous talk about this possibility upset him terribly and caused him to drink excessively. By the end of the season, Billy looked worn and haggard. George would talk about how worried he was about Billy's health while at the same time being the cause of his health problems.

Billy had stress from his job, but in 1983 he also had stress from his complicated, libidinous personal life, with both a wife and a steady girlfriend to support. With his big contract, Billy adopted a rich man's lifestyle. He took an apartment in Manhattan and a room at the Westbury Hotel. He hired a limo and a driver who was at his beck and call. Billy's lavish spending habits made his money disappear very quickly.

On the job Billy kept his nose clean in 1983 except for two run-ins with umpires that twice got him suspended. George was also involved in the umpire-baiting, which began when the Yankees press guide featured a picture of Billy kicking dirt on an umpire.

In front of Mike McAlary of the *New York Post* and Jerry Eskenazi of the *New York Times*, in spring training George put on a shocking display of boorishness during a game against the Pittsburgh Pirates. National League umpire Lee Weyer made a call at first base that went against the Yankees. Standing with the reporters, George said, "Those fucking National League homers." Both McAlary and Eskenazi wrote the story. Bowie Kuhn fined him $50,000.

In late May in a game against the A's, Dave Winfield was hit by a pitch, charged the mound, and was thrown out of the game. Steinbrenner dictated a press release calling the umpiring "a disgrace." When Lee MacPhail chastised him, Steinbrenner blasted MacPhail for not allowing him to exercise his freedom of speech. Steinbrenner was suspended from running the team for a week.

Then came the legendary Pine Tar game on the afternoon of July 24, 1983. With two outs in the eighth inning, George Brett of Kansas City hit what appeared to be the game-winning home run, only to have Billy protest that he should be out because the pine tar on the handle of his bat exceeded the legal height limit. When the umpires agreed and called Brett out, the Royals star put on an exhibit of ranting and raving that still gets replayed occasionally on ESPN for its entertainment value.

Four days later Lee MacPhail rightly ruled that the pine tar on the bat had nothing to do with Brett hitting the home run. He overturned the umpires and ordered the home run to stand and the game to be completed.

Steinbrenner began a one-sided war of words, charging that MacPhail, the former Yankees general manager, was "anti-Yankee."

The last four outs were played on August 18. Billy played pitcher Ron Guidry in center field. The Yankees lost. After the season, commissioner Bowie Kuhn fined Steinbrenner $300,000 for his remarks.

Then in late July, Billy declared war on the umpires. He had been ejected by Dale Ford after arguing about how many warm-up throws one of his pitchers could make. Billy was in a rage, brought on by alcohol. He charged that Ford had been out to get him.

When Moss Klein of the *Newark Star-Ledger* told Billy that Ford had a different story, Billy yelled at him, "Ford's a stone liar, a flat-out liar, and I know the commissioner and MacPhail will call me on it. But I'm telling the truth." Lee MacPhail suspended him three days for his comments.

More than anything in 1983, Billy wanted not to get fired, and all seemed to be going along just fine through June even though Billy rarely could or would do the foolish things that George wanted him to, because he knew he would be hurting his players and the team.

As an example of George's meddling, he sent Billy a letter dated June 9, 1983, in which George offered "a few thoughts about the practices and continuing work during the trip." He told Billy that Andre Robertson needed to work on his bunting, that Roy Smalley needed to practice his fielding at first, that Steve Balboni needed lots of extra hitting—George underlined the words "extra hitting." He told Billy he wanted to see Balboni hitting against more left-handers so he could "make a decision on him."

George added in his note that all players had to work on bunting, that catcher Rick Cerrone should "work on low pitches," that Steve Kemp needed to "work on fly balls," that Lou Piniella and Bobby Murcer should also take fly balls "just to stay in shape."

And there was more: George informed Billy that Don Baylor needed to DH on the road "as much as possible," and that he should use his relievers more if they were going to be effective. All players, moreover, needed instruction on baserunning, "as we discussed," and the team wasn't stealing enough bases. "Can Robertson be worked with?" he wanted to know.

George had "one more thought." Enforce the curfew and maintain strong discipline. "If you do this," he wrote, "we'll turn it around."

He then asked Billy to either tear up the letter or keep it confidential. Obviously Billy did neither. But letters like these made Billy's blood boil because George concentrated on the negative, and this combination of amateurish player critiques and "suggestions" for Billy made his life miserable, because on the one hand Billy knew George had no idea what he was talking about, but on the other George had the power to fire him if he didn't go along.

The beginning of the end of Billy III came because of Billy's promiscuity, his lack of respect for George's Knute Rockne–like mandates, and his penchant for yessing Steinbrenner and then not doing what he had said yes to, followed by George's anger at what he saw as Billy's challenge to his leadership.

In early June, the Yankees lost the final game of their home stand to the Cleveland Indians, and George ordered Billy to hold a workout the next day on what should have been an off day. Billy agreed, but he told the players the workout was voluntary for everyone, even the coaches, wink-wink. He didn't tell George that, though. Only three players showed up. Billy wasn't even in Milwaukee. He was back in New York, shacking up with his girlfriend, Jill. He would bring her to games, and one day, when she was wearing a revealing halter top and shorts, he passed notes to her and she passed them back to him with her toes.

All of the reporters saw it. No one wrote about it.

And no one would have, except that the resourceful Henry Hecht, who was writing a column for the *New York Post*, had called Yankees PR man Ken Nigro fishing for a story. Nigro, who protected Billy whenever he could, informed Bill Madden of the *Daily News* of Hecht's call. Everyone knew how much Hecht hated Billy, so his writing about the missed practice and notes from Jill's toes wasn't out of the question.

"Find out if Hecht is onto something," Nigro said to Madden.

Madden couldn't afford to be scooped by the *Post*. A suspicious sort, he was sure that Hecht had tipped off Mike McAlary and was going to run a story on the skipped practice and the notes between Jill's toes. When he called Steinbrenner to ask his reaction to the skipped practice and Jill's presence, Steinbrenner blew up and said he was thinking of firing Billy and hiring Yogi Berra to manage.

The next day Steinbrenner flew to Cleveland, where George and Billy met at the Pewter Mug, George's favorite hangout. George agreed to give Billy a reprieve so long as Billy "instilled discipline" in the team.

The next day George got back at Billy by firing Art Fowler, causing Billy enough personal misery to make him drink more. The hard drinking made him a little more paranoid and crazy than usual. He would show up at the ballpark for a night game after drinking all afternoon. That afternoon a young woman working the news side for the *New York Times* entered the clubhouse to conduct a survey on All-Star team voting. Billy didn't recognize her, and he threw her out of the clubhouse.

Upset with the way she had been treated, she called Steinbrenner to protest. If Billy had told her, as she claimed, "Suck my cock," Steinbrenner said, he would be gone that day. Steinbrenner questioned Coach Don Zimmer, trainer Mark Letendre, and pitcher George Frazier. Zimmer said he hadn't heard anything. Letendre and Frazier backed Billy.

Billy made it through another crisis fueled by George when he fired Fowler. But, unable to handle George, he was drinking more than ever as the disease of alcoholism worsened. In the past, Billy had reserved his imbibing for after games. This year he was drinking before games and even during them. Players were also beginning to notice that his memory wasn't always what it should have been.

Putting pressure on Billy to win and meddling was one thing, but when George fired his closest buddy on the team, Art Fowler, that was devastating. Said pitcher Shane Rawley, "That was the start of Billy not caring as much about his job as he could have. That being his payback to Steinbrenner for what he did to Art."

Without Fowler, Billy's lines of communication with the pitchers were effectively cut off. At the same time a paranoid, under-the-gun Billy was sure that the other coaches—Don Zimmer, Jeff Torborg, and Sammy Ellis, the ones picked by George—were plotting against him with George.

In early September the Yankees climbed to within four games of Baltimore, but then came a doubleheader loss to the Orioles, and they fell back. Billy was a mess. Once again, he knew he had done everything asked of him, done a better job than anyone else could have, and George still sought to make him look bad and then fire him. Ron Guidry, the Yankee ace who rarely got in the middle of the George-Billy feuding, was so disgusted when George fired Art that he announced he was dedicating the rest of the season to Fowler.

Billy knew George wanted him to quit. After one loss, Billy was talking to the writers in his office when the phone rang. Steinbrenner began screaming at him so loudly that all the journalists could hear what he was saying. After the writers left, Don Zimmer walked into Billy's office and found the hard-bitten manager sobbing at his desk. All Zim could do was put his arm around him to console him.

Not trusting Torborg or Sammy Ellis, Billy decided he'd run the pitchers himself, and the staff fell apart emotionally. Billy would second-guess the pitch selection of all the pitchers except Ron Guidry. The pitchers began to resent him.

Without Fowler, Billy would bring relief star Goose Gossage into the game a batter or two late. Graig Nettles and some of the other players noticed. But no one had the courage to confront Billy. When Goose stopped being effective, the team started to lose, and when that happened, the pitchers began complaining to George and in the press. Other players began complaining that Billy was too tough on them, and at this point it was only a matter of time for Billy.

George began planting stories in the papers about the players' gripes, greasing the skids for Billy's departure. In the end, the avalanche of stories in the papers planted by George made Billy's third firing acceptable to the public.

After hearing all the criticism, you'd think the Yankees hadn't won much in 1983. But that year under Billy Martin, the Yankees won ninety-one games, which was a fine performance. They didn't win the pennant that year because the Baltimore Orioles won ninety-eight games and went on to defeat the Philadelphia Phillies in the World Series. At the end of the 1983 season, a distraught, drawn Billy Martin checked himself into a Minneapolis hospital with a liver condition.

In one of his farcical press conferences after the season, George announced that Billy was being "shifted" into the role of consultant and that Yogi Berra would take over as manager in 1984. To keep Billy quiet, George promised he would retire his uniform number. Said

Graig Nettles, a student of human nature, "I guess George got tired of having to take a backseat to Billy again. I can't think of any other reason why he fired him. Now George can reconnect the phone to the dugout. Now he can come back into the clubhouse to give more of his rah-rah speeches."

When George fired Billy, the press made fun not only of George, who never could complete a season without firing a manager, but of Billy as well, for allowing George to humiliate him so badly. Why would Billy allow himself to be humiliated a third time, despite the excellent job he had done as a manager?

The answer, of course, was two-pronged: his pride in being the Yankees manager, and his fat contract. Adding to his woes was a thought process warped by alcoholism. To pay for his women and his jet-setting ways, he needed a lot of money. Billy believed that the only person willing to pay him the money was George Steinbrenner.

Friends warned Billy that the money came with a price. They saw how Steinbrenner would torture him, make him feel small and make him look bad in the press and in the eyes of the public. They warned him about what George was doing to his self-esteem.

Billy didn't care. The Yankees were what he cared about. He loved the Yankees deeply. He had come from nowhere to the New York Yankees, and he never forgot it and the pride it instilled in him. The Yankees had made him something. Yet the franchise he loved most would turn out to hurt him the most.

His friends told him, "Billy, you know you can't get anything out of this guy except money." But the money was enough. He needed the money, which gave him some clout, and which would be guaranteed even if he were fired.

If Billy had to accept another firing and spend the year 1984 scouting, he could do that for $400,000 a year. And he knew, of course, that there was another aspect of George's warped personality to give him hope. Billy knew George well enough to understand that before too long George's meddling would drag the team down and he would need him again to manage.

Perhaps George could afford to offend and anger his manager, even fire him. But the ones he could not afford to alienate were his players, and by the end of the 1983 season one of his best players, closer Goose Gossage, decided he had had it with playing for the Yankees. George had taken the fun out of the game for him, and he was determined to play someplace where it would be enjoyable again. His contract up, Gossage signed with the San Diego Padres. The reason he was leaving, he said, was George Steinbrenner.

In his self-protective mode, George accused the pitcher of fearing that he would be blamed for the firing of Billy Martin and hence wanting to play somewhere else. The explanation was ridiculous. Without the Goose, the Yankees would be weaker in 1984.

That was the year the Detroit Tigers, led by pitcher/organist Denny McLain, began the season 35–5. Yogi Berra was doing a nice job of managing, but there's little a manager can do when an opposing team runs away with things.

In July, the Yankees lost a game, and afterward Steinbrenner called a meeting of the manager and the coaches in his office at the stadium. His tirade was directed mostly at Yogi. Said George, "You guys have really let me down. I gave you want you wanted. This is your team, and look at it—look what's happening."

Yogi shouted, "This isn't my fucking team, it's your fucking team. You make all the fucking decisions. You make all the fucking moves. You get all the fucking players nobody else wants. You put this fucking team together and then you just sit back and wait for us to lose so you can blame everybody else because you're a fucking chickenshit liar." Yogi stormed out of the room. A minute went by, and Yogi, cooled down some, returned, only to begin screaming again. Every phrase had the word "liar" in it.

George kept his cool. He said a few things calmly, and after Yogi yelled himself out, he left. "I guess the pressure of losing is getting to him," said Steinbrenner.

After the All-Star break, the Yankees, led by a group of young kids from Columbus, went 51–29. The run made it impossible for George to fire Yogi, and he returned for the 1985 season.

The day before spring training began in 1985, George had a meeting with Yogi in Fort Lauderdale. George had reservations about Yogi, because he wasn't the taskmaster he wanted him to be. Yogi was a gentle soul, whose patient philosophy was summed up when as manager of the 1964 Yankees, his team trailing in the standings, he said, "It ain't over until it's over." And he was right. The Yankees caught up and won the American League pennant. But in 1985 Yogi's owner was not a patient man.

George announced, "I put a lot of pressure on my managers in the past to win at certain times. This will not be the case this spring." He also said, "Yogi will be the manager the whole year. A bad start will not affect Yogi's status." Back in 1982 George had promised Bob Lemon the same thing, and Lem had been manager for exactly fourteen games when he was fired. Berra made it to sixteen games.

The season began with two lopsided losses to the Boston Red Sox. Before the third game, George declared that the next game would be "crucial." The Yankees lost, 6–4. After winning five of the next six, the Yankees then lost three times at Yankee Stadium to the Red Sox, and they lost the first two games in Chicago to the White Sox to run their record to 6–10. When Yogi "defied" George by refusing to schedule a mandatory workout—the same foolishness that got Billy Martin fired in 1983—Steinbrenner fired him after spreading the charge that Yogi had been too "easygoing."

For the first two weeks of the season, George had been threatening to fire Yogi, one of the most revered heroes in Yankees history. Yogi was a Hall of Fame catcher. As a player, he had appeared in fourteen World Series. He had the record for most career at bats, hits, and doubles in the series, he was second in runs and RBIs, and he was third in homers and walks. Thirteen times Yogi Berra teams won the World Series. As a manager, he won pennants for the Yankees in 1964 and the Mets in 1973. Yogi Berra was a beloved idol to Yankees fans.

According to pitcher Phil Niekro, Berra's nerves were so shattered by Steinbrenner's constant meddling and second-guessing that in a game against the White Sox, the mild-mannered, easygoing Berra cracked, making inappropriate moves that lost the Yankees the game. Said Yogi, "It's his team. He can do with it what he wants. It was going to happen sooner or later, so we might as well get it over with now."

Yogi's wife, Carmen, wasn't so sanguine. After Yogi was fired, it was she who declared that as long as George Steinbrenner owned the Yankees, Yogi would never return to Yankee Stadium. And she meant it. When George held a day in Yogi's honor on August 21, 1988, a day when Yogi and Bill Dickey were to have their number 8 retired and plaques placed in Monument Park, Yogi was a no-show. Bill Dickey was honored alone.

On the day Billy was hired to replace Berra, Billy, through his lawyer, Eddie Sapir, told reporters, "George and I have talked a lot and we have an understanding. The main thing is, we want to win."

The next day Steinbrenner issued a press release to answer the players' anger over Yogi's firing. The message: don't blame me. "I didn't fire Yogi," it said. "The players fired him. The way the team played is the reason Yogi is no longer the manager. Today's players have changed because of long-term, guaranteed contracts. Players have soft jobs and they're lazy." As with Billy and his alcoholism, George was unwilling to admit that his narcissism was getting worse: his penchant for attention, control, and power seemed to be getting more pronounced. The difference was that Billy's problem hurt only himself. George's problem hurt many others and also soured the fortunes of the Yankee team.

Steinbrenner was making the fabled New York Yankees into a laughingstock. The Yankee fans who remembered the days of Casey Stengel and Ralph Houk knew that as long as George continued his policy of trading away all the great prospects and firing one or two managers every year, the Yankees would never win again. When Yogi left, it was Steinbrenner's twelfth firing in eleven years, a record for destructive, frivolous management. In running AmShip, Steinbrenner did the same thing, churning executives and secretaries with great gusto, but the public didn't know or care. Only the stockholders and the affected employees and their families suffered.

George was too powerful to depose. Yankees fans had no choice but to be subjected to his every devious and destructive whim until he had done to them what he had done to his players: taken the fun out of being a Yankees fan.

Even bringing Billy back on April 28, 1985, generated little enthusiasm among the fans, because it had become clear that Billy no longer was the little guy fighting against his powerful boss but rather a man who had sold out his principles to keep his job as Yankee manager. And they loved and respected Yogi.

When Billy joined the Yankees in 1985, he was talking about his role in the organization. He envisioned becoming George's right-hand man, becoming a vice president, and he told reporters he was grooming Lou Piniella as manager. Billy wanted to be someone who could troubleshoot for Steinbrenner, who would make recommendations and be taken seriously.

Of course, he was only deluding himself. Why would Billy want to be the right-hand man of a guy who thought of him as white trash? But Billy had bought into George's web of bullshit, and if George wanted him to scout, or be manager, or be general manager, or sell peanuts, he'd do it for $400,000 a year.

When Billy took over, the players were just as tepid as the fans about his return. Many players loved Yogi. They respected him for who he was and how gentlemanly he treated them and everyone around him.

"We had become a family under Yogi," said Don Baylor. "Guys felt greatly for each other, felt we could win it all in '85."

Unfortunately for the players and the fans, George continued to make moves at inappropriate moments, destroying cohesiveness and dooming the Yankees. Even the act of bringing Billy back didn't have the positive effect it once did. The players had enjoyed playing for the easygoing Berra, and they weren't looking forward to Billy's whip or his alcoholic excesses. They also didn't appreciate a new wrinkle: Billy and George had made a pact. George would stay out of the clubhouse and stop making his rah-rah speeches if Billy promised to fine the players more often. Billy agreed, and though he knew it was Mickey Mouse, he kept his part of the bargain.

He fined Phil Niekro for giving up a grand slam home run. He fined Rich Bordi for not trimming his mustache, and he fined Bobby Meacham one time for swinging at the first pitch. The players knew George was responsible, but Billy's ass-kissing cost him their respect.

By June, Billy was second-guessing the pitchers something fierce. Mimicking George, he was taking the fun out of the game. And without Art Fowler as a buffer, there was no intermediary. It got so bad that Niekro described Billy as "the maddest of the game's madmen."

By the middle of 1985, Billy was drinking heavily every day. In addition to having George on his back, he was bringing his girlfriend, Jill, on the road with him. The two had a contentious, sometimes violent relationship, and they would fight so loudly they could be heard down the hall of the hotel. Every once in a while during a game Billy would leave the clubhouse and go to a nearby bar for a drink.

Still, the Yankees were only a couple of games behind Toronto going into August. Martin, drunk or sober, was again proving his greatness as a manager. When the Yankees took the field, they expected to win. Once again, Billy proved his worth to his players.

On July 20, 1985, the Yankees were only a game and a half back. All George Steinbrenner had to do was sit back and keep his mouth shut. Instead, the next day he went on TV with Howard Cosell to tell everyone how important *he* was. He told Cosell, "If Dennis Rasmussen doesn't pitch well today, I'm going to send him to the minors."

Rasmussen was pitching very well, until Joe Cowley heard Steinbrenner's remark and told Rasmussen, and he gave up five runs in the fifth inning. Had the Yankees won, they'd have had the lead. With the loss, they fell to two and a half games back.

After the game, Steinbrenner told Cosell he was banishing Rasmussen to Columbus. Billy, who was supposed to be consulted by George, hit the roof. Steinbrenner's treatment of Rasmussen also affected the rest of the staff. Pitchers Ed Whitson and Cowley lost, and the team sank further behind.

Making a bad situation worse, Steinbrenner then fired pitching coach Mark Connor. Since Billy was acting as his own pitching coach, he wasn't bothered all that much. But Whitson, who was close to Connor, was very upset. Whitson hated Billy, but Connor had been an effective buffer between the two of them. After Connor was fired, Whitson suddenly lost his effectiveness.

After a game in Milwaukee in mid-September, George infuriated several of the players, including Ken Griffey, Don Baylor, and Winfield, when in a diatribe in front of the press he said, "Where is Reggie Jackson? We need a Mr. October or Mr. September. My big guys aren't coming through—Winfield, Baylor, Griffey. They're letting us down. That's a fact." Then George referred to Winfield, who that night had driven in his hundredth run for the fourth consecutive year, as "Mr. May."

If Steinbrenner thought his words were going to do some good, he was sorely mistaken. With twenty games left in the season, the team lost its way.

Said Baylor, "After Steinbrenner ripped the team, we lost focus." From September 13 to September 20 the Yankees lost eight straight games to fall six and a half games behind. Billy was then informed that

George had second-guessed him to Tom Boswell of the *Washington Post* in a game in which he brought Dave Righetti into the game in the fifth inning. This time, Billy decided to put his feelings about George ahead of the welfare of the team. For the first time in their stormy relationship, he made moves to show up George. He left starter Brian Fisher in while he got pounded for six runs as Righetti waited in vain in the pen. He allowed the Tigers to hit five home runs and score seven runs against Ron Guidry. And when he brought in a reliever, he didn't bring in Righetti. He brought in Dennis Rasmussen, back from Columbus. Eyebrows were raised among the players.

The next night Billy let a struggling Phil Niekro pitch the entire game. Commented Niekro, "George may have pissed Billy off too much this time, 'cause Billy has gotten really crazy with some of his thoughts and actions."

During that game, Billy made the strangest move of his entire career. With the game tied and runners on first and third and two outs, he ordered Lou Piniella to tell Mike Pagliarulo, a left-handed hitter, to go up to the plate and hit right-handed against lefty pitcher Mickey Mahler.

At first Pags thought Billy was kidding. A good soldier, he did as he was told. Batting from the wrong side, he looked lost, and he took a third called strike. The Yankees lost, and they lost the day after that.

Said Niekro, "I wonder if Billy really does want out of here or if he's just playing games with George's mind."

By the time the Yankees arrived in Baltimore for the last leg of the road trip, Billy was in a truly wretched mood. He told reporters he was passing over pitcher Ed Whitson because Whitson had a sore shoulder. When asked by reporters, Whitson said his arm had never felt better. In the clubhouse he was furious that Billy had shown him up.

That night, in a game the Yankees lost, Billy's blunder cost them the game. With the count 3–0 on Lee Lacy, a runner on first, and pitcher Rich Bordi struggling for control, Billy stood on the top step of the dugout and scratched his nose, the sign for a pitchout.

Catcher Butch Wynegar saw the sign but couldn't understand why Billy was calling a pitchout, but he was too cowed to say anything. Bordi pitched out, the runner didn't run, and Lacy walked, bringing up Cal Ripken Jr. and Eddie Murray, Baltimore's two best hitters. Both hit run-producing singles to win the game, bringing the Yankees their eighth loss in a row.

After the game, Billy admitted that he hadn't been thinking about where he was standing when his nose began to itch and said, "I scratched it."

Mentally, Billy was cracking up.

After the game, Billy headed for the bar of the Cross Keys Inn, where the team was staying. He was drinking with pitching coach Bill Monbouquette when two couples approached him. One of the couples had just gotten married. Billy bought them a bottle of champagne, but then got into a nasty argument with the groom when the liquored-up Billy was accused by the liquored-up groom of saying that his liquored-up bride had a potbelly.

"I did not say she had a potbelly," said Billy. "I said she had a fat ass."

The groom poked Martin with his finger, and Billy gave him a hard shove. Players got between the two. Said Billy to the groom, "We'll take this outside."

Billy followed after him, hoping for a one-punch KO, but the man had vanished, leaving Billy feeling unsatisfied.

The next day Billy's eyes were wild and crazy-looking. He accused George of hiring the groom to get him in trouble so he could fire him. He then went out on the town, and when he returned, he stopped at the bar at the Cross Keys Inn. Ed Whitson, who was sitting there, pointed to Billy and loudly said, "He's the man who's causing my problems." All season long Whitson had complained about Billy's calling pitches from the bench and pulling him out of games too soon. Whitson also hated that Billy second-guessed pitches and berated his fellow pitchers. He was sure Billy played favorites—and Ed Whitson was not one of Billy's favorites. Steinbrenner had given Whitson a contract worth $4.4 million. Billy saw Whitson more realistically as an overpaid journeyman.

When a fan at the next table pointed a finger at Whitson, the big pitcher grabbed him by the throat. Billy rushed over to try to break it up. Whitson's hatred for Billy was ruling his emotions, and he began swearing at Billy. He then said the magic word, calling Billy "a motherfucker." Billy, without warning, punched Whitson in the face, splitting the pitcher's lip. All hell broke out. Whitson and Billy poured out all of the season's frustrations on each other. When it was over, Billy had suffered a broken arm and two cracked ribs from Whitson's blows. Worse was the beating his ego had taken.

Though Billy wanted to suspend Whitson "for life," he softened. GM Clyde King sent Whitson back to New York for the remainder of the road trip. When Whitson returned to the team, Billy acted as though nothing had happened. He figured the guy had had too much to drink and was out of his mind. It had been true of both of them.

But Billy was beat up both physically and emotionally. Said his friend Bill Reedy, who flew up to Toronto to be with him, "It was all coming apart. He started to lose the zest for it. He was beat up. He looked like an old man." A week later Billy was still coughing up blood.

Despite George's interference, Billy's drinking, and the injuries to the players, the Yankees finished the season 91–54, only two games behind the Toronto Blue Jays. All season long Billy had tried to do what George had asked him, but George was the sort of person who was never satisfied, who when his demands were met, would then up the ante and ask for more. By the end of the season, Billy was looking for a confrontation. Only the entreaties of his lawyer, Eddie Sapir, kept him from being fired in mid-September when Billy agreed to meet with George to discuss the Toronto lineup and then decided that a meeting with George was stupid and that he wouldn't go.

Finally, Billy went up to see George, but during the entire meeting he refused to look at him. He was there, but he wasn't there. That day pitcher Joe Cowley got hit for three quick runs, and Toronto went on to win the division title.

George announced that GM Clyde King and his assistant, Woody Woodward, would decide whether Billy would be fired. King was ordered to search for a new manager. He interviewed Chuck Tanner, Bobby Cox, and Mets manager Joe Torre.

Three weeks after the season ended, Steinbrenner fired Billy and hired Lou Piniella. He said he fired Billy because of the Whitson fight but he felt bad about it. He announced that Billy would be a broadcaster in 1986. Billy had two more years on his contract. The money was good, and Billy stayed on.

George now had control over Billy's soul. Billy would just have to swallow a little bit harder. Finally, Billy was saying uncle. Steinbrenner was his boss. Steinbrenner was calling the shots. George now owned Billy, as he owned Hopalong Cassady and a lot of his other employees.

As a reward for Billy's going along, George paid him generously. He extended his contract for a total of $1.4 million. Billy had an escape clause, but he was making so much money—$300,000 a year to be a consultant to George—that the likelihood of his ever leaving the Yankees was slim. The next year he would sit next to George in his private box second-guessing Lou Piniella, telling Steinbrenner what he would do if he was managing. With George and Billy second-guessing away, the chorus of criticism would drive the excitable Piniella half crazy.

Insanity

Lou Piniella had had a taste of what it was like managing the Yankees during the summer of 1985 when in late July Billy Martin had severe back spasms. The doctor who gave Billy an injection accidentally punctured his right lung, and Billy was in severe pain. He was hospitalized in a Texas hospital, and Piniella was named interim manager. It was arranged for Billy to speak with Lou during the game from his hospital bed as he watched the game on TV. Only on George Steinbrenner's Yankees would such a wacky arrangement be possible.

The first night the Yankees beat the Cleveland Indians 8–2. Martin called eight or nine times, offering advice on shifting outfielders against certain hitters and on calling pitches. Reporters contended that Billy had been released from the hospital and was actually giving his instructions from a bar.

The arrangement was reported in the newspapers the next day. After splitting the doubleheader, Piniella was begging for it to end. He told Moss Klein of the *Newark Star-Ledger* that he was going to quit as manager and as coach and would seek another line of work. Piniella's problem was that he was too sane to be working for the Yankees. "I don't have any future in this game," said Piniella. "So I'm getting out. I just wanted you to know."

Piniella didn't show up the next day. He was serious about quitting, but his wife, Anita, talked him out of it, and so he returned. The Yankees lost to the White Sox, and after the game Steinbrenner, in an attempt to punish Piniella, fired pitching coach Mark Connor.

Piniella told Klein, "I have to be crazy to want to manage this team, absolutely crazy. I can make more money running my restaurants the right way. But I can't help it. I still want to be the Yankee manager one day." He would get his chance the very next year, 1986.

George began his remake of the team with the signing of Chicago White Sox starter Britt Burns, who had won eighteen games the year before. Yankees physician Dr. John Bonamo advised George not to do it, saying the pitcher was suffering from a degenerative hip disease and might have to quit the game soon. After the doctor left the room, Steinbrenner said, "What does he know about baseball? He's a doctor. We're baseball men."

In March, during spring training, Burns broke down and never pitched again.

"Don't worry," Steinbrenner told Lou Piniella and the coaches, "they're saying he's never going to pitch again, but I know some experts in the field of hip surgery at the University of Florida. I'm going to send him there. I think they may even be able to fit him with an artificial hip. He could be back this summer."

Said one Yankees executive, who didn't want to be named for obvious reasons, "When George started talking about this poor guy pitching with an artificial hip, I figured he had really gone over the edge. He just didn't want to admit that he had screwed up going ahead with that trade. Can you imagine a guy pitching with an artificial hip?"

Another executive decision George made was to not re-sign slugger Don Baylor. George predicted, "His bat will be dead by August." That year Baylor helped lead the Boston Red Sox to the pennant.

A third decision was whether to keep forty-five-year-old Phil Niekro. Piniella wanted to keep him. He had won sixteen games each of the last two seasons. The vote to keep him was 11–1. George consulted with his son Hank and they overruled the vote. Piniella was furious. "What are you even bothering to ask our opinion for? You know what you're gonna do anyway."

A decision also had to be made on Dennis Rasmussen, a big lefty. Piniella liked him and wanted him on the roster. In an exhibition game at Pompano Beach in a small bandbox, Rasmussen gave up three home runs. George ordered him to Columbus, but he returned, only because Tommy John got hurt. Rasmussen went on to win eighteen games for the Yankees and led the team in innings pitched.

During spring training, Piniella made a proposal to Steinbrenner. He said, "How would you like to be manager? From where you'd be sitting, you can give all the signs just as well as I can. I'll give you a few signs now. We'll make them easy. And tomorrow, you take over. You tell me the lineup, you decide how you want to handle the pitching, and you give the signs to Stick [Gene Michael]—hit and run, bunt, steal, whatever you want to do."

Steinbrenner did not back away. "Okay, let's do it," he said.

Piniella was very excited. Here was a chance for Steinbrenner to see for himself just how difficult managing a major league baseball team could be. But Michael, when he heard what Piniella and George were planning, was horrified. "How can you do this to me?" he asked. "If a guy gets thrown out stealing, he's going to say I got the signs mixed up. Whatever goes wrong is gonna be my fault. And God help me if I miss one of his signs."

The next day Piniella waited for George to arrive and take his seat near the dugout. Game time came, and George was a no-show. When Piniella asked George why he didn't show, George said, "Oh no, you don't. You're not gonna trick me that easily. I figured out what you were up to. You're the manager. You do the managing. I'm the owner. I'll do the second-guessing. That's the way it's supposed to be."

In 1986, the Yankees finished 90–72, five and a half games behind the Boston Red Sox. The next year the team, led by first baseman Don Mattingly's .327 average, 30 home runs, and 115 RBIs, went 89–73, finishing fourth behind the Detroit Tigers.

Before the 1987 season George's most overblown signing was pitcher Steve Trout. Steinbrenner told Piniella, "I just won the pennant. I got you Steve Trout." But once again, Steinbrenner was a terrible talent evaluator, in part because he never took into consideration how a player would react to the pressure of playing on a team in a big city with an omnipresent press owned by him.

Trout wasn't comfortable pitching in New York. He was a nervous wreck. In fourteen appearances he had a 0–4 record and a 6.60 ERA.

In forty-six and one-third innings, he allowed fifty-one hits and thirty-seven walks, and he threw nine wild pitches.

Incredibly, the Yankees were in first place at the All-Star break. They had a three-game lead over Toronto. Then it all fell apart when on August 2, 1987, George disrupted everything. He and Lou Piniella got into a heated argument because Steinbrenner wanted to send relief pitcher Pat Clemens, a pitcher Piniella liked, to Columbus and wanted to bring up Al Holland. Bucky Dent, the Columbus manager, told Piniella that Holland's arm was shot. But George wanted Holland brought up anyway because he was doing a friend, Tom Reich, Holland's agent, a favor. To justify the move, Steinbrenner told Piniella, "I've been looking through binoculars watching Clemens warming up in the bullpen, and I've never seen an athlete so scared. I coached football at Northwestern."

That night the Yankees lost a close game to the Indians in Cleveland. George called Harvey Greene, the Yankees PR guy, to tell Piniella "to be in his room for a phone call from me at two p.m. the next day."

If George and Piniella had one issue that divided them, it was George's insistence that Piniella always be available when he wanted to talk to him. It was something George insisted all his executives do. But Piniella needed time to himself, and he would go have lunch with friends or play golf in the morning when George wanted to speak to him. If George wanted to speak to you and you weren't available, there was hell to pay. In the days before cell phones, it meant his executives remained chained to their desks working in their offices hanging by their telephones just as he liked it.

On the day George wanted to talk to his manager at 2 p.m. sharp, Piniella had a lunch date at the Pewter Mug in Cleveland with Bobby Murcer and two of the Yankees' limited partners. Piniella dutifully told them he had to leave because "the Boss is calling me at two p.m." They talked him out of going. Piniella thought, *He probably won't call anyway*. But he did call, and when Piniella wasn't there to take his call, Steinbrenner was furious.

That night Al Holland pitched, and he gave up five walks and six runs in one and two-thirds innings in a 15–4 loss. The next day Piniella called GM Woody Woodward to discuss bringing up a catcher.

Said Woodward, "I'm not allowed to talk to you. Nobody here is. I suppose you're gonna have to straighten it out with him."

Thought Piniella, *How could George be so petty?*

The Yankees won the last game in Cleveland, and the team flew to Detroit. Piniella told the reporters what had happened. He knew better than to embarrass George publicly, but like Billy Martin, when Piniella was ruled by anger, sometimes common sense went out the window.

After losing two games to Detroit, Steinbrenner issued a profane two-page statement through Harvey Greene rebutting Piniella's charges. It read, "The simple fact is Piniella didn't even come back from lunch—if that was really where he was—to get a call from his boss at two o'clock. He didn't bother to call me or to get word to me that the time was inconvenient for him. I don't know of too many people—even sportswriters—who, if their boss told them to be available for a call at a certain time, wouldn't be there.

"As for me not talking to Piniella, that's pure horseshit. Ask Woody. I told Woody to put the plan to bring up [Joel] Skinner up in full action. Everything was set, but I just wanted to talk to Lou about it briefly. The fact is Piniella was all for the Salas–Joe Niekro trade. I opposed it, but I let Woody and Lou make the deal. Now all of a sudden, Skinner is the answer to our problems and Salas is a bum."

Then Steinbrenner did something truly reprehensible. He said, "As for the Rickey Henderson matter, I was leaving that in the hands of our team doctor and trainer until Woody called me and said Piniella wanted to disable him right now because he was faking it, his teammates were mad at him, and he wanted guys to play and he would win it all without Henderson. I said I wouldn't disable a man as punishment, and despite what Piniella thinks, I don't think we can win it without Rickey Henderson. I said we should talk to Lou. We did, and Piniella told us he wanted Henderson traded as soon as possible."

Among the writers, at least two, Bill Madden and Moss Klein, thought that Steinbrenner had "gone nuts." In the past, Steinbrenner had issued some wild statements and said some ridiculous things, but the reporters all agreed this was the most outrageous. With his statement he had destroyed any credibility Lou Piniella could have hoped to maintain with the sensitive, handle-with-care Henderson, driving a wedge between the manager and one of the team's star players. Steinbrenner was saying the team couldn't win without Henderson, but after airing all of the behind-the-scenes dirty laundry about how Piniella and the front office wanted to deal with Rickey's injury, how did he think Piniella could ever get Henderson motivated to play again?

Piniella called Woodward, seeking to resign. Woodward refused to accept his resignation. He said Piniella was the best man for the job.

At the end of the 1987 season, George fired Piniella and put him in the front office. Billy Martin was named manager for a fifth time. There was little reaction to the announcement.

When the 1988 season began, Billy handed out T-shirts that read "Billy V." The V stood for five, not victory. The fans were sure it wouldn't last, knew that George would oversee Billy's every move, were sure that Billy, too often ensconced behind a bar, would self-destruct sooner rather than later.

Sooner came on May 6 in Texas. In a 7–6 loss to the Rangers, Billy was thrown out of the game in the ninth inning for arguing an umpire's call. He dressed quickly. He and Mickey Mantle took a cab to Lace, a strip club not far from the Arlington ballpark. There Billy offended some cowboys, who beat him up, dragged him out an exit door, and put their boots to him. Then they threw him down a flight of stairs and out into an alley. The club put a bloody Billy in a cab, and the cabbie took Billy to his hotel.

It was three in the morning, and it was Billy's bad luck (and good luck) that someone in the hotel had hit the fire alarm, so everyone in the place, including George Steinbrenner and the Yankee players, was standing outside when Billy's cab pulled in. Billy had intended to sneak up to his room, but trainer Gene Monahan took one look at him and ordered him to the hospital. If he hadn't, Billy might well have bled to death that night.

His greatest concern when he got out of the hospital was how George was going to react. He was afraid he would be fired—again.

Of course, he was. It had happened four times before. After a Sunday afternoon loss to the Indians in Cleveland, Steinbrenner sent Clyde King to observe the team, and King, whom Billy always distrusted, fearing he was one of George's spies, was aghast at the way Billy was using his pitchers. He left Tim Stoddard in to take a beating. King advised George to fire Billy and bring in Dallas Green. The

Yankees then lost three games in extra innings to the Tigers, and on June 23, Billy was fired, replaced by Lou Piniella, who just ten days later expressed his regret at having taken the job again. Lou had signed a three-year contract that paid him $400,000 a year, but during a game George had called him on the phone to complain that he hadn't used Dave Righetti in an extra-inning loss to the White Sox.

As Billy had learned, Lou found out that George never changes, despite all of the promises and pledges to butt out. In late August, the pitching fell apart, and so did the Yankees.

Around that same time, Don Mattingly ripped Steinbrenner for showing the players no respect. "You come here and play, and you get no respect," he said. "They belittle your performance and make us look bad in the media. They think money is respect."

George demanded Mattingly apologize. He refused. George then issued a statement saying Mattingly was making excuses for his own shortcomings. He demanded that Piniella sign the statement. Lou refused—even though he knew it meant he would be fired as manager. The statement was never released.

A slump by the Red Sox kept the Yankees in the 1988 race until September. After the Yankees lost three of four to the Sox, they fell six and a half games behind. Steinbrenner then began one of his ugly smear campaigns, this time with Lou Piniella as his target.

He began by spreading rumors that he hadn't yet filed Lou's contract with the commissioner's office. When asked why not, George said mysteriously, "I have my reasons. You can't write it because it's a very sensitive matter."

The sensitive matter had to do with furniture sent to Piniella as payment for doing a radio commercial. George said, "If Lou is stealing from me, I've got to let him go from the entire organization. He's like a son to me, and I'm certainly not going to prosecute him, but he's got to go." Bill Madden in the *Daily News* wrote that George was interviewing Dallas Green for the manager's job. It was a front-page article predicting that the sensitive Piniella was going to be fired. Lou was crushed. He also was angry that George could possibly think that he would steal from him.

"Do you believe the son of a bitch thought I stole from him?" asked Piniella. "What the hell is ten thousand dollars worth of furniture to me? I'm making four hundred thousand." He explained that the furniture had been a gift to him in lieu of payment for doing a pre-game show for WABC radio back in 1986. According to the WABC exec who made the deal, Steinbrenner had known about it and had approved it.

In 1989, George decided to hire as his manager a new face, not a retread. He selected Dallas Green, and he hired as his general manager Bob Quinn. In five years as manager of the Philadelphia Phillies, Green had led the team to a division title in 1980 and a pennant and a World Series victory in 1981. George vowed to let Green and Quinn run the team, but against Green's wishes, he invited both Ron Guidry and Tommy John to camp.

Green was a big fan of pitcher Rick Rhoden, a horse who had led the Yankees staff the year before in innings pitched. But without consulting his new manager, George traded Rhoden to Houston for three minor leaguers with little potential. When Green asked George why he had traded Rhoden away, George made up an excuse. He told him he wanted to cut payroll. "And besides," he told Green, "you have enough pitching." George then made up an even more ridiculous excuse, that Rhoden was cheating by cutting the ball and that he was being investigated by Commissioner Bart Giamatti. George then invented yet another silly rationale: by shedding Rhoden's $900,000 salary, he could then re-sign outfielder Claudell Washington. But Washington signed with the Angels.

Steinbrenner then traded away slugger Jack Clark without consulting Green. The season had already started, and George had traded away Green's best pitcher and he had lost his two best sluggers. George then signed Guidry and John without consulting Green.

Adding to Green's woes was a herniated disk suffered by Dave Winfield. When shortstop Rafael Santana tore a muscle in his elbow, Green and the Yankees were really up against it.

George replaced Bob Quinn as GM even before spring training was over, signing Syd Thrift to replace him. When the story appeared in the *Daily News*, George ordered everyone in the Yankees organization to take a lie detector test so he could find out who leaked the story.

When Dave Winfield went under the knife to repair his herniated disk, Green told the press how much he admired the outfielder. The next day Steinbrenner told Green never to say anything nice about

Winfield. He demanded Green "hammer" Winfield instead. When Green refused, his days as the Yankees manager were numbered.

With Steinbrenner having destroyed the team with his moves, the Yankees got off to a 1–7 start, and then were 33–35 on June 21, when Steinbrenner traded Rickey Henderson to Oakland.

Making Green's life more miserable was George's penchant for second-guessing. He criticized Green's handling of pitchers all year long. On May 30, George called Green into his office for a meeting. There he displayed charts and graphs that bolstered his conclusion that when the Yankees trailed by six runs after the fifth, sixth, or seventh innings, they didn't win. From the chart George concluded that Green was leaving his starting pitchers in too long.

For the first time Green understood just how insane it was working for Steinbrenner.

At the meeting George told Green he was bringing up Deion Sanders. Why? Because Seattle phenom Ken Griffey Jr. had hit two long home runs off the Yankees the night before, and George wanted to bring up his own phenom.

Green had been hired because he was a martinet, but his attempts to impose law and order on the players failed miserably. When he berated his players, he sounded so much like Steinbrenner that they tuned out completely. The team was so bad that in mid-May after a loss to Anaheim, they went to Disneyland and purchased Goofy masks. On the flight from LA to Oakland they sang the Mickey Mouse theme song, but instead of saying "Mickey Mouse," they sang, "We stink." The players were so raucous on the flight that TWA sent the Yankees a $10,000 bill for damages. George questioned Green's ability to discipline his troops.

Green and GM Syd Thrift both were being treated for high blood pressure. Said Green, "Every day Syd would come down to my office from two thirty to three thirty and tell me about George's continual nit-picking. He beat on the coaches, second-guessing Lee Elia at third and Pat Corrales. He sent a list to down there about how many guys got picked off first base. He was also always going on about the pitching being .500. I told him, 'That's what you've got here, .500 pitchers.'"

The next day in the paper, Green called Steinbrenner "Manager George." From then on, every day Green had something negative to say about Steinbrenner. By then he didn't care if he got fired.

Green told Claire Smith of the *Hartford Courant*, "He should have learned from what happened before. If what you've tried for ten years hasn't worked, all the changing of managers and coaches and the criticism, you'd think you'd want to try some other way." Six weeks later he and his coaches were no longer wanted. The team fell from second to sixth place with a 56–65 record, and on August 18 George fired Green and his staff. Cynics suggest that George fired them when he did because two days earlier outfielder Luis Polonia had been arrested for having sex with a fifteen-year-old girl, and here was George's chance to knock Polonia from the headlines.

After he was fired, Green told Bill Conlin of the *Philadelphia Inquirer*, "He doesn't want anyone around he can't command. He couldn't make me change my lineup. He couldn't make me fine people or do anything I didn't want to do." He added, "George doesn't know a fucking thing about baseball. That's the bottom line." He also said, "Let's face it, there is absolutely no hope that their organization will be a winning organization as long as Steinbrenner runs the show. . . . It's sad. There is no organization there now. He has absolutely no pride. The ballplayers there now have no feeling of being a Yankee."

Commented Tom Boswell in the *Washington Post*, "The collective bar-stool wisdom is that the Yankees are, finally and not a moment too soon, a damned and doomed franchise, ruined now and for years to come, by the incompetence of their meddlesome owner."

George wanted Lou Piniella to replace Green, but Piniella had the good sense to say no. When George gave Bucky Dent the chance at his dream job, Bucky agreed. When the team went 2–11 with Dent as manager, the Yankee Stadium fans began to chant, "George must go, George must go." It was a daily occurrence at the stadium. Fans brought "George Must Go" banners, which were quickly removed by the fascistic security guards. Some fans wore paper bags over their heads. All the while, George was taking it out on Syd Thrift, the general manager. But Thrift had no control over the Yankee scouts or the minor league system. He couldn't even function as a true general manager.

George berated Thrift for not sticking up for him after Green's criticisms. In his first meeting with Thrift, Bucky Dent, and the new coaches, George lit into Thrift some more. On August 29, eleven days after Green was fired, Thrift couldn't stand it any longer. He quit. On that day the A's beat the Yankees 19–5. Said George, "We may have rushed Bucky. He might not be ready." Waiting in the wings: Billy VI.

A few days after the season, one in which the Yankees finished 74–87, in fifth place, fourteen games behind Toronto, George told the media, "Next year I'm going to be *more* involved."

Right after that Bob Quinn, a Yankee executive who had been replaced as GM by Syd Thrift, resigned. Quinn told Steinbrenner, "I've had it. I was the only general manager in baseball who went through spring training with no assistant and no regular secretary, and through it all you blamed me for everything. Then you brought in Syd Thrift over me, further humiliating me. And to top it all off, I haven't had a vacation in two years."

"Okay," said George, "You can have the month of December off."

The winter meetings were in December. Said Quinn, "George, I don't want your money. I've just had enough."

Lou Piniella also resigned, and he and Quinn went to the Cincinnati Reds as manager and GM. Dallas Green had been offered the Reds job before Piniella, but he turned it down. He decided to sit out the 1990 season and collect George's money instead.

For the 1990 season, George's choice again was Billy Martin. But on Christmas Day 1989, Billy was driving his Ford truck home from his favorite Binghamton, New York, watering hole, where he and his friend Bill Reedy had been since ten in the morning. Billy's truck hit a patch of ice and slid into a ditch not five hundred feet from his driveway. All Billy had to do was turn off the ignition and walk home, and he would have been fine. But Billy being Billy, he became angered at the ditch he was stuck in, and instead of walking away, he floored it. The truck lurched forward, and when the wheels wouldn't leave the ditch, the truck smashed head-on into a large pipe, breaking Billy's neck and killing him.

Reggie was gone, and now Billy, George's quick-turnaround artist. There was no one left to save George from himself.

This is stupid and venal, but I'm not going to throw him out of baseball. It's not the right thing.
—Baseball commissioner Fay Vincent

Howie Spira and Mr. May

On Thursday, January 19, 1989, the Reagan White House announced that George Steinbrenner was receiving one of ten presidential clemencies granted during Reagan's last two days in office, for Steinbrenner's conviction for making illegal campaign contributions to Richard Nixon. Steinbrenner hadn't been pardoned six months when on June 30, 1990, baseball commissioner Fay Vincent suspended him for life. It was the second time Steinbrenner was suspended from baseball for a significant period of time. This time it was for an unheard-of malfeasance. In an attempt to ruin the reputation of one of his players, Dave Winfield, he had paid a lot of money to a convicted gambler who once worked for the Dave Winfield Foundation to give him dirt on how poorly the Yankee outfielder ran his charity.

Even for George Steinbrenner this was a new low.

For most baseball owners, their most prized possessions are their players. Most owners feel that for players to give their best, they must be well paid and happy in the clubhouse. Not so with George Steinbrenner, who always seemed to be in a fierce competition with individual ballplayers, especially the ones who made headlines. George would become extremely jealous of his star players, resenting that they were getting more credit than he for the success of the team. His romance of and then divorce from Reggie Jackson was perhaps his most intense love/hate affair with one of his players. His feud with outfielder Dave Winfield, which smoldered over a ten-year period, was perhaps the most bizarre.

It had begun when Winfield's agent wrote a clause in his client's ten-year, $16 million contract that Steinbrenner either overlooked or didn't understand when he signed it. The clause called for Winfield's salary to increase as the cost of living rose. During the ten years of his contract, it rose a lot, and that cost Steinbrenner an extra $7 million. The clause came to George's attention in an article written by Murray Chass in the *New York Times*, and when he saw the article, he felt he had been made to look like a fool, and he exploded, demanding that the clause be rewritten. When Winfield refused, George was stuck. Winfield didn't know it, but he had made an enemy, one who would stop at nothing to get revenge. George grew hateful, and his actions would lead to his ban from baseball.

George's first salvo had come after Winfield made only one hit in the 1981 World Series, a series the Yankees lost. Steinbrenner disdain-fully referred to him as "Mr. May." In 1985, after the Yankees went into a tailspin, he twice reneged on sending checks to Winfield's foundation, checks he was contractually obligated to send because another clause in the contract provided that the Yankees each year would contribute $300,000 to the Dave Winfield Foundation. The organization, set up to help underprivileged children, was gathering the support of major corporations to help Winfield in his quest to show kids how to reject the lure of drugs. Dave Winfield was one of those caring athletes who felt strongly about giving back to the community. Any other team would have been honored to have a Dave Winfield on its roster. George Steinbrenner tried to blacken not only Winfield's reputation but that of the foundation as well.

Winfield was forced to go to court to sue him for the money. When George continued to refuse to pay, Winfield continued to press him for the money. George, a gutter fighter like Billy Martin, but one who used lawyers, PR men, and the press rather than his fists, struck back. Without revealing the reason behind his words, the bully in George surfaced. He wanted the public to know that not only didn't the Winfield Foundation deserve the money, but also that Winfield wasn't earning his $2-million-a-year Yankees salary, either.

George continued dogging Winfield through 1986. A number of times during the season he ordered manager Lou Piniella to platoon, bench, or remove Winfield from the fourth spot in the batting order. Piniella, who needed Winfield's bat in the lineup every day, refused, hurting his relationship with Steinbrenner. George also tried to trade Winfield, but the big outfielder had a no-trade clause in his contract, and he made George even crazier when he refused to allow himself to be traded.

Nothing much happened in 1987, but in 1988, Winfield's rather benign autobiography was published. Steinbrenner, who had traded Sparky Lyle and Graig Nettles after they wrote their autobiographies, wanted to dump Winfield too, but again the no-trade clause made that impossible.

Wanting what he wanted even if it was impossible, during spring training in Fort Lauderdale, George ordered Piniella to work a trade for Winfield anyway. Piniella arranged to trade Winfield to Toronto for Jesse Barfield or to Houston for Kevin Bass. In the middle of his discussion with Houston GM Bill Wood, Piniella was startled when Steinbrenner came storming into his office and ordered him to come with him. He led him outside the stadium, where hundreds of Yankees fans were milling around. As they approached the gate where the people with complimentary tickets were admitted, Steinbrenner pulled Piniella down behind a bush.

"Stay down," George ordered. "Don't let anyone see you." He then told Piniella, "I'm sick and tired of all these free passes being given out. There's too many people getting free passes, and I'm going to put a stop to it. Now, I want you to stay here and watch all the people who come through this gate. Count them and see who they are."

George then left. But because his search for the users of free passes had usurped his pursuit of a trade of Winfield, the issue was no longer pursued.

Steinbrenner ordered Billy Martin and Willie Randolph to speak out against Winfield's book, but all this talk did was increase sales. Steinbrenner attacked Winfield relentlessly, but the attacks made no impact. On the field, Yankees fans cheered Winfield as they never had before.

At the end of the 1988 season, Steinbrenner had to decide whether to exercise the option on the last two years of Dave Winfield's contract. He'd have to pay Winfield half its value, about $2 million, to let him go. Over the eight years he played with the Yankees, many while under attack by Steinbrenner, Winfield had hit a stellar .291, averaging 25 homers a year and 102 RBIs. He may not have been the straw that stirred the drink, but he was *damn* good. More than anything else, the fans respected him for standing up to Steinbrenner. In 1988, Winfield had hit .322, with 25 homers and 107 RBIs. How could George let him go free and risk his signing with a rival?

He couldn't. George exercised the option. Winfield would be George's bête noire for the next two years.

On January 6, 1989, Winfield sued Steinbrenner for again failing to make an annual $300,000 contribution to the Winfield Foundation, but this time Steinbrenner sued back, charging the foundation with "fraud, wrongdoing, and misappropriations." Steinbrenner had hired a retired IRS investigator to audit the books of the Winfield Foundation, and the investigator discovered discrepancies indicating that the foundation spent six dollars for every dollar it gave to charity.

Steinbrenner had an additional inside source who was providing him with information. He charged that money had been diverted from "the needy children of the city of New York" and given to Winfield and his friends. He also charged that "Winfield had made large loans at usurious rates of interest . . . and an individual he knew was engaged in heavy gambling." He demanded that Winfield make a $480,000 donation to the foundation, money he charged his outfielder should have given the foundation but didn't. Steinbrenner asked the court to place the foundation in receivership.

In response, Winfield told reporters accurately, "[He] can't steal my money, he can't run me out of town, so he's trying to ruin my reputation."

When Winfield suffered a herniated disk in his back during spring training, he was out for the entire 1989 season. On March 24, he had back surgery, and when he didn't visit the clubhouse the entire time, his teammates wondered how much he really cared about them.

On September 6, 1989, Winfield and Steinbrenner settled. Winfield agreed to pay $229,667 in delinquent contributions to the foundation; to reimburse the foundation $30,000 for monies taken from it; and to admit that certain allegations made by Steinbrenner were accurate. Steinbrenner agreed to pay the foundation $600,000 in back payments that had been placed in escrow.

That year George said to *Daily News* reporter Bill Madden, "You know, Winfield is the most selfish athlete I've ever known. He's nothing like Reggie . . . or even Graig Nettles. Nettles may have said a lot of nasty things about me, but he played hard, gave me his all, and was all for the team. I'd take him back any time."

On March 18, 1990, the thirty-two-day-long lockout by the baseball owners ended when Commissioner Fay Vincent brokered a deal with them. Vincent thought his nightmare had ended, but the next day there was an article in the *New York Daily News* in which a small-time gambler by the name of Howie Spira told the world that George Steinbrenner had paid him $40,000 to dish dirt on Dave Winfield.

Fay Vincent now had a second battle on his hands. Vincent had come to baseball as the assistant to baseball commissioner Bart Giamatti. But after five short months, Giamatti dropped dead of a heart attack at age sixty-one, and Vincent was thrust into the spotlight. Vincent, a Williams College graduate like George, was one of the sharpest lawyers in the business, and after working in government, he had been head of Columbia Pictures and Coca-Cola before joining Giamatti as baseball's top executives.

During the five months he was commissioner, Giamatti was very wary of George Steinbrenner and had asked Vincent to handle his fellow Williams graduate. And Vincent had. And it turned out that Steinbrenner wasn't nearly as difficult as Vincent thought he was going to be. Indeed, for a while, Steinbrenner was a stout supporter of theirs.

"George couldn't have been nicer when Bart died," said Vincent. "He said all the right things. And I remember shortly after I took over as commissioner, George and I went up to Williams for the Williams-Amherst game, and we appeared on a radio show up there, and George said, 'We have a star in Mr. Vincent, and I love him, and . . . ' He could not have been more fulsome and ebullient.

"On the other hand, I realized that George can be a loose cannon in baseball. I had met and gotten to know Al Rosen, the old Cleveland third baseman.

"He said, 'George basically is impossible if you are weak. He bludgeons little people, steps on little people, but he won't be able to do that with you. You are a very wealthy guy. You made a lot of money. You have a big position. He will not go after you at all.'

"And he was right. I said to myself, Al Rosen is a smart guy. George never made a frontal attack on me until we got into the mess over Howard Spira. Up until then, he was very deferential."

During the fall and winter of 1989–1990, in Fay Vincent's first battle as commissioner during his first winter in baseball, the owners locked out the players in an attempt to break the players' union. The owners had just colluded with one another to cheat the players out of hundreds of millions of dollars in salary, and the lockout was supposed to stick a dagger into the heart of the union. The problem was that the big-market teams, including the Yankees, were making too much money, and Vincent would get calls to end the lockout from George saying, "Fay, get this done. Just step in and do what you have to do. It's not worth blowing away part of the season. Let's play baseball."

Meanwhile, the small-market teams, led by Bud Selig, wanted the lockout to continue. Selig was telling Vincent, "Oh no, we have to really stand together and see if we can break the union. If we don't do it now, we're going to have to do it down the road, and we're screwed and we're going broke and we can't make a living."

In the end, Fay Vincent stepped in and got the issue resolved, and on the day the commissioner's office announced that the strike had been resolved, that the lockout was over, there was the article in the *New York Daily News* about Howie Spira and the $40,000.

Said Vincent, "I went to bed at two in the morning having resolved the lockout, and I woke up to the Howie Spira story in the paper. I went from dealing with the lockout to dealing with Steinbrenner. It was an uninterrupted nightmare."

In the article it was reported that Spira supplied information to George Steinbrenner because of his anger toward Winfield. Spira claimed that from 1981 through 1983 he did public relations work for the Winfield Foundation. Among his charges was that Winfield made him two loans totaling $21,000 to help him pay off gambling debts at a usurious interest rate and that at least once Winfield threatened him with a gun when he didn't pay the money back fast enough. Spira also accused Winfield of ruining his life. He said he provided Steinbrenner with the information in 1986. Apparently Steinbrenner sat on it for three years before using it against Winfield.

Winfield denied ever making loans to Spira, but when Spira displayed a check for $15,000 with Winfield's signature, the denial was proved false. For the first time people began to question Winfield's character, wondering whether perhaps Steinbrenner had been right about him and his foundation. Spira also let on that he was the one providing Steinbrenner with information on Winfield.

As soon as baseball commissioner Fay Vincent read the article in the *Daily News* alleging that Steinbrenner had paid for information to defame one of his players, he hired private investigator John Dowd to look into the matter. It didn't take long for Dowd to piece the story together. Vincent held a series of hearings with Judge Howard "Ace" Tyler sitting in, because Vincent knew George's first defense would be to charge that he wasn't getting a fair hearing. Tyler was protection against such a charge.

George's story was that he hadn't paid Spira the $40,000 willingly but only because Spira threatened to expose him if he didn't. It was a reprise of his blaming Jack Melcher for his Watergate troubles, though this time there was some evidence that after the first payment Spira did come back for more.

At the hearing Vincent said to Steinbrenner, "George, you have known me, knew I came from the government, you knew this guy was holding you up. This really is extortion in a criminal sense. Why didn't you come to me? Why?"

Steinbrenner answered, "I can't answer that. I should have."

"You certainly should have," responded Vincent.

Said Vincent about George's intentions, "He was so determined to bring Winfield down, he wanted to be able to destroy Winfield. This was George at his absolute worst. It was a miserable piece of work. And he did some other things he shouldn't have done. He went to Howard Cosell, the pillar of the church, who was writing a column for the *Daily News*. He fed Cosell all of the allegations against Winfield. Cosell, without doing a moment's investigating, printed the story as though Winfield had done all the things that George alleged. Winfield hadn't done any of them. And when we sent Dowd to Cosell to get the data from Howard, of course Cosell was devastated, because there wasn't any. It goes to show you the enormous power of owning the New York Yankees. Cosell loved going to ball games, sitting in that wonderful facility, and he wrote that piece. When Dowd pushed him, he had no information. So, typical of the world we live in, Cosell writes a book and just unloads on me. As though it were my fault. You can't tell me Cosell was a great person. You have to read the article he wrote. It was such bad work.

"Then Steinbrenner went to [New York district attorney] Robert Morgenthau, who is really a great man, and Morgenthau, on Steinbrenner's petition, starts a criminal investigation of Winfield. What's that all about? You can't do that. So it was a pretty ugly story. Here's a very powerful guy who was really pissed at Winfield, trying to destroy him, but his big mistake was climbing in bed with Spira, but he did it because he was desperate for facts, and he didn't have any."

Initially George came up with a string of rationales for what he had done. The first was that he had loaned Spira the money because he felt sorry for Spira's aging mother and did it "out of the goodness of my heart." Then he said he did it because he feared for the safety of his family, so much that he considered applying for a gun permit. He said another reason he did it was that he feared that Spira would reveal information about "two employees who stole from the team" and that he would talk about Lou Piniella's gambling habits. The two employees, Pat Kelly and Dave Weidler, took "great bulks of giveaway items" and sold them, said Steinbrenner, ratting out his own employees to the public. Why Spira would have known any of this was unclear. George then said the reason he gave Spira the money was so he would "take the money and get out of town."

"The reason was very clear why Steinbrenner did it," said Vincent. "Winfield took George to the cleaners in his contract, because George didn't understand what CPI [consumer price index] meant. At the time, President Carter drove the CPI through the roof, and it cost George a fortune, and then Murray Chass wrote a very, very dismissive article, in effect saying George should get a new brain or a new GM, that the contract was just awful, and when Chass insulted George so viciously and accurately, Steinbrenner went crazy. He was played for a fool, and that's one thing George never wanted to be, to look stupid."

One charge George made was that three times he had informed Commissioner Peter Ueberroth about the extortion threats by Spira, and three times Ueberroth had ignored him. He argued that since Ueberroth had ignored him, it wasn't his fault that he had given in to Spira's extortion demands, because when he tried to tell the commissioner about it, he got nowhere. The only problem with the story was that it was a complete fabrication. In July 1990, Ueberroth told Vincent that he had never heard Spira's name from Steinbrenner.

After a week of hearings, Steinbrenner's defense was the same one he used in the Watergate case: "I got bad advice." In the end he told Fay Vincent, "I did it. I'm sorry. Whatever the punishment, I'll take it."

At least one reporter urged the baseball commissioner to throw George out of baseball for life as Giamatti had jettisoned Pete Rose. Barry Bloom wrote in the *San Diego Union-Tribune*, "The man who turned the New York Yankees into dirt must face the music. Do it for all the Yankees fans who remember Mantle, Maris, and Whitey. . . . Do it for baseball. Do it because it is right. . . . Make him sell the Yankees. Put us all out of our misery. Push, Fay, push. The boss must go."

But Vincent wasn't convinced a lifetime ban was called for. He talked it over with his assistant, Steve Greenburg, and with Judge Tyler. He said, "This isn't Pete Rose. This looks like about a two-year suspension. This is stupid and venal, but I'm not going to throw him out of baseball. It's not the right thing."

What George didn't count on was that Fay Vincent and Steve Greenburg were able to anticipate any and all subterfuges George might use to circumvent the ban. One of those subterfuges was asking for a lifetime ban.

Said Vincent, "He'll figure he can outmaneuver us and run the team through his sons or someone else, and that way he won't be suspended, and he'll have made a good deal." Vincent suggested that Greenburg write up an agreement that was ironclad, in effect putting George out of baseball for life. "We were just trying to be good lawyers," said Vincent, "trying to be prepared for whatever happened."

Prepared they were. And that's what happened. On the day Vincent was going to pronounce the two-year suspension, George told him he had decided he wanted to leave baseball forever, that he would turn it over to his boys. When Vincent asked if he really knew what he was talking about, George insisted that he did.

"Later we met again. In came Steinbrenner with two different lawyers. One was a classmate at Williams, and I don't know who the other one was. The two of them didn't agree. The Williams lawyer was the deal man. He kept saying 'We'll work something out.' The other lawyer wanted to go to court and sue and challenge the authority of the commissioner.

"In the course of the meeting Steve and I pulled out the agreement we had made. We said, 'This is not negotiable. This is not an offer. Either you sign this and you're out for life, or I suspend you, and I don't really care which one you do. I have a press conference at five this afternoon.'"

The two lawyers argued back and forth, but at the last moment, George signed the lifetime ban.

"We were stunned, because it was trading a speeding violation into a life sentence," said Vincent. "It really made no sense, unless he really had had enough. But then what we heard later—this is not firsthand knowledge but I'm pretty sure it's right—he gets down to the car having signed this thing, and he calls Jerry Reinsdorf and he said, 'Jerry, I just made a great deal with Steve and Fay.' And Jerry, who is smarter than all of us, said, 'Really? What is it?' And George told Jerry the deal, and Jerry said, 'George, let me be the first to tell you. You got fucked. You made a horrible deal.'

"That was the opening. From that moment on, George realized he had made a disastrous mistake."

George thought it was a good deal because it protected him from getting bumped from the U.S. Olympic Committee, but what he didn't realize was how airtight Greenburg and Vincent had made the contract. He was sure he could still run the Yankees while he was out, but the agreement barred him from doing that, and it also barred him from appealing, suing, or in any way challenging the document. There was nothing legally he could do about it. Or at least that's what Greenburg and Vincent thought.

"We misjudged him, as usual," said Vincent. "He then got a couple of people to sue us on his behalf."

The lawsuits were bogus, but the amount of time Vincent's office had to spend defending the suits was substantial as George's lawyers made motions and took depositions and otherwise made life miserable for Vincent.

"They were manufacturing and causing trouble," said Vincent, "and then after about ten months George calls me up and he says, 'Fay, I want to come back to baseball.'"

Vincent refused to talk to him about it. "I said, 'George, look. I know what you did. You signed an agreement with me that you wouldn't sue me, and then you had some buddies of yours sue me.

It's not even close to being kosher, and it's not going to fly, and I'm not going to talk to you. You're out for life, George. You had very bad counsel. They were stupid, though they are eminent.'

"Later he called me back. 'What if I make the suits go away?'" Vincent told him he would consider it.

Later, Steinbrenner called Vincent back again, complaining that settling those suits was going to cost him a lot of money, but Vincent wouldn't budge. Finally, he called to say he had gotten rid of the lawsuits, which cost him a lot of money to settle.

A meeting was set. Steve Greenburg and Fay Vincent met George secretly. This time Steinbrenner brought a new lawyer, one not nearly as belligerent as his first two. Steinbrenner said to Vincent, "You and Steve were too smart for my other lawyers. You took us apart. I admit that. I got killed by bad lawyering. Now I have a new lawyer, and we're going to try to work something out."

"We'll work it out on my terms," said Vincent.

"What do you mean?" asked Steinbrenner.

"It was a two-year suspension," said Vincent. "At the end of two years I will talk about reinstating you." Which is exactly what happened. After Steinbrenner served his two years, on March 1, 1993, Vincent reinstated him. He explained why he did it: it was the right thing to do. "I can't imagine keeping a guy locked up just because he had bad legal advice."

Meanwhile, Steinbrenner went after Howie Spira in much the same way he had gone after Jack Melcher, his Watergate attorney. He had gotten Melcher to resign from the bar. In this case, he made sure Spira would go to jail. Spira had tried to hit up Steinbrenner for more money, and George, who had close ties to the FBI in Tampa, made a complaint that resulted in Spira's arrest. Howie Spira was tried and convicted and sentenced to three years in prison.

Steinbrenner also went after Fay Vincent. He joined forces with Jerry Reinsdorf of the Chicago White Sox, Bud Selig of the Milwaukee Brewers, and Charlie Brumback of the Tribune Company to get rid of Vincent as commissioner. They were ganging up on him for various reasons and because of his not-tough-enough stand against the union. They appointed a committee to determine whether Vincent had trampled on George's civil liberties. They were trying to find ways to embarrass him so he'd resign.

Said Vincent, "I kept saying to them, 'It's like the guy who pleads guilty and then claims the jury selection was improper.' George begged me to let him sign this piece of paper and not suspend him. And then he goes around and says he wasn't treated fairly. It doesn't make any sense. But that's the way he lived and played. The tragedy of George is with all his ability and all his good luck and fortune, he never could confront his own mistakes." In the end, George helped force Vincent out as commissioner. After he resigned, Bud Selig, determined to break the players' union, took over. Selig and his pit bull, Randy Levine, would be largely responsible for the disastrous player strike of 1994, a strike that caused the World Series to be canceled for the first time in baseball history.

For two years Steinbrenner would have to keep his nose out of the Yankees' business. For those two and a half years two talented baseball people, general manager Gene Michael and farm director Bill Livesay, would restore order to the team and put it on a foundation to win four more world championships. When the Yankees once again were able to rise to greatness, George Steinbrenner would be guaranteed a place in the Baseball Hall of Fame and in the hearts of Yankees fans. One result of the four Yankees world championships: the delirious fans and longtime critics would forgive him for the seventeen years of unabated craziness and for the Howie Spira incident that ended it.

I don't know about you boys, but I'll be eating
three meals a day.

—George Steinbrenner to union leaders

American Ship Goes Under

When Steinbrenner was suspended from running the
Yankees for two and a half years for the Howie Spira/
Dave Winfield mess in 1990, he was able to devote most of his time to
running American Ship Building. He had moved his home to Tampa
in 1976 and had been shifting the base of operations of American Ship
since then.

His move to Tampa had been provoked by media coverage in
Cleveland of his Watergate troubles, which had upset him very much.
When I interviewed George Steinbrenner in 1981, he made it clear
that he wanted to put the whole "Watergate thing," his first major
scandal, behind him.

"I'm a felon," he said. "I am, and I live with it. It's not easy to say to
people. And it hurts me. But you have to live with it, and I do live with
it. I suppose some president will feel I have a pardon coming, because
there are people being pardoned for a hell of a lot more than what
I did. A twenty-five-thousand-dollar contribution was at issue, when I
gave seventy-five thousand dollars of my own money."

He did admit, though, that he became so upset with the coverage
of the case by the Cleveland media that he decided to leave Cleveland

and relocate to Tampa, Florida. "I moved out of Cleveland [in 1976]. I moved to Tampa, Florida, and between Florida and New York, I couldn't be happier. I just don't have the feel for Cleveland anymore."

In 1972, George had bought the Tampa Ship Repair and Dry Dock Co., one of the nation's largest repair docks, adding it to American Ship Building's yards in Chicago, Cleveland, and Lorain. He also bought an 860-acre horse farm in nearby Ocala. In 1979, Steinbrenner moved American Ship Building's main office out of Cleveland, announcing on October 22, 1979, that he was relocating the headquarters to Tampa.

The reason he gave for the move out of Cleveland was that his wife's health wasn't good, and he wanted her to live in a more healthful place. Critics saw this for what it was: another Pinocchio moment. He was moving, they knew, because after all of the negative publicity about his underhanded attempt to funnel corporate money to the Nixon campaign, his ego couldn't take the stares of the locals who were looking at him thinking, *He's damn lucky he didn't end up behind bars.*

He also announced that the company's AmShip division, which built and repaired ships for the Great Lakes, would be moved from Cleveland to Lorain, Ohio.

George's biggest problem was that the landscape had shifted dramatically in the shipbuilding industry. By the end of the 1970s, Great Lakes shipbuilding was in as serious a bind as the automobile industry. There was no getting around it. The economy was becoming global, and it was a lot cheaper to build boats—and cars—in the Far East.

The Maritime Administration had passed a construction subsidy, which paid the difference between the cost of building the ship in the United States and building one abroad, but the subsidy was limited to 50 percent of the ship's cost. Yards in Japan quoted prices 60 percent below those of U.S. yards. How could the U.S. firms compete? Not easily. And as China and India emerged as industrial nations, the competition became more intense and the nation's ability to compete more impossible.

As a result, most American shipyards were in trouble because of lack of orders. In the late 1970s, more than fifty thousand dockworkers were laid off in the cities at the heart of the steel industry that stretched across the Great Lakes. Chicago, Gary, Flint, Detroit, Toledo, Cleveland, Akron, Youngstown, Pittsburgh, Erie, and Buffalo became known as the Rust Belt.

Moreover, American shipyards that were building boats were losing money because of high labor costs. By the late 1970s, only two Great Lakes shipbuilding companies had survived. American Ship was one of them, and the reason it had survived was that Steinbrenner had been able to get the Lorain Port Authority to float $7 million in tax-free revenue bonds for the firm to finance the building of a mammoth dry dock capable of building thousand-foot-long super ore carriers. In 1975 and 1980, the Port Authority floated two additional bond issues totaling $6.8 million for improvements to AmShip's yard.

Clearly, the era of ships being built in the United States was coming to a close. In 1981, AmShip's Chicago yard closed, and in 1983, its Toledo shipyard closed its door as a hundred workers were laid off. Almost a thousand workers were laid off at the AmShip Lorain plant that year. At the same time, forty-five hundred workers were laid off by Lorain's U.S. Steel pipe mill, sending unemployment in the city of Lorain to a whopping 36 percent.

Things were no better for the Great Lakes shipping business. A sudden drop in the production of steel in the United States resulted in a sharp decrease in Great Lakes shipping traffic. Only about half of the more than a hundred bulk carriers were operating in 1983.

In the summer of 1982, Steinbrenner went to Washington, where he promised Congressman Donald Pease of Ohio that he would bring nine hundred jobs to Lorain if Pease would help him gain support for a navy contract to build five cargo tankers that would bring the company $300 million in revenue. Pease said Steinbrenner promised him that if he got the contract, the work would be done in Lorain.

Pease went to work. He contacted the navy, and he arranged to have other members of the Ohio delegation send letters. Among those who used their influence was Senator Howard Metzenbaum of Ohio, who said that Steinbrenner had called him "with syrupy, sweet promises that he would do everything he could to keep the jobs in Lorain."

American Ship won the contract. But instead of bringing the work to Lorain as he promised, Steinbrenner went to the union leaders and demanded concessions on wages, fringe benefits, and work rules, threatening that if they didn't give in to his demands, he would shut the Lorain shipyard and throw them all out of work. Unless the unions gave in to his demands, he would do the work in Tampa, he said.

Said Senator Metzenbaum, "As usual with George Steinbrenner's promises, they soon turned to castor oil."

Said Pease, "I feel I was misled and double-crossed."

George told the union leaders, "I don't know about you boys, but I'll be eating three meals a day." Union leaders said negotiations were undermined by George's arrogance and his hostility toward the unions. During the eleven months of bargaining, Steinbrenner told the union leaders, "If you don't get in the ballpark, there isn't going to be any game." It wasn't an idle threat.

George complained of the high cost of doing business in Lorain. The union leaders countered by saying the higher costs were due to "stupid mistakes" and "mismanagement" of AmShip.

In the end, Steinbrenner's offer was a $2.50-an-hour pay cut from their salary or the complete loss of their health benefits. The members decided they would rather see the plant close than give in to blackmail.

When the union refused to give in, Steinbrenner had the ships built in Tampa. In December, a few weeks before Christmas of 1983, he announced he was closing the Lorain shipyard altogether—throwing more than fifteen hundred workers out of work.

"There's a real tragedy here, and it should be a national scandal," said James Ulger, president of the local Boilermakers union. "The American Ship Building Company isn't losing money; it's not facing hard economic times. They've got a record-breaking backlog of work. But they've thumbed their noses at everybody in Ohio and gone down South." He went on, "When you see the amount of misery this is caus- ing, it can literally rip your heart out. But there's nothing you can do."

Steinbrenner said later that American Ship Building had lost $30 million on the Lorain yard over the past five years. He positioned himself as one who battled his board to keep the yard open three years longer than everyone else wanted.

Said John Cole, the editor of the *Lorain Journal*, "He showed no loyalty to the city or the people, not to anyone but George Steinbrenner."

President Ronald Reagan in the end finished off the shipbuild- ing industry in the United States when he got rid of subsidies and tax breaks that allowed U.S. companies to compete with Japan, which could build ships far more cheaply because of inexpensive labor costs. More than forty shipyards closed in the 1980s. American Ship stayed open mostly on George Steinbrenner's misplaced belief that he could over-come any obstacle and succeed. He also kept it open because of pride: the industry had been in his blood since he was a child. Steinbrenner failed in the end, but one has to give him credit for trying.

After winning a navy contract to build five oceangoing cargo ships, in March 1983 Steinbrenner announced that Tampa-based American Ship would become a defense contractor. He also announced that AmShip would subcontract out some of the work to nonunion shipyards in New Orleans and Mobile, Alabama. Tampa workers were skeptical of Stein-brenner's promises. On the side of the one of the trucks at the Tampa shipyard was written the word "Lorain."

AmShip successfully completed the work on the five cargo tankers in 1985 at the repair facilities. The tankers came in on time and on budget. It would be the shipyard's first and last major success. After the tanker contract was completed, AmShip laid off twelve hundred of its fifteen hundred workers. The question was what to do next. The dry dock in Tampa had been built for the purpose of repairing ships. It did not have the capability to build them from scratch. But as with the Cleveland Pipers and with politics, George Steinbrenner had grandiose plans for the facility. In Chicago and Lorain, he had built ore carriers and other vessels. He wanted to be able to do the same thing at the Tampa Ship Repair and Dry Dock he owned in Tampa. The idea was that he was going to build supertankers. Tampa floated $23 million in bonds to improve the facilities to build them. But the orders never came.

In 1986, Steinbrenner, desperate for business, announced that AmShip had signed a contract to build two eight-hundred-passenger ships for the Hawaiian cruise market. In January 1987, he applied for $225 million in federal guarantees. If he had succeeded, AmShip would have been the first American company to build a cruise ship in the United States since the 1950s.

"I believe we have to do things that build this nation, not others," said Steinbrenner. It was a bigger pipe dream than signing Steve Trout and expecting him to win twenty games.

Others were contemptuous. Said the president of American Hawaii Cruises, C. R. Huang, "It's a fantasy. You can't combine high capital cost with high labor cost."

Huang was right. It was a fantasy. Steinbrenner tried to get both Lee Iacocca and former treasury secretary William Simon to invest, but both declined. The cruise ships never were built.

Financial World magazine, in listing its "Ten Worst Managed Companies in America," said the only reason American Ship Building didn't make the list was that "the company is simply too small these days to merit serious consideration in a contest of this gravity." The magazine noted that "George has taken it from $194 million in sales . . . to just $25.3 million in sales [in the last few years]." Acknowledging that the whole industry was in trouble, it noted, "It takes a special kind of talent to invest in cruise liners when nobody has built one in the U.S. for more than thirty years."

That same year President Reagan announced that he was eliminating subsidies for building U.S.-flag vessels. By 1988, construction of merchant vessels had stopped altogether. In 1987, AmShip lost $8.9 million, and Steinbrenner was desperate, so desperate that he, along with other executives, took stock instead of salaries.

Looking for a way to make some money, Steinbrenner bought a company that made gutters and sidings for houses, but a housing slump sunk it, and it was sold. AmShip announced a plan to design a four-hundred-foot-long, seven-story barge to follow Alaska's pollock fishing fleet and process the catch into frozen fillets called surimi, a high-protein, low-fat fish paste. The scheme never got off the ground. George swore he convinced his board members to kill it. His cruise ship plan backfired, and he didn't get his Maritime Administration loan.

Making things worse for the company, in 1987, Steinbrenner had a face-off with the unions. As in Lorain, he made a "last offer" to the union leadership, demanding 40 percent pay cuts. Union leaders said they would bend, but not that far. AmShip stock fell to nine dollars a share.

On November 18, 1988, Steinbrenner fired AmShip's president, Allen Fernstrom. He was the third president George had fired in the last five years. Edward Forbes and George Chandler were sacked before him. Steinbrenner, riding to the rescue, took Fernstrom's place.

"We've had several people as presidents and CEOs, and the board has asked me to step in again," said George. "I'm determined to turn it around, and I think that I will. I'm not happy with the company right now. But I'm confident. People have bet against me before."

The only construction left for the shipyards, Steinbrenner decided, would come from the U.S. Navy, but in March 1989 American Ship suffered a serious blow when the navy announced that a shipyard in New Orleans had won the bid to build three navy tankers that had been targeted for American Ship. The reason: AmShip's bid was $30 million higher than the lowest bid. So even though the navy was aware that the loss of the work probably meant a death blow to AmShip, it denied them the contract anyway. In 1989, as AmShip stock sank to three dollars a share, Steinbrenner was forced to lend the company $1.35 million of his own money to stay afloat. By the time of George's suspension from baseball in 1990, the stock in the company had fallen to $2.50 a share.

Steinbrenner got what he thought was a reprieve in April 1990 when AmShip was awarded a $49 million labor-only contract to refit two half-built navy refueling oil tankers, part of the six-hundred-ship armada commissioned at the height of Ronald Reagan's defense buildup in 1985. They were left half done with pieces lying on the ground because the first firm was so short of cash that a $25,000 donation by employees to the United Way was diverted to pay bills. When the navy terminated the contract, Steinbrenner pounced. He lobbied two friends in Congress, Senator Daniel Inouye, to whom he had donated laundered corporate funds during the Watergate years, and Representative John Murtha, then chairman of the House Appropriations Defense Subcommittee.

There were protests about giving the job to AmShip in that the company had never done this type of work before. The navy had to pay $10 million to transport the ships, which were unseaworthy, from Philadelphia to Tampa. One ship ran aground en route, incurring severe damage. When the ships finally arrived, Steinbrenner said he couldn't believe what "rust buckets" they were. Some twelve thousand tons of rusted parts arrived on dozens of railroad cars and more than a hundred trucks. The ships were in such bad condition that an executive of a competing company, who did the due diligence, concluded, "No prudent person would bid on that contract."

Maybe so, but George Steinbrenner impetuously had bid on the job and signed the contract, even though it had no provisions for cost overruns and even though the Tampa shipyard was a repair facility that couldn't have completed the complex task of building the ships without a major renovation. Machine shops were inadequate. Areas for building ship sections were too small. The yard had no warehouse. Tampa Shipyards lacked the planning staff to map out the work. And it had no trained workforce for the job.

"Ship building and repair are two different worlds that just happen to involve ships and dry docks," said Tim Colton, a consultant for the Port of Tampa. "It's like the difference between an automobile repair shop and an automobile production plant." Another expert, who studied the inadequate Tampa facilities, commented, "It was like a mouse trying to swallow an elephant."

"They didn't have the experience and didn't know what they were doing," said Mark Buse, legislative assistant to Senator John McCain, who opposed awarding the contract to Tampa. "Congress was responding to individuals using high-powered lobbyists."

Steinbrenner was so desperate he would have bid on anything, and four years later, after running through four CEOs, he ended up with an impossible job that he couldn't finish under budget, a canceled contract, and the death of his beloved company. Steinbrenner asked the navy for an additional $24 million in 1992 and was turned down. He then went back to congressmen on his payroll, who put $45 million into a defense appropriations bill. When troubles continued, Steinbrenner offered to finish the job using his own money. The navy said no, and in August 1993 canceled the contract when the ships weren't even close to being finished. As a result, AmShip filed for bankruptcy to protect it from creditors, and in 1995 the company was sold to Delphi American Maritime Inc., a Greek firm.

The bill for the two unfinished ships came to $450 million. The Senate Permanent Subcommittee on Investigations raised three key questions:

1. Why were the half-built ships awarded to Tampa Shipyards, a subsidiary of American Ship Building Co?
2. What role did the political connections of Yankees owner George Steinbrenner play in that decision?
3. Why were the ships never completed?

No report was ever issued.

24 I had to work a lot with the field coordinator,
and Mr. Steinbrenner kept firing them, for whatever reason.

—Mitch Lukevics, Yankee farm director

Gene Michael Rebuilds

During the period when George and Billy Martin were a dysfunctional couple, the Miller beer company decided to air a jaunty national commercial in which the two men bantered back and forth as to whether the beer tasted great or was less filling. Finally George says to Billy, "You're fired." Billy replies, "Oh no, not again." They laugh. It was supposed to be endearing, but few thought it amusing.

While on suspension after the Howie Spira debacle, Steinbrenner decided it would do his image good if he branched out into show business. On October 20, 1990, he hosted *Saturday Night Live*. This was the year his former manager Lou Piniella led the Cincinnati Reds to the world championship. In the opening sketch, Steinbrenner dreams that he is the manager, the coach, and all nine players. In another sketch, he chews out Al Franken for featuring him in a mock Slim-Fast commercial with Saddam Hussein, Pol Pot, and Idi Amin.

"They're ruthless characters," he complains to Lorne Michaels. "I'm just the owner of a baseball team."

In another skit, Steinbrenner is a store manager who cannot bring himself to fire an employee, no matter how inept or incompetent.

"How do you fire a man?" he asks rhetorically. "I just can't fire people; it's not in my nature."

In 1994, George appeared in the movie *The Scout*, with Albert Brooks and Brendan Fraser. In it Brooks, a Yankees scout, is sent as punishment to Mexico, where he discovers Fraser, the greatest player in the game. He brings him to New York to play for George Steinbrenner, who has a cameo. The movie went straight to video.

Then on May 19, 1994, George Costanza, played by Jason Alexander, was hired by the New York Yankees on the TV sitcom *Seinfeld*, the show about nothing. For four seasons, Costanza interacted with the team owner, George Steinbrenner. It was the role that would make the real George Steinbrenner nationally mega-famous. When Jerry Seinfeld called Steinbrenner personally to ask if he could use his name, Steinbrenner had no idea who the stand-up comedian even was.

The running joke throughout the final four years of the show was that no matter what idiotic, self-destructive thing George Costanza did while an employee of the Yankees, instead of firing him for it, the George Steinbrenner character would praise or reward him in some way. Larry David, the warped mind behind the caricature, left many memorable Steinbrenner moments for *Seinfeld* fans to savor.

In the first show in which the Steinbrenner character appeared, titled "The Opposite," George Costanza, a schlameil of a loser, decides that on the day he is applying to work for the New York Yankees he will take an opposite approach to everything he is accustomed to doing.

That morning he had been sitting on the beach, analyzing his life. He says to the Jerry Seinfeld character, "It became very clear to me sitting out there today, that every decision I've ever made in my entire life has been wrong. My life is the opposite of everything I want it to be. Every instinct I have in every day life, be it something to wear, something to eat. . . . It's all been wrong."

When the Yankees traveling secretary, a Mr. Cushman, interviews George to be his assistant, he asks George to talk about his previous work experience.

"Alrighty. Ah . . . ," George begins. "My last job was in publishing. I got fired for having sex in my office with the cleaning woman." (That happened in a prior episode.)

"Go on," says Mr. Cushman.

"All right, before that, I was in real estate. I quit, because the boss wouldn't let me use his private bathroom. That was it."

"Do you talk to everyone like this?" asks an incredulous Mr. Cushman.

"Of course," says George, still doing the opposite of what he'd normally do.

"I gotta tell you," says Mr. Cushman. "You are the complete opposite of every applicant we've seen."

At this point, the George Steinbrenner character makes his appearance. Mr. Cushman introduces George Costanza to the Steinbrenner character and tells him he is an applicant for the assistant traveling secretary's job.

"Nice to meet you," says the Steinbrenner character.

"Well, I wish I could say the same," says Costanza, "but I must say, with all due respect, I find it very hard to see the logic behind some of the moves you've made with this fine organization. In the past twenty years you have caused myself, and the city of New York, a good deal of distress, as we have watched you take our beloved Yankees and reduced them to a laughing stock, all for the glorification of your massive ego."

Without blinking, the Steinbrenner character shouts, "Hire this man!"

For many Yankees fans it was one of the funniest moments in the history of television.

In another episode, the New York Mets want to hire George Costanza as head of scouting, but they tell that him under league rules they can't offer him the job unless he gets himself fired from the Yankees first. Costanza goes to a staff meeting and in front of the George Steinbrenner character he takes out Babe Ruth's uniform, which he took from a display case at the stadium. He is eating strawberries, and he wipes strawberry juice from his fingers onto the jersey. He then drops another strawberry onto the uniform. End of scene.

Later the Steinbrenner character calls Costanza into his office.

"You wanted to see me, sir?" asks Costanza.

"I heard about what happened at the meeting this morning . . ."

"Oh yes," says Costanza, "I already packed up my desk, sir. I can be outta here in an hour."

"And I have to tell you," says the Steinbrenner character. "It's exactly what this organization needed."

Costanza looks stunned.

"We wanna look to the future. We gotta tear down the past. Babe Ruth was nothing more than a fat old man, with little girl legs. And here's something I just found out recently. He wasn't really a sultan. Ah, what do you make of that? Hey, check this out. [He stands to reveal he's wearing baseball pants.] Lou Gehrig's pants. Not a bad fit." [He has a thought.] "Hey, you don't think that nerve disease of his was contagious, do you? Uh, I better take them off. I'm too important to this team." [He takes off the pants to reveal his boxer shorts.] "Big Stein can't be flopping and twitching."

Costanza can't believe the Steinbrenner character is standing there in his underwear.

"Hey, how about some lunch," says the Steinbrenner character. "What're you going for?"

In his next scene, Costanza is standing outside Yankee Stadium wearing a body stocking. He's on the phone with Seinfeld.

"Jerry, I can't get fired," says George.

In the next scene, Costanza is driving around the Yankees' parking lot. On a rope trailing behind him is a large trophy, which bounces around on the tarmac. He is leaning out the window with a megaphone.

"Attention, Steinbrenner and front-office morons," he says. "Your triumphs mean nothing. You all stink. You can sit on it, and rotate. This is George Costanza. I fear no reprisal. Extension five-one-seven-oh." Classic and hilarious.

In the final scene, Costanza stands before Steinbrenner, eating something and shrugging at the Steinbrenner character's remarks.

"I heard what you did in the parking lot, big boy," says the Steinbrenner character, "and it is in-ex-cus-able. You personally insulted me, my staff. . . . I cannot believe that you could perpetrate such a disloyalty. Breaks my heart to say it. . . . Oh, who am I kidding? I love it. You're fi . . ."

The Steinbrenner character stops just before saying "You're fired." George Costanza looks at him, waiting for the end of the word, when Mr. Wilhelm, the general manager, walks in and interrupts. Wilhelm tells the Steinbrenner character it's all his fault, that he had put George up to it.

Wilhelm says he did it "because I'm tired of all your macho head games."

Costanza interrupts him. "He's lying, sir. *I'm* tired of all your macho head games."

"Macho head games?" asks the Steinbrenner character.

Wilhelm puts his arms around Costanza. "He's just being loyal to me," he says.

"Wilhelm, you're fired," says the Steinbrenner character. "Now if you gentlemen will excuse me, I'm not going to the game today. I'm gonna go outside and scalp some tickets. Owner's box. That's gotta bring in forty bucks, no problem."

When Costanza asks Wilhelm what that was all about, Wilhelm tells him, "I wanted to get fired, George. You are looking at the new head scout of the New York Mets." As he walks out the door, Wilhelm sings, "Meet the Mets, Meet the Mets, step right up and greet the Mets. . . ."

Yankees fans laughed so hard their sides split. But once the Steinbrenner character began appearing on *Seinfeld*, it was the start of the humanization of the real George Steinbrenner in the hearts and minds of Americans. As written by Jerry Seinfeld and Larry David, the voice of the Steinbrenner character in the show, the real George Steinbrenner took such a lampooning and was made to look so ridiculous and crazy that viewers began to think that the real George Steinbrenner must be a pretty good guy after all to be able to take all that abuse in good spirits.

With George Steinbrenner exiled from the Yankees for the Howie Spira fiasco, he had to find someone to run the organization in his place. Picking a stand-in wasn't easy. George's first choice, his elder son Hank, for self-protection needed to stay away from his father, who all his life had ridden him so hard that as a child Hank had a tic. His daily confrontations with his old man exacted a terrible toll on the boy.

After college, Hank chose to run the horse farm in Ocala, Florida, hoping to escape George's reach. One of George's constant criticisms was that Hank was "too easy" on the employees. One day George called the farm looking for Hank. He didn't get through for a while because the office manager had left to pick up his sick child at school.

George told Hank, "For Christ sake, that's women's work. You don't let employees leave the office for that. That's his wife's job."

They got into a big fight, and Hank eventually quit his job on the farm and moved to Clearwater to live with his wife's parents until his new home was ready. Hank and George didn't talk for over a year. George couldn't choose his younger son, Hal, to run the Yankees, because the boy was still in college, and so he selected his tax lawyer, Leonard Kleinman. When Fay Vincent nixed Kleinman's appointment, George then opted for limited partner Robert Nederlander, whom Vincent trusted implicitly to play by the rules. Joe Molloy, George's son-in-law, also helped run the team. Even with George gone, Yankee employees always felt he was looking over their shoulder.

George handed the decision making for the Yankees over to Gene Michael. It had been a long route back to the top of the Yankees executive ladder for Michael, about whom George once said, "He's like a son to me." Michael was thirty-seven years old when his playing career ended in April 1976. George called him in and told him, "I think you should stay in the game." Two years later, at George's insistence, he had joined Billy Martin's coaching staff.

George had made Michael, whose nickname was "Stick," the general manager in 1980 after a stint managing Columbus in 1979, but his term was marked by Steinbrenner's constant second-guessing. "Son" or not, Michael couldn't take the abuse, and he quit after two years on the job. Steinbrenner's meddling and firings led to a revolving door that brought fourteen different general managers over seventeen years. Only Gabe Paul, his first GM, had had any real authority. After Gabe left, George became the real GM, as the men with the title stewed under a barrage of second-guessing and abuse.

With George ordered to step aside, Michael, a capable, savvy baseball man, would be able to work his magic without any interference. When he took over on August 20, 1990, the Yankees were in serious trouble. George had spent recklessly and foolishly in 1989, signing Pascual Pérez to a three-year, $5.7 million contract. Perez finished the year 9–13. George had screwed up the team so badly with his whims and stupid trades and outrageous behavior that many major leaguers refused to even consider the Yankees after they became free agents. The Yankees finished the 1990 season with a 67–95 record, the worst in the majors. George's suspension had come just in time.

Michael, unlike Steinbrenner, had a plan. He would let prospects develop in the minor leagues. He could restock his young pitchers without fear that Steinbrenner would trade them all away for over-the-hill name veterans. He wanted to add more left-handed batters to the lineup. Don Mattingly was his one solid lefty bat, and Mattingly had a bad back. Michael filled holes in the lineup by signing solid but unflashy veterans Wade Boggs, Paul O'Neill, and Mike Gallego.

Michael drafted players as much on personality as talent. He was a believer in statistics determining future ability rather than what a player looked like. He believed in *Moneyball* long before Michael Lewis wrote his book about Oakland A's general manager Billy Beane fifteen years later. But what made Michael special was that he didn't just look at the numbers. As one longtime Yankee employee put it, "Gene Michael understood people's hearts."

Said the employee, "To look at a guy like Paul O'Neill, you wouldn't necessarily trade Roberto Kelly for him. But Gene saw something in Paul, the way he played, and he was able to project the kind of player O'Neill was. Gene also knew Lou Piniella, who was managing O'Neill in Cincinnati. Before he made the deal he spoke to Piniella about him. Gene saw those intangibles in players. Between O'Neill and Tino Martinez and Scott Brosius, that was the heart of those teams."

Michael liked O'Neill's intensity, Rock Raines's sense of humor, Joe Girardi's professionalism, and rookie Derek Jeter's confidence. They weren't superstars, though Jeter would turn into one, but as a group they were special.

During the two years George was suspended from running the Yankees, Michael's two managers were Stump Merrill in 1991 and Buck Showalter in 1992. Michael inherited Merrill, a gruff, grizzled minor league lifer who reminded you of Wilfred Brimley in *The Natural*. There was always a rumor that Merrill was keeping in touch with George throughout his suspension. He finished out the 1991 season, and on the final day Michael informed him he wasn't coming back. His replacement was Buck Showalter, a meticulous man who worked long hours. Often Showalter would sleep in his office. Had George been around, he would have loved that Buck knew the stats and the charts cold.

It was Showalter who convinced the players around the league that being a Yankee was once again a great thing to be. He also encouraged all the young players in the farm system, letting them know that if they worked hard they could become a Yankee.

Like Steinbrenner, Showalter was a micromanager, and his fastidiousness and nit-picking drove some of the players crazy, but he was respected for his preparedness. Like Michael, Showalter insisted on bringing in players who had character. He avoided or got rid of players with reputations for being selfish. He wanted those who would cheer for their teammates, players like Spike Owens, great people if not great athletes.

One player Gene Michael signed over Showalter's objections was Danny Tartabull. The reason he was signed: George, hiding behind the invisible curtain, demanded it. The Mets had signed free agent Bobby Bonilla, and George didn't want the Mets to monopolize the headlines with respect to player signings. Tartabull was given a five-year contract worth $25 million.

Showalter was manager when it was announced that George would return to his post on March 1, 1993. Showalter worried about he was going to deal with George, even though he was a dot the i's and cross the t's guy like George wanted. But with the return of George came the return of the intense pressure he put on everybody, and after George returned, Showalter did a lot of complaining in the press about that pressure.

The day George returned to the Yankees in 1993, his office staff ordered champagne along with a cake in the shape of Yankee Stadium. They invited family members in for a toast. They were sure it would be a joyous occasion. But when George found out the staff had arranged the celebration, he was angry and mean-spirited. Quickly they discovered that the man hadn't changed, except that he was much more reluctant to appear in the public eye. In private, he was just as critical and demanding as the day he left.

On his return, George wasn't quite as active with the Yankees as he had been before his suspension, and part of the reason was the crisis with American Ship Building. It was going broke, and George's reputation was at stake.

When George did call general manager Gene Michael on the carpet, Michael knew just how to handle him. If Steinbrenner criticized him, he would respond in his own defense with an honest, forthright rebuttal. If Steinbrenner kept at him, he would continue to return fire, something Steinbrenner respected.

If Steinbrenner ordered him to make a trade he thought unwise, Michael would say to him, "Hey, no problem, but I'm going to tell the reporters that it was your fucking idea." Usually Steinbrenner would back off, with the admonition, "You better be right." Michael was gaining a reputation as a shrewd judge of talent, and because of him, the reputation of the Yankees was improving so much around the league that in 1993 Michael was able to sign premier left-hander Jimmy Key, the first important free agent to sign in quite a while. Key, who had pitched well for Toronto, was impressed at how Michael and Showalter had put the Yankees on the right track, so he signed a four-year, $17 million deal with the team. In 1993, Key was 18–6, and the Yankees were 88–74. It was clear that Gene Michael was building something special.

Steinbrenner, though, had no clue, even though Michael had taken a team that was the worst in baseball when George left and brought it back to respectability. When he returned he said to Michael, "This team is messed up. The players are messed up, everything is messed up. This was in good shape when I left."

Responded Michael, "That's why we had first pick in the draft in 1991."

"Don't be a wiseass," said Steinbrenner.

As hard as Steinbrenner tried to undo Michael's handiwork, Michael managed to keep to his plan. Steinbrenner would demand changes, and Michael would argue vehemently against them. Michael was forced to defend every decision, which he did with facts and charts and statistics, and George usually went along. In 1995, Gene Michael's nerves were shot so badly because of George's criticisms and cursing that he ended up in the hospital for a week with shingles.

One of the players Steinbrenner wanted to trade was twenty-one-year-old outfielder Bernie Williams. Williams, who was something of a flower child, played the guitar and sang and spoke in a very soft voice. Steinbrenner had looked into the boy's eyes and declared him "too soft."

Steinbrenner ordered Michael to call every single general manager in an effort to deal him. And that's exactly what Michael did. Michael, obeying Steinbrenner's orders to make calls, got in touch with every single general manager, but he never once mentioned Bernie Williams's name. He told Steinbrenner the truth: he had spoken to every general manager and not one was interested in Williams.

The one youth-for-a-veteran trade Michael did make was a brilliant one, Roberto Kelly for Paul O'Neill of the Cincinnati Reds. Michael didn't think Kelly was anything special, and he loved O'Neill's intensity and character.

Another trade George ordered that Michael refused to make was twenty-one-year-old Mariano Rivera for veteran free spirit David Wells. When Michael saw that Rivera was throwing ninety-five miles an hour, all talks were off.

In 1994, the strike-shortened season, the Yankees were the best team in baseball. Unfortunately, they didn't get into the World Series because it was called off.

By 1995, the players were sick of Showalter's finicky nature. They wanted him gone. That was also the year George Steinbrenner had become an important character on *Seinfeld*. On the show the George Steinbrenner character fires Buck Showalter. Weeks later, George did it for real after the Yankees, a wildcard team, lost to the Seattle Mariners in the seventh game of the first round of the playoffs. George, in punishment mode, insisted that Buck fire two of his coaches, including hitting coach Rick Down. Showalter refused, and he was fired. George didn't stop there. In September 1995, he fired his talented minor league development staff, and at the end of the season he fired general manager Gene Michael. As self-destructive moves went, this was the worst of them all.

One of the architects of the Yankees resurgence under Gene Michael was Mitch Lukevics, who was the vice president in charge of the minor leagues. Lukevics got his start in the Chicago White Sox organization, where he signed as a pitcher in 1975. As a promise to his father, who worked in a steel plant, he earned his BA degree at Penn State in the off-seasons.

When he was released as a player in the spring of 1981, White Sox GM Dave Dombrowski offered him a job as a minor league pitching coach. His intention was to return to his hometown of Bethlehem, Pennsylvania, where he wanted to teach and coach in the public school system. But there were no jobs, and he had just gotten married, so he accepted the offer to coach. His first stop was the extended spring training program in the Gulf Coast League in St. Petersburg, Florida.

In November of 1985, the White Sox brought Hawk Harrelson to be general manager, and Lukevics's mentors, Dombrowski and Roland Hemond, were fired. So was Lukevics. When one of the administrators in the White Sox office was promoted to scouting director, the Sox needed to find an administrative assistant, and they asked Lukevics. He wasn't on the field, but the job gave him insight into how baseball worked from the inside.

After spending three years learning the job, in the fall of 1988, Lukevics was recruited by the New York Yankees. George Bradley, who had been a scout with the White Sox, was hired as vice president of player development and scouting for the Yankees, and he offered Lukevics the job of director of minor league operations. Lukevics had been a Yankee fan as a boy.

Lukevics relocated to Tampa, Florida, the home of the Yankees' minor league complex. By 1988, George Steinbrenner was spending 90 percent of his time in his Tampa office. He was on site, keeping a close eye on everything his employees were doing.

Lukevics had two vivid memories when he first joined the Yankees. "I remember the uniforms," he said. "The Yankee uniform stood out. And I couldn't believe the chaos that went on internally. That stood out as well." The chaos included the constant firings of important staff members.

The chaos could come from out of the blue. "In those days Mr. Steinbrenner had control over everything, and you never knew what might come up that would be a disruption, something you would no more think to be on top of that he would come up with, and you would be startled.

"I remember one of George's colleagues had a son who we had drafted, and we had let him go, and I had to bring him the reports, and when I got there he told me I was going to be George Bradley's ex-assistant. That was quite common. You never knew where it was coming from—well, you knew where it was coming from, but you never knew why. That was very challenging as an administrator. You just never knew. It wasn't a comfortable working environment.

"One of the funniest things that happened—it wasn't funny at the time—Mr. Steinbrenner called me down to the Radisson Bay Harbor, the hotel he owned. He used some funny words. He said, 'Get your ass down here now.'

" 'Yes sir.' It was always 'Yes, sir.'

"I drove from the Yankee complex to the hotel, and I was thinking, Ooooooooh. I sat down with him in the restaurant, and he proceeded to yell at me because one of our minor league players had his swimming trucks hanging from the balcony of the hotel. That's the detail our owner concerned himself with. Maybe he could have handled it differently, telling me and letting me address the players and moving on, but that wasn't how it usually happened. You usually got your fanny handed to you for half an hour, then moved on, shrugged it off you made an announcement to the players, and you went back to trying to develop players. But that was his attention to detail. He wanted it right in his mind. We all have different ways of getting things done. That was his way. And quite frankly, he was the owner. He was paying your salary. So you really grew to know the environment you were in after a short time. 'Yes sir, no problem, we will take care of it.' And you go limping back to the complex."

Another time Bill Livesay, who was in charge of player development, came to Mitch and said, "I have some good news and some bad news."

"Okay, what's the good news?" Mitch said.

"We're going to Fort Lauderdale to go to the big league camp."

"What's the bad news?"

"We have to leave with Mr. Steinbrenner in an hour and a half. He said to go home and get our clothes and to make sure we have our scouting reports, because we're going to have a meeting as soon as we get to Fort Lauderdale."

Lukevics said, "Go home? Have the scouting reports? Be on his jet in an hour and a half?"

"Yeah."

"Bill, that's impossible."

"I know," said Livesay.

As they left the Yankee complex with their briefcases and the scouting reports to go directly to the plane, they were handed Yankee shirts to wear as they went out the door.

"You look back," says Lukevics, "and that was funnier than heck."

It was yet another example of the way George Steinbrenner had his employees jump through hoops for him. "We did," said Lukevics, "but he made you a better manager. I truly mean this, even if it was out of fear. You didn't want to disappoint him, and you didn't want to get the wrath of Mr. Steinbrenner. It made you better. Absolutely."

But Steinbrenner's quickness to fire people made Lukevics's job much harder than it had to be. "I had to work a lot with the field coordinator," he said, "and Mr. Steinbrenner kept firing them, for whatever reason. I had heard about the turmoil on the Yankees, on the big league level, but when I got there—I wasn't there three months, and, oh my God. We had four field coordinators in the month of March."

Lukevics recalled how difficult it was for George Bradley, who was in charge of player development and scouting, to do his job. "I'd have to drop my kids off at school, and I'd get to the office fairly early, because their school was close by," Lukevics recalled. "The working hours were nine thirty to five thirty, but heck, I'd get in there early, and I can recall seeing poor George Bradley. His hair would be all ruffled, and I could only imagine the phone call from George that he had already gotten that morning. I'd go to my desk and think, Boy, that must have been a bad phone call. And I'd think, George didn't even have to be in this early. But we knew the environment. You knew the detail, and sometimes there was a price to pay."

It wasn't long before Steinbrenner fired George Bradley, put Brian Sabean in charge of player development and scouting, and named Bill Livesay scouting director. When Steinbrenner fired Bob Quinn as the Yankees general manager at the end of the 1989 season, Quinn took Sabean with him. Livesay became vice president of player development and scouting, and Kevin Elfrey became scouting director. Lukevics moved up in the hierarchy as well.

During the time Lukevics was with the Yankees, the men in charge of drafting and signing players did a spectacular job. Among the youngsters signed by Gene Michael's minor league team were Derek Jeter, Jorge Posada, Bernie Williams, Andy Pettitte, and Mariano Rivera.

"I'll never forget the first day Derek came to the Yankee complex," said Lukevics. "He was a high school senior who signed as the fifth pick in the country. He weighed a hundred sixty-two pounds. I was thinking, *What a tall, lanky guy*. In one of the first doubleheaders he played in the Gulf Coast League, he struck out five times. In his last game, he got two hits to finish the season at .202, but never once did you ever think he would not be a big leaguer. He showed you all the skills why he was selected, his attitude was terrific, his aptitude terrific. He was wonderful. All those kids were.

"Jorge was a second baseman, and to Bill Livesay's credit, he converted Jorge to a catcher, a career saver for Jorge. Converting a player isn't easy. Looking back, I wouldn't say it was a last resort, but it's a 'Let's give it a shot.' And Jorge had a great attitude. He worked hard. He had the power in the bat. Everybody saw the bat, and over the course of time he made a fine big league catcher.

"When Andy Pettitte, another wonderful young man, came, he had a good attitude, good aptitude, a good work ethic. He came with a fastball and a change-up, and I'll give Nardi Contreras, our pitching coordinator, credit. He helped Andy with his curve, and he got to the big leagues. Later Andy developed a cutter, which took him to another level.

"Bernie was a terrific athlete, but some of the scouts didn't think Bernie was tough enough. In the minor leagues, it's about the potential to perform. In the big leagues it's about performance. Bernie didn't perform all the time, but you saw the athleticism, and you were waiting for Bernie to catch up with his athleticism, and then boom, he took off, and if you look at the statistics, he became one of the greatest Yankees.

"And then there is Mariano Rivera, who came to us throwing a baseball into a thimble. That's how good his control was. He completely dominated until the day when he tore his ulna collateral ligament and had to have Tommy John surgery. You thought it was the end of the world, but through medical rehab he ended up stronger and tougher. He became a terrific relief pitcher in the big leagues.

"There was no surprise about what they accomplished in the big leagues. These guys had the work ethic, and they had the mental capacity. They all came at the same time, and it was through good scouting. Bill Livesay set the tone. He was the one who had the philosophy. He profiled every position. He was the quality control director. He talked to the scouts. If he didn't see a player himself, he would ask a barrage of questions, and they would have to meet a certain criterion, or Bill wouldn't give the go-ahead to sign that player."

The player development team was running on all cylinders, but the men in the scouting department were always in a state of concern because as long as George Steinbrenner ran the Yankees, general managers turned over often, and at any moment George, who served as general manager whenever he wished, could decide arbitrarily and unilaterally to trade away a young prospect for a veteran.

"Trading prospects always came up," said Lukevics, who to this day doesn't have it in him to place blame on George. Instead, he talked about "they." When I asked him who "they" were, he sheepishly had to admit, "George."

Said Lukevics, "They wanted to trade Bernie. They wanted to trade Mariano. They wanted to trade Mark Hutton. We had some great battles. I said 'Don't do that. They are your future.' But the MO was to trade them. And thank God, they didn't trade them."

One reason "they" didn't trade them was George's banishment for life from running the Yankees because of his dealings with Howie

Spira. He was kept away from the team for two and a half years of peace and quiet.

"Everything calmed down," said Lukevics, who was the farm director during Steinbrenner's banishment. "We had been in chaos, and then it did calm down, and Joe Molloy, George's son-in-law, and Gene Michael, the general manager starting in 1991, were very instrumental in that.

"The club wasn't winning at the time he was suspended. We had chosen Brian Taylor, the number one player in the draft, which tells you we were the worst team in baseball. He got hurt in a bar fight, which was sad, because Brian had a lot of ability. But there were battles over players during that time. George wasn't there, but you had to assume he was talking to Joe Molloy, his son-in-law, simply because they're family members. They couldn't stop him from seeing family members, but certainly Mr. Steinbrenner wasn't involved on a daily basis like he was before.

"We had good, spirited battles over whether to trade prospects. When you're in New York, there's a lot of pressure to win from the back pages of the newspaper, and we were a terrible team, the worst team in baseball, and there were a lot of spirited conversations about how to get the Yankees back to where they should be."

Under Gene Michael and Bill Livesay, the decision was made not to trade their talented kids.

"Was it easier to do that with George gone?" I asked Lukevics.

"A lot easier," he replied. "Absolutely. And the proof is in the pudding. The smartest thing they did is not move those kids." Those kids being Jeter, Posada, Williams, Pettitte, and Rivera. But they did trade other kids, and those kids landed them a group of talented veteran, gutty, lunch-pail players such as Joe Girardi, Paul O'Neill, Tino Martinez, Chuck Knoblauch, and Scott Brosius.

"Certainly what Bill Livesay and his staff did was instrumental in the Yankees' success for years to come," said Lukevics. "You can recite the roster of the 1996 team, the first World Series the Yankees won in quite some time. How did we get Joe Girardi? We got him for Steve Shumacher, a fourth-round pick, and Mike DeJong. Bill Livesay converted DeJong from a shortstop to a pitcher. How did we get Tino? We got him for Sterling Hitchcock and Russ Davis, who still has the best bat speed I've ever seen in a young kid. Chuck Knoblauch? We got him for Eric Milton, and Christian Guzman, who was discovered in our Latin program by Rudy Santeen, and another Latin player. We got David Cone for Marty Jansen, Michael Gordon, a tenth-round pick, and a thirteenth-round pick. Bill Livesay had a message: it's a farm system, and you keep the crops you want, and you take the ones you can take to the market and trade off and get something you need. That was the goal all along.

"Stick Michael did a great job getting Scott Brosius, and he traded Roberto Kelly and Rodney Hines for Paul O'Neill. Other players, Ricky Ledee, Shane Spencer, were homegrown. So you can see the making of that 1996 ball club was through player development and scouting. From the year 1988, when Bernie was signed, to when we were fired in Arizona in 1995, we kept telling George what we had, but he really didn't know what he had. Player developmentally, he didn't know what he had."

When Steinbrenner returned to run the Yankees on April 1, 1993, the nucleus of the four-time world championship Yankees was established so firmly that he could not undo it. Jeter and Rivera will be Hall of Famers, and Posada, Williams, and Pettitte became perennial All-Stars.

George is unhappy when things are going well and others are getting credit, so after the 1995 season, the first season a Yankees team made the playoffs in more than a decade, he felt underappreciated, and he decided to "go in a different direction." That was why he fired the entire player development team that brought the Yankees their World Series success, and general manager Gene Michael, the man who is most responsible for the future success of the Yankees.

"Bill Livesay, Kevin Elfrey, myself, and Joe Molloy all flew first class from Tampa to Phoenix, Arizona, for a farm and scouting directors' meeting," said Lukevics." I was thinking at the time, Boy, this is unusual. Someone in Joe's high position doesn't usually come to those meetings. We had never flown first class before. I was thinking, What's going on?

"We arrived the night before the meeting, which was scheduled for eight the next morning. Joe Molloy said to us, 'Let's meet in my room before we go.' We did that, and he said to us, 'George wants to make a change.' He gave no real reason, but in business sometimes there is no real reason. They just want to make a change.

"We were all in shock. Not surprised, but yet in shock. He was dumbfounded. Things were really clicking as far as development," said Lukevics, "not only with draft picks, but Bill Livesay and Rudy Santeen were starting to get a Latin program together.

"I have no idea why we were fired. You look back and you ask, Why did it happen? No one knows. There was no real reason given except that George wanted to make a change.

"They gave us a little severance, and that helped, and finding another job was difficult. I thought with my position I wouldn't have trouble finding another job, but I was wrong. I went from farm director to a Gulf Coast League pitching coach with the Tampa Bay Devil Rays.

"Brian Sabean had offered me a special assignment job with the San Francisco Giants as his assistant, but I was so beat up mentally and physically from working for George that I couldn't do a job that challenging. The environment was terrible. No disrespect to anyone, but that's how it was.

"It was real sad, because it was hard enough to get players into the big leagues, but with the Yankees the chaos and confusion that went on really took away from what you could do best. I give Bill Livesay a lot of credit, because he shouldered a lot of that on himself, shielding us from George, allowing us to concentrate on doing our jobs. He was the umbrella, but we were affected by it.

"When all was said and done, our nerves were pretty well shot. All of our nerves, but that was the environment of the New York Yankees. Despite all that, looking back, we got the job done.

"Mr. Steinbrenner gave us all the resources we needed to get the job done, and there was no excuse for not getting it done. But it didn't need to be as hard as it was.

"I'm very proud of the staff, and I credit Bill Livesay and what he did and the philosophy he put in place, and in the end a lot of people got World Series rings because of the guys who endured.

"None of us got rings. We were fired in September of 1995, and they won their first World Series in 1996.

"We were on the threshold of something great, but it all came to an end that September morning in Phoenix. And when I returned home, my kids cried and cried and cried—with joy—that they were getting their dad back. We all sacrificed for our families, because we had to provide for them, but when you worked for George, your kids grew up without your seeing them grow up. I'll never forget the day when my wife and kids came with me to clean out my office at the minor league complex in Tampa. They had tears—of joy. It was a relief."

In the winter of 2008, Mitch Lukevics was the head of player development for the American League champion Tampa Bay Rays, a team under new ownership. Before the arrival of the new management three years earlier, the then-named Devil Rays were so bad they never won more than seventy games in each of their first ten years. Lukevics and Bill Livesay headed up player development with the Rays, and with their help the perennial last-place doormats have been miraculously transformed into pennant winners. Lukevics in all sincerity credits George Steinbrenner for his success with the Rays.

"The education with the Yankees was priceless," said Lukevics, "and I mean that respectfully. George made you be on top of your game. He made you dot your i's and cross your t's. We worked every minute of our day to make the New York Yankees a better organization. Maybe you could argue we were successful because of the environment, but I don't believe that. The result came because of Bill Livesay's philosophy and plan and everybody being on the same page. The environment was a detriment. It's amazing how often work was disrupted, and yet after we were with Tampa Bay, Bill Livesay and I were reminiscing, and we wrote down the names of the Yankee minor leaguers who made it to the big leagues during the time we were there. We came up with sixty-two. In seven years. We were having fun making the list, because there is nothing more gratifying than having the players you draft make it to the big leagues. It was very gratifying. As much as getting fired hurt, we got the job done.

"I was with the Yankees from 1989 through 1995, and I have eleven minor league rings. We won in the minor leagues, though that wasn't our primary goal. Player development was our primary goal. I had back-to-back Triple A rings, back-to-back Double A rings, and in 1989, my first year, we won three league championships. We were developing players by winning. We got players to the big leagues who made an impact, and through trades of our minor league players, the Yankees got major league players who helped them win and helped them bring home four world championships."

After Gene Michael, Bill Livesay, and Mitch Lukevics were fired at the end of the 1995 season, from 1996 through 2008, not one single first-round draft choice made by their successors has made it to the Yankees. And after winning four world championships between 1996 and 2000, the Yankees have not won a World Series since. In 2008, they didn't even make it into the playoffs.

25

He's the owner, and he can say what he wants.
—Manager Joe Torre

Joe Torre Arrives

Another man who was instrumental in turning around the fortunes of the New York Yankees was a most unlikely one. Arthur Richman had been a longtime executive with the New York Mets. He and his brother Milt had been venerated newspaper reporters back when the Dodgers were playing in Brooklyn and the Giants in the Polo Grounds in Manhattan. Arthur's baseball career began with a friendship with the St. Louis Browns baseball team in 1945. For thirty years he had been involved in PR and promotions for the Mets, and after Harvey Green quit as director of public relations in 1989, Steinbrenner hired him to come and work for the Yankees.

When Steinbrenner fired Gene Michael as general manager, Michael, after spending five years building the team, swallowed his pride and took a scouting job. George asked Richman to make a list of GM candidates, and at the top of the list was Joe Torre. Richman had been very fond of Joe Torre when the two were together with the Mets, and he suggested that Torre might make an excellent replacement. When Richman told Steinbrenner that Torre came from Brooklyn, Steinbrenner liked the idea even more.

Joe Molloy, who was George's son-in-law and stand-in, called Torre and asked if he would be interested in the GM job. Torre flew to Tampa to meet with Molloy. Torre's wife was eight months pregnant, and with all the time a newborn took, he knew he couldn't possibly devote the number of hours that Steinbrenner would require, which as he described it was "twenty-five hours a day and thirteen months a year."

As a measure of how bad Steinbrenner's reputation was as a boss, a half-dozen candidates turned down the GM job when George called. Bob Watson, who was the Houston Astros' GM, finally agreed. To get him to say yes, Steinbrenner looked him in the eye and told him he was backing away from baseball.

"I took the man at his word," said Watson. My bad, as they say.

Bob Watson had played for Torre when Torre was managing the Braves. Watson had just survived prostate cancer. Torre called Watson to "congratulate" him on taking the job. "Did the doctors tell you you had six months to live? Is that why you took this crazy job?" he teased.

Torre wrote Steinbrenner a note thanking him for the GM interview. "Maybe someday we'll work together," he wrote. But before he could mail the letter, Arthur Richman called him to ask if he'd be interested in becoming the Yankees manager. "It looks like Buck Showalter is leaving," said Richman.

Torre put his note in the mail. A week later Steinbrenner called him to offer him the job. Joe could pick his own coaches, but George wanted Willie Randolph and Tony Cloninger to stay on. And Torre couldn't say anything until it was official that Showalter was leaving.

Showalter's contract expired on October 31, 1995, and Torre was hired the next day. He signed a two-year, $1.05 million contract. At the press conference Torre was at his bubbly best. He had heard the horror stories of what it was like working for George, but he had just been fired as manager of the St. Louis Cardinals, and his teams didn't win pennants because ownership didn't spend the money needed to do it. Torre knew one thing: Steinbrenner would spend the money to win a championship.

When Steinbrenner hired Joe Torre to replace Showalter, who was respected and appreciated by the press for his openness, there was an outcry. Steinbrenner began getting piles of hate mail, and some of the correspondents threatened his life. Fans were even sending their Yankees caps back to George.

Making things worse was that his choice to replace him wasn't at all popular. Joe Torre had managed the Mets and the Cardinals and had fared poorly. Yankees fans didn't want some National League loser. Hence the lamentations.

After five days of criticism, Steinbrenner, crumbling under the pressure, flew to Pensacola, Florida, where Showalter lived, and asked Showalter to return as manager.

"You just hired Torre as your manager," said Showalter.

"I'll find another job for Joe Torre," said Steinbrenner.

Showalter said no and took a job managing the Arizona Diamondbacks. Thus the year 1996 marked the first year of Joe Torre's fabled ten-year run as Yankees manager.

Torre had one qualification for the job that most lacked: his father, a night-shift detective with the New York Police Department, had been an abusive bastard. When Dad would come home, everyone would be on pins and needles. The experience was so terrible that as an adult Torre began the Safe at Home Foundation for victims of domestic violence. For Torre's part, the strain of dealing with the abuse underlay his two failed marriages. It also caused him to look to baseball for his self-esteem. If he made an out, it wasn't just an out. In his mind, with each one he was letting each of his teammates down. That's a tough burden for anyone who plays such a difficult and demanding game.

But being a victim of abuse enabled him to handle and endure the humiliations of another abuser, George Steinbrenner. It also enabled Torre to tutor his players, instructing them to ignore the impossible expectations and to put aside any failures in order to concentrate on the present. As a result, Torre became a father figure to his players and also became a Dr. Phil for all Yankees fans as he sought as well to teach them patience and understanding.

Under his steady hand, and in the face of Steinbrenner's relentless criticism and the fans' too-high expectations, the Yankees won four world championships and six American League championships. When he was hired, the press called him "Clueless Joe," but he turned out to be the perfect man for the job, worthy of enshrinement at Cooperstown along with the other legendary Yankees managers Miller Huggins, Joe McCarthy, and Casey Stengel.

Torre added Mel Stottlemyre as pitching coach, Chris Chambliss as hitting coach, and Don Zimmer as bench coach. The sixty-five-year-old Zimmer had just cashed his first Social Security check. The prideful Zim wanted to know if he was Torre's choice or George's choice. He would take the job only if he was Torre's choice. Billy Connor told him Torre wanted him. Torre and Zim were a perfect team.

When spring training opened in 1996, Torre decided not to read the New York newspapers. He had spent six years in the broadcast booth, so he had some understanding of the role of the media. He wanted to be open with the reporters and the radio guys, but at the same time he didn't want to fall into the trap that had waylaid many of the New York managers: they would read items in the paper and get so upset they would overreact badly, distracting them from their job. Early in the season Paul O'Neill didn't catch a ball Torre thought he should have caught, and he told him so. Late in the next game he took O'Neill out of the game. TV broadcaster Michael Kay asked Torre if he was punishing O'Neill. The next day in the middle of the clubhouse with players all around him he yelled at Kay, "Don't fuck with me. I don't appreciate you trying to stir up something in the clubhouse." Torre was angry.

O'Neill said to Torre, "I read in the papers I'm miffed at you."

Torre told him he didn't read the papers. "Are you miffed?" he asked.

"No," said O'Neill.

"So it really doesn't matter," said Torre.

In his own way, Torre was able to minimize the tension in the clubhouse. He was able to do that for nearly ten years, until in his final year George made it impossible for him to manage without an upset stomach.

George had another of his *Seinfeld* moments in the spring of 1996. Hillsborough Community College was playing against Indian River on field 1 of the Yankee spring training complex in Tampa because the college's home field was under construction, but they were supposed to be playing on field 2. George, seeing the game was on the wrong diamond, ordered one of his executives to go down to field 1 and move the game over to field 2, even though the game was in the fourth inning. When the executive demurred, George said, "I don't want to hear that bullshit. I own this fucking complex, and it's my field and I'm telling you to get them off the field."

"But Mr. Steinbrenner," the executive said, "you got parents out there and scouts . . . "

"Well, since you don't have the guts to do it, I will." And he did. George walked with the executive to the field. The first college kid he confronted was warming up in the bullpen.

"Hey you," George yelled. The kid just looked around. "Hey," George yelled, "get the fuck off of my pitcher's mound."

"I'm sorry, sir," said the player, "but my coach told me to warm up here."

"Do you know who I am?"

"No, sir. I don't."

"You don't know who I am?"

"No, sir."

Not being recognized was enough to drive Steinbrenner over the bend. "You don't know who the fuck I am?" he screamed. "I'll tell you who the fuck I am, you snot-nosed little fuck. I'm George fucking Steinbrenner, and I own this place, and I want you to get the fuck off my mound."

Everyone, meanwhile—the parents, scouts, players, coaches, fans—was watching. George then ordered the executive to walk over to the Hillsborough College coach, who explained to him that field 2 was being seeded and that he had been asked by the grounds crew to play on field 1. When the executive told that to George, he lost it completely.

Steinbrenner marched right into the grounds crew room, where four guys were playing cards and having coffee, waiting for the game to end so they could get diamond 1 ready again.

"Who's in charge here?" George asked.

"I am, sir," said one of them.

"Then you . . . are fucking fired. Get the fuck out of here." George then turned to the executive and said, "See, that's how it's done."

There was another outburst from George not long afterward that made onlookers wonder if he hadn't completely lost his marbles. George had hired Reggie Jackson as a special assistant, and during spring training of 1966, Reggie's mother became very sick and had to be moved from one nursing home to another, and it had to be done quickly. The first spring training game was March 1, 1996, the day when Legends Field in Tampa was to be dedicated. But Reggie needed to attend to his mother, and he flew to California to be with her, missing "Legends Day." When Reggie returned, he walked over to greet Steinbrenner, who responded by turning his back on his former star.

In front of a group of people, Reggie yelled, "Hey, Boss, what's the matter? You mad at me today? You don't want to shake my hand today?"

Embarrassed, George finally shook his hand.

It wasn't the first time George had snubbed Reggie. He had been signed as an adviser, but George made it very clear he didn't want any advice. When George had signed Darryl Strawberry the year before, Reggie criticized the signing. For a month George ducked Reggie's calls and refused to speak to him.

Then during the fall of 1996, there was a truly ugly scene. George had told Reggie he could make the trip to Texas for the first round of the playoffs. Reggie assumed he could go on the team plane with everyone else, but when he stepped onto the bus for the trip to the airport, George yelled at him, "Who gave you permission to be on this bus? This is the team bus."

"I'm supposed to be the special adviser," said Jackson. "Aren't I supposed to go?"

"You don't go anywhere unless I tell you," said Steinbrenner. "I'm still the owner of this ball club."

"I'm sick and tired of being embarrassed by you," said Jackson. "I'm sick and tired of you treating me like an animal." Jackson made an aggressive move forward, but Joe Torre intervened before a furious Jackson could do something he might have regretted.

From the start of spring training in 1996, Torre installed a rookie, Derek Jeter, as his shortstop over the veteran Tony Fernandez. Torre liked Jeter's poise and his character. Jeter, who called his manager "Mr. Torre," had been error-prone at Columbus, but Torre was determined to go with him. When Steinbrenner told Torre, "My advisers don't think Jeter is ready to play," Torre replied, "It's too late for that now, folks." Torre had committed himself and wasn't going to change plans. On opening day, Jeter was tremendous. He made a great catch on a pop-up, and he hit a home run. In 1996, Derek Jeter hit .314 and began to establish himself as one of the greatest players of his era.

Meanwhile, Steinbrenner stayed away from Torre. He made his suggestions, criticisms, barbs, and jibes to Bob Watson, who then talked to Torre, who ignored all of George's suggestions about line-ups and benchings. Watson, who had been a fine ballplayer in his own right, had enough cachet to be able to talk George out of bad trades. One habit of George's that bugged Torre was his penchant for blaming

Torre's coaches for the players' failures. If a hitter wasn't hitting, it was the fault of the hitting coach. If a pitcher didn't do well, it was the fault of the pitching coach. Torre knew how hard his coaching staff worked, and he tried to ignore George's criticisms.

George second-guessed game decisions, but Torre could remain unflustered because George rarely questioned the things that truly bothered him. In 1996, the Yankees were winning from the start, and according to Don Zimmer, "George stayed out of Joe Torre's way and trusted his judgments on most everything." It would stay that way for the next two years.

By July 28, 1996, the Yankees had a twelve-game lead. When the lead shrunk to eight, George began to panic. He warned Torre that if he blew it, he'd live in ignominy and be remembered like Ralph Branca, who gave up the famed home run to Bobby Thomson to lose the 1951 National League pennant.

By the end of August, the Yankees' lead was down to four games. There were twenty-four games to play. David Cone, their best pitcher, returned from the disabled list. After the 1995 season, Cone had become a free agent. At first Steinbrenner was lukewarm about re-signing him, but when Baltimore Orioles owner Peter Angelos came after Cone hard, George swooped in and gave in to the pitcher's demands before Angelos could finalize a deal. If he hadn't, the Yankees would not have won three world championships. But in the spring of 1996, Cone developed an aneurysm that could have killed him, and he missed most of the season. When he went down, George blamed his "baseball people." When Cone returned in September, no one knew how he'd do. In his first game back, he threw seven innings of no-hit ball.

Despite Cone's return, the Yankees' lead continued to shrink as Baltimore kept winning. With twenty games to go, the margin was down to two and a half games. Torre, an All-Star player who in 1973 was Most Valuable Player of the National League, was a calming influence with a knack for saying the right thing to his players. Unlike Steinbrenner, he never reacted to failure. He well knew that increasing the pressure on a player only made things worse. He rated his players not on their averages, but on how hard they hustled. Despite a shrinking lead, Torre kept positive, talking to his players about the importance of playing for the team. Steinbrenner, his panic growing, continued to pepper GM Bob Watson with memos and phone calls. He also came down on Watson for his trade with the Milwaukee Brewers for pitcher Graeme Lloyd, who arrived in New York with a sore elbow. He had a bone spur, which made it impossible for him to pitch effectively, and with George in his ear, Watson went to American League president Gene Budig requesting that the trade be voided. Making things worse, the other player the Yankees got in the deal, Pat Listach, arrived with a broken foot. Milwaukee agreed to pay the rest of Listach's salary. George wasn't satisfied. The deal placed Bob Watson in George Steinbrenner's gun sight. The talk was that if the Yankees didn't win the World Series, Watson would be fired.

"It's unfair that I lose my job because of this," said Watson on the Lloyd trade. "But if I do, that's fine. George doesn't want his general manager to have the appearance of being taken. He doesn't want the Yankees to be taken. . . . Is he cutting me any slack? No. I don't think he wants to cut the Milwaukee Brewers any slack."

In the 1980s, Yankee fans hated Steinbrenner because they saw that he was keeping the Yankees from winning. Beginning in 1996, as the Yankees once again became contenders, the fans embraced George and his philosophy of "Just win every day." A player who went 0 for 4 might get booed. A pitcher who was knocked out in the third inning would get booed. It was not easy playing in New York, and as the booing from the fans replaced the booing coming from Steinbrenner, some players had a hard time performing. Torre didn't have it easy, either. If the Yankees lost two games in a row, the fans would begin to get restless. If they lost six in a row, the fans would become positively panicky. You may not have read about George Steinbrenner in the papers every day anymore, but his influence was as strong as ever.

Not that Torre didn't hear complaints directly from Steinbrenner. He did every once in a while, but Torre knew just how to handle him. Torre would be scrupulous about not criticizing him to the press. He would tell reporters, "He's the owner, and he can say what he wants." Often Torre would anticipate a Steinbrenner phone call by calling George first. When Steinbrenner would criticize a player, Torre would laugh out loud in a way that let George know he didn't agree with his criticism. Torre's brilliance was to defend Steinbrenner to the world but in private to tell him he was full of shit.

Said bench coach Don Zimmer, "A big part of the team's success, if you ask me, has been Joe's inner strength, which is one of the reasons the owner, for the most part, has steered clear of him. Whenever Steinbrenner would come into Joe's office after a tough loss or when we were playing bad, it was to vent. Not at Joe, but at the circumstances. To the best of my knowledge, he never dared to second-guess or criticize Joe to his face, even though he'd be constantly doing that with anyone and everyone up there in his private box."

The Yankees held off the Orioles, and when on September 25 they beat the Brewers 19–2, the Yankees were Eastern Division champions.

While Torre was hugging his players, the phone rang. It was Steinbrenner calling. Torre know exactly who it was.

"Hello," said Torre, "this is Bobby Thomson."

The Yankees played the Texas Rangers in the first round of the playoffs. They lost the opener, then won the second game in extra innings on an error. Derek Jeter started the winning rally with a single, as he did in a game three win. Bernie Williams, whom Torre tried to pump up all year long, hit two home runs to clinch the finale.

Baltimore was the next opponent. Losing after seven, Jeter tied the game with the home run caught by Jeffrey Maier, the twelve-year-old kid who from his bleacher seat reached down and caught the long fly ball in his glove before it could drop into the glove of Orioles outfielder Tony Tarasco. The ball was in play, so it should have been fan interference. The umpires ruled otherwise. Said the Orioles' Bobby Bonilla, "I guarantee you if that ball was hit by us, George Steinbrenner would have had that kid's butt out of the stadium and his parents picking him up on some bridge."

Bernie Williams won it in the eleventh with a home run. After losing game two, the Yankees were losing to Mike Mussina with only four outs to go when a throwing error by Todd Zeile led to four runs and a victory. The Yankees won the next game, and then Andy Pettitte pitched a beauty. Cal Ripken Jr. grounded to Derek Jeter, who threw to first for the final out. Joe Torre had been in a major league baseball uniform for thirty-six years, and he was going to be involved in his first World Series. In the clubhouse afterward he bawled unashamedly.

The Braves won the opener 12–1 at the stadium. After the game George met with Torre, grumbling about how badly the team had played. Said Buster Olney about Steinbrenner, "He all but threw in the towel."

Before game two, the pessimistic George said, "This is a must game." Torre told him he should prepare to lose again. Then he said, "But then we're going to Atlanta. Atlanta's my town. We'll take three games there and win it back here on Sunday."

Steinbrenner didn't say a word. He didn't know what to say.

Torre's prediction was right on target as Greg Maddux shut them out in game two. Before game three, George called. "We can't be embarrassed," he said. "If we lose, all that we've accomplished won't mean anything."

"Well, I don't think so, George, but don't worry about it," Torre said. "We're fine."

"I hope you're right," George said. "I trust you." Then he recommended some lineup changes. He wanted Torre to skip over Kenny Rogers in game four, but Torre talked him out of it.

"Okay, I trust you," said Steinbrenner. As was his custom, George hung up without saying good-bye.

Torre was the one manager who had the ability to calm George's fears. He also was a manager with the Midas touch in the 1996 World Series. Everything he tried worked to perfection.

David Cone pitched beautifully in game three, winning 5–2. The Braves had the bases loaded and only one out in the seventh, but Cone pitched out of it, giving the Yankees momentum. In game four, Torre used every single player except three of his starting pitchers. It was the longest World Series game ever played. Kenny Rogers, George's whipping boy, started and had control trouble. He was behind 4–0 in the second inning. Before Torre pulled him in the third, he had given up another run. Atlanta scored another in the fourth to make it 6–0. The Yankees scored three to make it 6–3 in the eighth. A Jimmy Leyritz home run off hard-throwing Mark Wohlers tied the score at 6–6. The Braves were done the rest of the way. Wade Boggs, pinch-hitting, walked with the bases loaded to drive in the winning run, and the series was tied.

John Smoltz, the 1996 Cy Young winner, started game five for Atlanta. Torre surprised the experts by starting Charlie Hayes over Wade Boggs and Cecil Fielder over Darryl Strawberry. The two combined to score the only run of the game. Andy Pettitte outpitched Smoltz in a 1–0 victory. The Braves started the ninth with a double, and a groundout sent him to third. Torre brought in John Wetteland, who got Javy Lopez on a grounder to Hayes. He had Wetteland walk Ryan Klesko intentionally to pitch to Terry Pendleton. Luis Polonia hit for Pendleton. A fly ball to Paul O'Neill in right carried and carried and carried, but the gimpy O'Neill caught the ball. The series was returning to the Bronx with the Yankees one game away from victory.

The next morning Torre learned that the doctors treating his brother Frank had found a heart for a transplant. The operation was a success.

Game six featured the matchup of Jimmy Key and Greg Maddux. The Yankees took a 1–0 lead in the third on a double by O'Neill and a triple by Joe Girardi. A Derek Jeter single made it 2–0. Jeter stole second, and a Bernie Williams single made it 3–0. Ahead 3–1 in the ninth, John Wetteland closed out the game and the series. With two runners on and one out, he struck out Luis Polonia. Marquis Grissom singled to make the score 3–2. Mark Lemke, the next batter, lifted a high pop-up down the third base line next to the Braves dugout. It landed in the stands. And then he lifted another one in the same direction, and this time Charlie Hayes caught it, and Torre had his World Series victory. The entire team followed Torre in a victory lap. They ran around the edge of the warning track, waving to the fans.

Three million people witnessed the Yankees' victory parade down Broadway.

After Torre led the Yankees to a World Series championship, he became fireproof. But as with Billy Martin, Steinbrenner couldn't stand that Torre and Watson got most of the credit for winning it. Watson, who did his best to keep Steinbrenner away from Torre, took daily abuse from the owner. Watson had a particularly tough time because he was a sensitive, decent man who couldn't believe another human being could be so cruel and manipulative.

About a month after he was hired as GM in 1995, Watson told George he was going back home to Houston for Thanksgiving. He had no idea that George had a no-vacation, no-holidays-off policy for his employees, and that included Thanksgiving, Christmas, and New Year's. It was the day before the holiday, when most teams weren't working. Bob hadn't yet moved his family to New York, and he wanted to go home to be with his wife and kids for some turkey.

George was furious that Watson had considered leaving his post. George wanted to sign Roberto Alomar, and he knew the Orioles were after him. George asked Watson if he had called Alomar's agent.

"Yes," said Watson, "and he will call me tonight at home."

"Why are you waiting?" asked Steinbrenner. "Why the fuck don't you call him back now?"

"I'm getting ready to get on a flight back to Houston," said Watson.

"Wait a minute," said Steinbrenner. "You can always get on a flight. If you're gonna do this fucking job here, then get on the fucking phone until you get the agent and get Alomar signed. Then you can fly to fucking Houston. You know, Bob, you're starting to make me think that I made a bad decision hiring you."

George had a secretary change the flight to 7 p.m., and Watson didn't get home until very late. The Orioles ended up with Alomar anyway.

Watson had the title of Yankees general manager, but like other GMs, he learned that when George wanted to take over, he could and would do so, and often. During the winter of 1995–1996, George made more than fifty personnel, staff, and player changes, and half of those moves were made without Watson's knowledge. Agents didn't know whom to talk to, which was one reason the Yankees lost out on signing pitcher Jack McDowell.

Not long after Watson announced to reporters that he was done molding the pitching staff, Steinbrenner by himself and without consulting Watson signed pitcher Kenny Rogers. In a conversation with a Yankee employee (who did not want to be identified), he made it clear that he, not Watson, knew what was best for the Yankees.

One day late in December 1995, George, running late, yelled to the Yankee employee, "I'm out of here. I have to get this contract done."

"But Mr. Steinbrenner," said the employee, "I don't see any appointment on the calendar. What contract?"

"It's Kenny Rogers," said Steinbrenner. "I'm going to sign Kenny Rogers for four years right now. I've got to get this thing wrapped up."

"Isn't Bob handling that?" asked the employee.

"He's weak," said Steinbrenner. "He'll fuck it up if I don't go do it. He's a nice man, but he's weak, and Rogers's agent will walk all over him."

People who worked with Steinbrenner were pretty sure he was headed for a nervous breakdown during the 1996 season. In mid-April, Joe Torre set him off when he made a comment in the paper about the attendance at Yankee Stadium. Torre observed that the construction on the Major Deegan Expressway, the main highway leading to the stadium, was horrendous. He said he could understand why people stayed away.

When George read the comments, he went ballistic. He called Bob Watson and executive vice president David Sussman into his office. "Get in your goddamned cars," George screamed at them, "and drive up and down the Major Deegan highway for two fucking hours. I want to know what the fucking problem is out there, and I want to know everything about it." He instructed them to go from exit to exit, and from borough to borough, to determine just how much time it took to make those trips in their cars.

Even though Watson had been in negotiations, Steinbrenner ordered him to stop what he was doing and start driving up and down the expressway. They were two of the highest-paid Yankees executives, but they had to drop everything they were doing to make a full report to George on how many orange cones were blocking which traffic lanes.

Despite George's craziness, no one could stop the Yankee juggernaut. By the end of June, the Yankees were poised to run away with the division, a warning sign to his employees that with no major problems to solve, George would invent minor ones to drive them nuts. Even with the Yankees leading the league, Steinbrenner told a bewildered Bob Watson, "You've brought me nothing but fucking bad luck since you've got here. You don't know what the fuck you're doing with this team."

A couple days later he told Watson he was just kidding, but he wasn't. His hatred for those who succeeded—especially those in his own organization—is legendary. If Watson hadn't quit, he would have been fired, because he had done something George never dreamed he would do: succeed. Once Watson became a hero to Yankees fans, his days were numbered.

Watson's health from the pressure Steinbrenner brought to bear led to his resignation. For Bob Watson, a fine gentleman, it was either quit or die. Early in 1996 Watson suffered from chest pains, and he had to wear a blood pressure monitor to start the season. He had survived a bout with prostate cancer two years before that. Said Watson, "If you can survive cancer, you can survive anything—but being with George for a year runs a close second."

After fielding phone calls and getting memos almost every day from Steinbrenner and suffering intrusions and indignities, Watson quit in February 1998 after just over two years on the job. By the end of his tour of duty, Bob Watson was sure Steinbrenner was insane. In his last days with the Yankees, he joked that Steinbrenner's people were "voices running around in his head."

Watson was highly respected by everyone, and his resignation was met with such disdain that the *New York Times* went so far as to analyze it in an editorial on February 4, 1998. "Ask any fan about Steinbrenner's record," it read, "and you will hear a roll call of players, coaches, and managers—general and otherwise—who have been undercut, humiliated, fired or simply induced to resign. Bosses are bosses, it is true, but if all bosses were like Steinbrenner, the union movement would be booming today.

"A fan expects volatility. It is the condition of fandom. Teams rise and fall, and hopes rise and fall with them. Love is offset by loathing, even self-loathing at times. The perfections and imperfections of many men must come together to make a winning season in baseball, and a true fan grows to love the perfections and imperfections alike because together they define the identity of a team. The trouble with trying to love the Yankees is that no matter how volatile or imperfect the team is, its owner is more volatile, more imperfect still. At some point in the season, good or bad, it becomes necessary to believe that a team's fate lies in its own hands. With Steinbrenner's team, that illusion is almost never possible. Whenever New York embraces the Yankees, Steinbrenner steps in to break up the clinch."

As his final act, Bob Watson recommended Brian Cashman to replace him. He told Cashman he thought he was going to be offered the job.

"You've got a lot to think about, buddy," said Watson.

Brian Cashman's father had operated a horse farm in Ocala, and he had met Steinbrenner through a mutual friend. He was hired as an intern when he was eighteen, and his job was to compile reports and to work security. After he graduated from Catholic University in 1989, at age twenty, Cashman joined the Yankees full-time, and in 1992 he became assistant general manager to Watson. In February 1998 he replaced Watson as GM.

At a meeting at Steinbrenner's suite at the Regency Hotel, George looked Cashman in the eye and asked him, "Are you ready?"

"I'm your man," he said. At thirty years of age, Brian Cashman was the second-youngest general manager in the majors, behind Randy Smith of the San Diego Padres. He told Steinbrenner he wanted only a one-year deal so he could prove himself.

Cashman turned out to be an excellent choice, because the kid had seen Steinbrenner up close for ten years and knew just how to handle him: modest by nature, he would sit there as Steinbrenner bombarded him with criticism, vulgarity, and venom, and when it was over, he would blink back tears and pretend it had never happened, unlike the older men who had previously worked as GMs in other organizations—Clyde King, Cedric Tallis, and Bob Watson, who in time would begin to really despise Steinbrenner, and, once they no longer could take the abuse, would quit. Cashman would turn out to be a trouper. In the end, he would outlast both Joe Torre and Steinbrenner himself.

Torre and Cashman had an excellent working relationship. Torre at times would suggest improvements to the team. He would also make the suggestions to Steinbrenner just to keep him in the loop. Steinbrenner often would listen and oblige, making it easier for Cashman to do his job.

Cashman showed his smarts at the trade deadline in 1998. Seattle offered the Yankees star pitcher Randy Johnson, and in return they wanted Andy Pettitte, Ramiro Mendoza, and a couple of top minor leaguers. Johnson was going to be a free agent at the end of the season. And his salary was high. Cashman said no, but at the same time he made counteroffers to keep the Cleveland Indians from getting Johnson cheaply. The big pitcher ended up in Houston, where he couldn't hurt the Yankees. Pettitte and Ramiro were important cogs in the success of the 1996 Yankees as they won their first World Series since 1978.

The Yankees made it to the playoffs in 1997, but their cause was hurt badly when David Cone's shoulder broke down. He pitched badly against Cleveland in the playoffs. The Yankees lost the game and the series to the Indians when Mariano Rivera gave up a home run over the right-field wall to catcher Sandy Alomar.

The 1998 Yankees may well have been the best team in Yankees history, better even than the Babe Ruth-Lou Gehrig 1927 Yankees.

They started the 1998 season 61–20, and before it was over they won 125 games. They swept the San Diego Padres in the World Series. They were dominant and indomitable, crushing their opponents early.

A major reason the Yankees won so many games was the pitching of stopper Mariano Rivera, who became almost unhittable. From July 9, 1998, to September 11, 1999, he had a streak of not walking the first batter he faced after coming into a game. Darryl Strawberry, a Steinbrenner reclamation project, also was a factor. The Straw, who was battling drug addiction, hit twenty-four home runs in only 295 at bats in 1998.

Another key cog was third baseman Scott Brosius, whom Cashman acquired from Oakland over the winter in a trade for Kenny Rogers. Brosius had had a terrible season for Oakland the year before, but in 1998 he hit .300 and drove in ninety-eight runs during the regular season. He also hit two home runs in game three of the World Series and singled home a run in the finale to help the Yankees win their twenty-fourth championship. He finished with eight hits in seventeen at bats and was named Most Valuable Player in the series.

During the victory celebration, he held up his MVP trophy. The modest Brosius commented, "I don't know what to do with this thing. It's bigger and heavier than anything I've ever gotten."

In 1999, Brian Cashman took a beating from Steinbrenner when, in February, he lost arbitration cases to both Derek Jeter and Mariano Rivera. Steinbrenner always was livid when the Yankees lost in arbitration, and he let Cashman know it. He constantly belittled him, and he put him in a secondary position to his "baseball people" in Tampa. Those people included Mark Newman, who took over from Mitch Lukevics as vice president of player development and scouting. Steinbrenner more and more listened to Newman and not Cashman, but being a stubborn sort, Cashman perfectly understood Steinbrenner's ways, and he made up his mind to stay the course no matter how bad it got. In the end, Cashman's perseverance and his eye on improving the Yankees won out.

Steinbrenner's negative influence was felt constantly. The Yankees had acquired Hideki Irabu in a deal with San Diego after Irabu told the Padres he would only play for the Yankees. San Diego officials were sure that Steinbrenner had done something underhanded to get Irabu to say that. George gave Irabu a $12.8 million contract, hoping he would turn out to be Hideo Nomo. Instead, Steinbrenner became so disgusted with the way Irabu was pitching in spring training that he called him "a fat, pussy toad." Irabu's interpreter told Joe Torre, "He doesn't think he can pitch here anymore." Irabu was persuaded to finish out the season, then was traded to Montreal at a huge financial loss.

In the early part of spring training in 1999, Joe Torre became sick with prostate cancer. Don Zimmer took over as manager while he was recuperating. Zim had a bad knee and walked on crutches, traveling in a golf cart. He managed the team for five weeks during spring training, and it was during this period that he and Steinbrenner got into it over Irabu.

After Steinbrenner called the pitcher "a fat, pussy toad," before the game, Irabu told Zimmer he didn't want to pitch. A sympathetic Zimmer scratched out his name in the lineup card and replaced him with Ramiro Mendoza. Steinbrenner, furious, demanded that Zimmer start Irabu. Zimmer ignored him. Mendoza pitched eight shutout innings, and Zim brought Irabu in to complete the shutout. Steinbrenner, punishing Zimmer for disobeying him, didn't talk to him the last month he managed.

Said Zimmer, who refused to be bullied, "I'm sixty-eight years old. The worst thing I can do is go home. What are they going to do, shoot me? While I'm here, I'll do the best I can." It was the beginning of a four-year feud that would end with Zimmer's resignation after the 2003 season.

Joe Torre recovered and returned as manager in May. Steinbrenner would sit in his private box and grouse that Torre had lost the energy to do the job. He didn't change managers. He just complained and second-guessed.

In July, David Cone pitched a perfect game, but the victory came at a price. After that day, Coney made forty-two starts and won only six more times. After the perfecto, his ERA was 6.17. At the end of the season, Cone signed a one-year, $12 million contract. All the next summer, Steinbrenner blasted Cashman and Gene Michael for wasting his money on Cone.

In 2000, the Yankees' payroll hit $100 million, and in mid-June, the team was only 36–32. Steinbrenner and Cashman fought constantly. Steinbrenner wanted to buy slugger Sammy Sosa from the Cubs, but

Cashman felt the cost was too great. They switched to Juan Gonzalez, but Gonzalez didn't want to play in New York. The outfielder Cashman and Gene Michael wanted most, David Justice, was a perfect fit. Cashman traded Ricky Ledee, Zach Day, and Jake Westbrook for Justice. That summer Justice hit .305 with twenty homers and sixty RBIs in seventy-eight games.

Then there were the trades George wanted to make but Cashman didn't. George was offered outfielder Jim Edmunds by Anaheim if the Yankees would give up Alfonso Soriano, the talented rookie infielder. Cashman talked Steinbrenner out of it. After Edmunds went to St. Louis and became a leader on the Cardinals, Steinbrenner made Cashman send him daily reports on Edmunds's performance.

Another player Cashman refused to trade was Andy Pettitte. In midsummer, Pettitte's record was 5–7, and Steinbrenner ordered Cashman to trade him. The crack team of Tampa advisers was telling Steinbrenner that minor league pitcher Ed Yarnell was ready to fill his spot. Cashman, Torre, and pitching coach Mel Stottlemyre fought against trading Pettitte, and when Torre told Steinbrenner he was against using untried prospects, Steinbrenner finally backed off. Pettitte won seven of his last ten decisions, and he won two games in the playoffs. After seven seasons with the Yankees, his record was 115–65.

That year the Yankees won the pennant and beat the New York Mets in the World Series. The series clincher was won by the clever managing of Joe Torre. The game was at Shea Stadium, so there was no DH, and in the eighth inning Torre double-switched Luis Sojo into the lineup. José Canseco was available to hit, but Torre felt that Sojo was more of a contact hitter, and he batted against Al Leiter in the top of the ninth with the score tied, two outs, and two runners on base. Sojo bounced a single up the middle, and Posada scored the winning run. It was the last World Series the Yankees would win.

26

When we win, it's George's team, and when we
lose, it's Joe Torre's team.
—Don Zimmer

George Takes Back the Reins

T he 2000 World Series would be the last one the Yankees
would appear in, even though by 2001 the team's budget
would soar to $122 million, and that figure didn't include cash sent to
other teams in trades and money spent on buying international free
agents. In 2001, every starter was an All-Star except Alfonso Soriano and
Shane Spencer. The problem was that the farm system was barren,
and the many millions Steinbrenner spent on buying Latin talent was
mostly wasted.

Don Zimmer, for one, noticed that since Bill Livesay and Mitch
Lukevics were fired in 1995, the farm system had come up with only
two major leaguers, Jorge Posada, whom Livesay and Lukevics had
found, and Soriano. Zimmer, like Brian Cashman, was always hearing
about Steinbrenner's "baseball people" in Tampa. They were the ones
responsible for the farm system, and as far as Zimmer was concerned,
they were inept.

"All we kept hearing about were the great players they had in their
system," said Zimmer, "especially pitchers. Yet every time we needed
a pitcher at the major league level, they sent us someone who didn't

come close to getting the job done. We heard nothing but great reviews from Tampa on kids like Ed Yarnell, Randy Keisler, Ryan Bradley, Adrian Hernandez, Brandon Knight, and Jake Westbrook, to name a few who never lived up to those reviews. Joe [Torre] never complained, even to us. He just played the hand that was dealt and won anyway because we were fortunate to never be without our full quota of veteran, established starters for long periods of time. I wouldn't have complained either, except that I got fed up with Steinbrenner always giving Tampa the credit when we'd won, and Joe and the coaches the blame when we'd be in a losing streak. From what I could tell, the contributions to our success from Tampa were minimal, especially when it came to pitching. You'd think they'd find an acorn once in a while."

One top draft choice who was a complete bust was Drew Henson, the Michigan quarterback. The Yankees paid him $2 million to sign. Later they would give him a six-year, $17 million contract. Within a year and a half he would return to football.

Not a single player drafted in the first round from 1996 to 2001 by the Yankees made it to the majors. They top choice in 1998, pitcher Mark Prior, went back to college and eventually signed with the Chicago Cubs.

At the same time, most of the international free agents also turned out to be busts. The Yankees paid Jackson Melián, a Venezuelan outfielder, $1.6 million. Ricardo Aramboles was paid $1.2 million, and Edison Reynoso was paid $900,000. Willy Mo Peña, a Dominican, was paid $3.7 million, and Adrian Hernandez, a Cuban defector, got $4 million. Then in the spring of 2001, the Yankees signed another Cuban player, third baseman Andy Morales, sight unseen. They gave him $4.5 million. When he arrived in camp, infield coach Clete Boyer was hired to work with him. Boyer determined that Morales wasn't good enough to play major league ball. He was gone within a year.

"Who was responsible for the Yankees spending four million like that?" asked Don Zimmer.

The one Latin player who made the grade was Orlando Hernandez, El Duque, for whom the Yankees paid $6.6 million. The next closest bid was $3 million by the Cleveland Indians.

The money wasted by Steinbrenner's "baseball people" was more than what some teams spent on their entire rosters. General manager Brian Cashman was facing a tough decision. His contract expired at the end of the 2001 season, and he was getting fed up. Burdened by Steinbrenner's drumbeat to "win now; win today; win every day; win every year," he worked fifteen-hour days, and during and after games he would get phone calls from Steinbrenner, even when the team was on the road, complaining that the team wasn't good enough, always warning him that if something went wrong, it was his fault. Complicating the situation was a sense that something was wrong with Steinbrenner's mental facilities. More than once Steinbrenner ordered Cashman to fly to Tampa or to join the team on the road, and when he'd get there, Steinbrenner would ask him why he was there. After the 2001 World Series, which the Yankees lost to the Arizona Diamondbacks in the final game, both Baltimore and Toronto wanted to talk to Cashman about becoming their GM, but in the end he signed a three-year extension at $1 million per year to stay with the Yankees. He would be paid well for doing a job in which his performance was never good enough, no matter how hard he tried.

The Yankees came very close to winning it all in 2001. They hit two of the most dramatic home runs in their history. In game four, down by two runs with two outs in the ninth, Tino Martinez homered to tie a game the Yankees would go on to win. Then the next night, again with two outs in the ninth and down by two runs, Scott Brosius hit a two-run homer to tie a game the Yankees went on to win. In the end, they were defeated in the ninth inning of the seventh game of the World Series on a flare hit by Luis Gonzalez off Mariano Rivera just over the head of shortstop Derek Jeter, who was playing in to cut off the run. In one of the hardest-fought series in baseball history, the two teams had played each other tooth and nail.

All Steinbrenner could see was that the Yankees had lost. He stood in the clubhouse after the final defeat, and all he said was, "There will be changes, that's all I can say. There will be changes."

The final game was the swan song for several Yankees, including Paul O'Neill, Chuck Knoblauch, Luis Sojo, Scott Brosius, and Tino Martinez. According to journalist Buster Olney, the Yankee dynasty ended on the night of their defeat to Arizona as the good relationship between Steinbrenner and Joe Torre and his staff began to deteriorate.

Once Steinbrenner decided to take back the reins, the craziness of the past returned as once again he made moves based on impulse and whim. David Wells was a free agent, and Brian Cashman and the staff were against signing him, in part because he had a bad back. But Wells arranged to meet Steinbrenner for lunch, and after Wells told him how much he wanted to become a Yankee, Steinbrenner signed him without consulting anyone. Wells was 19–7 in 2002, only encouraging George to make more decisions. But a year later, Wells published a book in which he admitted to having been drunk when he pitched his no-hitter, and Steinbrenner fined him $500,000. George also gave the rotund pitcher the silent treatment. Said Wells in response, "What I did hasn't come close to some of the shit he's gotten into."

Asked Jon Heyman in *Newsday*, "We have our question to consider: Who has gotten into more shit? The fat man or the big man?" Heyman mentioned that Wells had some criticism for teammates in his book. Then he wrote, "Steinbrenner has authored some unfair criticisms of his own. He's publicly ripped or embarrassed every decent player who ever played for him except the most perfect one [Don Mattingly]. Oh, that's right, he even ripped into that one." Heyman then recounted Steinbrenner's disparaging behavior, the firings, and his breaking of rules, including a mention of Watergate and Howie Spira.

Heyman concluded, "After carefully considering Wells' considerable challenge, I think he actually may be right. Perhaps Steinbrenner has gotten into more shit."

His next signee was Raul Mondesi, whom Toronto wanted to get rid of because he wasn't worth the $24 million he was getting paid. At age thirty Mondesi no longer was the player he once had been. He was hitting around .200 in June, but when injuries struck and supersub Enrique Wilson made an error in left field, Steinbrenner decided to acquire Mondesi. Cashman was dead set against it, but George did it anyway. The Yankees agreed to assume $13 million of his salary. The Blue Jays could not have been happier.

In 2002, when most of the other teams cut payroll, the Yankees' rose to $150 million. They won the East in 2002, but they lost in the playoffs to a red-hot California Angels team.

Commented Don Zimmer, "See, this is what Steinbrenner never is able to understand. He thinks that spending money on players should assure him of winning. When you get into these sudden-death, short postseason series, it doesn't matter a hoot what your players are earning. In baseball, the postseason is a crapshoot, especially that best-of-five round."

Anything *can* happen, and in 2002 the Angels won. As punishment, Steinbrenner didn't give Joe Torre's coaches raises. A week after the series, Brian Cashman told Zimmer, "You can come back if you want to." Zim knew he would be needed to give Joe Torre comfort from Steinbrenner's criticisms and second-guessing. He told Cashman, "I'm not looking for a raise."

Two weeks after the season, Steinbrenner fired twenty-five employees, saving him a million dollars. His cost-saving was derided in the face of his wastefulness when it came to signing ballplayers. He was accused of being callous and petty.

In the winter of 2002–2003, Steinbrenner began to rely more and more on his "baseball people" in Tampa, and less and less on Brian Cashman and his New York staff. Cashman had three years left on his contract, but little influence. Some of Steinbrenner's execs saw this New York–Tampa tug-of-war for what it was—a vehicle Steinbrenner used to humiliate his employees.

The year 2002 was the first year of the salary tax, which was aimed squarely at the Yankees. Any team with a salary above $117 million had to pay at a rate of 17.5 percent. The labor contract was approved 29–1. The one no vote was George's. With a $150 million payroll, the Yankees had to pay $61 million to other less well-to-do teams.

In response to the tax, George thumbed his nose at the league and just kept on spending. He ordered his director of international scouting, Gordon Blakely, to sign pitcher José Contreras no matter what the cost. Contreras had never pitched in the major leagues, and the Yankees gave him a four-year, $32 million deal. Owners of other ball clubs were furious and outraged as the Yankees salary in 2003 soared to $180 million.

The year 2002 was the last season that Steinbrenner and Joe Torre got along, as Steinbrenner became more and more jealous of his manager's rising popularity. Torre stoutly protected his players from Steinbrenner's wrath, and whenever Steinbrenner started in on how any one game was "the big one," Torre let his players know that no game was any bigger than any other game. Torre had few rules. He only asked that they play hard.

At the start of the 2003 season, Steinbrenner decided to go after Joe Torre's coaching staff in the press. He questioned their work ethic. During the winter after the 2002 season, Don Zimmer ran into Steinbrenner at the Tampa Downs racetrack. George made a point of ignoring him because he was sure Zim had leaked to George King of the *New York Post* that the Yankees had signed José Contreras. It was a strange, unfounded conclusion, perhaps another sign his mind was slipping. For Don Zimmer, 2003 began as the last year had left off. In spring training he learned that Steinbrenner was taking the company car from him. Two days after the news spread around the league, Steinbrenner, embarrassed, apparently relented. Zim was told he could have his car back. Zim told PR director Dave Szen he had his own car. "He can take the keys to this one and stuff them up his ass," said Zim.

Zimmer was seeing firsthand how petty and vindictive Steinbrenner could be once he decided he didn't like someone. What he didn't know was that this was just the beginning.

In addition to feuding with Don Zimmer, George angered pitching coach Mel Stottlemyre, telling him how he wanted José Contreras used. Joe Torre, for the first time since he signed on as manager in 1996, complained publicly about how he was being treated. He told George King, "I'm not having much fun." Part of the problem was that Steinbrenner once again was shuttling players in and out, and Torre was having a hard time developing personal relationships with them. His contract would expire in 2004, and Torre fully expected to play it out and leave.

In early May, Zimmer was stricken with diverticulitis and was hospitalized in Manhattan. The Yankees were heading for the West Coast for six games. Zim wanted to go, but the doctors said no. After the Yankees lost their first game in Seattle, Steinbrenner called Zim.

"What are you doing?"

"I'm all right," said Zimmer.

"Well," said Steinbrenner, "I'll tell you one thing. You better get your ass on a plane to Oakland for the weekend because my manager and my pitching coach don't know what the hell they're doing."

Zim was stunned. After everything Steinbrenner had pulled the year before, he was surprised he had the nerve to talk to him. Zim also was hurt. These were close friends Steinbrenner was talking about. Zim called Dave Szen and asked him to book him a flight the next day to Oakland.

Brian Cashman found out and called Zim. The Yankee doctor, Stuart Hershon, also called him. They ordered him not to go. And he didn't.

Said Zimmer in his book *The Zen of Zim*, "How goofy is this man Steinbrenner? He's sitting home there in Tampa, frustrated and upset over us losing a couple of games on the West Coast, and he's so mad at Joe and Mel, he calls me—the SOB he wants to get rid of—and tells me to get out there because they can't do the job. It's almost scary."

A couple of weeks later Steinbrenner went after the coaching staff anew. In one newspaper, a cartoonist had drawn a picture of six ducks lined up in a row with the faces of Torre and his coaches. Zim went on Michael Kay's TV show to talk about the cartoon, saying it was unfair. When he arrived at the ballpark, his anger was growing. He told reporters, "When we win, it's George's team, and when we lose, it's Joe Torre's team." It was not a new sentiment. All through the season whenever the Yankees would lose two games in a row, Steinbrenner would say in the papers, "This is Joe's team. We gave him everything he wanted." All the while there was speculation he was getting ready to fire Torre. During the season, *USA Today*'s publisher, Al Neuharth, wrote an editorial highly critical of Torre. Zimmer was sure Steinbrenner was behind it.

"Where else would Neuharth come up with those kinds of mean-spirited and downright dumb opinions?" he wondered.

When the writers ran to get a reaction from Steinbrenner to Zimmer's quote, he refused to comment. But he didn't refrain from reacting. George ordered the YES Network producers not to put Zimmer on camera and ordered the announcers not to mention his name. Steinbrenner also changed Don Zimmer bobblehead day to Hideki Matsui bobblehead day. After the season, Brian Cashman told him Steinbrenner had in fact nixed it.

It was a year of constant criticism from Steinbrenner. Reporters remained on the "Steinbrenner Watch," as Christian Red of the *Daily News* called it. Red, in his first season covering the Yankees, waited by the Stadium Club after an 8–4 loss to the Red Sox, just in case George had something to say after the game. He didn't have to wait long.

Steinbrenner was in full critical mode. He opined that starter Jeff Weaver should be sent to the bullpen, that José Contreras should start, that Jason Giambi's personal trainer had no business being in the clubhouse, that Hideki Matsui needed to "step up." According to Red, Steinbrenner went on with his critique for ten minutes. Then he turned to the reporter, jabbed his index finger into his chest, and said, "Don't bet against us." He got in the backseat of his Town Car and his chauffeur drove off.

The Yankees won 101 games in 2003, and they met the Minnesota Twins in the first round of the playoffs. Five innings into game two, they had missed on repeated scoring opportunities when Steinbrenner went off on GM Brian Cashman. "You're horseshit, and you're over-paid," screamed Steinbrenner. "No one will take your contract off my hands. Maybe the Mets will talk to you. You have permission to talk to the Mets."

Despite Steinbrenner's fears, the Yankees defeated Minnesota and went on to defeat the Red Sox to win the pennant. The Red Sox, under the ownership of John Henry and the wizardry of general manager Theo Epstein, had become a much stronger team. The series went the full seven games, and the Sox were leading late in the finale, but they blew their lead, and when Aaron Boone homered in extra innings, the Yankees again were pennant winners and the Red Sox, who hadn't won a World Series since 1918, again were long-suffering losers.

Beating the Red Sox in 2003 was one of the most satisfying victories for Joe Torre and Don Zimmer, who in one game was thrown to the ground in a scuffle with Boston pitcher Pedro Martinez. And yet, after the pennant clincher, George Steinbrenner was nowhere to be seen. He had derided Cashman, saying the team had too many holes to win, and he had continually criticized Joe Torre and his coaches, all of whom had proved him wrong.

"Everyone in New York was spent over [beating Boston]," said Zimmer in his book. "And yet, where was Steinbrenner? Why didn't he come down to the clubhouse to congratulate Joe and the players? It was my thinking he'd made enough comments and treated enough people like dogs that he didn't want to show up. The only conclusion anyone could draw from this is that he just didn't like us. Why, I'll never know. All we ever did was win four World Championships and six American league pennants in eight years for him."

All season long Steinbrenner had complained about the coaching staff. But the Yankees ended up winning 101 games and winning the pennant in 2003. How bad could the coaches have been?

After the Yankees beat the Red Sox to win the pennant, a reporter approached Zimmer to ask how he felt. Zimmer unleashed all his anger at what had been going on all year long. He as much as said he was quitting. He loved the players, he said. He loved the manager. He loved New York and its fans. He was quitting because of George Steinbrenner.

When Yogi Berra phoned him to ask him to reconsider, Zimmer replied, "You're a fine one to talk. It took you fourteen years to get over what he did to you."

The Yankees played the Florida Marlins in the World Series. Steinbrenner was tense and irritable throughout one of the greatest World Series in history, won by the Marlins in six games. By the eighth inning of the finale, Steinbrenner was seething. He went to see Brian Cashman, barking, "There will be a meeting in Tampa in forty-eight hours."

After the series, Don Zimmer, the baseball lifer, quit the Yankees to take an advisory position with the Tampa Bay Devil Rays. Said Zimmer in his book, "There's a reason I'd spent fifty-four years in baseball. I love the game, and I always had fun. In 2003, George Steinbrenner took the fun out of it for me, in the same way he took the fun out of it for so many other good baseball people like Yogi Berra, Dick Howser, and Bob Lemon, to name three. To this day I still don't know what it was that I did to him to have him turn on me and treat me like he did."

After Zimmer quit, Steinbrenner gave Joe Torre a three-year, $20 million contract. Zim didn't know it, but the George Steinbrenner reign of terror was about to end. In a couple of months his mental health would take a sharp turn for the worse, and the bark of the Boss would be silenced forever.

27

I have seldom in my life seen a crueler individual.

—Leo Hindery

The Gold Mine

Ted Turner was the one great financial genius in sports in our lifetime. He was the owner of the Atlanta Braves, but more important, he was the first to recognize that it was critical to also own a television network on which to broadcast the team's games. Turner put up the TBS satellite, carried the Braves games on his cable network, and made so much money he was able to marry Jane Fonda and buy half of the state of Montana.

Turner once told former baseball commissioner Fay Vincent, "Look, I paid ten million dollars for the Braves. Let's suppose I get their programming for five years, and I write off the cost of the programming on a five-year basis. Since I own them both, I get the programming forever. By the time the five years has come and gone, the cost of the programming to me is zero. No cost, and it's all been amortized."

Another financially brilliant sports team owner has been Charles Dolan, the owner of Madison Square Garden's New York Rangers and New York Knicks. In addition to Knicks and Rangers games, Dolan's MSG Network aired Yankees and then Mets games. Dolan said to himself, I'm paying a fortune to carry the Yankees and Mets games. Why don't I buy a team? But Mets owner Fred Wilpon wouldn't sell. Dolan came within a whisker of buying the Yankees for $500 million when Steinbrenner backed out. Later Dolan tried to buy the Boston Red Sox, but lost out when baseball commissioner Bud Selig rigged it so John Henry would end up with the team instead.

If CBS had one failure while it owned the Yankees—and it had many—it was in not recognizing the gold mine it owned. The Yankees played in the largest market in the country, and the Yankees fan base was large and extremely loyal, considering that the team had been a powerhouse since Babe Ruth joined them in 1920. But CBS owner Bill Paley wasn't much of a baseball fan. Paley, who moved successfully from radio to TV, didn't have the imagination to go from TV to cable TV. He didn't see the world changing, and so not only didn't CBS take over the Yankees' broadcasts, but in the end he sold the team to George Steinbrenner for $10 million, a song. An irony: in November 2001, the Yankees sold the rights to televise twenty games a season for three seasons to CBS for $36 million. If fans wanted to watch the rest of the Yankees games on TV, they had to get cable. The next month the Yankees sold their radio rights to CBS-AM, in a five-year deal worth $8 million a year to the Yankees' coffers. Had Paley been alive, he would have been mortified.

Paley wasn't the only owner who didn't understand the importance of owning the means of broadcasting the team's games. For a long time, only Ted Turner and the Tribune Company, which owned both WGN and the Cubs, did. That was it. When Bob Luria, the owner of the Florida Marlins, sold his programming to Fox, then–baseball commissioner Fay Vincent called him on the phone and told him not to do it.

"What you're doing makes no sense," said Vincent. "Over time you want to own your own programming."

Luria told him, "I get a lot of cash. It cleans up my balance sheet. I need the money."

Said Vincent, "Can you get out of the deal in five years? Suppose I'm right and you're wrong, and it's a terrible mistake? Can you get out?"

"Oh, no," said Luria, "I'm in for a long time."

Said Vincent, "In five years you will call me and say you're really sorry you didn't listen to me. I guarantee you the value of your programming will go through the roof, and Fox will have a fixed price. Don't do it. Well, he did. They are all richer than I am, so why am I so smart?"

It took George Steinbrenner thirty-five years to figure it out, but better late than never. For years, Steinbrenner sold the TV rights to the Yankees games to WPIX, Channel 11, and then to Charlie Dolan's MSG Network. Steinbrenner certainly knew the importance of making money from the television broadcasts. In 1983, in a conversation with *U.S. News & World Report*, he told the interviewer, "Television is the key to all sports, and the reason why most owners are in sports today. Owners are looking forward to the entertainment dollar coming from the packaging of sports for TV, whether on cable, pay per view or over the air. In my opinion, the most important thing is not owning the cable-television companies themselves but owning the product that TV needs to fill its time— and baseball has that product. For my money, we've got the number one product in America."

When in 1989 he signed a ten-year $500 million deal with Dolan's MSG Network, George was sure he was doing just fine. But as it turned out, he wasn't making anywhere near the money he could have made from TV. All those years Steinbrenner didn't know what he had, until one day he woke up and said to himself, *I get it. I want to own the distribution facility. That's where the money is.*

In November 1998, the New Jersey Nets were purchased by a partnership group led by financiers Ray Chambers and Finn Wentworth. When the group decided to build a regional sports network, it negotiated with George Steinbrenner to include the New York Yankees in the project. On September 23, 1999, the regional sports network called YankeeNets was born. The Yankees' share was 60 percent, the Nets' 40 percent. In order to succeed, YankeeNets had to outmaneuver Cablevision, the regional cable giant owned by Charles Dolan. The man they hired to give the group credibility was Dr. Harvey Schiller, who had once run Turner Sports and who was a bigwig on the U.S. Olympic Committee. George, another member of that committee, signed Schiller to a five-year deal.

In the spring of 2000, Dr. Schiller made a fatal mistake. He gave an interview to *Forbes* magazine in which he represented himself as "the boss of the Boss." "You know, people can always spot a pilot," Schiller said, referring to his time as an air force pilot in Vietnam. After the interview, he was asked by a friend, "Harvey, do you really want to do that? I don't know how this is going to go over."

It went over like a lead balloon. After the article came out, Steinbrenner excommunicated him, refusing to take his phone calls. George felt that Schiller had shown him up, and the good doctor was toast. Said an executive close to George, "George didn't just believe in an eye for an eye. He didn't stop at an eye. He wanted his head."

At this point, because of George's flagrant overspending on salaries, the Yankees were barely breaking even, and George was in serious financial trouble. That's why he almost sold the Yankees to Cablevision's Charles Dolan in 2000 for $500 million. As part of the deal, Dolan was going to give him a five-year employment contract. For George, the deal would have been a disaster.

A year later he received $600 million for 40 percent of his team from the investment firm of Goldman Sachs and the group led by Chambers and Wentworth. Goldman Sachs then hired longtime cable wizard Leo Hindery to be the CEO of the network. If the network took off, George would never have to worry about making payroll again. It was up to Hindery to make it happen.

As founder of the YES (Yankee Entertainment System) Network, Leo Hindery had the job of putting together a cable station that would carry most of the Yankees games and the twenty-four-hour programming that was all Yankees all the time. After the Yankees' long-term deal with Charlie Dolan's Cablevision expired in 2000, the YES Network became a competitor in 2001. If the start-up had one glitch, it was that Cablevision in the spring of 2001 refused to make a deal to carry the YES Network because Dolan didn't want to pay two dollars a customer for the programming, which was to appear on basic cable. Dolan wanted the Yankees to be on a pay channel where he could get eight dollars a head from subscribers. Hindery was adamant that the Yankee games appear only on basic cable.

The standoff and public feud between Jim Dolan, Charlie's son, and Hindery, former close friends, lasted the entire 2001 season. Just as the 2002 season was starting, Cablevision finally capitulated. Without the Yankees programming, it was losing millions in value as its stock plummeted. The three million unhappy Yankees fans who had Cablevision in their homes finally were able to see the Yankee games, and all was right with the world. By the 2008 season, the YES Network had become the most successful regional sports station in the country, earning the New York Yankees more than $200 million a year.

An executive close to the network who asked not to be identified nevertheless wanted it to be known that it was Leo Hindery's skill and savvy that was responsible for the success of the YES Network. "Hindery was the guy who was the engineer, who marshaled the troops and fought with the networks and brought the talent to bear, who basically won our freedom from the Cablevision guys," he said.

"I had no impetus to be Leo's ally until we became partners, and it was only through diligent effort that I recognized what he was doing. His work effort was tremendous, for the two years through the completion of 2001 and all of 2002, and then the launch of the station. He had been on the board of Cablevision, and now the guy was taking crap from guys he's known throughout his cable career. Dolan was attacking him because he was acting in our interests. I remember going with Leo to Trenton and rallying to get a bill passed that wasn't going to let the Cablevision guys operate in New Jersey unless they broadcast competitively sporting teams. It wasn't anyone else's efforts but Leo's."

Leo Hindery had a bird's-eye view of the workings of George Steinbrenner's Yankees. He discussed the founding of the network and what he recalled most vividly about his time working with George Steinbrenner and the Yankees.

"Ray Chambers used to own the New Jersey Nets," said Hindery. "His financial partner was Bill Simon. They had one of the early private equity funds, and they made a ton of money. Ray is very philanthropic, New Jersey born and bred, with lots of affection for his home state. When the Nets threatened to move out of the state, he and some friends bought the team. A couple years later he proposed to George that they form something called YankeeNets, and they would put the two teams together. The Yankees would own sixty percent, and the Nets would own forty percent, and everything would be commingled. The deal was, 'I'm going to put my basketball team in, and you put your baseball team in.' George said, 'You run your basketball team, and I will run my baseball team.' Well, that only works if both of the guys are doing the right thing.

"The Yankees don't make any money, as you know. They actually lose money. Year after year George has the highest payroll, and the Yankees make no money. He pays himself and family members high salaries, and everything he does is for the glorification of the

Steinbrenner family. So George paid ten million for the Yankees, ran it largely to break even, took his own salary out, which is high, but if you are one of the investors, you make no money. If you are an investor, you don't even get financial statements. You get nothing. Absolutely nothing. The wealthy investors who own forty percent of the team have never gotten a nickel in thirty years. You get nothing. Nothing. Sometimes you don't even get seat preferences. If George gets mad at you, he takes your seats away.

"George is the only one making money. At the same time, the value of the Yankees keeps rising to where it's worth $800 million, so for George, it's a good deal. But for Ray Chambers, it was a nightmare. It was ridiculous. George's payroll was $200 million a year. Why couldn't it have been $150 million, where the Yankees could have made a profit of which Ray would have gotten a percentage? So it was making Ray completely crazy. It was a complete disaster, because Ray was brilliant and George was an autocrat.

"While they were still partners I came along and proposed the YES Network. I was introduced to George and Ray through Fred Wilpon of the Mets. Some years ago I oversaw the development of what is called regional sports networks when I was president of TCI. We sold them to Rupert Murdoch en masse. And New York was left out of the mix because there was this long-standing contract entered into very badly with the Dolan family of Cablevision.

"I had retired from TCI and AT&T, and I was blessed with having made quite a bit of money, and my family office is located here in New York. Fred Wilpon wanted to buy the other half of the Mets from Nelson Doubleday, who was going to sell his piece to five families at ten percent a piece. He invited me to be one of those five families. We grew to be very fond of each other. I said to Fred, 'Don't do this. I'd love to buy ten percent of the Mets, but you shouldn't sell it to me. I will show you how in a few years you can turn your own holdings into a wholly owned baseball team with your own regional sports network.

"We became dear friends, and he introduced me to George. I went to see George and Ray Chambers, and we started the YES Network on September 10, 2001, the day before the Twin Towers tragedy. The opening headline in the *New York Times* the morning of 9/11 was about the YES Network. It was on the front page. Goldman Sachs, Providence Equity, and I put up $335 million, and we acquired forty percent of the YES Network. That money was given to YankeeNets and distributed sixty–forty. So Chambers owned forty percent of YankeeNets. Since YankeeNets owned forty percent of the YES Network, Ray owned twenty-four percent of the YES Network and George owned thirty-six percent. And the financial investors owned forty percent.

"It wasn't easy making money from whole cloth, but it was one of the great success stories of all time as we turned the YES Network into the most profitable regional sports network ever created. It's now worth two and a half billion dollars. The YES Network makes $200 million a year, of which sixty percent belongs to the Yankees, and forty percent to the financial investors. Once the YES Network was up and running and you could see it would be widely successful, wildly profitable, Chambers went to George and said, 'I can't work with you anymore. You never listen to me. You treat partners badly. I always knew you ran the baseball team, but I didn't think you would run it badly. I didn't think you would never listen to me when I said, 'Maybe there is a better way to run it.'

"In 2006, because of YES, the Yankees had more money than they ever had, and they cut the health and welfare benefits for their employees. At a point where they were paying $210 million in payroll, they cut the dental plan. The Yankees employee handbook does not provide for holidays. If they had been written down, they would have to give them. Chambers is a sensitive, generous guy, and he said, 'I can't live like that.' And so they broke up YankeeNets. Chambers and his partners sold the Nets to Forest City Ratner, which is moving the Nets to Brooklyn, but Ray kept his piece of the YES Network. So Ray Chambers owns twenty-four percent of the YES Network, Steinbrenner owns thirty-six percent, and the limited partners of the Yankees and the financial investors own forty percent.

"When I came in and started the YES Network, we had to find an understanding that would isolate and insulate the network from George. Some of that was just drawing a line in the sand and saying, 'This isn't your world. It's your team playing in our world.' But I also had to rely on MLB and revenue sharing when I would say to George,

'You cannot interfere with the network,' because if he did interfere, those monies could have been included in revenue sharing.

"The rich teams share with the poor teams. They share their rights fees. If a TV station pays George $55 million a year to carry the Yankees on TV, that is revenue to him that the poorer teams can get their hands on. If George owns the TV station that paid the $55 million, the profits of the TV network—in this case the YES Network—are immune provided George can show there is a Chinese wall, that he is not in control of the management of the network. He could own a large portion of it, but he can't run it. And so the YES Network makes George $200 million a year free and clear—if he keeps away. If he had control of management, he would have to declare another $120 million in revenue.

"In any event, we would not have tolerated him getting involved. You cannot work for George. You cannot work for Bruton Smith. You cannot work for the Dolan family with Cablevision and Madison Square Garden. But there are a million people who want to hang around these clubs and work for them and have a shot at getting a ring on their finger. And if you're a sadomasochist, which George is, there is nothing in the world like owning a ball club, because it's a completely proprietary asset. Nobody can screw with you. You can't get forced out. You can't have a bad performance that will cost you your job. So George found the perfect outlet back in the 1970s for his personality. Where can you have a franchise for life, not be fired by anybody, a macho environment—no women allowed—where the need to fuel your ego and your untouchability come together in a single place? There is no place like that except professional sports.

"I never had any problems with George, because with the relationship he and I struck, I was immune, which was the only way I could hang around him. But I have seldom in my life seen a crueler individual. There's a TV show, *What Won't You Do for Money*. The abuse he heaps on people, and then finds some reward either psychic or monetary. In the case of a lot of his top executives, it's no more than rings on their fingers. He will mercilessly excoriate a waiter, but then he'll whip out a hundred-dollar bill as he walks out the door just to break him.

"He's cruel. Everyone, from players to GMs to people in the clubhouse who pick up towels, has been a target of a George and now a Hank tirade. Howard Rubenstein keeps getting shorter and shorter.

In all the years he has represented George, Howard has said fewer things to the press since last fall than anytime in all the years he was with him, and because Hank is so impolitic, he doesn't even understand the desirability of having deniability and a buffer. George would use Howard to say something outrageous, and if it flew, it did. If it didn't, George would say, 'Howard had no right to say that.' And then it was, 'Oh, by the way, Howard, here's a whole lot of money so I can abuse you.'

"Did you hear the story about the wedding anniversary? George requires that Lonn Trost, his COO, be at the stadium when the Yankees are playing, even during away games. He's not allowed not to be there.

"Lonn Trost had a significant wedding anniversary coming up, and he asked if he could have the night off, and several times George said no. Finally, he conceded that Trost could have the night off if Randy Levine, the president, stayed at home with his cell phone in case George needed to call. Lonn took his wife to Lincoln Center for his anniversary.

"Levine is sitting at home with his cell phone, and Trost is at Lincoln Center with his cell phone off. He comes out at about eleven o'clock at night to find a series of voice mails on the phone, and it's quite clear that what George has done is get the two phone numbers mixed up. So he's been calling Randy Levine, but using Trost's phone number while Levine sits at home and gets no phone calls.

"The first phone call says, 'Randy, it's George. Call me.'

"The second one is, 'Goddammit, Randy, it's George. Call me.'

"The third one, 'Fuck you, Randy. Where are you? If you don't call me, I'm going to fire you.'

"By the fourth call he does fire him. And then he proceeds to keep calling him back, telling him what he thinks about him now that he's fired and what he really thought about him all this period of time.

"They were both fired for a couple of days, and the only reason this thing blew over was that they finally were able to convince George he had dialed the wrong number because they didn't delete the messages.

"Ray Chambers, the owner of the New Jersey Nets at the time, and some of his people actually heard these recordings. They told me this story. They said, 'George's phone messages were simply profane.' But they are hilarious, especially the one that said, 'Now that I've fired you, let me tell you what I've thought about you all these years you worked for me.'

"I can remember one of the greatest lunches I ever attended. It was at 21 in the last week of Rudy Giuliani's administration. It was myself, George, Lonn Trost, Randy Levine, and Howard Rubenstein, George's PR man. In the course of the lunch George fired, in sequence, the other three guys.

"Giuliani is a great Yankee fan. He also is quite corrupt. George and Rudy were going to sign a sweetheart deal with the city of New York in terms of land improvements and things of that sort for the new stadium in the Bronx. [A week later, when Mike Bloomberg took over, he reneged on it.] But at this meeting George was angry. He didn't think the agreement was rich enough for what he wanted. As much as they had gotten greased, it wasn't enough. I was along because the press conference was going to be on the YES Network. I thought I was being invited to a social lunch, and then we would go down to city hall where Giuliani would shake George's hand on the new deal.

"At lunch the waiter brings the food, and George starts yelling at him that the food isn't right.

"George then starts asking questions about what had been agreed to and how the thing was going to progress. He said, 'I don't like that,' or 'You have to change that.'

"Randy Levine said, 'We can't change it. It's going to be announced in two hours.'

"And then, 'You're fired.'

"Trost was the second guy who was fired. Howard then tried to tell George, 'You can't just fire these guys. How are you going to explain this in two hours that they are gone?'

" 'I'll do whatever I want,' said George. 'And you're fired.'

"It was a scene out of a Hitchcock movie. We're at 21, and George has screamed and yelled so loudly that the entire restaurant is aghast. Customers are getting up and leaving as he's firing these guys.

"I had no skin in this game. This was so far above my pay grade. I was just sitting there eating.

"At which point George says to me, 'You and I will go to the press conference.'

"I said, 'I'll go, but I'm not saying anything.'

"He paid the bill, put a tip on it, and he handed this poor waiter who stood there shaking in his boots a hundred-dollar bill.

"We went outside, and standing on the sidewalk were the three guys who have been fired. They aren't talking to each other, and in under an hour there's going to be this press conference announcing this deal. George says he wants me to get in the limo and go with him, but I refuse and go back to my office. The four of them pile into the limo and have this press conference with Giuliani, who signs this give-away on behalf of the city of New York.

"And everybody gets their jobs back.

"So George finds this amazing vehicle that suits an abusive person-ality, a vehicle that is all male all the time, all testosterone, white males largely, and so he finds this perfect world. He finds ways to control this perfect world. It plays into all his ego issues, all of his sense of self-worth and lack of self-worth, and he really is untouchable. The only time he's ever been dusted up was with CREEP under Nixon and with Dave Winfield. For all of his bullying, the aggressiveness, he comes out of this smelling pretty good.

"What's so fascinating about it is that history repeats itself. Steve Swindal was a bridge between the daughters, who are very bright, but would have no direct role, and the idiot sons. Steve would have suc-ceeded George as head of the Yankees but Steve couldn't survive that cut, because George's world is very black and white. George him-self can have serial affairs and interests, but if he catches someone he can point a finger at, he's very quick to do so. The problem is that George's illness was coincident with Steve's problems. George became non compos mentos exactly when Steve Swindal fell into problems. Steve is actually trying to get back with Jennifer. With George not being around, they are trying to save their marriage. We are all quite fond of Steve.

"Hank and Hal were persona non grata in the eyes of their father, and sadly, the brains of the family are in the daughters, but it's a family that both in terms of how it made its original money and then the pat-tern George chose to continue, there is no role for women in baseball or in horse racing or in any of the other things that fascinate George.

"So Steve got popped, and who takes over but Hal, who has fine features, very quiet, a handsome guy. Hal is virtually untalkative. He's almost mute, but instantly he was dominated by Hank, who was sweeping out the barns at the horse farm. Hank is absolutely his father's physique, and we think he is meaner than his father ever was. Hank stayed scared shitless of George until his father disappeared.

"Hank has Howard Rubenstein pulling out what little hair he has left, because Hank is trying to prove, 'If you think my father was mean, I'm a lot meaner than that.' In the last seven or eight years, George wasn't as aggressive with the club as Hank has been in a single season. Hank demanded that Joba Chamberlain become a starting pitcher. The only way you understand this kind of interference is that there is a gene in the pool that seems to pass from one generation to another. George was abused by his father, who sent him off to military school. For George it's, 'I'll show you, Dad. I'll send my own kid off to this same military school.' So instead of being the best parent, George becomes the same parent.

"My sense of all of this is that it's Shakespearean. George's story has every human failing. It's Gatsby. F. Scott Fitzgerald could write this stuff. There is rudeness and haughtiness and cruelty, and it just repeats. This book is more fun than any piece of fiction."

28

Who is going to lead us? Will the new Yankee brain trust spend money
like George Steinbrenner did? What is going to happen to our team?
—The thoughts of Yankee fans

Silent George

George Steinbrenner began showing signs of slowing down
in 2001. For the first time he didn't go to games as often
as he once did. Where he once attended all the spring training road
games, he started cutting back. He only went to games within an hour
of Tampa. When the regular season began, he didn't travel to most of
the away games as he once had. And if he did fly, he wouldn't take the
flight right after the final game of the home stand with the rest of
the team, but instead he went home and slept and flew out the next
day. People didn't notice any physical problems; they just noticed his
drop in involvement. Not that he wasn't just as involved in running
the team as always.

In the winter of 2003–2004, without consulting Brian Cashman
or Gene Michael, the baseball professionals he had hired to run the
Yankees, George decided that the slugger the Yankees needed to win
the World Series was Gary Sheffield. He paid the thirty-five-year-
old veteran $39 million for four years. Cashman was certain it was a
mistake. His feeling was the team needed to go younger, not older.
Cashman wanted Alfonso Soriano to play the outfield and Kaz Matsui
to play second base. When Sheffield waffled on his deal, Cashman

moved to sign Vladimir Guerrero instead. At least Guerrero at age twenty-seven was younger. But Steinbrenner killed the Guerrero negotiations. He wanted Sheffield, and that was that. But by courting Sheffield so resolutely, he neglected to pay any attention to Andy Pettitte, who had become a free agent. He never even gave him a phone call. Pettitte, a fixture in the Yankees rotation who was tired of how dysfunctional the Yankees were, signed with Houston, and when another fixture, Roger Clemens, learned his buddy had gone home to Texas, he decided to go with him. To replace one of them, the Yankees had to trade two highly prized prospects, Nick Johnson and Juan Rivera, to the Montreal Expos for Javier Vasquez.

Steinbrenner wasn't finished with the Sheffield signing. He made a trade that Cashman knew was a bad move. He sent Jeff Weaver to the Los Angeles Dodgers for Kevin Brown, a difficult man whom Cashman considered a cancer on a ball club. Cashman wondered how Brown, a nasty guy, would do under the microscope of the New York media. The 2004 Yankees began the season with no left-handed pitchers and no minor league prospects.

Only one thing could slow the irrational actions of George Steinbrenner, and that came without warning. Otto Graham, the great Cleveland Browns quarterback and one of Steinbrenner's longtime football hero buddies, had moved to Sarasota, Florida, after his days as coach of the Coast Guard Academy, and they had remained close. They were golfing partners, attended banquets together, and gave to each other's charities.

In late December of 2003, Graham lay in a Sarasota hospital dying. He was weak and couldn't talk. Graham's wife, Beverly, called Steinbrenner on the phone and asked him to speak to her husband. He said a few words, and Beverly told Steinbrenner the monitor registered a jump in his heart rate. The next day, December 17, Graham died. He was eighty-two.

Nine days later a memorial service was held for the legendary quarterback at the Church of the Palms in Sarasota. At the reception, which was packed with mourners, Graham's grandchildren were showing a series of slides, including one from the 1960s of Graham and Steinbrenner together, when Steinbrenner stumbled, reached for a chair, missed, and fell face-first onto the floor.

As he lay unconscious for a few seconds, a witness described him as being ashen-faced. He was turned faceup, and his tie and collar were loosened. A dozen or more people reached for cell phones and called 911.

An ambulance came, and he was whisked to the Sarasota Memorial Hospital. A fire department spokesman talked as though Steinbrenner was going to be okay. He spoke of Steinbrenner's being in good spirits and talking.

But Steinbrenner wasn't okay. The word around Tampa was that he had had a stroke. He rarely made himself available for interviews, and his pronouncements thereafter would come in the form of releases read by public relations guru Howard Rubenstein.

Steinbrenner would continue to run the Yankees from Tampa. His mercurial decisions would continue to negatively affect the team. Joe Torre would still get memos. What would stop would be the constant barrage of phone calls.

In the early months of 2004, the big question was whether Yankees general manager Brian Cashman was going to quit. For months he had expressed his unhappiness and desire to leave, but like Billy Martin, he was unable to separate himself from his first love, the Yankees.

In 2004, the Yankees came within one game of winning the American League pennant. They won the first three games of the Boston playoff series, but then, in a most improbable way, lost four in a row to give the Boston Red Sox their first pennant since 1986. The Red Sox went on to defeat the St. Louis Cardinals to win their first World Series since 1918, when Babe Ruth was pitching for them. The Curse of the Bambino was broken, but for Yankees fans, the winter was one of the toughest in memory. After the loss, experts extolled the Red Sox for being a real team, while blasting the Yankees for trading away so many prospects for veteran stars who were just a bunch of guys playing together. The criticism wasn't entirely fair. After all, the Yankees came oh so close to the pennant with the players they did have.

By 2005, George Steinbrenner had become a recluse. Once he had commanded headlines every day. Now he was invisible like every other baseball owner. Torre and the players knew of his presence through his memos, but Yankees fans wondered whether Steinbrenner's health was so bad that he no longer was running the team.

After five weeks of the 2005 season, the Yankees were 11–19 and playing so badly that they were tied with the Tampa Bay Devil Rays. Considering that the Yankees had a salary of $208 million and the Rays' salary was $25 million, the Yankees were in line to become the most expensive flop ever. There were comparisons with the movies *Heaven's Gate* and *Waterworld*. The papers reported that Steinbrenner was blaming pitching coach Mel Stottlemyre for the sorry state of affairs. The fault, however, hardly lay with Stottlemyre, who was fighting multiple myeloma, a form of bone cancer. In May, Brian Cashman called up Chien-Ming Wang from Columbus, and he was looking to trade for pitching help, but after he brought up Wang the minor league cupboard was bare, and the trade market was dormant. By June, Bernie Williams had made it obvious that he no longer had the speed to play centerfield, and when Torre called for minor league help, there was none to be had. Memos from Steinbrenner indicated he had wanted to fire hitting coach Don Mattingly and pitching coach Mel Stottlemyre since May, but was talked out of it for PR reasons. Why Stottlemyre should be blamed for injuries to pitchers Jaret Wright, Kevin Brown, and Randy Johnson no one could figure out. It certainly wasn't his fault that there were no pitchers ready to come up from the farm system.

There were calls for George to do something, but there was nothing that could be done. George and his Tampa cronies had once again screwed the team up very badly. The Yankees were paying their pitchers $220,000 an inning. On June 28, 2005, Steinbrenner called a meeting in Tampa of his "baseball people." He turned to Brian Cashman and asked, "What are we going to do? What can we do?"

Not wanting to trade any more prospects, Cashman replied, "We made our bed, and now we have to sleep in it."

Those close to the organization say Steinbrenner stopped blaming trades he made on others, in part because Alzheimer's began taking over his mind. He no longer could remember who made which trades. He became more forgetful, and no longer was he the micromanager he once had been, because he couldn't remember the details he needed in order to micromanage.

He almost never returned phone calls to reporters, and when he did, he never said much, except perhaps, "We have to play better." Papers assigned reporters to follow Steinbrenner to assess his mental health, but Steinbrenner never stopped to talk. He retreated to his private box, and he hired a security guard to make sure he wasn't disturbed.

There was other evidence that at age seventy-five his reign was coming to an end. He was being interviewed on local TV when a group of fans began shouting, "We love you, George." He began to quiver and weep.

"Nature made him change," said cartoonist Bill Gallo, a friend.

Steve Swindal, George's son-in-law, would be his eventual successor, he said in August 2005. Swindal was a very capable executive who had played a big role in starting the YES Network and in planning for the new Yankee Stadium, but the next March Swindal's wife, Jennifer, filed for divorce, and Swindal was forced out, necessitating a new successor. His departure was a huge loss for the Yankees.

An executive close to the Yankees recalled Swindal's role. "Before it became widely known George was sick, my sense was when Steve Swindal, the son-in-law, left [in 2006], they lost the brains of the operation for the past eight years. Basically when the YES Network was being formed, George at that point deferred entirely to Steve. The guy who represented Yankee Holdings was Steve. Once Steve left in February of 2006, that was such a dramatic loss because no matter how they wanted to portray him in a negative light, anyone who was involved with the team on the business side knew for the eight years he was there that Steve was the anchor. The guy was understated, not bombastic, a listener, and he could follow the numbers and understand what the realities were. He was very good."

When Swindal was kicked out, the Steinbrenner sons, Hank and Hal, took over. Said the same executive, "I'd say there's no logical way the next generation can measure up. Did you ever hear of 'Itchie and Twitchie'? Hal and Hank. If you took both kids' feet together at the same time, they couldn't fit into George's shoes."

Along with Hank and Hal, the two Yankees executives with designs on running the Yankees are Randy Levine and Lonn Trost. The executive, who was close to the situation, saw Levine and Trost as men who did their best to sour Leo Hindery's relationship with George and to take credit for Hindery's success. He was contemptuous of both of them.

"Did you ever hear of the pharaoh syndrome?" he asked. "In Egypt, every pharaoh wanted to have his own pyramid built. But the pharaoh didn't himself understand the engineering, the calculus, and the math required to do it, so he got someone to build the pyramid, and do you know what happened to the guy at the end of the day when the pyramid was done? They killed him and buried him in it. And so there was a good bit of pharaoh syndrome in the story of the YES Network. The guy who was the engineer, who marshaled the troops and fought with the networks and brought the talent to bear, was Leo Hindery.

"And I would say frankly the way Leo was treated by the likes of Randy Levine and Lonn Trost was really disgusting. They spread rumors to George Steinbrenner that were unfounded. They said Leo was a liar. They represented that Leo wasn't telling the full story. Meanwhile Leo was doing cartwheels and backflips to make things happen relative to getting the network up and running.

"Randy had zero economic investment in the YES Network, but he was president of the New York Yankees, and so as George got more retired, as his health started to drop, Randy was in New York, and George's absence gave him more room to play. Randy had freewheeling access and he wanted to be the voice, and Levine got very jealous that Leo Hindery was on the radio, Leo Hindery was on television, and Leo Hindery was getting the credit that he rightfully deserved.

"Lonn Trost had been a partner at Shea, Gould, and was hurting financially after the law firm went belly up. Trost was a smart money man down on his luck, a guy George knew would be loyal and would work like a dog." According to the executive, in the *Seinfeld* episode where George Costanza was building a bed under his desk, the show was lampooning Trost, who often would work from dawn to dusk.

The Yankees made it to the American League Division Series in 2006 but lost to the Detroit Tigers in four games. Rumors abounded that Joe Torre would be fired and Lou Piniella would replace him.

Torre didn't get fired after 2006, but 2007 was not an easy year for Joe. The Yankees, with a $195 million payroll, were in last place at the end of April. Again plagued by injuries to their senior-citizen players, the team was six and a half games behind the Boston Red Sox.

On May 6, the Yankees signed Roger Clemens out of retirement for $18.3 million ($4.45 million a month). After the game, Bob Sheppard introduced him, and the crowd went wild. It was a perfect George Steinbrenner moment, and he wasn't there, which told everyone all they needed to know about his health. When reporters asked to interview George, Howard Rubenstein said that he had declined. Rubenstein was right about that, but not the way he intended.

Clemens's twenty-fourth season turned out to be a bust for his $18 million, as he finished the 2007 season with a 6–6 record.

The Yankees made the playoffs again, and they faced a young, hungry Cleveland Indians team. After the Yankees lost the first two games, on October 7, 2007, George Steinbrenner spoke to a reporter and threatened that if the Yankees didn't come back and beat Cleveland, Torre would be fired. "His job is on the line," he said. "He's the highest-paid manager in baseball, so I don't think we'd take him back if we don't win the series."

Two days later Cleveland eliminated the Yankees from series contention. The Yankees lost because rookie pitcher Joba Chamberlain couldn't contend with a swarm of tiny, annoying bugs called midges, which attached themselves to his face and neck while he was trying to pitch. He gave up the tying run on a wild pitch. The Indians won in the eleventh. It was the third year in a row the Yankees were eliminated in the first round of the playoffs.

The one Yankees win came in game three, and afterward Torre told reporters, "Every time we go to the postseason, there's nothing that's going to satisfy anybody unless you win the World Series. And that's very difficult. . . . I understand the requirements here, but the players are human beings, and it's not machinery here. Even though they get paid a lot of money, it's still blood that runs through their veins." For Joe Torre, it was all about the players.

Employees thought there was something fishy about the whole Torre affair. Why would George threaten to fire him after the Yankees trailed two games to none? That seemed like a cheap shot, even for George.

According to at least one employee who knew the situation, Yankee president Randy Levine was the one pushing George to fire Torre. Said the employee, "Randy knew how to push George's buttons. If you want to get George very upset, it's very easy. If you're sitting in George's office and the game is on, and someone screws up, you can say, 'What the hell was he thinking?' and then George will get all riled up. Or you can sit there and not say anything or downplay it. If you want to suck up to him, just bad-mouth a player or a decision by the manager. 'What was the pitching coach thinking?' 'What was Torre thinking?'

"The manager puts in a pinch hitter. If you want to second-guess and make yourself look good in George's eyes, you say, 'What's he doing that for?' And chances are that seven out of ten times you will be right. If you second-guess it and the guy strikes out or hits into a double play, you look good, because you're smarter than the manager.

You've put the manager down, and you look good in George's eyes, and George gets all fired up, and he likes you because you're on his side. Randy would do that all the time.

"Heaven forbid you get stuck in an elevator with George. You'd be in there with him after a loss, and he'd say, 'Your team really stinks.' My answer would be, 'We did tonight, but don't worry, we'll be all right. We're going to win this thing.' And he'd go, 'You're crazy.' I'd say, 'No, I guarantee it.' And then he'd move on to something else. Or you could go down that elevator ride with him and bash everyone in sight and get him all fired up like Randy did."

According to the employee, who was close to the situation, Levine saw himself as Steinbrenner's successor, and when George became incapacitated, Levine used his position with Steinbrenner to push Torre out.

"They are respectful of Randy because they know he made the Yankees a lot of money with the new stadium deal, but I do know Hank and Hal have clipped his wings and told him to calm down, and he's not in charge of everything like he thinks he is. There's a little bit of limbo going on, not knowing who's in complete control, but the sons are cementing their power and control.

"If you go back to when George said that if the Yankees didn't win the World Series, Torre would be fired, it was after the Yankees had lost the first two games to the Indians," said the employee. "What did they think was going to happen? So it was really a cheap shot. And Randy was the one who arranged for the writer of the article to have access to George. Before that they had been very careful about people having access to George.

"Randy is one of the most stubborn people around. He's irrational. He had the players' union so pissed and seeing blind that he forced them into a strike in 1994, and he was happy to do it. That's the kind of guy he is. Just about anyone else would have worked something out to avoid losing the World Series. You never heard anyone make that connection, but Randy was the head of the owners committee when they lost the World Series."

Instead of firing Torre and incurring a PR debacle, Hank offered Torre a contract that cut his pay 33 percent but provided for incentive bonuses. When Torre said he was insulted, Hank expressed surprise. Torre took a job managing the Los Angeles Dodgers, and in 2008 led them to a division title. When Torre wasn't even mentioned during the ceremonies commemorating the final game at Yankee Stadium, the Yankees looked petty and vindictive.

Hank Steinbrenner told Alex Rodriguez that if he didn't re-sign with the Yankees, it would be good-bye, and the ploy paid off handsomely after he walked away on the advice of agent Scott Boras and suddenly discovered he had made a mistake. Rodriguez fired Boras and negotiated personally with the Yankees for three more years. The Yankees would have been paying ARod $50.7 million over the next three years if he hadn't ripped up his contract (the Rangers were stuck with $21.3 million plus $9 million in signing bonus money), so the Yankees in effect added a seven-year, $224.3 million extension. In addition, ARod will get more than $25 million in bonus money if he should break Barry Bonds's career home run record of 762 home runs. ARod should do that around the summer of 2013.

Meanwhile, by 2007, it had become clear that George Steinbrenner had faded from the picture, his mind no longer functioning. Alzheimer's had taken its toll. When Steinbrenner rode in a cart around the field during the 2008 All-Star game he looked like a figure from a wax museum. He handed baseballs to Yankee Hall of Famers Yogi Berra and Reggie Jackson, but no words were exchanged, no sentences uttered. Berra and Jackson, who had suffered terribly at the hands of George Steinbrenner during their careers, both kissed him on the cheek. They could forgive him because the lights had gone out inside George Steinbrenner.

His sons, Hank and Hal, took over the reins, and they left it to Brian Cashman to put Humpty Dumpty back together again. Whether he is up to the task remains to be seen, though his acquisitions of outfielder Xavier Nady and catcher Ivan Rodriguez during the summer of 2008 to replace the injured Hideki Matsui and Jorge Posada seemed inspired. The rap on Cashman is that he's a numbers guy who will look at two players and always pick the guy with the best stats. Whereas Gene Michael might see the intangibles in a player, Cashman sees only the numbers. Another criticism is that Cashman always leaves himself an explanation if something goes wrong. Why the Yankees don't put the team back into the hands of Gene Michael is a question a number of observers have posed.

As I finished writing this after the 2008 season, the Tampa Bay Rays have won the American League East over the Boston Red Sox, and

both finished far ahead of the Yankees. Hank Steinbrenner was wring-
ing his hands and gnashing his teeth over the Yankees' not making the
playoffs for the first time since 1993. In mid-September, he was heard
to say he intended to convene an "advisory panel" to make baseball
decisions. It was Brian Cashman's worst nightmare.

The next day Hank said, "We're going to have to look at what has
been done wrong over the last five years, which I've had one year to
try and figure out." Added brother Hal, the quiet one, "Clearly, a lot
of mistakes were made." George would have been proud.

Yankee fans are nervous. They want to know: *Who is going to lead
us? Will the new Yankee brain trust spend money like George Steinbrenner
did? What is going to happen to our team?*

Yankee fans, stop worrying. If money can buy happiness, it ought
to be able to buy pennants, unless Hank and Hal screw it up, which
is possible but not likely. Neither Hank nor Hal has the certainty that
George had that only he knew what he was doing. Hank and Hal know
they don't have a clue (why should they?), and like the smartest owners, they will let their general manager do his work. What is certain
to happen is that the New York Yankees, thanks to deals orchestrated
by George Steinbrenner, will have more money than Bill Gates (well,
maybe not that much) when in 2009 they move from the House that
Ruth Built into the House that George Built, the Taj Mahal of baseball stadiums. The team, which as of 2008 was worth $1.3 billion and
in 2007 had revenues estimated at $327 million, will become a whole
lot richer—the yearly take, according to experts, is expected to at least
double. All fifty-two thousand tickets for 2009 are likely to sell out.
The best box seats, which used to cost $250 a seat a game, will sell in
the new stadium for ten times that. That's $2,500 per ticket per game.
It's not a misprint. If you want to take your date and sit by the dugout, it'll cost you $5,000 a game—if you can get seats, because those
seats were going fast to season-ticket buyers in late 2008. Multiply that
by eighty-one home games for the cost of one season ticket along the
playing field. The fifty-six luxury suites are expected to bring a whopping income of $850,000 each per season.

The team will make another $70 million from concessions, and the
Yankees at the moment are cozying up to the federal government for
another $366 million of tax-exempt financing. Then there's the money
to be made from the YES Network, from selling Yankees gear, and

more millions from mlb.com and DirecTV. The Yankees will be awash in cash, and if the team is run intelligently, all of baseball better watch out. The only question is: how many lifelong Yankee fans are going to be priced out of the market and will have to watch their beloved Yankees on the YES Network or DirecTV? When I was kid, I would buy a box seat for $3.50 and shmear an usher I befriended ten bucks to let me sit in Dan Topping's box. A beer and a hot dog now cost more than that.

Making the stadium deal even sweeter for the Yankees, the debt service on the $962 million the Yankees are borrowing will be counted against the luxury-tax dollars. So will $25 million in maintenance expenses. Tampa Bay, Kansas City, and Pittsburgh can forget that luxury-tax money. That's $77 million a year the less wealthy teams won't be getting from the Yankees.

Estate planning experts say it appears that George has made plans for his succession. If he were to pass away, the Yankees could be placed in a trust in his wife Joan's name for the rest of her life, and then be passed on to the children, who would have fourteen years to pay off the tax on Steinbrenner's portion of the club.

In the fall of 2008, the Yankees made two bold moves to return to the top of the American League. They paid a king's ransom for two ace pitchers, signing Cleveland's C. C. Sabathia for $161 million for seven years and Toronto's A. J. Burnett for $82.5 million for five years. Combined, the Yankees gambled $243.5 million on two arms. In 2008, they had opted to start the season with two talented rookies, Ian Kennedy and Phil Hughes, but neither panned out, and when Chien-Ming Wang got hurt, they missed making the playoffs for the first time since 1993. If Sabathia and Burnett can stay healthy, the Yankees will have a powerful starting rotation.

A week after the Yankees signed Sabathia and Burnett, they surprised everyone by signing first baseman Mark Texiera to an eight-year $180 million contract. That's $423.5 million dollars committed to three players. Add that to Alex Rodriguez's $32-million-a year contract, and it's pretty clear that George's sons, despite a crippling recession, are determined to put a championship team on the field in 2009.

Meanwhile, until the Yankees return to pennant contention, their fans will continue to harangue Alex Rodriguez for his inability to hit in the clutch, and they will brand manager Joe "Mr. Sunshine" Girardi or his successor "idiot," "imbecile," or "moron." For Yankees fans, as it was for me in the 1950s and early 1960s, winning the pennant and going to the World Series has become their birthright. Nothing short of that will be acceptable. In the end, that will be the lasting legacy of George Steinbrenner.

From whole cloth George Steinbrenner turned a drab New York Yankees team into the gold standard of sports franchises. He's had his ups and downs, but his influence on the sport has been great. When a thoroughbred horse wins the big race, you can't lose sight of the fact that the jockey had to whip that horse, and that's what George did with this franchise.

People have argued that he's in the biggest market. Look at the advantage he has. But the New York Mets have had the exact same market and advantage. The only thing George had over the Mets was history. At the time George bought the Yankees, the Mets had recently appeared twice in the World Series. They were way ahead of the Yankees in fan appeal when he came in, and George blew them off the map. Other big-market teams such as the Chicago White Sox, the Chicago Cubs, and the Los Angeles Dodgers and Angels, haven't come close to doing what George has done with the Yankees. Cleveland fans will forever wonder what George would have done with the Indians had he and Vernon Stouffer been on better terms.

And so despite George's personality disorders, which cost his team more pennants and world championships and caused his employees headaches and heartaches, George Steinbrenner's teams won enough that he should be a first-ballot selection to the Baseball Hall of Fame. The next big push should be for two legendary Yankee owners to go into the hall: the long-forgotten Colonel Jacob Ruppert, who owned the Yankees during the era of Ruth and Gehrig, and the owner who oversaw two great teams almost twenty years apart—the Bronx Zoo teams led by Reggie Jackson and the Evil Empire teams led by Derek Jeter—the blustery George Steinbrenner. Hate him or love him, we are certainly going to miss him.

There probably will never be someone like George
Steinbrenner ever again.

—Former Tampa mayor Dick Greco

29

George the Munificent

While living in Tampa, George has done things to ruffle feathers. When American Ship closed its doors in 1995, there was a howling heard among the dockworkers. For reasons no one can explain, there have been times when he hasn't paid his bills or has failed to fulfill a business promise.

In the early 1990s, for instance, George decided he was going to go into the magazine business. Regional magazines were the rage at the time, and the one he decided to buy was one that combined lifestyle and business for residents of Tampa Bay's Sun Coast. It was owned by a father and son in Clearwater. Because the owners were undercapitalized, it was a hand-to-mouth operation when Steinbrenner called to say he was interested in purchasing it. Steinbrenner and his financial adviser had several meetings with the owners of the magazine, and in the end Steinbrenner agreed to buy the magazine for approximately $300,000.

Recall the case of Ben Fleiger, who was promised a contract after he agreed to be the general manager of the Cleveland Pipers, only to wait for months until after the team folded to get one and to get paid. Steinbrenner did the same thing with the father-son owners of the magazine. After he took control of the magazine, he had his lawyers stall the negotiations. The former owners would sit with Steinbrenner's money people, who kept raising points for the lawyers of the old owners to solve, only to raise other points. The lawyers for the old owners were convinced Steinbrenner's tactic was to make sure a deal never was signed. Without a signed deal, he wouldn't have to pay what he had promised.

The old owners sued Steinbrenner, as did creditors of the magazine. If the old owners won the suit, the creditors then would get paid. Faced with a lawsuit, Steinbrenner's defense was that he and the magazine owners hadn't agreed on a concrete price.

Dan Joy, the lawyer for the creditors, put Steinbrenner's financial adviser on the stand. He was a hostile witness, and Joy peppered him with leading questions in an attempt to get him to admit that Steinbrenner had indeed made a verbal commitment to buy the magazine. Joy was in his face, and for most of four hours the man kept denying that Steinbrenner had made any such deal.

By the end of the afternoon Joy had boxed him in, and reluctantly he confessed to being witness to a deal that called for the old owners to get paid $300,000 for the magazine. When George's financial adviser made the fatal admission, the eight jurors in the box turned their heads as though tied together on a string and stared at Steinbrenner, who was in the courtroom.

The following morning when court resumed, Steinbrenner was absent.

"He didn't have enough time for this," said George's lawyer, "and while he is confident his side will prevail in court, he doesn't have the time to be distracted."

Said Joy afterward, "We're not stupid. Regardless of what the lawyer said, when Steinbrenner didn't show up in court, we knew he had thrown in the towel. The reason he didn't show up for day two: he knew it was lost."

Steinbrenner's lawyer asked for time to settle the case, and Judge Morris Buck gave the two parties the morning. By noon, the plaintiffs had won all they were seeking.

Joy, who lives in Sarasota, was told the story of an acquaintance who had gone to a local Tampa tailor, who told the acquaintance that Steinbrenner had ordered five suits but that he hadn't paid him.

"There is a common denominator," said Joy. "The guy doesn't pay his bills, and he abuses people he perceives to be inferiors. That's the key. He preys on small fry."

There was a footnote. Before the trial Joy forcefully, relentlessly questioned George about the terms of the agreement for the better part of an afternoon. Steinbrenner's usual response was that he couldn't remember. Joy was pleased that Steinbrenner had taken that tactic, because he felt that Steinbrenner had removed the greatest asset from the lawsuit: himself. "Strategically, it was a dumb move," said Joy.

When the deposition ended after four hours, Joy and Steinbrenner were chatting. Joy commented, "Tomorrow I'm heading for Boston." He was going to Cape Cod to take a break. Said Joy, "The first thing out of his mouth: 'We're at Fenway this week. Can I get you tickets?' Even after four hours of cross-examination, he could turn on the charm!"

A friend of mine, who covered George Steinbrenner as a reporter in New York, said to me, "I have never known an asshole who so many people speak well of as George Steinbrenner."

There is a reason for that. Away from the baseball arena, there is a separate and different George Steinbrenner who is praised and revered by the many recipients of his largesse. In Cleveland, New York City, and Tampa, hundreds, perhaps thousands, of boys and girls have been helped by the generosity of the man. In Tampa alone, both a high school and a street are going to be named after him. Legends Field, the winter home of the Yankees, already has been renamed George M. Steinbrenner Field.

When I interviewed him, Steinbrenner told me, "I have a great sense of compassion for people less fortunate, and I got that from my mother. My dad did good things, but he never understood. I was always for the underdog, maybe because I always felt I was an underdog and a maverick.

"I've always felt the strong need—there's an old saying, 'The good you do for others always comes back to you.' John Greenleaf Whittier. It's very true. My life has been that way. Every time I go out of my way to do something for somebody else or do a project for people who needed it, I've gotten rewarded tenfold."

When you add it up, what George Steinbrenner has done for people, especially children, is mind-boggling. His work helping youngsters began with the Junior Olympics in Cleveland. He helped start the program, and as he became more prominent in the community he spent a lot of his money to finance it so Cleveland boys and girls could compete in track in order to stay out of trouble. He helped many young Cleveland-area athletes like John LeCourt by offering them college scholarships. He also endeared himself to those who saw his generosity.

George contributed generously to causes in the New York metropolitan area. He gave heavily to the Police Athletic League, the Catholic Youth Organization, and the Silver Shield Foundation, which pays college tuition for all children whose fathers died in the line of duty as police officers or firefighters in New York State and in Hillsborough County in Florida. Started by Steinbrenner, the foundation is funded by a hundred supporters who each donate one thousand dollars a year. Hundreds of youngsters, many of whom would not have been able to afford them, have received college educations as a result.

For years, George funded the Whitney M. Young Classic, a football game at Yankee Stadium between Grambling College and another historically black college. Grambling's coach, Eddie Robinson, had no place to play in 1974 because Yankee Stadium was being refurbished. Steinbrenner agreed to cover all expenses for the game, which continued for many years as a result. Grambling awarded Steinbrenner an honorary degree.

Wrote Robinson in his autobiography, "I fell in love with George Steinbrenner in 1976, and love him even more today. His generosity to Grambling has been remarkable. No one really knows these things about him."

A lot of people, many who started out as strangers, owe him a lot. On a hot July day in 1973, eighteen-year-old Ray Negron went with his half brothers and cousins, tough street kids from the Hunts Point section of the Bronx, to Yankee Stadium. Spray-painting graffiti on walls was big in urban neighborhoods, and Negron's cousins had brought a can of white paint to leave their mark. Ray, a gentle kid who sported a tall afro, had begun spray-painting a big "NY" on the wall of the hallowed stadium when a black limousine pulled up. Everyone except Ray saw the big man get out of the limo. Before the teen could run, George Steinbrenner grabbed him by the scruff of the neck and marched him inside the stadium to a holding cell. Negron had no idea who Steinbrenner was, but he pleaded with him, "Cut me a break." He told Steinbrenner, "I'll never do anything like that again. Give me a chance, please."

Steinbrenner left the terrified boy in the cell for ten minutes. When George returned, he took him into the Yankees locker room and ordered the clubhouse manager to give him a uniform.

"He's got damages he's got to work off," said Steinbrenner, who made him a bat boy for a couple of days. When one of the regular bat boys got sick, Negron stayed on and never left. He has been a Yankees employee on and off ever since.

He enrolled at New York Institute of Technology, but after two semesters was going to quit because of a fear of tests. Steinbrenner told him, "If you don't graduate, you're fired."

Later George told him, "I have plans for you. You never have to worry about a thing, not as long as I own the New York Yankees."

With Steinbrenner's blessing, Negron worked in the Yankees' audiovisual department and was a gofer and chauffeur for manager Billy Martin and the players, especially Reggie Jackson. When Jackson left for the West Coast to play for the Angels, Negron went to Hollywood for several years to try his hand at acting, and after he appeared in a minor role in the movies *The Cotton Club*, *Liquid Sky*, and *The Slugger's Wife*, George brought him back to the Yankees, where he became a drug counselor to Dwight Gooden and Darryl Strawberry. After going to work for Cleveland and Texas, after the 2003 season he returned to work for George. In 2006, with George's blessing, he published a children's book, *The Boy of Steel*, about a young cancer patient, Babe Ruth, and the Yankees.

George's many acts of charity often have been random and kindhearted. When he heard in 1988 about a twenty-year-old Sarasota construction worker who was killed by a stray bullet during a nearby argument over a drug deal, he paid for the man's funeral. In 2006, Steinbrenner read an article in the *Daily News* about a thirteen-year-old Arkansas boy who gave a thousand dollars he had earned working to his debt-ridden middle school rather than use it to travel to New York on vacation. George made the boy a special guest of the Yankees on Old-Timers' Day. George flew him to New York, wined and dined him, and sent him a $1,000 check.

Then there was the case of the man whose four children died in their home in the Bronx when a space heater sparked a fire. Steinbrenner paid for the funerals.

When he heard of the plight of the thousands left homeless in Homestead, Florida, by Hurricane Andrew, the next day, August 24,

1992, he got in a truck and drove from Tampa to Miami with a load of bottled water for the victims. He got there in the middle of the night, unloaded all of the water, and drove back to Tampa. He arrived early in the morning, and he heard there was a charity drive under way at a local mall to get baby formula and diapers for the victims. He drove to the shopping mall, got on the radio and TV in Tampa, and begged people to donate. He personally donated $20,000, and a couple of days later he drove a shipment of baby formula and diapers back to Homestead.

George did more. He discovered that the Salvation Army trucks didn't have air-conditioning, and he donated the money to install air-conditioning in every single one of them. He does a lot of great work with the Salvation Army in the Tampa area.

One day George went to a Tampa Yankees game when a young boy approached him with a ball for an autograph. George asked the boy what he wanted on the ball. No answer.

"What's the matter, son? Cat got your tongue?" George said.

The boy's mother came along and told him that the boy was deaf and couldn't speak. George was so upset at his faux pas, he sent the whole family to New York for a weekend of baseball at Yankee Stadium. He paid for plane tickets, a chauffeur-driven limo, and a stay at the Regency Hotel. When they got home, he paid to give the boy speech therapy. George keeps the boy's picture on his desk.

He gave $50,000 for toys to a needy orphanage on Christmas Eve.

One time he drove past a broken-down school bus on a Florida highway. He paid for the repair and for all the kids on the bus to have lunch at McDonald's.

The number of high school athletes George has helped is large. One such athlete, Tony Fossas, had talent but no money to go to college, and Steinbrenner arranged to pay for all four years at the University of South Florida. Fossas later went on to have an eight-year major league career.

There were bumps along the way. There were times George would promise to fund something, and then when the time came, for reasons no one could understand, he'd wait for weeks to actually pay the bills. He did that with Olympic swimmer Ron Karnaugh, whose father died during the 1992 Olympics. George volunteered to pay for his medical school tuition. When George went weeks without paying, a desperate

Ron sometimes didn't know whether to enroll for another semester or not. With forbearance by the school, eventually George paid, and Ron graduated.

Sometimes he didn't pay what he promised. When Olympic skater Nicole Bobek was having trouble paying her bills, George volunteered to sponsor her and pay for her ice time, coaching, living expenses, and training. She and her mother were supposed to get monthly checks, which were weeks late in coming until they stopped altogether. According to an employee close to Steinbrenner, he had heard something negative about Bobek's personal life and decided to withhold the checks.

One time his munificence led to scandal. After he gave money to Olympic skater Tonya Harding, it turned out that some of the money was used for the "hit" on rival skater Nancy Kerrigan. When George heard that, he wanted to hunt down Harding and get his money back.

In Tampa, George Steinbrenner is beloved and revered. He founded and funded the Hillsborough County coaches foundation, which honors public and private high school coaches and their wives; he has rescued middle school sports that would have been cut had he not stepped in and paid for them; he provided lights for a number of Little League fields as well as for fields at the University of South Florida, the University of Florida, Florida State, and Eckerd College, named after fellow Culver alum Jack Eckerd.

He has been so generous to the schoolchildren of Hillsborough County that on December 17, 2007, it was announced that a high school that was to be built in Lutz would be named after him. The groundbreaking for the $60 million Steinbrenner High School is scheduled for January 2009. "If you're going to name a school after anybody in Tampa, it should be him," said Derek Jeter.

Dick Greco, who has served four terms as mayor of Tampa, is one of the most popular local politicians in recent memory. He is part of George's Tampa posse, and he has come to appreciate George's approach to life and the good he has brought to the Tampa community. Here's what Greco had to say about all that George has done:

"I met George many years ago when he first came here, and he always was a friend. He was as nice as he could be. What I remember most about him: if he liked you, he was your buddy. About twenty years ago I went through a hard time. Someone had written a crazy story about me in a magazine. I was chairman of the board at

Metropolitan Bank, and it closed. I had taken the position because I was working for [real estate mogul] Eddie DeBartolo at the time, and he owned a piece of the bank, and it wasn't something I normally did, and the magazine blasted me in the article. George called me, and he said, 'I want to have lunch with you.'

"I arrived, and two of my other close friends, Tom McEwen and George Levy, were there, and George said to me, 'I wanted you to know that I'm here for you, pal. And that article was a bunch of bull crap, and I just wanted you to know that you're okay. Anything you need, just ask.' I was so touched. I will never forget that.

"George always contributed to my campaigns. I never asked anyone for money in my life. I never had to. I never even sent out letters asking for donations. But every time I ran there would be a check in the mail from him. And I'd see him, and he'd say, 'Listen, pal, if there is anything you need, just let me know.' That was it. You knew it was sincere and it was real. And if ever I did need something, I knew all I had to do was call, and he'd do it in two seconds. That's the way he is with a lot of his friends. People who don't know him have no clue what he's all about. He has a good heart, and he really understands loyalty, and that's not a word used today very often.

"One thing about George, he's a hundred percent winner. I went to his house to play tennis. His partner was Phil McNiff, a retired FBI agent who is still with him. I was playing with E. C. Smith, and I didn't realize when we started that George had just started playing. He had taken a couple of lessons. I had been playing a while, and so when I served to him, I didn't want to hit it as hard as I would have to McNiff. By the second serve I hit to him it had become obvious. He said, 'What are you doing?'

"I said, 'What?'

"He said, 'Hit the damn ball.' He did not want to be treated any differently. He played so hard. We were playing on an asphalt court, and I was afraid he was going to dive to get the ball. George is a born winner. He gives everything he's got.

"I remember Tom McEwen, Phil Alessi, and I took George fishing on a boat off Pass-a-Grille [just south of St. Pete Beach]. I didn't realize it, but George had never fished before. I just assumed that everyone in Florida had fished. We went with a guide, and he didn't know how to cast. It was a little difficult, because we were using a fly line, no lead, and you have to flick the thing over your head to make it go any distance.

"The guide took George's rod and cast it for him. The next time, the guide went to do it again, and George said to him, 'I'll get it.' The first time he didn't cast it very far, but the second time it went a little farther, and from then on no one said a word to him. He did not want anyone to help him, even though he didn't know how. Not only did he cast his own rod, but he baited his own hook, and he got to catching fish like everyone else.

"Phil, Tom, and I would take breaks and talk, but George kept fishing. He ended up catching the most fish, and he caught the biggest fish, which was important to him. He caught a great big snook, and he said to the captain, 'That's the biggest one, isn't it?'

"The captain said, 'Yeah, I think so.' He was so tickled. That was so important to him. That's the way George thinks. Everything is a contest, and he doesn't want to be at the bottom. He didn't want anyone helping him, any more than he wanted me serving softly to him. He's a very unusual man in that respect.

"But underneath it all, he has this soft side he doesn't want anyone to see. I was with him at a Tampa Bay Bucs football game, and we were sitting on the east side of the field and the sun was going down, and he said to me, 'Look at that sunset. Isn't that beautiful? Why wouldn't anybody want to live here?' You wouldn't think he would say something like that.

"George did so many good things around here that no one could ever imagine them. During spring training if they had a banquet for the Boys Club or another organization, many of the Yankee players would show up. It was something he demanded. They showed up en masse, all the stars, too. He wanted it to happen, and he required it, and he was always there.

"He loved the police department, and he started that Silver Shield club for kids of policemen who are hurt or killed to go to college. Every year he puts money into that, along with other people. If it weren't for the fact there was no way to keep it quiet, you never would have known his involvement in it. That's true of many of the things he does.

"One night a house burned down in Tampa, and two little black children perished, and I'll never forget, I went to the scene, and the firemen were sitting outside crying because there was nothing they could do. When they arrived, the place was engulfed in flames. It was in the paper that an anonymous Good Samaritan paid to redo the house and to bury the children. Later I found out it was George. These were people he had never met. He just did it.

"He would read about something in the paper: a Little League would have a break-in, and someone would steal all the equipment, and they'd lose everything, and the next day George would take care of the bill and never say a word to anyone. He constantly, constantly, constantly did things like that.

"Another time someone brought to my attention a woman in her eighties, a longtime Yankee fan who had come down for spring training from the North year after year. She was ill, and this was going to be her last visit, and her greatest dream was to meet George Steinbrenner. I called George, and not only did he meet her, but he gave her a seat of honor at the game and announced her presence. That meant so much to her. George is a many-faceted guy who doesn't want anyone to see the soft side of him.

"The last couple of times I saw him it hasn't been easy for him to get around, but he keeps plugging. When they dedicated Legends Field to him, he was in a golf cart, and they drove him around and he waved at everyone. I thought it was a fine thing to do.

"A couple years ago he sent me a bat with his name on it in a Plexiglas case, and I thought that was strange, because he never promoted himself. I wondered whether he was saying good-bye because it was so unusual for George to do a thing like that. And I will keep it forever.

"I really cherish his friendship. Always have and always will. He has done so much for this town, for baseball, for life in general. He's a real giver and a real pal, as he puts it. No question about it: I love the man.

"He's a many-faceted person and a very good friend. You can't mention the game of baseball without mentioning George Steinbrenner. He created a persona for baseball and probably helped make baseball what it is. People expect him to be out front, making noise, raising hell, whether you win or lose. You don't see that a lot. There probably will never be someone like George Steinbrenner ever again."

Notes

1. Henry and George

People whose interviews contributed material to this chapter are George Steinbrenner, Ike Ganyard, Frank Treadway, and Patsy Stecher.

2. Culver Military Academy

Interview sources for this chapter are Ket Barber, Don Martin, George Steinbrenner, Lee Robinson, Pam Thomas, Warren Ornstein, Pete Hensil, George Steiner, Jim Beardsley, A. Coke Smith, and Mr. Morris.

3. Williams College

This chapter uses interview material from Robert Simpson, George Steinbrenner, Charlie Glass, Don Martin, Dick Kraft, Len Watters, Jack Brody, Frank Treadway, Steve Blasky, Peter Callahan, Bill Callahan, Tony Butterfield, Bruce Breckenridge, and Pete Smythe.

28 George's separated shoulder: When I asked Culver track coach A. Coke Smith whether George had separated his shoulder senior year, he said, "Not that I know of, and I would have known." When I asked the same question of Culver assistant football coach Morris, he said, "I don't remember that. He played through the whole season." But it is certainly possible that George could have dislocated his shoulder and not told anyone.

4. Lockbourne Air Force Base

This chapter uses interview material from Bob Stecher, William Mixson, Jeanette Montgomery, Jerry Adams, and John Moore.

45 John Moore: This is a pseudonym. He agreed to talk to me on the condition that I not reveal his identity.

45 Charlie Wilson: Charles Erwin Wilson was born in 1890 in Minerva, Ohio. A boy mechanical genius, after he graduated from Carnegie Tech he designed the first automatic starter at age twenty-two. During World War I, he helped develop dynamotors and radio generators for the armed services. In 1928, when he was thirty-eight, he became the youngest vice president in General Motors' history. In 1941, he became its president.

During World War II, his company played an important role in turning out tanks, armored cars, machine guns, and diesel engines. In 1944, he was named to the War Production Board, where he and Henry Steinbrenner worked together to ship products for the war effort.

More than anyone else, it was Charlie Wilson who put the United States on a permanent war economy as we entered the missile age. He was still head of GM when President Eisenhower named him secretary of defense in January 1953.

For more on Charlie Wilson, see *Time* magazine, October 6, 1961.

45   Colonel Jerry Adams was happy to confirm what I knew, but reluctant to add to it. Thus the following dialogue:

"I was told George was instrumental in the lights' being put up on the baseball field."

"I suspect that's true," he said.

"I was told George said, 'If the air force won't pay for it, I will.'"

"That sounds like George."

"Bo Dougher found the money to pay for the lights."

"I expect that's true."

"Were you aware that Bo was protecting George?"

"Yes. Dougher was very politically conscious of the Ohio political scene, and George's father was prominent in Ohio."

50   General Dougher was awarded his second star on March 10, 1958. He retired on March 15, 1961, and died on December 19, 1978.

5. Coach George

This chapter uses interview material from John Moore, Dr. Jim Hull, Harold Zeig, Tom Keys, Don Martin, Bob Sudyk, John LeCourt, Tony DeSabito, Lou Saban, Paul Hornung, Ben Froelich, George Steinbrenner, Dan Mason, and Len Dawson.

52   After George bought the Yankees, he hired his friend Hopalong Cassady to work for him at the stadium. Steve Blasky, a fellow Williams College alum, was George's guest at the stadium. He tells this story:

"One day at Yankee Stadium when I was in George's box, there was a man who didn't look too much younger than I did, a very nice-looking man, and he was acting like a waiter. At least George treated him like one. The man looked familiar. And George was treating him like shit: 'Come on. Move your ass. Get the drinks.'

"All of a sudden I said to this guy, 'Aren't you Mr. Cassady?'

"He said, 'Yeah, I'm Hopalong Cassady.'

"I said to George, 'George, that's Hopalong Cassady. He won the fucking Heisman Trophy. How can you treat this guy like that? He's a hero of mine.'

"He said, 'Well, he's working for me.'"

54   *he also had played a year of pro ball with the New York Giants.*   "It was interesting that George was telling people he played for the Giants," said his friend Joe Bennett. "I had a good friend, Bill Albright, who went to Wisconsin and played on the Giants. I said to Bill at a Wisconsin reunion, 'I know somebody who played for the Giants. George Steinbrenner.' Bill said, 'What are you talking about? I know who I played with. I never heard of him.'"

60   LeCourt did not last long at Ohio University. He got married, dropped out, and enlisted in the armed services. He later became the longtime recreation director for the town of White Hall, a suburb of Columbus.

61   *Years later George would hire Saban to be president of the Yankees.*   Milt Northrop, "Loyal Steinbrenner Still Repaying Saban for Favor," *Buffalo News*, March 25, 2003, p. E1.

6. Come to Papa

This chapter uses interview material from Joe Bennett, Frank Treadway, Bill Crippin, Ben Fleiger, Patsy Stecher, George Steinbrenner, Otto Graham, John Nagy, and Bill Callahan.

70   When I interviewed an assistant football coach at Park View High School in Bay Village by the name of Kitzerow, he said to me, "One time George was considered for the head coaching job at the Coast Guard Academy before Otto Graham got it. He had a choice to make. He was either going to be president of American Ship or be a coach, so he took the presidency." Obviously George had told him this, because when I said to Otto Graham, "I heard a rumor that George was going to be coach at the Coast Guard Academy," his reply was, "Somebody is pulling your leg, believe me."

7. The Cleveland Pipers

This chapter uses interview material from Jack Adams, John McClendon, Dan Swartz, Bob Sudyk, Mike Cleary, Ben Fleiger, Frank Treadway, Dick Brott, Bill Sharman, John Schanz, Bob Stecher, Bill Gabriel, and Bud Shockley.

85   On playing for George Steinbrenner: When I called Roger Brown twenty years later to ask him about what it was like to play for George Steinbrenner and the Pipers, he said, "I'm not interested in talking to you about George Steinbrenner. Sorry." And he hung up. When I asked Coach McClendon, "Which was worse, playing in Russia or working for George?" he answered, "You knew you could always get out of Russia!"

8. George Builds an Empire

This chapter uses interview material from Robert Sauvey, Frank Treadway, Harold Zeig, Pete Smythe, Bob Sudyk, Jack Melcher, and Charles Mosher.

9. Vernon Stouffer's Revenge

This chapter uses interview material from Gabe Paul, Shelley Guren, Jack Melcher, Ben Fleiger, Frank Treadway, Joe Bennett, Bob Sudyk, and George Steinbrenner.

10. Buying the CBS Yankees

This chapter uses interview material from Michael Burke, David Halberstam, Tom Evans, and Fred Bachman.

107   *Burke said it was a terrific idea.*   Michael Burke, *Outrageous Good Fortune* (New York: Little, Brown, 1984), p. 236.

11. George Takes Charge

This chapter uses interview material from Gabe Paul, Sparky Lyle, and Pete Callahan.

12. Watergate

This chapter uses interview material from Jim Polk, Jack Melcher, Tom Evans, Tom McBride, and Roy Meyers.

13. George's Short Exile

This chapter uses interview material from Catfish Hunter, Maury Allen, and Pete Callahan. In researching this chapter, I also relied on *Hardball* by Bowie Kuhn and Marty Appel (New York: Crown, 1987).

14. Wooing Billy

This chapter draws on an interview with Billy Martin. Much of the material was also taken from my book *Wild, High and Tight* (New York: St. Martin's Press, 1991).

15. George's First Pennant

Billy's quotes come from my conversations with him while we were working on his autobiography, *Number 1*. The quotes from Lyle come from my conversations with him while we were writing *The Bronx Zoo*.

16. The Bronx Zoo

My primary source for this chapter was *A Whole Different Ball Game* by Marvin Miller (New York: Birch Lane Press, 1991). Interview sources for the chapter include Gabe Paul, Billy Martin, and Pearl Davis.

17. "One's a Born Liar . . . "

This chapter draws on an interview with Billy Martin.

18. George in Charge

This chapter uses interview material from Jim Bouton, Sparky Lyle, Billy Martin, Joe Flaherty, George Steinbrenner, and Burt Sugar. For more information on Reggie Jackson, see *Reggie* by Reggie Jackson and Mike Lupica (New York: Villard Books, 1984).

19. The Fans Chant
This chapter draws on an interview with Graig Nettles.

20. Hello, I Must Be Going
For this chapter, I relied on the following books: *Don Baylor* by Don Baylor and Claire Smith (New York: St. Martin's Press, 1989), and *Knuckle Balls* by Phil Niekro and Tom Bird (New York: Freundlich Books, 1986). The chapter also uses interview material from Graig Nettles and Shane Rawley.

21. Insanity
239 *"You're not gonna trick me that easily."* Bill Madden and Moss Klein, *Damned Yankees* (New York: Warner Books, 1990), p. 81.
244 *"And besides, you have enough pitching."* Ibid., p. 252.

22. Howie Spira and Mr. May
This chapter draws on an interview with Fay Vincent.

23. American Ship Goes Under
This chapter draws on an interview with George Steinbrenner.
263 *"The American Ship Building Company isn't losing money"* Michael Isikoff, *Washington Post*, February 5, 1984.
263 *"He showed no loyalty"* Thomas Maier, *Newsday*, January 15, 1989, p. 4.
267 *"It was like a mouse trying to swallow an elephant."* Steve Huettel, *Tampa Tribune*, July 23, 1995, p. 1.
267 *"They didn't have the experience"* John Mintz, *Washington Post*, May 2, 1995, p. A1.

24. Gene Michael Rebuilds
This chapter draws on an interview with Mitch Lukevics.
You can read all of the scripts from *Seinfeld* at Seinfeld.com.
276 Gene Michael outfoxes George: For more on how Michael bested Steinbrenner, see Buster Olney, *The Last Night of the Yankee Dynasty* (New York: Ecco Books, 2005), p. 60.

25. Joe Torre Arrives
299 he joked that Steinbrenner's people were *"voices running around in his head."* Buster Olney, *The Last Night of the Yankee Dynasty* (New York: Ecco Books, 2005), p. 150.

26. George Takes Back the Reins
304 *"All we kept hearing about were the great players they had in their system"* Don Zimmer and Bill Madden, *The Zen of Zim* (New York: St. Martin's Press, 2004), p. 58.
310 *"How goofy is this man Steinbrenner?"* Ibid., pp. 23–24.

311 *"You're horseshit, and you're overpaid"* Olney, *Last Night*, p. 2.
311 *"Everyone in New York was spent"* Ibid., pp. 62–63.
312 *"You're a fine one to talk."* Ibid., p. 31.
312 *"There's a reason I'd spent fifty-four years in baseball."* Ibid., pp. 27–28.

27. The Gold Mine
This chapter draws on interviews with Fay Vincent and Leo Hindery.
315 *"Television is the key to all sports"* *U.S. News and World Report*, April 11, 1983, p. 67.
315 *Dr. Schiller made a fatal mistake.* Dyan Machan, "The Boss' Boss," *Forbes*, May 15, 2000, p. 156.

28. Silent George
335 *Estate planning experts say* T. J. Quinn, "Life After the Boss," *New York Daily News*, February 8, 2004.

29. George the Munificent
This chapter uses interview material from Dan Joy, George Steinbrenner, Alex Belk, and Dick Greco.

Bibliography

Baylor, Don, and Claire Smith. *Don Baylor* (New York: St. Martin's Press, 1989).

Berton, Pierre. *The Great Lakes* (Toronto: Stoddart Publishing, 1996).

Bowen, Dana Thomas. *Lore of the Lakes* (Cleveland: Freshwater Press, 1992).

Burke, Michael. *Outrageous Good Fortune* (New York: Little, Brown, 1984).

Condon, George E. *Cleveland* (New York: Doubleday 1967).

Golenbock, Peter. *Wild, High and Tight* (New York: St. Martin's Press, 1991).

Jackson, Reggie, and Mike Lupica. *Reggie* (New York: Villard Books, 1984).

Kuhn, Bowie, and Marty Appel. *Hardball* (New York: Crown, 1987).

Lyle, Sparky, and Peter Golenbock. *The Bronx Zoo* (New York: Crown, 1979).

Madden, Bill, and Moss Klein. *Damned Yankees* (New York: Warner Books, 1990).

Martin, Billy, and Peter Golenbock. *Number 1* (New York: Delacorte Press, 1983).

Miller, Marvin. *A Whole Different Ballgame* (New York: Birch Lane Press, 1991).

Nettles, Graig, and Peter Golenbock. *Balls* (New York: G. P. Putnam's Sons, 1984).

Niekro, Phil, and Tom Bird. *Knuckle Balls* (New York: Freundlich Books, 1986).

Olney, Buster. *The Last Night of the Yankee Dynasty* (New York: Ecco Books, 2004).

Pluto, Terry. *The Curse of Rocky Colavito* (New York: Simon & Schuster, 1994).

Rose, William Ganson. *Cleveland* (Cleveland: World Publishing, 1950).

Stokes, Geoffrey. *Pinstripe Pandemonium* (New York: Harper & Row, 1984).

Torre, Joe, and Henry Dreher. *Joe Torre's Ground Rules for Winners* (New York: Hyperion, 1999).

Torre, Joe, and Tom Verducci. *Chasing the Dream* (New York: Bantam Books, 1997).

Zimmer, Don, and Bill Madden. *The Zen of Zim* (New York: St. Martin's Press, 2004).

Index

Page numbers in *italics* refer to illustrations